SECTARIAN VIOLENCE

To JOANNE , VICTORIA, ROSLYN
and, most of all, EVELYN

SECTARIAN VIOLENCE

THE LIVERPOOL EXPERIENCE, 1819-1914

An aspect of Anglo-Irish history

Frank Neal

Newsham Press

First Published by Manchester University Press
Oxford Road, Manchester M13 9PL, UK
ISBN 0-7190-1483-2 HB

Reprint 1991 by Manchester University Press
ISBN 0-7190-2348-3 PB

Published by Newsham Press in 2003
St. Anthony's, Newsham Street
Scotland Road, Liverpool L5 5BD
ISBN 0-9545013-0-6

British Library cataloguing in publication data applied for
Library of Congress cataloging in publication data applied for

Printed in Great Britain
by The Reprographic Unit, University of Salford

Contents

Tables and maps

Maps

Preface

The central concern of this book is the origin, scale and nature of sectarian violence on the streets of nineteenth-century Liverpool. The period covered could be described as Victorian but the tensions existing in working-class Liverpool arising from sectarian bitterness survived until comparatively recently. The reasons for writing the book were visceral rather than academic, an attempt to exorcise childhood ghosts. Anyone born and raised in working-class Liverpool in pre-slum clearance days could not fail to be aware of religious differences within that society and, in many instances, these had deleterious consequences for friendships and families.

However, the study has to be set in some kind of explanatory framework. In attempting to identify the probable causes of sectarian violence in Victorian Britain generally, several themes stand out as particularly relevant. The constitutional settlements following the Reformation not only embedded the Church of England into the nation's political system, they also were instrumental in giving rise to the view that the British constitution was as near perfect an arrangement for safeguarding the peace and well-being of all Britons as could be achieved. According to this viewpoint, the Established Church imparted a necessary religious dimension into political life. It was the challenge to this privileged position of the Church, from a rising tide of Dissent, Utilitarianism, Radicalism and Catholicism, which by 1800 produced a reaction among Tory ultras which was an important factor in explaining the appearance of Orangeism in England by 1798. The strength of this Tory adherence to the belief in the superiority of the Anglican theological-political arrangements has been underlined by the appearance of J. C. D. Clarke's *English Society, 1688-1832* (1985). Clarke argues persuasively that the defence of Anglicanism was integral to the durability of the Ancien Regime, which lasted until its defeat in 1829 over Catholic emancipation. This episode and its repercussions form an important part of the background to events in Liverpool up to 1852.

However, the sectarian violence which forms the substantive content of this work must also be seen from the perspective of studies of crowds and their behaviour. Though preceded by earlier works, G. Rude's books, *The Crowd in History* (1964) and *The Gordon Riots* (1974), both provide an explanatory scheme for examining crowd behaviour, with a central conclusion that crowds or 'mobs' are rarely purposeless. John Stevenson's work, *Popular Disturbances in England, 1700-1870* (1979), provides a valuable analysis of the types of riots and disturbances over this period, reinforcing Rude's view that rioters are rarely without objectives. The idea of 'bargaining by riot' also informs the more recent work by John Bohstedt, *Riots and Community Politics in England and Wales, 1790-1810* (1983). One of Bohstedt's conclusions which seems relevant to the Liverpool experience is that rapid growth, overcrowding and urban stress are factors in producing violence on the streets. These works are obviously not the totality of studies on riots but they are most important references for students new to this field of scholarship.

Other considerations inform this study. The consequences of Irish immigration into Victorian Britain following the famine of 1845-49 resulted in profound and permanent changes in the social structure of certain towns, Liverpool and Glasgow in particular. The experience of the influx of famine Irish was traumatic in both places and in the case of Liverpool it will be argued that this was an important factor in engendering sectarian bitterness. From 1850 to 1886 the consequences of Irish immigration into Liverpool were the major source of sectarianism in Liverpool, but this anti-Irish prejudice could by then be legitimised in terms of defence of the Church and Constitution. Scholars such as S. Gilley, J. M. Treble, Lynn Hollen Lees and W. J. Lowe have contributed greatly to the history of the Irish in Victorian Britain; a recent work, S. Gilley and R. Swift (eds.), *The Irish in the Victorian City* (1985), provides an excellent collection of essays on this theme and is a highly recommended survey of 'the state of the art'. Surprisingly, Liverpool was not a subject covered in that collection, mainly because so little had at the time been published on the Liverpool Irish. In particular, the experience of the famine Irish in Britain in the immediate aftermath of the tragedy awaits its historian. Worthy of note is Dr Papworth's monumental study of the census data, 'The Liverpool Irish, 1841-'71' (unpublished Ph.D., Liverpool, 1982). Also important in the context of understanding English anti-Catholicism is E. R. Norman, *Anti-Catholicism in Victorian England* (1968). Another influence on the sectarian conflict in Liverpool was the Ritualist dispute within the Church of England, and the essentials of this controversy need to be grasped in order to have any understanding of events on the streets in Liverpool after 1886. Strongly recommended is J. Bentley, *Ritualism and Politics in Victorian Britain* (1978).

The Irish Orange Order provided the model for ultra Tories in England who wished to harness working-class support in defence of the Church and Constitution. The English Orange Order also awaits its historian, and the only comparatively recent work is H. Senior, *Orangeism in Ireland and Britain, 1795-1835* (1966). This draws heavily on the Select Committee Report on Orange Lodges (1835) and devotes only two chapters to Britain. There is no central body of archives available to the scholar and the source material for this study is eclectic in the extreme, mainly because its prime concern is the actions of working men and women, history from the bottom. The details of Orange lodge activities, parades, meetings and the like have had to be obtained from an extensive search of the local press. However, it is hoped that the material concerning the early English Orange Order provided here will prove a valuable starting point for further studies and that the study as a whole will be a useful addition to the history of the working class in Britain.

The most important work on Liverpool of recent years is Phillip Waller's *Democracy and Sectarianism* (1981). This excellent book describes in detail the process by which the Liverpool Conservative Party harnessed Protestant fears and prejudices for political ends and the individuals involved. It also analyses the role of the Liverpool Orange Order in sustaining working-class Toryism. Our periods overlap but it is hoped that the present work, with its concentration on the violent aspects of the sectarian conflict, will complement Waller's political study. Finally, a broadly narrative style of treatment has been deliberately adopted in the hope that the book will be of interest to a wider readership than professional historians, in particular my fellow Liverpudlians.

Acknowledgements

I should like to record my sincere thanks to the Nuffield Foundation for financial assistance with respect to a research project into the economic and social consequences of Irish immigration into Victorian Liverpool.

I am also greatly indebted to Dr John Papworth for permission to use two tables and one map from his unpublished Ph.D. on the Liverpool Irish, which makes extensive use of census material. This work is the definitive source for anyone wishing to know the geographical distribution of the Irish in Liverpool. I should like to thank the Home Office for permission to use certain files connected with the religious disturbances in Liverpool between 1900 and 1909. The staff of Salford City Local History Library have been extremely helpful in my using their newspaper archives, while John Percy of the University of Salford library was unstinting in his assistance. Two colleagues, both lawyers at the University of Salford, Harcourt Concannon and Brian Doyle, have given their time most generously in my pursuit of statutes and an understanding of public order and ecclesiastical legal issues. In addition Marnie Mason gave me unrestrained use of her extremely skilled detective abilities in tracing newspaper reports while Gustavus Dobrynski of the Department of Geography at Salford University contributed his skill as a cartographer. To all these friends and colleagues, many thanks. I should also like to express my appreciation to Phillip Waller, who allowed me to read a draft of his fine book before its publication. To Celia Ashcroft and her incredible skills with the word processor and her unfailing cheerfulness, I am eternally grateful. Lastly, and most of all, I would like to record my heartfelt thanks to John Stevenson of Sheffield University for giving his valuable time and expertise as a historian to encourage and advise an outsider. The deficiencies in this book are entirely my responsibility.

F. N., Salford, 1986

Chapter I   **The social background**

I

Sited on the eastern bank of the river Mersey in the north-west of England, Liverpool faces Ireland and, beyond, the Americas. This geographic position was to have immense social and economic consequences for Liverpool during the eighteenth and nineteenth centuries because of the rise of North and South America as trading areas and the ease with which the Irish could cross over. The shipowners and merchants of the port revealed an unparalleled ability to grasp every opening that presented itself and by 1851, by any criteria, Liverpool was the first port of the empire.[1]

The first quarter of the nineteenth century witnessed technological developments in the application of steam power to shipping which were to strengthen greatly the connection with Ireland. Steam power brought a regularity of channel crossings that sail could not, because of its dependence on the strength and direction of the wind. The new steam packets were fast and, because of competition on the Irish routes, cheap. By 1822 the Irish could cross over to Britain with comparative ease.[2]

The growth of the port was mirrored by a corresponding increase in its population. In this respect it is useful to note that before 1835 the parish and the borough were identical, but after the passing of the Municipal Corporations Act the boundaries of the borough were extended in 1835, 1895, 1902 and 1905, taking in outlying districts. (In 1881 Liverpool became a city.) Thus the population statistics in Table 1 do not refer to a constant area, but the picture they present is clear enough in indicating the rapid growth of the town.

Many other towns experienced rapid growth during the nineteenth century but the scale of Liverpool's development is better appreciated if the ten top boroughs of England and Wales in 1851 are listed by size of population (Table 2). Even if the population of Salford (the fifteenth

TABLE 1
The population of Liverpool, 1801-1911

Year	Population
1801	77,653
1811	94,376
1821	118,972
1831	165,175
1841	286,656
1851	375,955
1861	443,938
1871	493,405
1881	552,508
1891	517,980
1901	684,958
1911	746,421

Source: Census reports.

largest borough) is added to that of Manchester, it still gives a total of 367,232, which was less than that of Liverpool. The sheer pressure of population produced results that placed Liverpool at the head of every list of indices of bad living conditions. By 1842 it had been publicly indicted as the 'unhealthiest town in England', yet this 'black spot on the Mersey' was to become the point of arrival for hundreds of thousands of starving Irish.[3]

TABLE 2
The ten largest boroughs or cities in England and Wales by population, 1851

City or borough	Population
Liverpool	375,955
Manchester	303,382
Birmingham	232,841
Leeds	172,270
Bristol	137,328
Sheffield	135,310
London (City)	127,869
Bradford	103,778
Newcastle-upon-Tyne	87,784
Kingston-upon-Hull	84,690

Source: census report, 1851

II

Figure 1 indicates the borough boundaries as they existed in 1851 and the main thoroughfares that are important markers in the social geography of the town. That part of the borough north of a line running east from the Princess landing stage, now known as the Pier Head, is still referred to by Liverpudlians as the 'North End'. This is the district north of Water Street, Dale Street and London Road. South of the line is 'South End'. By

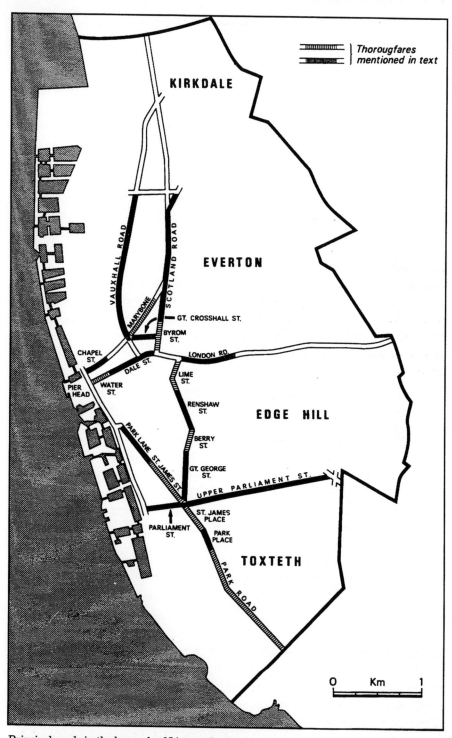

KIRKDALE

EVERTON

EDGE HILL

TOXTETH

VAUXHALL ROAD

SCOTLAND ROAD

MARYBONE

GT. CROSSHALL ST.

BYROM ST.

CHAPEL ST.

LONDON RD.

DALE ST.

PIER HEAD

WATER ST.

LIME ST.

RENSHAW ST.

BERRY ST.

PARK LANE

ST. JAMES ST.

GT. GEORGE ST.

UPPER PARLIAMENT ST.

PARLIAMENT ST.

ST. JAMES PLACE

PARK PLACE

PARK ROAD

Thorougfares
mentioned in text

0   Km   1

Principal roads in the borough of Liverpool, 1851

1851 the streets in the North End between Vauxhall Road and Scotland Road contained the greatest concentration of Irish immigrants in England, while in the South End, in the streets between the docks and a line running along Park Lane, St James's Street and Park Road, a relatively smaller but still large Irish community was to be found. The boundaries of the Anglican parish were not identical with the boundaries of the borough in 1851, the parish being slightly smaller, but the inner dockland areas were all within the parish. A more useful geographical unit of reference is the political ward, because its boundaries remained constant over a fairly long period, unlike, for example, ecclesiastical districts. Much statistical material published in the reports of social investigators refers to political wards, and the map, Fig. 2, shows the sixteen wards existing in 1851.

The population statistics in Table 1 hide the fact that Liverpool experienced the greatest *density* of population in the country during the first half of the nineteenth century. In 1841 the average for England and Wales was 275 persons per square mile. For Liverpool the estimate was 138,224 in the built-up areas.[4] The corresponding figure for Manchester was 100,000 per square mile. In fact the figures did not reveal the true extent of the overcrowding in some districts. For example, Dr Duncan, the Medical Officer of Health, claimed that between Great Crosshall Street and Addison Street, in the North End, a population of 7,938 occupied 811 houses, covering an area of 49,000 square feet, giving a ratio of 657,963 persons per square mile! This was double the previously published figure relating to the most crowded parts of London.[5] Such a degree of overcrowding, when combined with a housing stock lacking basic amenities in terms of sewage disposal, water supply and refuse collection, resulted in the appalling public health record and mortality rate revealed by Duncan. If we assume that houses let at £10 a year or less represented the only housing available to the working class, Table 3 gives some idea of the amount of such housing and its dispersal throughout the wards of the borough in 1849, a year in which the town was still struggling with the immediate consequences of the influx of famine Irish.

The 23,970 houses rented at £10 a year or less represented 24% of the borough's housing in 1849. Duncan had estimated that in 1840 70% of the population was working-class, and in view of the greatly increased numbers of Irish in the town by 1849 the proportion is unlikely to have declined.[6] It seems reasonable to conclude that at least 72% of the population in 1849 was 'working-class', while the cheaper property available to them was only 24% of the housing stock. Dr Taylor has shown that Liverpool's notorious slum problems had begun to emerge in the last decade of the eighteenth century *when the Irish born population of the*

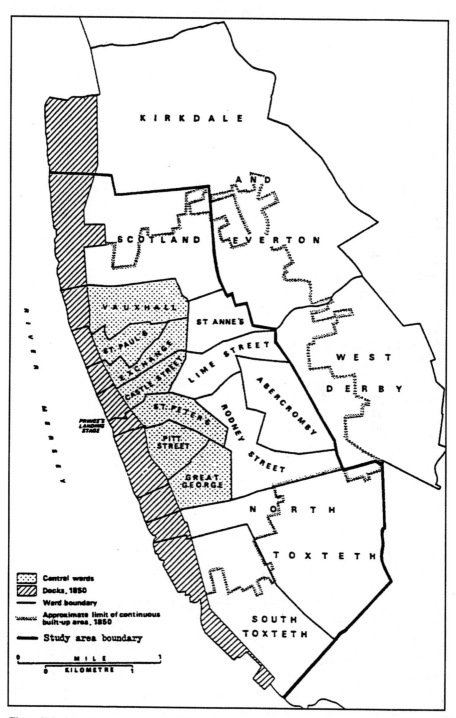

The political wards of the borough, 1851

TABLE 3
Percentage of the housing stock in each ward of the post-1835 borough which in 1849 was let at £10 or less per annum

Ward	Total No. of houses	No. of houses let at £10 or less	% of such houses in each ward
Kirkdale	1,379	407	30
Scotland	10,219	6,349	62
Everton	4,418	1,250	28
Vauxhall	3,724	2,662	71
St Pauls	2,522	1,157	46
Exchange	2,295	1,142	50
Castle Street	1,495	475	32
St Peters	1,623	123	8
Pitt Street	1,870	387	21
Great George Street	2,856	1,182	41
Rodney Street	3,334	642	19
Abercromby	3,394	725	21
Lime Street	3,149	1,012	32
St Annes	3,822	1,660	43
West Derby	3,853	1,192	31
South Toxteth	5,543	3,425	62
Total	55,496	23,790	24

Source: Health Committee, Minute Book, 28 June 1849

borough was quite small.[7] By 1841, in the parish as a whole, a total of 75,702 people lived in courts or cellars in contrast to street houses.[8]

TABLE 4
The distribution of the population living in courts and cellars through-out the political wards of the parish of Liverpool, 1841

Ward	Population resident in			Population	Residents of courts and cellars as % of population
	Courts	Cellars	Courts and Cellars		
Vauxhall	11,585	3,253	14,838	26,146	57
St Pauls	5,209	1,981	7,190	18,002	40
Exchange	3,975	2,491	6,466	17,769	36
Castle Street	1,829	570	2,399	9,691	25
St Annes	5,588	1,983	7,571	18,882	40
Lime Street	4,079	900	4,979	18,848	16
Scotland	10,628	3,166	13,794	35,613	39
St Peters	1,589	499	2,088	9,533	22
Pitt Street	1,742	2,103	3,845	15,263	25
Great George	4,590	1,337	5,927	19,645	30
Rodney Street	2,567	903	3,470	15,202	23
Abercromby	2,153	982	3,135	15,899	20

Source: First Report of the Commissioners of Inquiry into the State of Large Towns and Populous Districts, appendix 'Liverpool', p. 24.

Not surprisingly, the wards with the largest number of people living in cellars were, in 1841, those with the greatest proportion of cheaper housing. The prominence of Vauxhall ward as an area of poor housing is evident, with 57% of its population living in cellars and courts, although in the Pitt Street ward 14% of the population lived in cellars, compared to 12% of Vauxhall. In the Scotland ward, though the proportion of the population in courts and cellars was less, at 39%, than in Vauxhall, in absolute terms they numbered 13,794. The concentration of court and cellar dwellers in the North End is evident, with Vauxhall, Scotland, Exchange and St Pauls accounting for 42,288, or 56%, of the total. At the time fifty-two of every hundred Liverpool children died before their fifth birthday.[9]

III

The rapid growth of Liverpool's trade and shipping from the mid eighteenth century onwards attracted people of all classes from all over Britain, drawn by the prospect of making a fortune in the mercantile economy where the purchase of a ship was well within the means of a small partnership.[10] This drawing power increased in the first half of the nineteenth century, and among the upper echelons of shipowners and merchants such 'in-migrants' predominated. This inflow of entrepreneurial talent was a major factor in the growth of the town's economy, but the greatest number of people who flooded in was unskilled and poor. Of these, the most important single group was the Irish.

It is useful to distinguish between the Irish-born citizens of Liverpool and the Liverpool Irish. The latter term is used here to mean both the Irish-born people of Liverpool and the English-born children of Irish parents, brought up in Irish communities in the town and absorbing the outlook and attitudes of the Irish. Thus the Liverpool Irish, as a group, were greater in number than the Irish-born Liverpudlians. The size and significance of this latter group is best appreciated if seen in the context of Irish immigration as a whole. While there was always some movement of unskilled Irish into Britain during the eighteenth century, it was on a fairly small scale and predominantly seasonal, as the Irish came over to help with the harvests. There was a relatively large community in London by the last quarter of the century, but it was the nineteenth that was to witness the large-scale emigration that resulted in the establishment of many large communities outside Ireland.[11] The significance of the great famine of the 1840s is revealed by the fact that, from 8,175,000 in 1841, the population of Ireland had fallen to 6,552,255 by 1851.[12] In the main, the exodus was precipitated by the potato famine, and multitudes went to America or, to a lesser extent, Canada and Australia. Britain also had to absorb large numbers (Table 5).

TABLE 5

The Irish-born population of England, Scotland and Wales, 1841-61

Area	Nos. of Irish-born residents (nearest 1,000)	% of population Irish-born
1841		
England and Wales	291,000	1.8
Scotland	126,000	4.8
1851		
England and Wales	520,000	2.9
Scotland	207,000	7.2
1861		
England and Wales	602,000	3.0
Scotland	204,000	6.6

Source: census reports

In the twenty-year period 1841-61 they rose by 311,000 in England and Wales or 107%. From 1861 onwards the numbers declined until an upsurge in the 1930s. The aggregate figures in Table 5 must be broken down further to gain a full understanding of the impact on England. For example, the figure of 520,000 Irish-born citizens in 1851 does not seem unduly dramatic in a British population of over 18 million, but when we look at their geographical distribution a pattern presents itself that has different implications. Of the 520,000 Irishborn residents recorded in the 1851 census, over 20% lived in London; of the rest, 299,640 lived in the seven northern counties, and, together, these represented 58% of the total Irish immigrants. The county that exceeded all others in the number of Irish-born residents was Lancashire. The distribution of the Irish in the North of England is shown in Table 6.

Though there was hardly a town in Britain that did not experience an influx during the decade 1841-51, the major centres of immigration were clearly London, Liverpool, Glasgow, Manchester and Salford, and they remained so throughout the nineteenth century. (Table 7.)

Though London had the largest number of Irish-born people within its boundaries in 1851, as Dr Lees has shown, their impact on the community at large was much less than in the case of the other towns because they were spread out over a much greater area.[13] Outside London, Liverpool had the greatest *number* of Irish-born within its boundaries and also the greatest *proportion* of its population who were Irish-born; the four towns - Liverpool, Glasgow, Manchester and Salford-accounted for 42% of all the Irish-born community in Britain in 1851. The concentration of the immigrants into these towns is emphasised dramatically when they are compared with sixteen other large towns in which the Irish had

TABLE 6
Irish-born population of the nine northern counties, 1841 and 1851

County	Irish-born residents 1841		Irish-born residents 1851	
	No.	%	No.	%
Lancashire	105,916	70	191,506	64
Cheshire	11,577	8	22,812	7½
West Riding	15,177	10	36,307	12
East Riding	1,945	1	6,052	2
North Riding	905	½	1,323	½
Durham	5,407	3½	18,501	6
Northumberland	5,218	3	12,666	4
Cumberland	4,881	3	9,866	3
Westmorland	242	-	607	-
Total	151,268	100	299,640	100

Source: census reports, 1841 and 1851

TABLE 7
Irish-born residents of Liverpool, Glasgow, Manchester, Salford and London, 1841-91

Town	1841	1851	1861	1871	1891
Liverpool (borough)					
Population	286,656	375,955	443,938	493,405	517,980
Number of Irish-born	49,639	83,813	83,949	76,761	66,071
Irish as % of population	17·3	22·3	18·9	15·5	12·6
Glasgow (burgh)					
Population	274,533	329,097	-	477,156	565,840
Number of Irish-born	44,345	59,801	-	68,330	60,182
Irish as % of population	16·1	18·1	-	14·3	10·6
Manchester and Salford (borough and town)					
Population	306,991	401,321	460,428	379,374	703,507
Number of Irish-born	33,490	52,504	52,076	34,066	32,270
Irish as % of population	11·06	13·1	11·3	9·0	4·6
London					
Population	1,873,676	2,362,236	2,803,989	3,254,260	4,211,743
Number of Irish-born	73,133	108,548	106,879	91,171	66,465
Irish as % of population	3·9	4·6	3·8	2·8	1·6

Source: census reports, England, Wales and Scotland

established themselves (Table 8).

The total number of Irish-born in these sixteen towns, taken together, was *still* fewer than the number in Liverpool. Indeed, the concentration in Liverpool was greater than the statistics reveal. For example, in 1851, parts of the township of West Derby (now part of

TABLE 8
Irish-born population of sixteen large towns, 1851

Place	Total population	No. of Irish-born	Irish as % of total
Edinburgh (inc. Leith)	191,221	12,514	6·5
Birmingham (borough)	232,841	9,341	4·0
Bradford (borough)	103,778	9,279	9·0
Leeds (borough)	172,270	8,446	4·9
Newcastle (borough)	87,784	7,124	8·1
Bristol (city)	137,328	4,761	3·5
Sheffield (borough)	135,310	4,477	3·3
Sunderland	13,897	3,601	5·6
Merthyr Tydfil (town)	63,080	3,051	4·8
Kingston upon Hull	84,690	2,983	3·5
Gateshead	25,568	2,195	8·6
Newport (borough)	19,323	2,069	10·7
Nottingham (borough)	57,407	1,557	2·7
Swansea (borough)	31,061	1,333	4·3
Tynemouth	29,170	1,108	3·8
South Shields	28,974	922	3·2
Total	1,413,702	74,761	5·2

Source: census report, 1851: birth places of the people

Liverpool city) were outside the borough boundary but adjacent to it. The Irish-born population of West Derby was 16,380, while in the next parish, Prescot, there were an additional 9,341 Irish-born.[14] Thus adjacent to the borough of Liverpool were at least another 25,271 Irish, giving a total of 109,534 for the whole district, an area still smaller than London. Many of the immigrants came from small towns and rural areas, and on arrival in Liverpool they found more Irish gathered together than most of them had ever previously experienced. The Irish-born population of Liverpool exceeded that of any Irish town except Dublin, Cork and Belfast.

The census of 1841 was the first to record the place of birth of the enumerated population, so that estimates of the Irish-born population in Britain before that date are less accurate. In 1836 the *Report on the State of the Irish Poor in Great Britain* was published, giving estimates of the Irish Catholics in certain towns, using Catholic baptism records.[15] The figure for Liverpool in 1833 was 24,156. Given this estimate, the number of English-born children of Irish parents must have been relatively large by 1851, so that the *Liverpool* Irish certainly exceeded in number the 84,000 Irish-born recorded by the census. One proxy for the size of the Liverpool Irish community is the number of Roman Catholics. If we assume that the few Irish Protestants equalled in number the few English Catholics, we can ignore both groups and assume the number of Roman

Catholics equals the numbers of Liverpool Irish. In 1855 the Catholic Institute put the number of Roman Catholics in Liverpool at 90,000.[16] In trying to understand the attitudes of many Protestants in Liverpool towards Catholics, the precise number of Liverpool Irish is not the crucial factor. What mattered was what the numbers were *thought* to be, as is the analogous situation today with regard to immigration statistics. To poverty stricken Protestants living in, or near, the numerous streets filled by Irish newcomers the town must have seemed like a part of Ireland.

The simplest way to illustrate the geographical distribution of the Irish in Liverpool in 1841 is to point out that the largest concentration of immigrants was in the North End political wards, specifically Vauxhall, Exchange, Scotland and St Pauls. All these areas were less than a kilometre from the docks and so within easy walking distance of the main source of employment. A smaller but still relatively large number of Irish had settled in the South End wards of Pitt Street, Great George and North and South Toxteth - and again, they massed in the streets running down to the docks, in this case the Wapping area. Table 9 shows just how big the Irish community was in the North End.[17]

TABLE 9
The geographical distribution of Irish-born residents in fourteen political wards,
1841 and 1851

	1841			1851		
Ward	Total population	Irish-born	Irish as %	Total population	Irish-born	Irish as %
Scotland	35,290	6,095	17·3	60,065	18,275	30·4
Vauxhall	25,330	8,529	33·7	25,663	12,115	47·2
St Pauls	18,086	3,853	21·3	14,051	3,539	25·2
Exchange	17,652	6,115	34·3	16,935	7,965	47·0
Castle Street	9,742	2,382	24·5	8,746	2,186	24·9
St Peters	9,511	2,236	23·5	9,278	2,074	22·4
Pitt Street	15,393	3,793	24·6	12,144	3,328	27·4
Great George	19,331	4,354	22·5	20,181	6,009	29·8
Rodney	15,072	1,136	7·5	17,892	1,504	8·4
Abercromby	15,669	1,248	7·9	21,701	2,060	9·5
Lime Street	18,753	1,837	9·8	17,570	2,181	12·4
St Annes	18,862	1,850	9·8	22,706	3,503	15·4
North Toxteth	21,714	2,275	10·5	28,270	3,681	13·0
South Toxteth	18,241	1,769	9·7	31,667	4,558	14·4
Total	258,646	47,472	18·4	306,869	72,978	23·8

Source: J D Papworth, 'Liverpool Irish, 1841-1871', unpublished Ph.D. University of Liverpool, 1982,

In 1841 the Irish-born population of Vauxhall, St Pauls, Exchange and Scotland wards totalled 24,592, and by 1851, following the famine, the number had increased to 41,844, more than lived in most Irish towns. The dramatic rise in the number of immigrants is particularly striking in the case of Scotland ward, which experienced a threefold increase. In the cases of Vauxhall and Exchange, 47% of the population in each ward was Irish-born, so that the Liverpool Irish in those areas must have accounted for well over 50% of the population. In the South End wards of Pitt Street, Great George, North and South Toxteth the Irish numbered 12,191 in 1841 and 17,756 by 1851, not only fewer in absolute numbers but also reflecting a slower rate of increase. However, this was still a large community when compared with other towns listed in Table 2. A major factor in the clustering of such large numbers of immigrants in the North End was the dock construction and operations, which continued to increase after 1851, providing job opportunities. Also, the Irish steamers came in at the Clarence Dock, making the North End streets easier to reach than those in the South.

The St Bartholomew's ecclesiastical district overlapped both the Vauxhall and Exchange wards. In 1841 the number of Irish in the district was surveyed. One result of the survey is shown in Table 10. Many of the streets run off the Vauxhall Road and were the heartland of the Liverpool Irish (see Fig. 3). The fourteen streets in Table 10 had a population of 9,115, of which 52%, 4,712, were Irish born. In the case of Midgehall Street and Stockdale Street, 90% of the inhabitants were Irish, a total of 1,028. Oriel Street, incredibly, had 1,777 inhabitants, of whom 1,278 were Irish - more than many Irish villages. These figures refer to the situation in 1841, four years before the immense emigration from the famine. In all cases the proportion of Catholics in a street would be greater than the number of Irish-born people.

TABLE 10

The distribution of Irish-born in St Bartholomew's ecclesiastical district, 1841

Street	Total population	Irish population	% Irish	Proportion of Irish total
Pickup Street	161	47	29·1	0·9
Marlborough Street	527	153	29·0	3·3
Midghall Street	867	387	44·6	8·2
Midghall Lane	131	118	90·1	2·5
Banastre Street	1,202	721	59·9	15·3
Stockdale Street	1,008	910	90·3	19·3
Freemason's Row	640	228	35·6	4·8
Gladstone Street	231	22	9·5	0·5
Naylor Street	935	398	42·6	8·5
Oriel Street	1,777	1,278	71·9	27·1
Cherry Lane	401	238	59·4	5·1
Paul Street	526	212	40·3	4·5
Vauxhall Road	364	-	-	-
Marybone	345	-	-	-
Total	9,115	4,712	51·7	100·0

Source: Second Report of Commissioners of Inquiry into the State of Large Towns and Populous Districts, appendix, p. 88

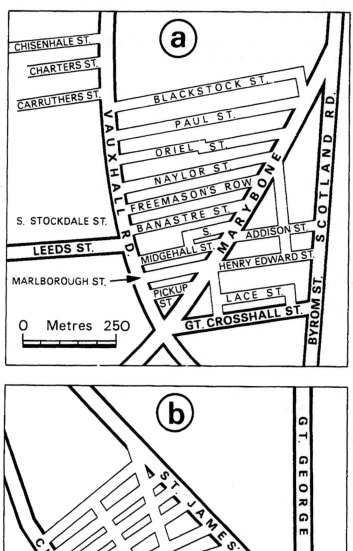

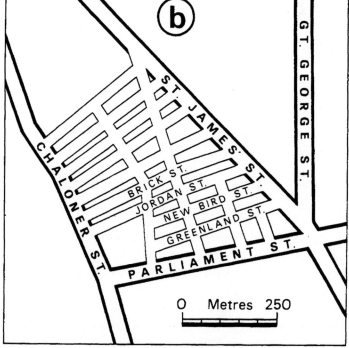

Principal streets in (*a*) the North End and (*b*) the South End

In 1850 Canon Abraham Hume, assisted by lay readers, undertook another survey, this time of the Vauxhall and St Stephen's ecclesiastical districts, and produced more detailed information concerning the Irish in the area. (The districts were not identical to the political wards.)

TABLE 11
Irish-born population of streets in Vauxhall ecclesiastical district, 1850

Street	Total population	Irish	% Irish
Carruthers Street	120	33	27·5
Chartres Street	803	543	67·6
Chisenhale Street	1,539	1,269	82·5
Clement Street	458	169	36·9
Cockspur Street	261	95	36·4
Dickson Street	37	10	27·0
Eaton Street	577	313	54·3
Eccles Street	286	97	33·9
Gascoyne Street	1,028	172	16·7
Highfield Street	821	309	37·6
Key Street	163	68	41·7
Leeds Street	881	130	14·8
McVicar Street	66	38	57·6
Milk Street	224	151	67·4
Northampton Street	349	113	32·4
Pall Mall	613	193	31·5
Plumbe Street	652	175	26·8
Pownall Square	155	121	78·1
Prussia Street	482	56	11·6
Pumpfields	39	19	48·7
Ray Street	867	156	17·9
Smithfield Street	597	413	69·2
Tithebarn Street	204	70	34·3
Upper Milk Street	497	268	53·9
Vauxhall Road	318	116	36·5
Westmoreland Street	674	346	51·3
Wigan Street	93	46	49·5
Worfield Street	224	60	26·8
Total	13,028	5,549	42·6

Source: A. Hume, *Missions at Home, or, A Clergyman's Account of the town of Liverpool*, Liverpool, 1850.

The total population of the district was 13,028, of whom 5,549, or 43%, were Irish. At the street level, nine of the twenty-eight streets, representing a population of 5,132, had Irish inhabitants who accounted for 50% or more of the total street population. Chisenhale Street stood out, with a population of 1,539, of whom 83% were Irish-born, while in Milk Street, Upper Milk Street and Pownall Square, huddled together off Vauxhall Road, there were 560 Irish, 62% of the inhabitants. Other streets in the North End displayed a similar pattern of concentration, illustrating the fact that the term 'little Ireland', used in other towns to describe a particular group of streets in which the Irish lived, had little meaning in Liverpool, where such areas were common. A year later the census returns reflect the same widespread pattern of Irish settlement in other streets in the North End. The streets listed there were close to those surveyed by Canon Hume in 1850, and so support the contention that practically every street in the Vauxhall area contained Irish inhabitants. Of the twenty-five streets in Table 12, six had Irish-born populations that accounted for 50% or more of the total inhabitants.

TABLE 12
Irish-born population of selected streets in the North End, 1851

Street	Total population	No. of Irish born	Irish as % of total
Edgar Street/Bow Street	269	38	14
Cavendish Street	860	497	58
Milton Street/Back Milton Street	1,240	645	52
Harrison Street	520	417	80
Sawney Pope Street	1,397	740	53
Addison Street/Fontenoy Street	947	695	73
Marybone/Bevington Bush	208	94	45
Bevington Bush/Scotland Road	319	48	15
Comus Street	639	182	28
Rosehill/Plover Street	315	58	18
Scotland Place	68	6	9
Hare Place	92	45	49
Bent Street/East View	495	264	53
Ben Jonson Street	684	252	37
Nash Street	204	48	24
Richmond Row	314	47	15
Rose Place	203	32	16
Gay Street	244	61	25
Total	9,018	4,169	46·2

Source: J. D. Papworth, 'The Liverpool Irish, 1841-71', unpublished Ph.D., University of Liverpool, 1982, p. 269.

IV

A letter, dated 19th June, appeared in the *Liverpool Mercury* in 1819 under the heading 'Orange Lodges'. The anonymous writer claimed that an Orange procession was planned for 12th July and, if it took place, it would be attacked by Irish Catholics.[18] On the morning of 12th July an estimated ninety men attended a service at St Peter's Church, where a sermon was preached in celebration of the battle of the Boyne in 1690. After the service the Orangemen formed a procession, accompanied by a band, and set off for the town centre. At the bottom of Dale Street a crowd of Irish Catholics had gathered, estimated at 2,000 in number. Dale Street is near the Vauxhall Road, where the poorest Irish lived in large numbers, and so the procession was heading into certain trouble. When the parade reached the end of Dale Street a savage attack was launched on the Orangemen. The affair was over fairly quickly, leaving many of them dreadfully bruised and several seriously injured. Liverpool had experienced its first Orange-Catholic riot.[19]

There is general agreement among both Orangemen and students of Irish history that the Irish Orange Order came into existence in September 1795. The most recent work on the history of Orangeism in Ireland and Great Britain is that by H. Senior.[20] It deals in detail with the appearance and growth of Orangeism in Ireland up to 1835 but allots only two chapters to the English Orange Institution. Senior draws heavily on the most important source of evidence concerning the early history of Orangeism, the 1835 report of the Select Committee on Orange Lodges. An earlier work is Sibbert. This two-volume study covers the history of Orangeism from 1688 to the early twentieth century.[21] Sibbert, as an Orangeman, draws on the 1835 report but also had access to early Orange lodge records which give the book additional value. However, it is an uncritical account and contains little material on the English Orange Institution.

The defeat of the Catholic military potential in 1690 led to the establishment of the Protestant Ascendancy in Ireland, that is, political power held by a relatively few wealthy Protestant settlers, staunch supporters of the Anglican Church of Ireland and the Protestant monarchy. The term 'Protestant Ascendancy' took on a more sinister meaning when, following the victories of William of Orange, a series of harsh laws were passed, penalising Roman Catholics in a comprehensive manner.[22] These penal laws became less rigorously enforced as the eighteenth century wore on but their mere existence exacerbated bad feeling between Catholics and Protestants in what was increasingly becoming a polarised society. In September 1795 a clash took place between Catholics and Protestants at Dan Winter's inn, at a place called the Diamond in County Armagh. The Protestants were defending the inn while the Catholics were attacking in considerable numbers. The result was an estimated forty-eight dead or wounded on the Catholic side and no reported deaths among the Protestants. Immediately after the clash, many of the Protestants involved met and decided to form an organisation to protect themselves and their interests as they perceived them. Out of their discussions emerged the Orange Order.[23]

Significantly, as many of the founder members were Freemasons, the signs, ceremonies and rituals of Masonry were adopted by the Orangemen. The basic unit of organisation was the lodge, and a lodge came into

existence by the issuing of a warrant by the officials of the new organisation. A leading personality in the setting up of the Order after the battle
of the Diamond was James Sloan, an innkeeper of Loughall, and he issued
the early warrants. The fact that Sloan was an innkeeper is significant in
that, from its inception, the Orange Order was characterised by a membership that was drawn overwhelmingly from the lower strata of the
Protestant Irish community.[24] Intending members had to undergo an initiation ceremony at which oaths had to be sworn, and it was the nature of
the oaths which later gave rise to legal difficulties. Matters had progressed
sufficiently for the first Grand Lodge to be formed in July 1797, and a
Colonel Blacker became the first Grand Master.[25] The Grand Lodge was to
be responsible for the granting of warrants and the imposition of discipline on the Irish lodges. On 10th November 1798 the first set of rules and
regulations for the use of all Orange societies was issued. On 12th July
1797 the first large-scale procession had taken place in Ireland to celebrate William III's victory at the Boyne in 1690, and this event was to
become a permanent feature of the Protestant calendar.[26] It was this single
feature of lodge activities that was to provoke most physical violence. To
Orangemen, they were exercising the right of free men to parade on the
king's highway in celebration of events they held to be of crucial importance to the well-being of their country. To Irish Catholics, the overwhelming majority of the population, excluded from political power,
almost excluded from land owning and subject to the penal laws, such
parades were intended to remind them of the Protestant Ascendancy.

V

The sense of crisis that permeated the life of Irish Protestants at this time
was shared by many members of the establishment in England, though for
different reasons. Events overseas played their part in rattling Tory and
loyalist nerves. The loss of the American colonies in 1782 was followed by
the French revolution in 1789, an event which stimulated and encouraged
those in England with strong republican sympathies. Given the French
dalliance with Irish rebels and the abortive landing in Ireland in 1798,
French and republican sympathisers were doubly suspect in the eyes of
Church-and-King loyalists. Parallel with the emergence of changing political aspirations which were causing strains in English society, there were
also developments in the industrial sector which produced additional challenges to existing economic and social relations.

The campaign for political reform and the emergence of an embry-
onic trade union movement were not the only causes of concern among
those who wielded political power in the eighteenth century. The growing
challenge to the Church of England's claim to be the national Church was

alarming that large number of Anglicans who regarded the Church as an integral part of the combination of Monarchy, Parliament and Constitution which had, in their opinion, produced a near perfect political system. Following the Reformation, the passage of legislation strengthening the position of the Church of England embedded it in the national power structure. The erosion of Anglican privileges had been going on throughout the eighteenth century, and it was the dismantling of this legislation which fuelled the Tory Anglican backlash which, in turn, was instrumental in the appearance of Orangeism in England.[27] For many of the leaders of English society, latitudinarian by disposition, the Church remained an essential part of their concept of a nation united by a common set of political and religious values. Any attack on the established Church was to be resisted at all costs. In the view of the ultras, grudging concessions might be made to Dissenters, who were increasing not only in numbers but also in wealth and education, but there were to be no concessions to the most feared institution, the Roman Catholic Church. As long as Catholicism was confined to the relatively small number of recusants it posed no threat, but the incorporation of Ireland by the Act of Union in 1801 at a stroke increased the Roman Catholic population by about 4 million. This event thrust the 'Catholic question' to centre stage of English politics, where it stayed for the first half of the nineteenth century.

By 1800 Orange Lodges had made their appearance on the mainland. Before the formal setting up of the English Orange Institution in 1807, lodges operating in England came into existence in one of three ways. Most important was the military lodge. English and Scottish regiments had served in Ireland during the 1798 rebellion, and in several regiments the Grand Lodge in Ireland had granted warrants to individual soldiers, who then enrolled others in the lodge. These military lodges consisted almost entirely of noncommissioned officers and privates. From 1799 onwards several regiments within which there were Orange lodges returned to Lancashire, and by 1803 it is highly probably that ex-soldiers were responsible for the appearance of lodges in Oldham, Bury, Ashton-under-Lyne, Rochdale and Wigan.[28]

Another way in which an English lodge could come into existence was for a civilian to apply to the Grand Lodge in Dublin for a warrant. Thus between 1798 and 1807, the year in which the English Orange Institution came into existence, Orange lodges in mainland Britain grew in number. They were concentrated almost entirely in the Lancashire cotton belt, with no central organisation and outside the control of the Grand Lodge. To confuse the situation, some Irish Protestants in England formed Orange clubs which were not Orange lodges in the strict sense. The potential to be exploited by enrolling ex-soldiers in the service of the forces of law and order was not lost on some members of the middle and aristocratic classes, who, at a time of widespread unrest, feared the existing social order was on the point of collapse. In particular, four men in Manchester recognised the possibilities of the Orange Order as a vehicle for counter-revolutionary activities. In 1807 they set about organising the existing lodges in Lancashire and progressed sufficiently to set up the first Grand Lodge of the English Orange Institution.

The member of the quartet about whom most is known is Ralph Fletcher, who conformed to the popular view of a reactionary 'backwoodsman'. He was born in 1757, the son of John and Mary Fletcher of Bolton, ten miles north-west of Manchester in the Lancashire coal and cotton district. The family was not one of the landed dynasties. John Fletcher was the son of a coal merchant and was himself a partner with Richard Guest in several pits in and around Atherton (also known locally as Chowbent), some four miles south of Bolton. Thus coal was the economic base of the Fletchers' family wealth.[29] Ralph Fletcher was sufficiently well established in local society to become a justice of the peace in 1797, and he also became the colonel of the Bolton local Volunteers, a title he used for the rest of his life. It was in this joint capacity as both magistrate and commander of the local Volunteers that he obtained his notoriety as a ruthless opponent of worker combinations and reformers in general. In the first two decades of the nineteenth century the industrial unrest unnerved a number of magistrates, who bombarded the Home Office with reports of secret meetings of workers intent on revolution and sedition. Among these Fletcher stands out. Using Home Office files, both the Hammonds and E. P. Thompson have highlighted his activities as a zealous proponent of law and order who appears to have been particularly obsessed with the activities of Luddites, real or imagined.[30] Commenting on Fletcher's career after his death in 1832, the radical *Bolton Chronicle* stated:

> The whole policy of the spy system, of which, in this part of Lancashire he was the prime mover, is too well known .. : suffice it to say, that the scenes which occurred under that system in 1812, can never be forgotten . . . We contend he was morally liable for all the results that accrued from that agency. It is difficult to trace the causes of human action to their primary source . . . We should perhaps find, that in the instance of Colonel Fletcher, this particular policy resulted from the circumstances of his being an inveterate Orangeman, and consequently illiberal in his religious feelings, and from a belief that the absolute ascendency of the Orange or Protestant interest, was necessary to the safety of what he called the British Constitution.[31]

Precisely when Fletcher joined the Orange Order is not known but it must have been at the latest in 1807, for in that year he became an official of the newly formed County Grand Lodge in Manchester. A staunch Anglican all his life, he was a founder member of the *Bolton Church and King Club*.

Though Fletcher was prominent as a reactionary, he was not the driving force in bringing together the disorganised individual Orange lodges in England under the umbrella of a distinctive English Orange Order. As revealed by the correspondence in the minutes of evidence of the 1835 report, this role was undertaken by a rather shadowy figure, Ralph Nixon.[32] However, the report contains no biographical details of Nixon at all. In fact he was a fustian manufacturer in Manchester and was only nineteen years of age when, in 1807, he took the initiative in the formation of the English Orange Institution. How he came to know Fletcher and Taylor is not known; in 1807 Fletcher was fifty and Taylor thirty-five; both were magistrates. Nixon appears to have been a reckless character, and by 1820 he had lost his business. He appears to have fallen out with Fletcher and Taylor and had probably left the Orange Order by then, despite his central role in its formation. In May 1821 he was arrested on a charge of stealing a watch and other articles from the Turk's Head public house in Hanging Ditch, Manchester. At the time he was reduced to living in lodgings, and when the police searched his room they found a set of professional burglar's tools. While awaiting trial he appears to have been a troublesome prisoner and, because he was so well known, his appearance in court attracted a great deal of attention. The press reports confirm that he had been the secretary of the Orange Order. Interestingly he was sentenced to seven years' transportation by the. Rev. Hay, a leading Tory in Manchester and someone who might have been expected to be sympathetic to Orangemen, which reinforces the view that by this time Nixon had fallen out with his former Orange colleagues. Hay confined himself to the comment that Nixon was a talented man who could have made his way in the world.[33] These events throw some doubt on the accuracy of Sibbert's account of the early history of the English Orange Order. He describes Nixon as the Rev. Robert Nixon of the collegiate church, Manchester. This is now the cathedral and there is no record in its archives of a Rev. Robert Nixon. Later Sibbert describes him as the Rev. Richard Nixon, again erroneously.[34]

The Taylor family were modest landowners in Moston, which in 1807 was north-east of the township of Manchester. In 1776 Samuel Taylor bought Moston Hall, and the young Samuel Taylor, born in 1772, was brought up there. Little is known of him. In 1801 his father died, and on the death of his mother in 1802 Taylor, aged twenty-nine, inherited the estate. He appears to have enjoyed country pursuits, kept a pack of foxhounds and hunted the country around Moston. One manifestation of his patriotism was that he raised and financed the Manchester and Salford Rifle Regiment of Volunteers, of which he was the colonel.[35] The regiment served in Ireland during the 1798 rebellion and this is probably the way in which Taylor came across Orangeism. Taylor became a magistrate but does not appear to have been an active political figure. Of W. A. Woodburne, the solicitor, nothing is known except that he had offices in Deansgate and acted as legal adviser to the Orange Order for a while.

The decision to organise the lodges in England seems to have been taken early in 1807, a time of continuing unrest among weavers in the Manchester area. It is possible that the decision was precipitated by the attack on an Orange lodge during a 12th July procession to the collegiate church. When the processionists left the church they were attacked by the Irish and a fierce clash took place, with several injured. The fight ended only when troops intervened to help the police.[36] Press reports of the riot give some indication of the activities of the Orange lodges in Manchester at the time. They suggest that 12th July processions had taken place before 1807 and had been stopped, and we know that the 'Twelfth' was celebrated in Oldham in 1803.[37] The July riot in 1807, however, was the first major confrontation in England between Orangemen and Irish Catholics and it seems to have happened at a time when, in Manchester at least, there was a rising level of popular anti-Catholicism.[38]

On 2nd December 1807 Nixon wrote to John Verner, the Grand Master of the Irish Orange Order, telling him that the lodges in the Manchester area had formed a Grand County Lodge, presumably with the objective of co-ordinating the activities of lodges in the surrounding districts.[39] Verner subsequently disapproved of this development, probably wishing to keep control in Irish hands, but Nixon's entrepreneurial zeal was undiminished. In January 1808, accompanied by James Lever of Bolton, he went to visit a London lodge. The object was to see if an English grand lodge could be formed, covering all lodges in England. However, the small number at the lodge and the fact that they were 'not respectable' in Nixon's view, led him to conclude that any English grand lodge would have to be in the north, where most lodges were.[40] In May 1808 it is probable that discussions along these lines were under way, for Nixon sent Samuel Taylor a copy of the Irish rules and regulations, 'which will assist you to elucidate the principles and design of the Orange Association'. In his letter Nixon indicated that the lodges operated as benefit societies and, more important, revealed his real objective in espousing Orangeism:

> . . . have not the society [Orange] a right to claim the countenance and support of government? Undoubtedly they have, but especially at this crisis, when the overgrown power of an implacable enemy threatens to

overwhelm us; and when internal dissatisfaction is not altogether extinguished, surely the good policy of supporting those who are sworn 'to assist the civil and military power in the just execution of their duty' cannot be disputed.[41]

Nixon's words are important because they encapsulate what was, and continued to be, the Orangeman's perception of himself as not only a defender of the established Church but also an upholder of law and order. It was later to be a matter of total incomprehension on the part of Orangemen that the authorities were to disapprove of their organisation and that they were labelled law-breakers and disturbers of the peace. What finally convinced Nixon that the lodges in England needed a separate Orange institution was the virtual disappearance, by 1808, of the Irish Grand Lodge.[42] In that year, an English Grand Lodge was set up in Manchester with Taylor as the Grand Master, Fletcher as the Deputy Grand Master, Nixon as Grand Secretary and Woodburne as Grand 'Treasurer, The new institution adopted the Irish rules and regulations, pass-words, oaths, etc., and the organisational structure of private, district and county lodges answerable to the Grand Lodge was retained.[43]

There is little doubt that the appearance of this organisation would have passed unnoticed but for the hostility shown towards the Irish Orange Order by influential people both inside and outside government. Groups of uneducated working men meeting once a month in a public house was, in political terms, a paper tiger but in Ireland the Orange Order had demonstrated it had teeth. Violent incidents involving Orangemen and Catholics had raised the fear that these antagonisms could spread to English streets and so hostility was also directed at the English Institution. The riot in Manchester in 1807 seemed to confirm these fears and it was to be the violence associated with Orange lodges that distinguished them from other Tory organisations. In addition, events in Ireland raised doubts about the impartial administration of justice in cases where magistrates were also Orangemen, and the opponents of English Orangeism feared the same results. However, the Orange Order might well have passed into obscurity but for the fact that it was, for a short time, espoused by a group of aristocratic Tory ultras, led by Lord Kenyon and patronised by the Duke of York and, afterwards, the Duke of Cumberland. This kind of support, and the fact of Orange lodges existing in some army regiments, guaranteed the full glare of public attention between 1821 and 1835.

In 1808 Nixon's immediate problems were threefold. First, there was the simple organisational problem of calling in all Irish warrants held by the lodges in Britain and their replacement by warrants issued by the English Grand Lodge. Without the power to threaten to withdraw a lodge's warrant, the Grand Lodge would not be able to exercise discipline over individual lodges. Second, the rules and regulations needed to be revised, in particular the type of oath administered at initiation ceremonies, to avoid the risk of prosecution as an illegal society under 37 Geo III, cap. 123, and 39 Geo III, cap. 79. Third, and equally important, Nixon wanted to solicit aristocratic support in order to give the Orange Order respectability and political influence. By 1814 changes in the rules and the removal of the swearing of oaths seemed to have safeguarded the Order's legal position.[44] With regard to aristocratic support, one important success could be claimed, not by Nixon but by Fletcher. In 1815 Lord Kenyon, who was to later lead the Tory ultras opposed Catholic emancipation, joined the Orange Order as a direct result of Fletcher's persuading him to do so. Kenyon told the Select Committee that Fletcher convinced him of the important part played by the Orange Order in maintaining law and order in the Bolton area at the time of the industrial unrest, giving credence to the argument that Orangemen acted as government spies.[45]

What was the numerical strength of the Order? Neither the 1835 Report nor the minutes of evidence give any idea of the size of the English Orange Order at this time but fortunately, an Orange Grand Master, probably W. Nuttall of Rochdale, published a book in 1815 called *The Orange Miscellany or Orangeman's Guide*.[46] This is a comprehensive guide to the Orange Order's rules and regulations, the manner in which lodge meetings were to be conducted and the words of Orange songs and toasts. More importantly, it lists the lodges in existence in 1815. These were seventy five in number, including three in Manchester, seventeen in Lancashire, seven on the Cheshire and Derbyshire borders, close to Manchester, twenty-two military lodges and nineteen others spread around the country, from Newcastle upon Tyne to Exeter. This information is of interest on a number of counts. Even if one assumed one hundred members per lodge, a total of 7,500 Orangemen throughout Britain hardly posed a threat to the lawful authorities, yet opponents of the Orange Institution were to level this charge. Of the fifty-three civilian lodges, thirty-five were in the north of England, north of a line from Chester to Hull, twenty-five of them in and around Manchester. Of these, all were in textile towns, as were five of the seven Yorkshire lodges, and all were places of industrial unrest. It was at this juncture in the affairs of the Institution that Ralph Nixon appears to have left the Orange Order to appear next before the public as a prisoner in the dock en route for Australia.[47]

Little is known of the activities of the Orange Institution between 1814 and 1821. Despite the efforts of Fletcher, Nixon and Taylor to recruit more influential members, the overwhelming majority remained labouring men. For lodge officials and the more respectable Orangemen, a major activity was attending the innumerable dinners to celebrate important dates in the Orange calendar, such as the victories of William III at the Boyne and Augherim, William's birthday, the anniversary of the raising of the seige of Londonderry, and so on. These dinners were the occasion of much toasting, rounds of Kentish Fire and drinking using rhetoric common to Tory clubs in general.[48] For example, in May 1821 the Manchester Pitt Club held a meeting, and in his speech the chairman used language indistinguishable from that of Orangemen.[49]

By 1821 the Orange Institution was still a provincial phenomenon. There is no evidence that it represented an organised, influential instrument of Tory policy. Numerically it was certainly less important than Benefit and Friendly societies. Individual lodges pursued an independent existence and were often beyond the control of the Grand Lodge in Manchester. The most prestigious recruit, Lord Kenyon, gave time and money to build the Institution up into an effective vehicle of ultra-Protestant opinion and action. However, it is highly probable that, but for the crisis over Catholic emancipation, the English Orange Institution would have remained in provincial obscurity. From 1821 to 1835, however, the Institution was taken over, at its highest level, by a group of aristocratic extreme Protestants who managed to obtain royal patronage, thus drawing Orangeism into the national political arena for a short time (see Appendix 1). The issue which precipitated this development was the Catholic question.

Essentially the 'Catholic question' in English politics centred around the issue of what concessions could be made to Catholics in order to obtain a reduction in violence in Ireland without, at the same time, provoking a Protestant backlash in England, politically damaging to those who made the concessions. The Act of Union in 1800 had failed to assuage Catholic grievances, and in 1801 and 1806 Catholic Relief Bills has been defeated in Parliament. Between 1815 and 1829 Catholic Emancipation became the central issue in English politics, mainly because of continuing unrest in Ireland.[50] The fissiparous nature of party politics at the time meant that Tories would hold quite different views on the problem. There were those who were prepared to accept change once the case for it had been overwhelmingly demonstrated and were willing to live with the consequences. Others were indifferent, but the ultra Tories were implacably opposed to change, whether it be electoral reform, agricultural protection or Catholic Emancipation. The ultra aristocrats included Lords Kenyon, Mansfield, Winchelsea, Salisbury and Falmouth, the Duke of Newcastle and the Duke of Gordon. The ultras have generally been portrayed as bigots, solely concerned with mindless opposition to change and party in-fighting, but a recent study has gone some way to modify this view. Writing of the ultras in 1829, Dr Simes concludes:

> The ultra Tory 'party' had begun as a small pressure group but it evolved into something closely akin to a true political party. It had developed a recognised leadership, a system of regular meetings which ensured solidarity in Parliament and a complex network of Orange lodges, Brunswick Clubs and 'electoral' machines which organised its popular following in a way not too unlike that adopted by the later Conservative Clubs and Constitutional Associations. It had formulated a clear-cut and consistent constitutional and social ideal and had financed a major press interest to publicise it . . . Far from being a factious clique of bigots and 'borough managers', the tory group was, at least before 1831, intellectually respectable and organisationally formidable, [51]

The ideals referred to involved the view that under the British constitution, the benefits of peace, property and religious toleration, were enjoyed by all and would be endangered if Catholics were given access to political power.

It is probable that the ultras' efforts to mobilise opposition to Catholic emancipation was the reason why, in 1821, Kenyon persuaded the Lancashire leaders of the Orange Institution to approach the Duke of York to become the Grand Master.[52] The purpose behind such a move was to raise the social standing of the Institution and so persuade other influential figures to become Orangemen. It is probable that Kenyon believed it would give the Orangemen some influence at court, to be used to persuade the King to oppose Catholic Emancipation. In February 1821 Woodburne, the Grand Secretary, wrote from Manchester asking the duke to accept the offer. The duke agreed on condition Kenyon became Deputy Grand Master.[53] The duke's appointment caused no embarrassment to the incumbent Grand Master, Taylor, because he was in ill health and in fact died later in the year. The Grand Lodge was moved from Manchester to London for the duke's convenience, and several more influential aristocrats became active members of the Orange Institution. In retrospect, there is something incongruous about a situation in which a small group of aristocrats and a member of the royal family set themselves up as leaders of an organisation consisting overwhelmingly of uneducated labouring men, mostly lacking the vote, whose main activities were drinking and, increasingly, street fights with Irish Catholics. One can only conclude that it was an *assumed potential* of the Orange Institution that appealed to Kenyon, based on a totally erroneous belief that events in Ireland had some relevance to life in England.

It was some time before the duke's appointment leaked out, but when it did it was greeted with astonishment in the radical press.[54] However, the Duke of York's tenure of the office was short-lived. On 21st

June 1821 he resigned, following a decision of the law officers of the Crown that the oaths sworn by members rendered Orange lodges illegal.[55] The subsequent appointment of the Duke of Cumberland, Commander-in-Chief, as Grand Master, and an increasing concern over the existence of military lodges, led to a conspiracy theory taking hold.[56] Kenyon had continued to chair the meetings of the Grand Lodge as Deputy Grand Master and the Duke of Cumberland was appointed Grand Master in 1828. Royal patronage does seem to have encouraged the recruitment of a few more influential men into Orangeism, but most influential Tories, ultras and others, held aloof.

Between 1821 and 1829 the English Orange Institution was preoccupied with administrative issues, in particular changing the system of oaths in order to avoid prosecution. In Ireland the Orange Order ceased to exist between 1825 and 1828 through fear of prosecution, and during this period the English Grand Lodge issued warrants to Irish lodges, thus keeping the Irish movement alive despite legal proscription, a move which brought English and Irish Orangeism closer together.[57] To accommodate this situation the Grand Lodge in London changed its title to the Grand Lodge of the Loyal Orange Institution of Great Britain, and Irish members sat on the Grand Committee. By 1827 the campaign for Catholic Emancipation was coming to a head under the pressure of events in Ireland. In that year the *Test and Corporation Acts* were abolished and the Tory ultras made preparations for a last ditch stand on the Catholic issue; meetings, petitions and newspapers were all mobilised in the campaign. However, even at this time of crisis some anti-Catholic Tories could not bring themselves to join the Orange Institution, not because of the low social status of its members but because of the allegations of illegality. To accommodate such people 'Brunswick' clubs came into existence to propagate the anti-Catholic views of the 'respectable' Tory diehards. All was in vain, the ultras were outwitted by the Duke of Wellington and Peel, and in April 1829 a Catholic Emancipation Bill became law. The episode demoralised Protestant opinion of all shades and caused a rift in the ranks of the Tories. For the next three years the Orange Order was moribund. [58]

One possible measure of an organisation's influence is the size of its membership. How big was the Orange Institution? The 1835 select committee investigation revealed that the record-keeping of the Grand Lodge was lax, and it could not tell the committee how many Orangemen there were in Britain. One member claimed 40,000 in London alone, and possibly 200,000 in total.[59] These figures were preposterous, and had the committee carried out the most rudimentary arithmetical calculations they would have realised it. We have noted that in 1815 there were seventy-five lodges. In 1830 there were 260; of this number, thirty were military lodges and 230 civilian. A rough estimate of total membership can be made, because the minutes of evidence give the membership of eight lodges, with numbers ranging from twenty to sixty-one, an average of thirty-seven. In a further piece of evidence a table listing the district groupings of lodges gave, in some cases, the total membership of the district. In this instance the average membership was twenty-three per lodge.[60] If we assume an average of thirty men per lodge, using both pieces of evidence, then, given 260 lodges, the total membership would be 7,800.

The geographical distribution of the lodges in 1830 is given in Table 13. The concentration of lodges in the north of England is

TABLE 13
The geographical distribution of civilian Orange lodges, November 1830

Region	No.
Lancashire	77
Scotland	39
Yorkshire	36
London	13
North East England	9
Cheshire	5
Derbyshire	5
Westmorland	4
Rest of country	40
Foreign	2
Total	230

Source: Report on Orange Lodges (GB), 1835, appendix 19, pp. 141-4.

immediately apparent and in fact the concentration is far greater than at first appears. For example, all but three of the thirty-six Yorkshire lodges were in the West Riding textile belt, not far from the Lancashire border, while all the Derbyshire lodges were near Manchester, for example, Glossop, Mottram, Tintwistle, Chapel en le Frith. The distribution of lodges within Lancashire is given in Table 14. Within this distribution there are quite distinct groupings. Wigan, Skelmersdale and Upholland are all close to each other, while Oldham, Middleton, Prestwich, Gorton, Denton, Newton Heath, Blackley and Worsley are all clustered around Manchester. A third grouping was Bolton, Bury, Rochdale and Colne. Interestingly, Liverpool was totally separate from the centre of Orangeism. Despite the increase in the number of lodges since 1815, demoralisation set in following the passage of the Catholic Relief Bill, and many lodges ceased to exist; even the Grand Lodge met infrequently. The aristocratic leadership had never shown much interest in the running of the organisation and the life of the Orange Institution remained rooted in the northern towns.

Into this vacuum stepped an extraordinary character, Colonel William Blennerhasset Fairman, who was appointed Grand Secretary in

TABLE 14
The geographical distribution of Orange lodges in Lancashire, November 1830

Town	No.	Town	No.
Blackley	1	Manchester	10
Blackburn	3	Middleton	2
Bolton	10	Newton Heath	1
Burnley	4	Oldham	7
Bury	7	Preston	1
Chowbent	2	Prestwich	1
Colne	1	Rochdale	9
Denton	1	Skelmersdale	1
Gorton	1	St Helens	1
Hindley	2	Upholland	1
Liverpool	3	Wigan	5
Leigh	1	Worsley	1
Lowton	1		
Total			77

Source: Report on Orange Lodges (G.B.), 1835, appendix 19, pp. 141-4.

1832, following the sacking of the previous secretary, Eustace Chetwoode, who was accused of inefficiency and of being a papist.[61] More so than Fletcher and Nixon twenty years before, Fairman was obsessed with the idea that the nation faced imminent rebellion and widespread sedition. Like the Manchester men, he wanted to recruit more aristocratic support for the Institution, and these obsessions led him to canvass potential leaders vigorously. For example, on 29th July 1832 he wrote a long letter to the Marquess of Londonderry, arguing that with such aristocratic leadership the pitmen of the northeast would join the Institution, making them less likely to ally themselves to trade unions and similar seditious groups, 'no less to the preservation of private property than to that of public peace'.[62] Fairman was taking a line consistent with that of the founding fathers of English Orangeism, i.e. the working class could be recruited in the defence of law, order and private property. Such sentiments were not in themselves exceptional but Fairman's language alarmed the authorities:

> By a rapid augmentation of our physical force, we might be able to assume a boldness of attitude which would command the respect of our Jacobinical rulers ... If we prove not too strong for such a government as the present is, such a government will soon prove too strong for us; some arbitrary step would be taken in this case for suspension of our meetings. Hence the necessity of laying aside that non-resistance, that passive disobedience which has hitherto been reluctantly enforced to our own discomfiture. The brave Orangemen of Ireland rescued their country from rebellion, and their gallant brethren in England would as heroically redeem their own from such perils.[63]

Here we have again the obsession with events in Ireland, the transference of lessons there to an English setting. Fairman's capacity for fantasy is revealed in a further letter in which he told the Marquess, 'we have the military with us so far as they are at liberty to avow their principles and sentiments'.[64] Thirty army lodges, representing about 1,000 men, mainly privates and noncommissioned officers, hardly posed a threat to anyone. Yet in the feverish atmosphere of the times the mere existence of military lodges, a Commander-in-Chief as Grand Master and the extravagant language of a senior official, caused questions to be asked in the House of Commons and the setting up in 1835 of the Select Committee on Orange Lodges in Great Britain. In particular there was a scare that the Order planned an uprising with the intention of placing the Duke of Cumberland on the throne. The Select Committee's report, published in 1835, unequivocally condemned the Order:

> The obvious tendency and effect of the Orange institution is, to keep up an exclusive association in civil and military Society, exciting one portion of the people against the other; to increase rancour and animosity too often unfortunately existing between persons of different religious persuasions-to make the Protestant the enemy of the Catholic and the Catholic the enemy of the Protestant - by processions on particular days, attended with the insignia of the Society, to excite breaches of the peace and to bloodshed - to raise up secret societies among the Catholics for their own defence and for their own protection against the insults of Orangeism-to interrupt the course of justice, and to interfere with the discipline of the army, thus rendering its services injurious instead of useful when required on occasions where Catholics and Protestants may be parties. . .[65]

Though the committee went on to claim that the Institution interfered with the political process and the administration of justice, it produced surprisingly little evidence to substantiate such allegations with respect to England, Scotland and Wales. In retrospect it is not easy to appreciate what all the fuss was about. An organisation of less than 10,000, spread throughout England, Scotland and Wales, ostensibly led by a small group of Tory diehard aristocrats, revealed to be inefficiently administered, hardly posed a threat to the State. Again, one cannot escape the conclusion that the committee's views were totally distorted by the quite different situation, in Ireland. Nor did they draw a distinction between the statements and activities of the aristocratic and middle-class leadership and the reality of what actually happened in Orange lodges outside the few that had gentlemen as members. However, in its contention that the activities of the Orange Institution increased tension between Catholics and Protestants the committee were correct, and in two towns, Liverpool and Glasgow, the numbers of Irish Catholics produced a situation more analogous to Ireland, and in which the emergence of Orangeism produced predictable consequences.

The riots on the occasions of the 12th July processions in 1807 (Manchester) and 1819 (Liverpool) were a portent of what was to come. In 1820 the Liverpool lodges had held another 12th July procession. The mayor had pleaded with the Liverpool lodge officials not to hold it, and wrote to the Grand Lodge officials in Manchester, asking them to intervene. The request was ignored and the procession went ahead, one banner carrying the inscription 'Protestant Ascendancy'. Another riot followed when Irish Catholic soldiers of the Connaught Rangers objected to some Protestant members of their regiment marching with the Orangemen.[66] In 1822 three Orange lodges paraded in Glasgow and came under attack from Irish Catholics.[67] In 1822 the Liverpool lodges decided not to hold a 12th July parade and confined their celebrations to public houses. However, the event had so quickly taken on the features of a confrontation between Orangemen and Catholics that Irish Catholics went round the pubs looking for Orangemen, and there were some disturbances. In 1824 these public-house clashes occurred again on the anniversary of the battle of the Boyne.[68] In Manchester no processions had been held following the 1807 riot, but in 1830 a serious disturbance took place because Irish Catholics thought an Orange procession was to be held, and again in July 1834 an Orange procession was accompanied by rioting.[69] In July 1835 the Manchester lodges were asked not to hold a parade. They refused to comply but agreed not to carry banners. Seven divisions of police were on duty as the Orangemen marched to St George's, Hulme. Inevitably there were continual skirmishes, although the Irish Catholics were unable to launch a full-scale attack.[70] In Liverpool a far more serious riot occurred the same week as Irish Catholics went on the rampage, searching for Orangemen (see pp. 41-3). Such clashes as those referred to above did little damage to property. Their significance was that the 12th July celebrations were becoming a regular event in some northern towns, providing a set piece confrontation between Catholics and Orangemen. In that sense the *Edinburgh Review* had got it wrong when in 1836, after discussing Orangeism in Ireland, it said:

> We now turn our views to England. The first essential difference consists in the proportion of Protestants to Catholics. This alone alters the character and tendency of British Orangeism; added to which, the long established respect for law and order, and for public opinion, preclude those perturbations which we view as a matter of course in Ireland. In England, Orangeism is little more than faction wearing the mask of bigotry; it has no substantial body of Catholics of which it can even pretend to be afraid. Politics are its real end and influence.[71]

Though these motives could be ascribed to the aristocratic leaders of the Orange Institution, to the working-class Orangemen, in Liverpool particularly, after the famine influx, *they* might well have felt they *were* living in Ireland. In their case, to misquote the *Review,* Orangeism was economic rivalry wearing the mask of politics. Obviously, this aspect of Orangeism was beyond the experience of the well-to-do Tories meeting in London houses to discuss high affairs of state. The contention of the select committee report that the existence of Orangeism would affect the administration of law and order was not without foundation. Following the 1835 disturbances in Manchester, a meeting of the leypayers on 30th July was held and a speaker called attention to the need to revise the list of special constables because a considerable number of them, he claimed, were Orangemen. Another speaker alleged that special constables who were Orangemen had been deliberately antagonising Irish Catholics in order to arrest them.[72]

To conclude this review of British Orangeism over the period 1800 to 1835, the obvious question to be posed is, why did working men join an organisation led by people whose primary concern was the protection of property, the maintenance of the existing order and the preservation of the established Church? Most lodges met in public houses, and drinking and socialising were important factors (see pp. 170-1). Benefit society activities were also sought. However, there were other, more potent reasons, one of which was the desire for more obvious material gain, as far as the least well-off Orangemen were concerned. Where the officials of a lodge were local mine owners, manufacturers, warehouse owners and so on, jobs would be given to Orangemen. This is not surprising, Catholics, where possible, exercised the same kind of patronage. Fletcher had absolute control over the lives of the miners who worked down his pits in Atherton, so membership of the Chowbent lodges would be a valuable element in job security. Publicans who were Orangemen could obtain custom particularly if the public house was used for lodge meetings and dinners. This system of patronage spread upwards through the Orange Order. The select committee report stated:

> It appears by the correspondence that the institution has been considered by some Orangemen a source of patronage, and there are various applicants from the brethren for the influence and assistance of the dignitaries of the Imperial Grand Lodge (which influence and assistance appear frequently to have been used) to procure licences for public houses, pensions in the artillery and situations in the police and docks. . .[73]

The volume of requests for help had become so great by 1833 that the Deputy Grand Secretary had to remind members of the Grand Committee that it was never the intention that the Orange Order should be used for private gain. It is almost certain that the patronage exercised by the members of the Grand Lodge was much less than that exercised by local officials in the provinces. In Liverpool the docks and warehouses became the battleground for jobs between Catholic and Orange equivalents of the *mafiosi*.

It would be wrong, however, to assume that economic gain was the only factor attracting recruits. For many men in humble circumstances the religious ceremonies attached to Orange lodge activities provided colour and a sense of mystery, legitimised by the adoption of the trappings of Freemasonry. Probably more important was the fact that men at one level of society could mix with those who were considered socially superior. At lodge meetings labourers could mix with local tradesmen, businessmen and Anglican clergy. These same tradesmen and business-men could, if senior lodge officials, attend Grand Lodge meetings in Lord Kenyon's house in Portman Square, in the company of Lords, Marquesses and a member of the royal family. This attraction of Orangeism should not be underestimated, and flattery of the lower orders was a technique later to be used with great success by Liverpool politicians. Another reason why the Orange Order attracted working men was that it provided a focus for anti-Irish antagonisms given a spurious legitimacy by expressions of anti-Catholic feeling. Where anti-Catholicism was propagated by middle-class clergy and laity, economic rivalry among the working class would be chan-nelled into anti-Irish prejudice. Another possible reason is the immigra-tion of Protestant Irish into England and Scotland. Before 1835 the Protestant Irish probably provided a significant element in Manchester Orangeism. The collapse of the linen industry in Ulster was followed by the emigration to the Lancashire cotton towns of Irish hand-loom weavers, but in Liverpool this was not the case. In fact Irish Protestant workers had little to do with the growth of Lancashire Orangeism. In 1833 and 1834 Colonel Fairman undertook a tour of Orange lodges in the north of England and Scotland and confirmed that the membership was English and Scottish.

The failure of both English Orangemen and Tory ultras to prevent Catholic Emancipation was followed by a gradual falling away of aristo-cratic interest, and after 1835 Orangeism returned to its plebeian roots in the northern industrial towns and the lowlands of Scotland. As an organ-ised body it almost disappeared until a revival in 1851. In some towns it provided a rallying point for working-class discontent which manifested itself in anti-Catholicism and anti-Irish prejudice: Orangeism never became a national political force, as in Ireland.

Notes

1   T. Baines, *History of the Commerce and Town of Liverpool and of the Rise of Manufacturing in the Adjoining Counties* (Liverpool, 1852). See also S. Mountfield, *Western Gateway-a History of the Mersey Docks and Harbour Board* (1965).

2   F. Neal, 'Liverpool, the Irish steamship companies and the famine Irish' , *Immigrants and Minorities*, Vol. 5/1 (March 1986), pp. 28-61.

3   Neal, op. cit., pp. 34-5. Between 1847 and 1853, inclusive, 1½ million Irish landed at Liverpool, of whom 586,000 were officially designated paupers.

4   *First Report of the Commissioners of Enquiry into the State of Large Towns and Populous Districts* (1844), appendix 'On the physical causes of the high rate of mortality in Liverpool', Dr Duncan, p. 16.

5   Duncan, op. cit.

6   For a detailed analysis of the market in working-class housing see J. H. Treble, 'Liverpool working class housing, 180I-1851', in *The History of Working Class Housing-a Symposium*, ed. S. D. Chapman (1971), pp. 167-220.

7   I. C. Taylor, 'The court and cellar dwelling; the eighteenth century origin of the Liverpool slum', *Transactions of the Historic Society of Lancashire and Cheshire*, Vol. 122 (1970), pp. 67-90.

8   *First Report of the Commissioners of Enquiry into the State of Large Towns and Populous Districts* (1844), appendix, table 10, p. 24.

9   Duncan, op. cit., p. 21.

10   F. Neal, 'Liverpool shipping in the early nineteenth century' in *Liverpool and Merseyside: Essays on the Economic and Social History of the Port and its Hinterland*, ed. J. R. Harris (1969), p. 175.

11   For an account of the Irish in eighteenth-century London see M. D. George, London Life in the Eighteenth Century (1966), chapter 3.

12   Irish census reports.

13   Lynn Hohen Lees, *Exiles of Erin: Irish Immigrants in Victorian London* (1979), chapter 3.

14   1851 census, North Western Counties: Birth Places of the People, p. 661.

15   B.P.P., *Report on the State of the Irish Poor* (1836), Vol. XXXIV, appendix G.

16   *Catholic Institute Magazine*, No. 2, Vol. 1 (November 1855).

17   I am greatly indebted to Dr John Papworth for permission to reproduce Table 10, which is from his unpublished Ph.D 'The Liverpool Irish, 1851 - 71' (1982). This thesis is an essential starting point for anyone studying the size and geographical dispersal of the Irish in Liverpool.

18   See also *Liverpool Mercury*, 6th August 1819. In a comment on the letter (reproduced in this edition) the Mercury claimed there had been no processions until 'the last few years'.

19   For a full account of the riot see *Liverpool Mercury*, 16th July 1819; *Billinge's Liverpool Advertiser*, 19th and 26th July 1819; *Manchester Mercury and Harrap's General Advertiser*, 20th July 1819, Examiner, 18th July 1819; H. C., Hansard, 21st December 1819, pp. 1390-93.

20   H. Senior, *Orangeism in Ireland and Britain, 1795-1836* (1966). This devotes only one chapter to mainland Britain.

21   R. M. Sibbert, *Orangeism in Ireland and throughout the Empire,* (1939). Vol. II covers the period 1828-1938. In 1835 two distinct committees were appointed to enquire into Orange lodges and their activities in Ireland, Great Britain and the colonies. The Committee on Orange Associations in Ireland did not produce a report but their minutes of evidence were published. The committee investigating the Orange Association in Great Britain and the colonies published both a report and minutes of evidence. Hereafter the Irish minutes of evidence will be referred to as S.C. while the British reports will be referred to as S.C. (G.B.). Senior draws heavily on the minutes of evidence for both committees, as does Sibbert. However, as an Orangeman Sibbert

also had access to some Orange lodge archives, but his book is an uncritical account of Orangeism.

22   For example, a Catholic could not legally possess a horse of greater value than £5. A Catholic priest could not celebrate mass, under the threat of severe penalties. However, mass was frequently celebrated in the hedgerows and fields. See *Catholic Encyclopedia,* Vol. XI, p. 8 (1911). 'Penal laws in Ireland', pp. 614-16.

23   S.C. Minutes of Evidence, Colonel William Blacker, q. 8924-39. Also Colonel Verner, q. 74-5, and Sibbert, op. cit., Vol. I, p. 281. For a different perspective see P. Gibbon, 'The Origins of the Orange Order and the United Irishmen', *Economy and Society,* Vol. 2, No. 2 (May 1972), pp. 135-62.

24   S.C. P. McConnell, q. 6470. Sibbert, op. cit., p. 385.

25   Blacker was one of the few gentry to join the Orange Order in its early days. He was for a while Deputy Lieutenant for the County of Armagh and a magistrate until his activities as an Orangeman resulted in his dismissal from those offices, S.C. (G.B.) Report, p. xxiv. Sibbert, op. cit., Vol. I, pp. 365-7. Sir Frederick Steven, Inspector General of Police in Leinster, expressed the opinion that the gentlemen in the Orange Institution had little control over the 'lower orders' in the organisation, who comprised the majority. S.C. q. 4658-4659.

26   At the time of writing (December 1986) the British government is planning to take legal action to curtail Orange processions, as a part of a strategy aimed at reducing communal tension in Northern Ireland. See *Guardian,* 2nd December 1986, 'Tougher R.U.C. curbs on Orange marches'.

27   For a recent and stimulating view of the Anglican place in the establishment and English society and the reaction of Anglicans to challenges to this role see, J. C. D. Clarke, English Society, 1688-1832 (1985) particularly chapters 4 and 6. See also E. J. Watkin, *Roman Catholicism in England from the Reformation to 1950* (1950), chapters 2, 3 and 4. Also A. D. Gilbert, *Religion and Society in Industrial England* (1976), in particular chapter I. E. R. Norman, *Church and Society in England, 1770-1970* (1976), chapter 3.

28   Sibbert, op. cit., Vol. I, pp. 479-480; Senior, op. cit., p. 151.

29   For biographical details of the Fletcher family see 'The Hollins leases, 1756 - 1829, and reminiscences of the Hollins, 1832-42', James Watkins (grandson of Ralph Fletcher) in Bolton Local History Library. These records have little to say about Fletcher. See obituary, *Manchester Guardian,* 25th February 1832.

30   E. P. Thompson, *The Making of the English Working Class* (1963), pp. 536, 557, 592, 621, 623, 633, 743. J. L. and Barbara Hammond, *The Town Labourer* (1920), pp. 25n, 45, 54, 163, 173, 178, 189, 199. Also id., *The Skilled Labourer,* 1760-1832 (1919), pp. 78, 275-85.

31   *Bolton Chronicle,* 25th February 1832. In 1821 several hundred Orangemen marched in the coronation procession with Fletcher at their head. *The Catholic Advocate* said that its correspondent recognised many many spies among the marchers. See *Catholic Advocate,* 22nd July 1821,. p. 269.

32   S.C. (G.B.) Minutes of Evidence. These contain practically all that is known of Nixon's activities. There are no biographical details.

33   The arrest and trial of Nixon was reported over a period of months and these reports contain the only available background material on him. See *Manchester Guardian,* 26th May 1821, *Manchester Mercury,* 7th August 1821. I am grateful to Margaret Mason, of the Manchester Family History Society, for drawing my attention to these press reports.

34   Sibbert, op. cit., Vol. II, pp. 481-2.

35   Fr. B. Searle, The Moston Story (1984), chapter 8.

36   *Wheeler's Manchester Chronicle,* 18th July 1807, *Iris* (Sheffield), 21st July 1807; *Cowdrey's Manchester Gazette and Weekly Advertiser,* 18th July 1807.

37   J. Foster, *The Class Struggle and the Industrial Revolution: early Industrial Capitalism in three English Towns* (1974), p. 219.

38   *Cowdrey's Manchester Gazette and Weekly Advertiser*, 25th July 1807. This edition complains of No Popery slogans appearing on walls in the town and of bands accompanying army recruiting parties playing anti-Catholic tunes such as 'Croppies lie down'.

39   The letter of 2nd December is referred to in a letter from Nixon to Verner on 3rd September 1808. S.C. (G.B.) Minutes of Evidence, appendix 21, p. 174.

40   Ibid., p. 175, Nixon to Verner, 21st November 1808.

41   Ibid., p. 174, Nixon to Taylor, 20th May 1808.

42   Ibid., Nixon to Verner, 3rd September 1808.

43   S.C. (G.B.) Report, pp. iv and v.

44   S.C. (G.B.) Minutes of Evidence. Appendix 21, p. 177. Nixon to John Gifford (Dublin), 11th February 1811. On 11th June 1814 Nixon wrote to J. J. Stockdale, Master of a London lodge, expressing doubts about the Orange Institution's safety from prosecution.

45   S.C. (G.B.) Minutes of Evidence. Lord Kenyon, q. 2598-605.

46   *The Orange Miscellany or Orangeman's Guide* (1815), Manchester Central Reference Library (Local History).

47   Lancashire Record Office, QS. 502/190 Order Book, 1821. Ralph Nixon, late of Manchester, Labourer, transported for seven years.

48   In November 1819 Ralph Fletcher chaired a meeting at the King's Head tavern in Manchester, also attended by James Watkins, an Orangeman from Bolton. The toasts were all in praise of the constitution and damning revolutionaries. *Manchester Chronicle*, 13th November 1819.

49   *Wheeler's Manchester Chronicle*, 2nd June 1821. The chairman praised William Hulton, a leading Protestant ultra and chairman of the committee of magistrates and who gave the Yeomanry the order to charge at Peterloo. At a meeting of the Metropolitan Pitt Club the toast of 'the Protestant Ascendancy' was drunk with 'great enthusiasm'. See G. I. T. Machin, 'The Duke of Wellington and Catholic emancipation', *Journal of Ecclesiastical History*, Vol. 14 (1963), p. 199.

50   The campaign by Tory ultras to stop the granting of Catholic emancipation was the main reason why some Tory aristocrats flirted with Orangeism. See G. F. A. Best, 'The Protestant constitution and its supporters, 1800-1829', *Trans. Royal Historical Society*, Vol. 1 (1958), pp. 105-27. Scott Bennett, 'Catholic emancipation, the Quarterly Review and Britain's constitutional revolution', *Victorian Studies*, Vol. 12 (1968/69), pp. 283-394. R. W. Davies, 'The Tories, the Whigs and Catholic emancipation, 1827-29', *English Historical Review* (January 1982), pp. 89-98; G. I. T. Machin, 'The No Popery movement in Britain, 1828-29', *Historical Journal*, Vol. 2, 1963, pp. 193-211; G. I. T. Machin, *The Catholic Question in English Politics, 1820-1830* (1964). E. R. Norman, *Anti-Catholicism in Victorian England* (1968).

51   D. G. S. Simes, 'The Ultra Tories in British Politics, 1824-1834', unpublished D. Phil. (Oxford, 1974).

52   S.C. (G.B.) Report, p. vi, letter to Woodburn from Duke of York dated 8th February 1821, accepting office of Grand Master. See also Minutes of Evidence, Lord Kenyon, qq. 2631-7, and C. E. Chetwoode, qq. 60-70. Chetwoode's claim that he approached the Duke of York *after* Taylor's death cannot be true, as the duke accepted the office in February 1821.

53   Lord Kenyon, op. cit., q. 2637.

54   Manchester Guardian, 26th May 1821.

55   S.C. (G.B.) Report, letter from Duke of York to Lord Kenyon, 2nd June 1821.

56   Sibbert, op. cit., Vol. 2, p. 193 and 198-9. The District Grand Master of Sheffield, J. Heywood, accused Fairman of sounding out opinion regarding the overthrow of William IV and putting the Duke of Cumberland on the throne. The split between the

Grand Lodge and the Sheffield lodges led to the Sheffield lodges breaking away in 1835. See *Sheffield Iris*, 28th July 1835 and 22nd December 1835.

57 S.C. (G.B.) Report, Minutes of Evidence, Lord Kenyon, qq. 2832-42.

58 G. I. T. Machin, 'The Duke of Wellington and Catholic emancipation', *Journal of Ecclesiastical History*, Vol. 13 (1963), pp. 190-208. See also S.C. (G.B.) Minutes of Evidence, C. E. Chetwoode, qq. 253-9.

59 S.C. (G.B.) Report, appendix 19. This contains a complete list of all lodges in existence in 1830, indicating which town each lodge was in.

60 S.C. (G.B.) Report, appendix 20, p. 145, District Warrants existing on 22nd August 1835. Appendix 21, Membership of numbers of lodges Nos. 3, 21, 40, 49, 204, 256, 223, 224.

61 S.C. (G.B.) Report, Minutes of Evidence, appendix 2. Chetwoode was suspended from the Orange Institution at a meeting of the Grand Committee on 4th June 1832. At a meeting of the Grand Committee on 15th February 1833 he was cleared of the charge of being a Papist but was dismissed on the grounds of financial ineptitude.

62 S.C. (G.B.) Report, Minutes of Evidence, appendix 21, Fairman to Marquess of Londonderry, 29th July 1832.

63 Ibid.

64 Fairman, op. cit. Letter to Marquess of Londonderry, 30th July 1832.

65 S.C. (G.B.) Report, p. xviii.

66 *Liverpool Mercury*, 14th July 1820; also S.C. (G.B.) Report, p. xix.

67 Manchester Guardian, 27th December 1822.

68 Liverpool Mercury, 16th July 1824.

69 *Wheeler's Manchester Chronicle*, 17th July 1830, 19th July 1834; *Manchester Guardian*, 19th July 1834; *Liverpool Journal*, 19th July 1834.

70 *Manchester Guardian*, 18th July 1835.

71 *Edinburgh Review*, Vol. 62, No. CXXVI (January 1836), p. 501. This edition contains a useful contemporary review of the select committee report on Orange lodges.

72 *Manchester Guardian*, 1st August 1835.

73 S.C. (G.B.) Report, p. x.

Chapter II   **No Popery politics,** 1800-44

On 15th July 1842 Catherine Carney, a native of Donegal, was murdered. She was kicked and beaten in a street in the South End of Liverpool. Before she died she told the police that two men had attacked her, calling her both an Orange and an Irish bastard. In the everyday life of the port such a killing caused little comment.[1] The motive was unknown and the attack would probably have been carried out no matter who the victim, but its significance lies in the killers' words. The sectarian conflict in Liverpool gave many people an excuse to indulge in gratuitous violence, providing labels by which the victims could be singled out. Even within families, at times of stress, the terms 'Catholic', 'Irish' or 'Orange' were frequently the precursor of physical attacks.

I

It is highly improbable that such deep-seated 'religious' antagonisms within the working-class community arose spontaneously, even taking into account the endemic anti-Catholicism of Victorian England. We shall examine the influences and events of the period 1819-46 which were instrumental in establishing religion as a potent weapon in political affairs in the town and, simultaneously, as a divisive element in the working-class community. The choice of period is based on a number of factors. The Orange Order made its appearance on the streets of Liverpool in 1819 with consequences that established the Orange procession as a set-piece confrontation between Irish Catholics and Orangemen. In 1835 the reform of local government meant that the fight for political control of a wealthy corporation was open to a wider electorate, and in that fight religious tensions were utilised as a political weapon. In particular, party organisation moved towards greater coordination of effort and a Tory leader of considerable ability emerged, a leader for whom the 'religious' issue was the most important, locally and nationally. Lastly, 1846 provides a natural break because 1847 was Liverpool's year of the Irish famine, with consequences that had permanent economic, social and political effects and which require extended treatment in later chapters.

Among the factors most responsible for virulent anti-Catholicism three stand out. They were an ultra-Protestant Conservative caucus on the town council and their supporters; the coterie of Irish evangelical clergy who held livings in Liverpool and Birkenhead, led by Hugh McNeile, and, lastly, the Orange Order. Membership of these groups overlapped after 1835. Some Conservative councillors were members of the Orange Order, all were Anglicans, some of the Anglican clergy though not McNeile - were Orangemen and all were Conservatives. They shared common objectives, the defence of the Church and the Constitution, no concessions to be made to the Roman Catholic Church and the defence of the union of Ireland with the rest of Britain. These objectives were to be achieved by ensuring the return to Parliament of 'Protestant' candidates, and 'No Popery' was raised to the status of a successful vote-catching slogan in Liverpool politics for nearly a century. In appealing to the electorate on all these issues the Tories successfully tapped the latent hostility of many among the non-Catholic working classes to the presence of a large Irish Catholic population.

Professor Fraser had demonstrated convincingly that the large Victorian towns provided political arenas where men of ability and wealth could use their talents in the exercise of power on a grand scale.[2] In Liverpool, where the corporation dock estates and town dues generated huge revenues, this was particularly true.[3] However, until the reform of local government under the Municipal Corporations Act, 1835, many men of talent were excluded from the direct exercise of political power. Until 1832 the parliamentary vote in Liverpool was confined to enrolled freemen of the borough, while the freeman monopoly of the municipal vote lasted until 1835.[4] Until then the affairs of the corporation were run by the Common Council, which consisted of forty-one freemen, of whom three carried out the duties of mayor and bailiffs. The majority of freemen were drawn from the ranks of labourers and tradesmen. For example, in the 1806 parliamentary election, of the 3,000 electors, 83% were described as working men.[5] The remainder consisted of a group of wealthy members of old established merchant and shipping businesses. These old 'corporation' families included such names as the Tarletons, Gildarts, Aspinalls, Cases, Gregsons, Clarkes and Branckners, many of them having made their fortunes in the slave trade. The councillors were drawn mainly from these families and constituted a self-elected Anglican oligarchy. At the passing of the Municipal Corporations Act all forty-one members of the Common Council were members of the Church of England and thirty-six of them were supporters of the Tory cause.[6] Elected for life,when a vacancy occurred on the council the sitting councillors themselves elected the successor. The majority of freemen were thus excluded from council affairs.[7] At times of parliamentary elections their votes were solicited but, as many of them worked for councillors or other freemen, they were frequently under duress to vote the same way as their employers.[8]

Opposition to the unreformed council came from two quarters. There were merchants and gentlemen in Liverpool who shared the same political and economic views as the councillors but who were excluded from power, and they frequently constituted an anti-corporation party. A second group of men, of similar wealth and standing, also excluded from power, but of radical or whig views, represented the opposition to Toryism of the Church-and-King kind. The more important of these were William Rathbone, William Roscoe, the Heywoods, Boltons, Booths and Fletchers. The fluidity of party groupings at the opening of the nineteenth century meant the contest of general elections at Liverpool reflected the particular issue or personalities involved rather than party alignments, and the freemen could be bought with drink and money. There is little evidence that the Anglican oligarchy on the Common Council was particularly anti-Catholic. The Roman Catholic schools in Seel Street were built on land leased to the Church on generous terms from the corporation. Significantly, however, the unreformed corporation did pay the stipends of many Anglican priests, using corporation funds. This was challenged after the election of the first reformed council in 1835. In a tight political situation, however, any weapons would be used, including anti-Catholicism. In the 1807 general election William Roscoe was opposed by Banastre Tarleton, a member of an old corporation family. Tarleton campaigned under the slogan 'Church and slave trade for ever'. Roscoe, like most of Liverpool's Jacobins, supported the abolitionist cause, and during the campaign he was mobbed by unemployed sailors. He was also accused by the Tories of having supported Catholic emancipation, and probably as a result of these factors he lost his seat.[9] As far as local elections were concerned, the unreformed council had no need to resort to anti-Catholicism because they did not need the freemen's vote.

Against this political background, how do we explain the appearance of the Orange Institution on the streets of Liverpool in 1819? It is extremely unlikely that the wealthy corporation families on the Common Council, though staunch Church-and-King Tories, had anything to do with initiating Orange lodges. They had no need of Orange support in municipal elections, and the low social status of Orangemen would have proved unacceptable to them anyway. Similarly, Tory merchants, shipowners and gentlemen outside the ruling elite had little need of Orangeism.

They had no factories to defend against Luddite attacks, nor any mass labour combinations to contend with, factors that may have overcome any social inhibitions they possessed.

It is most probable that the first public display of Orangeism in Liverpool was organised by Ralph Fletcher and the officials of the Grand Lodge in Manchester.[10] Woodburne, the Grand 'Treasurer, was reported as having been in the procession and subsequently to have prosecuted the Irish prisoners in the trial which followed.[11] It is reasonable to assume that if any local person of standing had been in the procession the press would have picked it up, but no mention was made of any such presence. Among those giving evidence for the prosecution at the 1819 riot trial were a customs officer, a cooper, a shoemaker, a ropemaker and a shipwright, the trades that were subsequently to provide the mainstay of Liverpool Orangeism. In fact the ships' carpenters were to join the Institution in such numbers that for a while the 12th July procession became known as 'Carpenters' Day'.[12] It was claimed that one of the leaders of the Liverpool Orangemen in this early period was a draper's clerk.[13] Because of the presence of Manchester Orangemen in the procession, the number of Liverpool Orangemen must have been small. It has been noted that in 1815 there was one lodge in Liverpool and by 1830 there were only three. (Appendix 3). The significance of the 1819 procession was not the numbers involved but in the mere fact that a procession had taken place at all. It was an important stage in the process by which sectarian violence became institutionalised in working-class life. In Liverpool and Glasgow this 'tradition' had become firmly established by 1851.[14] An influence on the decision of local Protestants to hold Orange parades in the case of Liverpool may have been the fact that in the 1820s the Irish held an St Patrick's day parade every year. Though such an event was in principle for all Irishmen, in practice it was a Catholic celebration, and this demonstration of Catholic numbers may have impelled the Orangemen to counter-measures. For example, in 1824 it was claimed there were between 10,000 and 12,000 in the St Patrick's day parade, something which, at that time, the Orangemen could not rival. The sheer size of the parade was probably the reason it was never attacked.[15]

The Irish attack on the 1819 procession did not deter the Orangemen, and on 12th July 1820 they organised another parade. The number involved was still small and the leadership unidentifiable but, significantly, the procession attracted a large following of 'supporters' drawn by the prospect of trouble.[16] Sir John Tobin, the mayor, had communicated with the local officials of the Orange lodges and with Fletcher, asking them not to hold a procession, but had failed to dissuade them. In exasperation he had the local Grand Master arrested but a grand jury concluded there was no case to answer.[17] No further processions were held until 1842, but the idea of confrontation on 12th July had been implanted. The absence of processions did not mean a cessation of hostilities. Disturbances in public houses occurred on 12th July in 1821, 1822, 1823 and 1824.[18] Such rows, specifically between Protestant and Catholic working men, were a new feature. Rows in public houses were common but after 1819 the 'religious row' emerged. Though the unreformed council did not adopt a particularly anti-Catholic viewpoint, there were Tories who were attached to the ultra-Protestant cause, but they do not appear to have been vociferous or influential. The campaign against Catholic emancipation was a low-key affair in Liverpool, mainly involving the collecting of signatures for petitions.[19] The local lodges probably suffered from the same apathy and sense of betrayal as ultra-Protestants elsewhere following the passing of the Act, and by 1830 the three lodges in the town probably consisted of no more than a hundred members at the most.

Despite this stagnation in the affairs of local Orangeism and the cessation of Orange parades, the situation remained volatile. Among the Irish Catholics there were always many who had recently arrived with news from Ireland, and the constant arrival of steam packets ensured that the Liverpool Irish were up to date with events. This had the consequence of keeping hostility alive towards Orangemen. In 1835 the Irish rioted on 12th July. To many people living in the areas affected the experience was terrifying, and it was this and similar experiences, rather than concern over the established Church and the Constitution, which shaped attitudes towards the Irish. Hence it is necessary to understand the extent and nature of such disturbances. It is difficult to measure their effects on the attitudes of the local English population but there can be little doubt that they increased hostility among many and contributed to the polarisation of the community that was to be brilliantly exploited for political ends.

During the week preceding 12th July 1835 rumours swept the Irish districts that the Orangemen were to hold a procession on the 12th.[20] The rumour was untrue, but it persisted. On Sunday 12th July large crowds of Irish gathered in the North End in the vicinity of Tithebarn Street, Vauxhall Road and Marybone (see Fig. 1). According to some newspaper reports, many appeared to be drunk. During most of the day they simply milled around looking for a non-existent Orange procession and, apart from inconvenience to traffic, caused little trouble. At about 10.00 p.m., however, a row broke out in Ben Jonson Street and the night watchmen, though greatly outnumbered, arrested one of the ringleaders. Immediately the crowd attacked the watchmen, rescued the prisoners and chased the watchmen away. Almost simultaneously, a disturbance occurred in Great Crosshall Street, near by, and officers of the night watch in surrounding districts were sent to quell what had become a riot. However, the fury of the Irish had increased, and the reinforcements of watchmen, greatly outnumbered, were driven up Great Crosshall Street towards Tithebarn Street. The violence of the Irish now became so great that the watchmen had to take refuge in the Vauxhall Road bridewell, which was immediately surrounded by an estimated crowd of 2,000, most of them armed with bludgeons and other weapons.

The leading group of rioters attacked the outer gate of the bridewell with hatchets and heavy staves and, though it was stoutly built, the door gave way under the ferocity of the attack. The defenders retreated up into the loft and rang the alarm bell in an effort to secure assistance. Fortunately the fire station in Hatton Gardens was not far away and the alarm was heard by Michael Whitty, superintendent of the night watch and fire police. Whitty was a Catholic Irishman, of powerful build and great courage. Assuming there was a fire, he took a coach and drove to the bridewell. Entering the yard through the shattered outer gate, he found himself in the middle of the riot. Fortunately for him the defenders inside managed to open a door, allowing him to get into the building, and, remarkably, none of the rioters tried to follow. He sent messengers to gather his men from all over the town, and when they arrived they launched a fierce attack on the Irish, he himself being prominent in the fighting. The reinforced night watchmen, with some fire police among their ranks, succeeded in driving the rioters away from the Vauxhall Road bridewell and arrested three of the ringleaders. However, the victory was short-lived because the rioters regrouped and attacked again.

By this time the authorities were thoroughly alarmed, and all the forces they could immediately muster were being called upon, although the disturbances were still confined to the North End. Whitty and his watchmen and fire police were joined by William Parlour, governor of the day police, with some of his men and a large force of firemen. With these reinforcements Whitty and Parlour led yet another attack on the rioters, and this time the Irish were forced to retreat. Whitty was joined by Mathew Dowling, superintendent of the dock police, who had arrived with 100 men, followed shortly by the mayor and Alderman Sir Thomas Brancker, together with 200 troops of the 80th Regiment. This large combined force ensured that by midnight the Vauxhall Road area was quiet, but in the fighting several watchmen had received severe injuries.

Though the Irish had been beaten off by late Sunday night and the large force of law officers had secured the arrest of many of the ringleaders, the trouble was not over. While the prisoners from the North End were in court on Monday morning, large crowds of Irish were gathering in

Park Lane in the South End and the rumour of an intended Orange procession persisted. At about 9.30 in the morning Parlour and a body of police went to Park Lane, where shopkeepers and other business people were extremely alarmed at the sight of the gathering crowds of Irish. Shops and businesses were closed in anticipation of a riot. Parlour told the Irish that there was to be no Orange procession and the magistrates would not allow any. It seemed to make little impression, however, and the Irish continued to gather in large numbers, many carrying staves and other weapons. In an effort to defuse the situation Parlour and his men started to disarm them but, under the urging of ringleaders, the crowd turned on the police and started to drive them from Park Lane. Seeing that the situation was out of his control, Parlour called for reinforcements. The mayor sent for troops of the 80th Regiment, who paraded the streets in a show of force. This seemed to bring some semblance of order to the South End but the Irish threatened the mayor that if the prisoners taken on Saturday night were not released the bridewell would be attacked. As a promise of their intent, the mob marched through the town to Vauxhall Road, where they joined a large number of Irish from the North End already assembled near the bridewell.

Despite the large force already at their disposal, the authorities were even more alarmed and swore in 100 special constables. By 2.30 p.m., however, the situation was becoming so threatening that the prisoners in Vauxhall, under a strong escort of police, were marched to the main bridewell, which was more easily defended. The mayor, however, was still not convinced that the situation could be contained, and even though the Irish had not recommenced attacking the Vauxhall Road bridewell or the police, he swore in another 400 special constables. Thus by teatime on Monday 13th July the forces at the disposal of the authorities were the fire police, night watchmen, day police, dock police, 500 special constables and 200 troops of the 80th Regiment. This was by far the greatest show of strength the corporation had ever had to call on in order to preserve the peace and though large crowds of Irish continued to gather throughout the town there was no further serious disturbance.[21]

II

The first municipal elections held in Liverpool under the 1835 Act took place on 26th December 1835. The Act had enfranchised the non-freeman merchants and many tradesmen, and the result was an overwhelming victory for the Liberals. Of the forty-eight seats in the sixteen wards, they took forty-three, and leading representatives of Liberal families were elected as councillors, including William Rathbone, Joshua Walmsley, Hugh Hornby, William Earle, Thomas Bolton and William Wallace

Currie.[22] Inevitably, the majority of the newly elected Liberal councillors had little experience of running affairs and, more significantly, were unused to the rough-and-tumble of political life. To grasp power in the reformed council the Tories also had the new experience of having to fight for seats but they adapted rapidly to the system. By 1841 the Liberals had lost overall control of the council and did not regain it for forty years. The main reason was an injection of anti-Catholicism into local politics on a scale unparalleled in England and Wales, and the driving force behind it was a group of Irish clergymen led by Hugh McNeile.

In their enthusiasm for reform the Liberals opened up the two corporation schools to the children of all denominations, totally underestimating or simply not comprehending the hostile reaction among the Anglican clergy. It is probable that the affair would have blown over, with a compromise being reached between Archdeacon Campbell, the junior rector of Liverpool, and Rathbone and his colleagues. However, it was the misfortune of the Liberals that there had just arrived in Liverpool an Irish Anglican priest by the name of Hugh McNeile. He was a brilliant controversialist, intelligent, eloquent and pugnacious, and he was utterly opposed to Roman Catholicism. He immediately seized on the schools issue and established himself as the undisputed leader of ultra-Protestantism in Liverpool and power broker within the local Conservative Party. The history of the schools controversy has been covered in detail elsewhere.[23] However, the controversy was so important in its political and sectarian consequences that the outlines need to be repeated here.

The unreformed council had opened two schools in 1827, one each in the North and South End. Though it was never explicitly stated that the schools were Church of England establishments, in fact they were. Under the rules and regulations for their general management the school day opened and closed with prayers; all pupils were taught the catechism and all the Bible readings were from the Authorised Version. On Sundays all children had to attend worship at an Anglican establishment. This regime meant that in practical terms most Roman Catholic children were excluded, even though the schools were financed by the ratepayers in general, including some Roman Catholics. In 1835 the average number of children attending the corporation schools was 1,300, of whom 'not more than two or three' were Catholic.[24] Immediately on coming to power, the Liberal-controlled council set up a committee under the chairmanship of William Rathbone to look at the problem of making the schools acceptable to the parents of children of all denominations.

The council was particularly interested in the Irish national education system, introduced in 1831. It provided for the education of Catholic and Protestant children together by drawing up a scheme acceptable to the leaders of both religious groups. The joint religious content of the scheme was based on undenominational instruction using 'selected' readings from the scriptures. In addition, one day a week, other than Sunday, was made available to clergymen of the various denominations to undertake the religious instruction of their own children. Readings from both the Authorised Version and the Douai Bible and the saying of prayers were counted as religious instruction and took place on the day set aside for it.[25] This was the model influencing the Liberal councillors when, on 6th July 1836, they approved new regulations concerning the running of the corporation schools. The motives of Rathbone and his colleagues were entirely honourable, if politically naive. They wished to provide some educational facilities for Roman Catholics as well as Protestant children and, equally important, to foster better relations between them. The formula eventually agreed upon by the council was that the day would begin for all children with readings from a selection of scriptures, followed by the singing of a hymn. After this, normal lessons would begin, and finish at four in the afternoon. Then, for an hour, the children were to be taken by their own clergy for religious instruction, including Bible readings from the Authorised and Douai versions by Protestants and Catholics respectively.[26] The Liberals were totally unprepared for the hostility the proposals met.

Hugh McNeile was thirty-nine years old when, in October 1834, he was inducted into the living of St Jude's, Liverpool.[27] He was born in Antrim, of wealthy parents, and entered Trinity College, Dublin, in 1810, where, for a while, he contemplated a legal career. In Dublin he seems to have led the life of a gentleman and, significantly, displayed a keen interest in the theatre; many of his later performances in the pulpit and on the public platform had a strong theatrical content. After graduation he entered Lincoln's Inn but in 1819 decided to enter the Church, and in 1820 he became a curate in Ireland. From the outset McNeile established himself as a powerful and compelling preacher, and, following a sermon he gave in London in 1821, he was offered the living of Albury in Surrey. The post was not a taxing one and during his time there he undertook and published a considerable amount of scholastic work before moving to Liverpool in 1834. McNeile was a fighter by instinct and a political parson by principle and, supported by a confidence derived from considerable personal wealth, he was his own man. Throughout most of his thirty-three years in Liverpool he was embroiled in bitter controversy, not only with Roman Catholics and their supporters but also with many of his fellow clergy. The impelling force behind his actions and utterances was two basic propositions, the truth of which he believed in totally. First, that the

Roman Catholic Church was the enemy of Christianity and the Pope the Antichrist. He had difficulty in bringing himself even to use the word 'religion' when referring to Roman Catholicism.[28] Thus, in his view, it was the duty of a Christian to oppose the Roman Church at all times and in all places. Individual Roman Catholics were not to be persecuted, because, in his view, they were victims of a cruel deception who needed the love and compassion of Christians to help them find true religion. Second was his belief that the Roman Catholic Church was engaged in a political conspiracy. It did not, in his view, recognise the supremacy of temporal rulers and would, whenever possible, grasp political power and use it to crush heresy. Any political concessions to Roman Catholicism had to be opposed because, in his view, the Roman Church was evil and, to the extent that it obtained political power and influence, true religion would suffer.

On arrival in Liverpool he quickly nailed his colours to the mast. In October 1835 the clergy of the Church of England in Liverpool met to form a branch of the Protestant Association.[29] It was at this meeting that McNeile emerged as a force in local politics. In the course of a speech defending militant Protestantism, he was reported as saying:

> ... They were asked why they would not keep quiet and allow Protestants and Catholics to live quietly together; his answer was that the Roman Catholic system was opposed to the perfect law of God and the gospel of his saviour. The law of God declared that all who transgressed in one point was guilty of all, there was no distinction in it between venial and mortal sin, a distinction without which the abuses of Popery crumble into the dust. The law of God taught the full and free forgiveness of sin by the blood of Jesus Christ, having therefore no place for purgatory of the soul, without which the whole system of Popery crumbles into the dust. That was a system with which they would not and ought not to live in peace.[30]

The cry that the 'Bible was excluded from the schools' proved a potent political slogan and rallying cry for the demoralised Tories many of whom evinced an attachment to the Church of England which had not been apparent before. Despite their victory in the 1835 elections, it quickly became apparent that the Liberals were not unassailable. Then they had polled 58% of the total votes cast, but in the 1836 elections their share dropped to 50·3%. Of the seven seats they retained in this contest, four had majorities of under twenty. As Table 15 illustrates, the Liberal share of the vote fell steadily until 1841 when the Conservatives regained overall control of the council and the Liberal share of the vote had fallen to 47%.[31]

It is clear that small majorities frequently won council seats for either party, and the party with the best electoral organisation would reap the benefit. The Conservatives appear to have grasped this fact

TABLE 15

Election majorities in each of the sixteen wards between 1835 and 1841, distinguishing between Liberals (L) and Conservatives (C)

Ward	1835		1836		1837		1838		1839		1840		1841	
	L	C	L	C	L	C	L	C	L	C	L	C	L	C
Everton and Kirkdale	108	—	—	5	—	15	6	—	1	—	—	21	—	127
Scotland	204	—	—	30	13	—	—	33	—	41	1	—	—	10
Vauxhall	52	—	—	19	22	—	—	22	—	19	—	22	62	—
St Paul's	68	—	—	23	8	—	—	31	—	1	—	10	—	44
Exchange	124	—	4	—	—	11	62	—	1	—	—	30	28	—
Castle Street	510	—	103	—	u	u	u	—	23	—	22	—	9	—
St Peter's	165	—	7	—	24	—	65	—	—	—	20	—	—	25
Pitt Street	129	—	—	—	21	—	44	—	3	—	—	1	—	42
Great George	279	—	—	31	—	41	u	—	—	21	—	2	—	20
Rodney Street	17	—	—	20	14	—	9	—	—	49	—	58	—	71
Abercromby	125	—	13	—	5	—	—	23	—	8	—	37	—	131
Lime Street	366	—	22	—	76	—	62	—	—	34	—	4	—	8
St Anne's	276	—	15	—	9	—	45	—	—	19	4	—	—	10
West Derby	10	—	—	27	—	24	u	—	—	62	—	60	—	10
South Toxteth	75	—	89	—	5	—	43	—	6	—	6	—	—	44
North Toxteth	335	—	—	24	41	—	u	—	1	—	—	7	—	36
Total votes cast	2,927	2,117	2,717	2,682	3,093	2,946	2,565	2,338	3,290	3,485	3,210	3,409	3,804	4,283
As % of total	58·0	42·0	50·3	49·7	51·2	48·8	52·3	47·7	48·6	51·4	48·5	51·5	47·0	53·0

Note. u = uncontested.
Source: Newspaper reports of elections

the more quickly and between 1835 and 1841 developed an effective electoral machine, based in the wards and consisting of Conservative Associations, Tradesmen Conservative Associations, Operative Conservative Associations and more important, a nexus of Protestant organisations, all brought together to present a co-ordinated opposition to the Liberals and their Roman Catholic allies. Central to the success of this campaign were the efforts of McNeile and a group of fellow Irish clergy who put their time, church pulpits and school halls at the disposal of the Tories, which, combined with their fanaticism, overwhelmed the Liberals. This 'Irish clique', presided over by McNeile, included the Rev. Thomas Nolan, McConkey, Joseph Baylee, Dr Butler, William Falloon and Fielding Ould. By contrast, Rathbone, Walmsley, Blackburn, Bolton and the other wealthy leaders of Liberalism failed entirely to understand the tensions among the working class created by the large Irish population and by economic change. The new breed of Tory politicians, including in their ranks shopkeepers, publicans, brewers and tradesmen, were closer to the grass roots, and realised the political potential of such a situation. Of particular importance in the Tory success were the Protestant Association, the Operative Protestant Association and the Orange Institution.

The Liverpool branch of the Protestant Association was formed in October 1835 and McNeile became its chairman. Its membership was drawn from the ranks of middle-class Anglicans, in contrast to the Operative Protestant Association and the Orange lodges. These two organisations were the primary means whereby the Liverpool Conservatives maintained a dialogue with the Protestant working class, and the success of this strategem was due mainly to the Irish evangelical clergy. The first Liverpool branch of the Operative Protestant Association was formed in 1838, and within three years at least six branches were flourishing and were an indispensible part of the Tory political machine.[32] Essentially, the aims of this particular branch of the Church Militant were to defend the Church of England and the British constitution against Catholic conspirators and their allies, and to help individual Roman Catholics throw off the spiritual shackles imposed by their Church. For example, at a meeting called to form a branch of the Protestant Operative Association in the Pitt Street and Great George wards, the Rev. H. Carpenter stated its aims to be:

> To enlighten the members of the Church of England on those great and fundamental truths on which themselves and the Church of Rome were at issue and to lay before members of the Church of Rome, the errors in which they were involved, in order that by contrasting those errors with the Gospel of Christ, they might embrace the truth.[33]

In practice, the meetings of the Operative Protestant Associations were used by McNeile and his followers to politicise the Protestant working class. This was achieved in two stages. First, a non-stop stream of lectures and sermons on the evils of Popery included the thesis that there was a conspiracy to overthrow the Church of England and re-establish the Roman Catholic Church. If successful this would lead to the loss of the liberties enjoyed by Englishmen. In McNeile's view, the Liberals' school policy was simply part of the same process of undermining the position of the Church of England, and the whole conspiracy had to be fought politically as well as from the pulpit. Second, having convinced Protestant working men that the Church of Rome was the enemy of Englishmen and that Liberals were Catholic sympathisers, it was a simple step to urging those with votes that it was their Christian duty to vote for Conservative candidates. These were, by definition, 'sound Protestants'.

During the six years following the 1835 Liberal victory the No Popery campaign was carried on with a virulence which dismayed many of the English Anglican priests in Liverpool and caused a rift to develop between McNeile and his Irish clerical supporters on the one hand and the English clerics on the other. Typical of the ferocity of the language used was a sermon preached by the Rev. D. James, vicar of St Mary's, Kirkdale, a McNeile supporter, following the 1837 parliamentary election. In the wake of this he stated :

> I tell you that if any of these liberal councillors belonged to my congregation, I should feel it my duty to refuse receiving them to the communion of the Lord's supper. And I tell you further, that if any man amongst you votes for a Liberal candidate, let him be anathema, himself, his wife and children forever.[34]

McNeile himself displayed character traits which caused his enemies to accuse him of inconsistency and duplicity. For example, at the height of the schools campaign he suggested that a solution would be for the corporation to provide schools for Roman Catholic children, thus enabling the Church of England to retain control of the two existing corporation establishments. This was certainly inconsistent with his basic position that no concessions were to be made to Roman Catholicism.[35] Such inconsistency was to be politically embarrassing later. An even more damaging incident, outside his circle of friends, was the so-called Fisher Street 'martyr' affair. In September 1838 McNeile publicised a letter purporting to have been signed by a Roman Catholic woman married to a Protestant named Stephenson, living in Fisher Street in the South End. The woman described herself as a Roman Catholic who, 'thanks be to God', had seen the light. Her husband, a true Protestant, and herself were having breakfast, it was claimed, on a Friday morning. She alleged a crowd of Roman

Catholic neighbours attacked her because she was eating meat: and her husband, in rescuing her, was struck by a stone and was seriously ill. The incident was recounted by McNeile to an audience of Protestants and, according to the *Liverpool Mercury,* his theatrical talents were used to the full to describe the incident of 'papist' intolerance.[36] Reporters from the *Mercury* went to Fisher Street and discovered, contrary to McNeile's allegations, the street was predominantly Protestant. The neighbour knew the Stephenson family, who had left, and explained that the affair had been an altercation between the Stephensons and a neighbour over children playing in the street. The next day the neighbour signed a statement for the *Mercury*, saying that Mrs Stephenson had told her that McNeile and a Mrs Johnson had visited her husband, as she said he was sick. Stephenson alleged she was given five shillings. The *Mercury* published signed testaments of six neighbours, three Protestant, three Catholic, that the alleged event had never occurred. McNeile was challenged publicly to respond to the charge of not checking the facts. In the minds of many, not all political enemies, the affair raised doubts about his integrity.[37] In 1840 Charles Trevelyan attended a church in Liverpool and heard McNeile preach. He was so horrified at what he heard that he published a pamphlet attacking the No Popery campaign.[38] In it, he claimed that it was in Liverpool that he saw political bigotry carried to its greatest height. Of McNeile's sermon he said it was a declaration of war on Roman Catholics. Trevelyan stated that in the sermon it was said:

> The time has come when everybody must choose between God's side and the devil's. We must fight even unto death. We must lay down our lives rather than submit. The struggle was to end only in the subjection of either Catholics or Protestants.[39]

In a report of a speech made at a meeting called to form a Church of England Metropolitan Training Institute, the *Liverpool Mercury* claimed that McNeile stated, 'He hated Popery, he was born and bred to hate it. He hated it through life and he would continue to hate it until death.'[40] Given the violence of such speeches, it is not surprising that it inflamed the passions of the Protestant working classes, and just before elections the stream of sermons given to branches of the Operative Protestant Association increased.[41]

The success to be attached to this stream of anti-Catholic propaganda can perhaps be judged by the perceptions of the shipwrights concerning the nation's problems, as revealed in a letter to McNeile on 23rd September 1840. They requested him to accept the office of president of a new branch of the Protestant Association to be formed in South Toxteth.

... We the undersigned members of the provisional committee, beg leave to inform you that the shipwrights of this town, desirous of being united in the defence of our Protestant constitution, the safety of which is so much endangered by the secret treachery of professional fiends, have determined in forming a branch of the Protestant Association.[42]

Propagation of the conspiracy theory concerning the established Church was not confined to the specifically Protestant organisations. At a meeting of a branch of the Operative Conservative Association, organised to petition against the corn laws, the chairman asked the audience:

Are we not banded together to defend the Constitution of our land? Are we not banded together to defend our Church? Yes, and we will defend our National Church because she is the holy, just, the tolerant, the divine Church.[43]

In addition to ostensibly political meetings there was a non-stop round of talks and discussions, all reinforcing the general atmosphere of anti-Catholicism. Thus, for example, in May 1837 the Ladies' Irish Island Society in Liverpool had been addressed by a speaker who told the ladies that many Catholics in the islands off the west coast of Ireland worshipped the Virgin Mary not as a saint but as a fish. The same meeting was addressed by Hugh Stowell, a close friend of McNeile's and Manchester's leading No Popery orator. He spoke of his happiness at the formation of a branch of a society with the aim of disseminating the word of God among 'Our deluded Irish fellow subjects'.[44] In the same month an Irishman by the name of O'Brien advertised a talk to be given on the subject of the system of education given at the Catholic seminary of Maynooth. In the advertisement it was stated ladies could not attend, as the subject matter was too indecent.[45] Soon after another meeting was called under the title of 'Justice for Ireland'. The tenor of the speeches was that Irishmen and women need rescuing from the spiritual bondage of the Catholic Church and a collection was taken to finance the taking of the scriptures to Connaught.[46]

It is not clear to what extent these activities were co-ordinated but there can be little doubt that there was some degree of organisation both within Liverpool and with sympathisers elsewhere. William Hulton, the Protestant ultra from Bolton, addressed meetings of the Protestant Association in Liverpool, Hugh Stowell was a frequent visitor from Manchester and there was an endless stream of speakers from Ireland.[47] McNeile was quite clear in his own mind as to the political nature of his mission-speaking in 1840 at the meeting in Toxteth called to form a branch of the Protestant Association, he exhorted his audience to live lives beyond reproach as an example to the 'poor, deluded and defrauded

Romanists'. This, he argued, was the way to restore the Protestant Ascendency in Britain:

> I believe that it can be gained in no other way. I believe that by our men in authority it is not to be regained because one and all . . . have proved faithless to the great principle of Protestant Ascendency; and the only way to regain it is by cultivating Protestant democracy. That is the way to regain Protestant Ascendency. It is to be regained by the people or it cannot be regained at all. The power is given to the people-the middle classes of society have the power; and if they will become a Protestant people, we shall have a Protestant Ascendency again, the Bible in the ascendent and the principles of the Bible supreme in the legislative of our country. Who appoints our legislators? You and such as you select them . . . We shall have a regenerated House of Commons, a Protestant House of Commons.[48]

McNeile was addressing a large gathering of shipwrights, ship's carpenters and coopers, mainly freemen of the borough. This was the section of the working class who possessed the vote and whom McNeile won over to the Tory party. Later the *Liverpool Standard*, the leading Protestant paper in Liverpool at the time, repeated the view that it was the creation of a 'Conservative Democracy' which had restored power to the Tories after the 1835 defeats. Unlike McNeile, however, it claimed it was the Protestant working classes which secured the Conservative triumphs.[49]

The political dividends from the No Popery campaign over the six years following the 1835 Act were immediate in the case of both municipal and parliamentary elections. As Table 15 illustrates, from 1837 the Tories began to pull back their losses on the council until in 1841 they regained a majority of seats. They were successful also in the 1837 parliamentary election, returning Sandon and Cresswell, and the victory in the 1841 parliamentary elections demonstrated that the success was no passing phase. In the municipal elections between 1835 and 1841 Tory councillors had to prove to the electorate they were 'sound Protestants'. The ambitious Tory contender for office could establish his credentials in a number of ways, apart from simply attending church. One obvious ploy was to join the Protestant Association or the Operative Protestant Association and attend meetings, especially as a speaker. McNeile noted carefully which councillors attended his meetings.[50] Interestingly, over this period, the Orange Institution was little in evidence. However, membership of the Orange Order became an increasingly important vehicle of political advancement, although shunned at the time by the majority of Tory councillors. It is possible from studying reports in the local press to identify the councillors who were Orangemen.[51] In view of the tensions that were later to develop within the council it is useful to establish that, by 1842, of the thirty eight Tory councillors, only six were Orangemen.

David Hodgson was elected to the Everton and Kirkdale ward in 1837. A man of independent means, he had been a Quaker and a lifelong Liberal until he heard McNeile preach, an event which converted him to Conservatism.[52] Joseph Cooper, an ironmonger, was elected to the council in 1837, in Great George ward. He enjoyed the patronage of James Lawrence, a brewer with influence in the ward. Cooper was also an Orangeman.[53] John Sheppard, an Irishman, was a close associate of McNeile and the other Irish clergy. He was a property owner of some substance and had been a magistrate in Ireland. He had made two attempts to win a seat in South Toxteth, in 1839 and 1840, but in 1842 he was successful in North Toxteth, probably because he too was an Orangeman. Interestingly, at a ward meeting in support of Sheppard, a speech by Charles Horsfall, a wealthy merchant and Protestant hardliner, echoed McNeile's view of the political nature of the religious campaign. He argued that while the town council was ostensibly concerned with municipal affairs, it was in fact a political body dealing with wider issues of the day, including the future of the Church of England. On that basis alone, he argued, Sheppard warranted their support.[54] The Tories in Liverpool believed that Rathbone and the Liberals were using the schools experiment as a prototype for a national education scheme.[55] In 1841 S. Lee Trotman, an Orangeman, beat William Houlbrooke Tayleur in South Toxteth. Tayleur was the son of Charles Tayleur, the partner of Robert Stephenson in the Vulcan Foundry.[56] This campaign was fought entirely on the schools issue and Tayleur was defeated by the relatively large majority of forty-four. Trotman was a wealthy West India merchant. A noted Orange councillor was Ebeneezer Rae, partner in a firm of ship's stores dealers. He won St Peter's ward in 1841.[57] James Parker, a brewer, was elected to the council, for St Anne's, in 1841 and was particularly reliant on the Orange vote. The most prominent member of the Orange Order to be elected to the council at this time was Richard Harbord, a warehouse owner. He secured North Toxteth for the Tories in 1840. He was a strong supporter of McNeile and became the deputy Grand Master of the Liverpool district of the Orange Association in 1844. His brother, H. G. Harbord, a surgeon, was also, for a while, a committed Orangeman who was eventually elected to the council for the Great George ward in 1847.[58] In 1839 the contest in the Exchange ward was fought by another Orangeman, Ambrose Lace, an attorney. He lost on that occasion but won a seat in South Toxteth in 1842.[59] It is important to remember that militant Protestantism was not a monopoly of Orangemen, McNeile and McConkey were not members of the Orange Order. T. T. Glazebrook, a supporter of McNeile, was elected to a seat in South Toxteth in 1843. A No Popery campaigner, he also was not a member of the Orange Order, although he felt it necessary to explain that this was only because of pressure of work.[60] (See Appendix 2.)

III

There can be no denying that McNeile's campaign paid handsome political dividends, though the majorities in many wards, both before and after 1841, do not justify White's contention that 'elections lost most of their significance, at least from a party point of view'.[61] Equally, there can be no doubt that the campaign inflamed antagonisms between the Catholic and Protestant working class, many of whom had no vote. Kirk has suggested that the unskilled English working class turned away from Chartism, to the rural Tories, for a leadership which offered a vision of a stable society unthreatened by technical change. In Liverpool a large section of the non-Irish working class turned to the Tory bourgeoisie for a similar vision at a time they were also under threat from technological and economic change.[62]

A useful starting point in tracing the causal chain leading from theological dispute to street warfare is the case of the ship's carpenters. The trade of ship's carpenter involved undertaking all the repair work to ships which involved working in wood. It is to be distinguished from that of the shipwrights, who worked specifically on shipbuilding and who, like the carpenters, worked in timber. Most of the timber yards in Liverpool were adjacent to the Mersey in the South End, and large numbers of carpenters and shipwrights lived in the area around Grafton Street. In an age of wooden vessels there was work for thousands of these tradesmen, many of whom, significantly, were freemen. This fact alone meant that they were antagonistic to Rathbone and his fellow Liberals. The Liberals had supported abolition of the slave trade, which, it was feared at the time, would reduce the volume of shipping in the port and so reduce demand for carpenters and shipwrights. The Whig government had, in the 1832 electoral reforms, destroyed the monopoly vote of the freemen in parliamentary elections, and in 1833 Rathbone led a campaign to remove their privileges.[63] During the campaign for Catholic emancipation the Liberals in Liverpool had taken the lead in the local agitation, thus associating themselves unambiguously with the Catholic cause. Later their support for Daniel O'Connell in his movement to repeal the union of Ireland and England increased their identification with Irish Catholic aspirations.[64] The years 1835-41 were a time of increasing concern on the part of carpenters and shipwrights. The apprenticeship system was breaking down. Thomas Price, a Liverpool ship's carpenter, claimed in 1841 that, of 700 apprentices in the London docks, three-quarters had not served their time with a master, while in Liverpool apprentices were doing the jobs of unemployed carpenters. The carpenters wanted government action to enforce the apprenticeship system, but the Whig Ministry had shown little interest.[65] Another cause of concern was the fact that the iron-framed hull had made its appearance and, though still in its early stages of development, it represented a threat to the trade.[66] In addition, the advent of steam-driven vessels in 1814 had produced new trades such as engine-makers and boilermakers, a new labour aristocracy.[67] Lastly, worry about the effects of Whig trade' policies on the shipping industry compounded their concern.[68]

Most of the Irish Catholics were unskilled labourers and did not represent a threat to the jobs of carpenters and shipwrights, although there must have been some Irish who were carpenters. However, the identification of the Liberals in Liverpool with the defence of Catholic liberties made Catholics guilty by association in the eyes of working men whose political wings had been clipped by reformers and who perceived their jobs to be threatened by Whig trade policies. Another factor, more difficult to monitor but probably important, was simple xenophobia on the part of sections of the English working class. McNeile and his allies, clerical and lay, provided a self-justification for those Protestants who became involved in street warfare against Irish Catholics. An undeniably important factor in provoking this backlash was the behaviour of the Irish themselves.

The 1835 riots had not involved clashes between Catholic and Protestant working men but it had been a terrifying experience for Protestants' who lived in the affected streets. The events of 1835, however, were followed immediately by the controversy over the schools, and its corrosive effect on the fabric of the working-class, community was demonstrated during the 1837 election. The rioting on election day, 25th July, clearly marked the polarisation of the two communities. Also, from the point of view of the public-order consequences of the emerging sectarian violence, the events of the day illustrated the considerable problems facing the police, arising from the fact that large numbers of Irish were dispersed throughout the whole borough. The contest for the two seats was between Lord Sandon and Cresswell for the Tories and Elphinstone and Ewart for the Liberals. Of the total of 18,025 votes cast, the Tories obtained 52% and it was clear that most of the freeman votes, some 71%, had gone to them, emphasising the need of the Liverpool Conservatives to woo this section of the working class.[69] The riots were claimed to be the worst witnessed in Liverpool elections till then, and Rathbone and other Liberal leaders admitted that their Irish supporters had initiated the disturbances.[70] The Liberal *Liverpool Mercury* expressed the belief that they had caused some Liberal waverers to vote Tory.[71]

Early on the morning of the election, large numbers of Irish gathered in the Vauxhall ward, armed with bludgeons.[72] Michael Whitty, now Head Constable, led a body of police who dispersed the crowds and arrested the ringleaders. However, soon after more trouble broke out in Vauxhall and he had to send reinforcements. At the same time an estimated 1,000 Irish gathered in Park Lane in the South End and a fierce battle took place with the police, who took a severe beating and had to retreat. Elsewhere in the South End another body of police were struggling with the Irish in Great George ward, and after dispersing them joined up with more police and returned to Park Lane, where they launched a strong attack on the rioters. Meanwhile in the North End Whitty was involved in yet another fracas, having been trapped by a mob of Irish. He literally knocked his way through the crowd and returned with more police, who gave the Irish such a beating that Whitty had to call them off. To complicate matters, in the South End young ship's carpenters went on the rampage, attacking anyone who wore Liberal colours and, more ominously, seeking out Irishmen for special treatment. A particularly fierce conflict between police and Irish took place in St James's market place in the South End, and nasty incidents continued throughout the rest of the day. In Greenland Street, in the South End, an old woman, an Irish Protestant, was beaten up by Irish who, it was alleged, were yelling 'Murder the bloody Protestant.'[73] Amazingly, there was no large-scale conflict between the carpenters and the Irish. The police force, led by Whitty, had acquitted itself well. Though special constables had been sworn in, the army had not been used.

In the recrimination afterwards the Tory press accused the Liberals of importing Irish bludgeon men from Dublin while the Liberal press, though admitting the Irish had started the trouble, blamed McNeile for the excesses of the ship's carpenters. The myopia of all the disputants was revealed when in his victory speech Lord Sandon is reported to have said:

> It was a victory of freedom of religion, of the country and the Queen . . . the electors of Liverpool had set a good example to the country which he insisted the whole country would follow - an example of sincere and earnest attachment to their ancient constitution, to the hereditary privilege of the House of Peers, and to the hereditary privileges which as freemen they possessed themselves. There was one peculiar element of their success to which he looked with no small satisfaction, the deep, sincere, religious feeling which had existed in the town.[74]

He attributed the electoral success to the Liberal 'attack' on the corporation schools. As in 1835, the disturbances had been frightening and, significantly, marked a growing polarisation along ethnic lines. They also initiated a big increase in hostility between ship's carpenters and the Irish.

For example, between 9th and 12th June 1841 the police were on stand-by continually because of expected clashes between the two groups.[75] The Anti-Corn Law Association called a meeting in Liverpool and a large number of Irish attended as supporters of the reformers. A number of carpenters and shipwrights also attended with the intention of disrupting the meeting, McNeile being vociferously opposed to the league. Despite a large police presence, fighting broke out between carpenters and Irish and the carpenters had to retreat. Some of them attacked St Patrick's Catholic church in the South End, breaking a number of windows. The police dispersed the carpenters but news spread round the Irish areas that St Patrick's had been damaged, so police reinforcements were put on stand-by in anticipation of communal disturbances. The actual attack on St Patrick's was almost certainly the work of young lads, possibly drunk, but in the strained atmosphere of the No Popery campaign the event was a dangerous escalation of the conflict. In an attempt to defuse the situation the three priests at St Patrick's issued a placard urging Catholics not to seek revenge.[76] The next day another meeting of the Anti-Corn Law Association drew an estimated 20,000, including several thousand Irish. Again there were disturbances and afterwards a large number of Irish marched to the South End and smashed the windows of St James's Anglican church, then attacked several public houses known to be used by carpenters. Again, a large body of police was needed to disperse the crowd. By now the streets in the South End were in a highly disturbed state and Whitty had to have men on permanent stand-by. The next morning he was told carpenters were assembling in large numbers in the South End and he despatched police armed with cutlasses, who confronted an estimated 2,000 carpenters marching to the town centre. They stopped the procession and after some negotiations a delegation of carpenters were allowed through to present a petition to the mayor, demanding protection from Irish attacks.[77]

From the public order point of view the incidents were particularly unfortunate, as they occurred in the lead-up to the 1841 parliamentary election. This time Sandon and Cresswell were opposed by Joshua Walmsley and Lord Palmerston, with the central issue the schools question. Again, the election was an occasion for widespread disturbances of an even more sectarian nature than in 1837.[78] Large numbers of men were on the streets wearing Orange ribbons. This had not been a feature of the 1837 election, and during the day an Orange band paraded, playing 'Boyne Water', one of the favourite tunes of Orangemen. In the town centre Sandon and Cresswell were stoned by an Irish mob, while in the South End carpenters were terrorising anyone wearing Liberal colours. In one incident a large group of carpenters attacked Irish homes, breaking all the windows, and late in the day gangs of Irish and carpenters clashed in the South End in a series of vicious fights. Near the docks a ship's carpenter by the name of Casement kept a public house. Large numbers of Irish attacked the building, and Casement, after warning them, opened fire with a pistol, wounding four.[79]

The difficulties of the police were particularly well illustrated by an incident in the South End. Carpenters and Irish were fighting in New Bond Street, Crosbie Street and New Hall Street. When a detachment of police arrived both Irish and carpenters turned on them. During what was reported to be a two-hour battle a method of fighting that was to become common in Liverpool was first reported. The Irish climbed on to the roofs of houses and used slates as weapons. In one such incident George Myers, a Protestant was killed.[80] In another fracas in the South End, Whitty led a mounted police charge to disperse battling carpenters and Irish. By any standards this had been disorder of a serious kind and had been openly sectarian, Catholic working man against Protestant working man. The *Liverpool Albion* commented that the No Popery orators had convinced the shipwrights that they were the natural enemies of Irishmen.[81]

Sandon and Cresswell again won the two seats for the Tories and these successes were followed by the return of a Tory majority in the municipal elections in November. This Conservative triumph did nothing to dampen McNeile's or his allies' enthusiasm for the sacred mission to defeat the conspiracy to return England to Rome. *The Liverpool Standard,* commenting on the 1841 municipal election results, warned Protestants against any easing of the No Popery campaign.[82] Increasingly the Tory press began to use more scurrilous language when speaking of Irish Catholics. The *Liverpool Mail,* referring to Daniel O'Connell, raged:

> One of the many obnoxious vices of popery is that where it prevails, it generates hosts of filthy and importunate mendicants—the vermin of the human race.[83]

The growing tension on the streets during the No Popery campaign was instrumental in increasing the determination of Orangemen to reestablish the annual 12th July procession, last held in 1821. In particular, Protestants were angered by the holding of St Patrick's day parades. In March 1841 some 5,000 Irish had taken part, including one society called the *Sons of Irish Freedom.*[84] The day passed off peacefully, Orangemen making no attempt to disrupt the proceedings, but the anger felt by some surfaced in a letter to the *Liverpool Standard* from an official of a local lodge. He called upon Protestants and Orangemen to hold a 12th July procession in 1842 to demonstrate Protestant attachment to the cause of Church and King.[85] The conflict during the elections of 1841 showed that the potential for disorder if such a procession were held was considerable, and when, on 23rd June 1842, the Liverpool lodges decided to hold a procession, the mayor and magistrates were very concerned.

John Shaw Leigh, the mayor, was a Conservative councillor for West Derby, but a majority of the magistrates were Liberals.[86] At a meeting on 28th June between magistrates and Orange officials, the Orangemen were told the magistrates disapproved of any kind of Orange procession because of the danger of disorder.[87] The Orange officials eventually agreed to cancel the parade, but on returning to their lodges they found that there was such strong grass-roots support for a march that it was not clear that members would obey them. The magistrates were sufficiently worried to write to the Home Office to inform Sir James Graham of their action in trying to stop the Orange demonstration.[88] Meanwhile Michael Whitty asked the magistrates to explain what powers he had to deal with any procession.[89] During negotiations it became widely known in the town that an Orange procession *might* take place, and for the younger men in both communities it was something to be looked forward to.

Early in the morning of Tuesday 12th July large crowds gathered in anticipation of trouble. Two Orange public houses were attacked, and by 10.00 a.m. several thousand Irish had gathered in Vauxhall with the intention of marching to the South End because, it was believed, some Toxteth lodges would march, mainly carpenters.[90] The police dispersed them but in the afternoon a body of Irish marched to the docks and persuaded dockers to walk out and join them in attacking any Orange procession which might take place. A procession of sorts did occur, accompanied by an estimated 2,000 people, mainly carpenters, and sporadic fighting took place with the Irish. Orange officials had tried to dissuade the Orangemen from marching. In one incident Orangemen came out of a public house armed with pistols and were stopped from using them only by police intervention. Throughout the day there were many small but vicious confrontations. Characteristic was the incident in the North End in which two men known to be Protestants were pursued by an Irish mob who assumed they were Orangemen. The two took refuge in the house of a courageous Irishwoman, but the door was beaten down. One man escaped over the back wall but the other, a carpenter, was dragged out and badly beaten up.[91] Elsewhere gangs of carpenters were roaming the town looking for Irishmen who, when found, received similar treatment. Another carpenter was badly beaten in Lime Street by a large gang of Irish while a mob of Protestants ran down Mount Pleasant shouting, 'We're Orangemen-we'll have No Popery—down with the Popery Bible.' This gang became engaged in several fights and the leader, when arrested, was found to have a large, newly sharpened carving knife.[92] Throughout the day the police, under Whitty, maintained overall control but the town was still in a disturbed state the following day. On 15th July Catherine Carney was murdered.

The No Popery campaign, initiated in 1835, had paid handsome political dividends, but the rising level of conflict between Protestant and Catholic was an increasing source of concern to many middle-class supporters of McNeile. Though he constantly reiterated the claim that he preached no harm against individual Roman Catholics, his working-class adherents drew no subtle distinction between the Church and the individual. It is clear that by 1842 neither McNeile nor Orange officials were in control of working-class passions, but at no time did McNeile ever admit that anything he said was in any way responsible for acts of violence. Among militant Protestants there was no concession that Irish Catholics could, reasonably, find Orange processions offensive, and if they did the view was they should stay away. The Orangemen equated the 12th July parade with St Patrick's day, St David's day and the parades of Total Abstinence lodges and benefit societies. The stipendiary magistrate, Edward Rushton, was anathema to militant Protestants. The son of a well known Liverpool radical, he had made himself unpopular with Orangemen by taking a tough line on the holding of Orange parades and the flying of flags and banners which could be offensive to Catholics. Given his Liberal leanings, his attitude was seen as partisan.[93]

Because of the sectarian overtones of all the municipal election campaigns and the return of several Orangemen to the council, it is not surprising that the bitterness spread to the council chamber. It came to a head in the clash between magistrates and members of the Watch Committee. The Municipal Corporations Act authorised borough councils to appoint a Watch Committee; which had the responsibility of appointing members of the police force and supervising their operations. The Head Constable was in operational command but it was not clear under the Act to whom he was ultimately responsible. The magistrates had a duty to maintain the peace, while in the background was the Home Secretary with his own responsibility for public order. It was against this confused administrative background that sectarian conflict shifted from the schools issue to the question of who controlled the police. Following the passing of the 1835 Act, the borough police force had come into existence, with Michael Whitty appointed Head Constable and Matthew Dowling and William Parlour his deputies, over a force of 390 constables. The appointment of Whitty, a Catholic Irishman, was a deliberate gesture on the part of the new Liberal council, and he turned out to be a good choice.[94] Despite his undoubted professionalism, by 1842 there was a growing feeling among Catholics that some policemen were not impartial in dealing with sectarian disputes. During 1844 St Patrick's Church had been subjected to a number of attacks by carpenters, and the parish priest asked the mayor for more protection, a request which would normally have gone to the Watch Committee. It was passed to Rushton.

In April 1844 the mayor received a complaint that sixty policemen were members of Orange lodges and as such would not be impartial in carrying out their duties. Again, this type of complaint could have been put before the Watch Committee but in fact a meeting took place on 17th April between the mayor, the town clerk and Rushton. They discussed the complaint and drew up a resolution to the effect that any policeman who was a member of the Orange Order, or a Ribbon society, should either resign or be dismissed.[95] Whitty was then asked to find out how many members of the force belonged to these societies. At no time was the Watch Committee informed of what was going on. Rushton may have been influenced in excluding the Committee because Richard Harbord, Deputy Grand Master of the Liverpool lodges, was a member, as was James Parker, another Orangeman. On 22nd April Rushton and the mayor met all the magistrates and told them of the resolution that had been drawn up while Whitty reported that, of 503 police officers, only nine had admitted to being Orangemen.[96] It was 27th April before the Watch Committee was informed of these matters and a bitter row broke out in the council chamber, Rushton being accused of exceeding his powers. In the debate Gladstone, a Liberal, argued that if a policeman was considered unfit to carry out his duties because he was an Orangeman, it followed that Richard Harbord was unsuitable as a member of the Watch Committee.[97] The matter blew over quickly but the issue of who was ultimately responsible for the police force remained unresolved, and the partiality of the police force continued to be questioned by Liberals and Catholics. For example, in September 1844 all officers in the borough had to state their religion and it was recorded in a book.[98]

The row over the magistrates' resolution concerning membership of the Orange Order was followed almost immediately by the Parker affair.[99] On 31st October 1844, on the eve of the municipal elections, James Parker went to the Rosehill bridewell and asked the keeper if information had been laid against a John Connor. Connor was a Liberal voter in Parker's St Annes ward, who had been in trouble with the police, and Parker implied that as he needed votes he would like Connor arrested, thus removing a Liberal voter. On being told no warrant had been made out he left. In a member of the Watch Committee and an Orangeman such behaviour was indiscreet, to say the least. On 5th November Superintendent Jones was called to a beerhouse where Orange flags were displayed from the windows.[100] A hostile crowd was gathering, and Jones went inside to persuade the owners to remove them. He was met by a group of Orangemen, all drunk. They refused to take the flags down. The publican refused to remove the flags, saying that he was an Orangeman and Orangemen were his best customers. If he offended them he would be driven out of business. One of the men, an ex-policeman, claimed the Orangemen of Liverpool put the councillors in power, implying that the policeman had better watch his step. Parker went to the bridewell later that night and asked whether a charge was to be brought against the men and, it was alleged, implied the police were partial towards the Irish. On hearing of these incidents Rushton interpreted Parker's behaviour as an attempt to interfere with a police officer in the execution of his duty and called a meeting of magistrates. The result was another resolution, stating that any officer who was the object of any attempt to interfere with him in the execution of his duty must report the matter to his superiors; any failure to do so would lead to dismissal.[101] The magistrates ordered that the resolution be entered into the borough police regulations. Again the Watch Committee was not consulted, they were simply told.[102] While not admitting any intention of interfering with the police, Parker apologised to the council, but the issue of police impartiality was far from dead (see pp. 129-46).

Physical conflict between Irish Catholics and Protestants on the occasion of 12th July processions was not the only sign of the growing entrenchment of sectarianism among the working class in Liverpool. By 1842 newspaper reports reveal a new form of coat trailing, the Orange funeral. For example, in September the burial of a lodge master was accompanied by a procession of several thousand, many wearing Orange sashes.[103] In December 1842 another Orange funeral was accompanied by a parade, both before and after the internment, and again most mourners wore Orange sashes.[104] In Liverpool it was almost impossible to avoid streets in which Irish Catholics lived, and Orange colours were inevitably taken as a challenge to combat. On 6th July 1845 an Orange funeral procession, estimated at 400 strong, marched down Scotland Road in the North End to bury a brother Orangeman in St Mary's Church yard, men and horses wearing Orange colours. On returning past the end of Great Crosshall Street they were stoned by some Irish, and young men at the rear of the procession broke off and attacked them. This triggered off a four-hour riot which police later described as one of the worst street clashes they had had to deal with. Peace was eventually achieved only when Catholic priests persuaded the Irish to stop fighting.[105]

The overall majority of the Conservatives on the town council following the 1841 municipal election represented the scaling of a plateau, in terms of McNeile's political success and popularity. On 1st January 1842 the Education Committee submitted new regulations for the running of the corporation schools which required all children to read the Authorised Version of the Bible. Within a week most Catholic children were withdrawn, following a statement issued by the Roman Catholic clergy of the town.[106] McNeile had succeeded in his object of getting rid of 'Popery on the rates' and in securing a Conservative council. Among many Protestants he was a hero, and in 1841 his admirers subscribed towards an engraved portrait, 'most admirably suited for cabinet purposes'.[107] By September 1845 grateful middle-class subscribers enabled the foundation stone of McNeile's new church to be laid, St Paul's, Princess Park, in Toxteth. This project provided work for the Conservative builder, Samuel Holmes.[108] At the same time McNeile was having built a 'large and elegant' house in the wealthy suburb of Aigburth, and Samuel and James Holmes were the architects.[109]

The question arises as to what extent the fanaticism displayed by Protestant activists over the years 1835-46 represented genuine religious conviction as opposed to political opportunism? Neither conviction nor opportunism is easily measured. It is probably true that the clergy involved, and many of the laymen who were not contenders for council office, were genuinely concerned for the future of the Church of England and Reformation principles. An illuminating example of the depth of feeling is that of Captain Crichton, a ship's master. Addressing the meeting held in Toxteth in 1840 to establish a branch of the Protestant Association, he said that he was once asked to allow six young men to travel on his ship to India. On establishing that they were Roman Catholics he had refused to take them as he always maintained 'Christian discipline' on his ships and it was impossible to connect true Christianity with Popery. On another trip he was asked to take four young Chinese from China to Naples, where they were to be trained as Catholic priests. He had refused, as he would not have fixed upon him 'the mark of the beast'.[110] In 1844 a free-trade meeting in Toxteth was disrupted when Richard Harbord led in a gang of carpenters. Harbord was a wealthy man with no need to prove himself a militant for economic gain, and such behaviour could be taken as an index of commitment to the Protectionist cause. It *was* the kind of behaviour which embarrassed moderate Conservatives and alienated many who shared the same beliefs.[111]

For contenders for councillor status there *were* economic advantages to be gained. Membership of key committees could bring patronage and business. Contracts for supplying the police force and the fire service with uniforms and equipment were lucrative. Membership of the Dock Committee was especially desired, as the committee was involved in decision-making that affected vital business interests throughout the town. The position of churchwardens for the parish was important in that the two wardens were influential in the fixing of the Church rates, and in 1850 Richard Harbord and Thomas Dover, both Orangemen, occupied the office.[112] Membership of other bodies, such as the Select Vestry, also carried economic benefits. In 1845 James Parker received the contract to supply the workhouse with ale and porter. It is not evidence of corruption, but his being a prominent Orangeman was not a disadvantage.[113] The Liberals attacked Samuel Holmes, accusing him of benefiting from public works projects because of his political allies.[114] No potential Tory councillor could hope to achieve public office unless he established himself in McNeile's eyes as a 'sound Protestant' and there is reason to doubt the religious conviction of many. McNeile himself recognised this and attacked some Tory councillors as 'political Protestant songsters'.[115] Showing preferences for one's co-religionists was not confined to Orangemen. Roman Catholics did the same, but the main difference was that individually they had less economic power and, municipally, possessed none at all. Catholic partisanship occurred mainly in the allocations of jobs in those spheres in which they could compete, particularly dock labour.

The network of Protestant organisations also meant that membership could buy rewards outside the sphere of municipal activities. In February 1846 the *Liverpool Mercury* carried a correspondence alleging that jobs at the railway station in Kirkdale were being handed out to Orangemen on the recommendation of an Orange clergyman, and calling for an enquiry.[116] The councillors had plenty to occupy them besides the sectarian squabble. The reactions to the various reports in the early 1840s revealing problems of housing, sewage disposal and water supplies also cut across party allegiances, but the sectarian problem did not disappear under the pressure of matters of social administration. The *Liverpool Standard,* commenting on the forthcoming municipal elections in 1846, made the point that the Liberals, having been routed by the Tories over the religious question, were attempting to regain power by adopting a less political stance:

> They feel the hopelessness of an open attack upon the sound Protestant principle of the people of Liverpool; and they are making the sanitary questions, water questions, drainage, sewerage and other non-political matters, a kind of Trojan horse, for their introduction to the citadel, when the blow is to be struck against the object of their intense hatred.[117]

Following the elections, the council consisted of thirty-four Tories and fourteen Liberal councillors and sixteen Tory aldermen, so that on the council as a whole there were fifty Conservatives and fourteen Liberals. Despite this, there were weaknesses in the Tory position.

IV

The clergy continued to stress the need for voter registration before parliamentary elections, as a Christian duty. Addressing a meeting of the Protestant Operative Association on 7th July 1845, the Rev. David James, a committeed McNeilite, moved the resolution:

> That as a good Christian is a good citizen, it is the duty of all Protestants enjoying the elective franchise, to pay all taxes due to the government before the 20th July and ensure themselves the privilege of voting for a sound Protestant at the next Parliamentary election.[118]

McNeile's personal standing seemed unchallenged and his influence was all-pervasive in Liverpool Conservative political circles. An example of this was the mayoral election of 1845, in which his nominee, David Hodgson, an Orangeman, was elected over G. B. Lawrence, a Tory generally considered to be next in line for mayoralty. It seems likely that by 1845 McNeile could rely on between ten to twenty-seven council members to support the 'Protestant' cause in the council chamber.[119] Not all No Popery men were McNeilites - for example, Samuel Holmes, a leading member of the Conservative Party: there was no doubt about his militancy. Speaking to a meeting of working men in 1840, he argued that to attack the beliefs and practices of the Roman Catholic Church was not a sign of intolerance:

> Popery is a double evil. It is a political evil, for it enslaves instead of giving liberty. It is a religious evil, for its creed is false and it withholds the scriptures from the people, for the Pope knows well that popery and the free circulation of God's holy word cannot be co-existent . . . Two antagonistic systems are struggling for ascendency in Britain - the Church of England and the Church of Rome.[120]

Following the 1841 Conservative victories in the municipal and parliamentary elections, and despite the emergence of a group of moderate Conservatives hostile to McNeile and supported by the *Liverpool Mail*, anti-Catholicism continued to be the fuel that fired the Tory political machine.

Divisions within Tory ranks were opened up by two major issues which led people to take opposite sides. One was the emergence of the 'Catholic' party within the Anglican Church. The Tractarians were a group of Anglicans, mainly Oxford clerics, who wrote and published ninety tracts between 1833 and 1841 in which they set out their views on the nature of the Church of England and its doctrines.[121] In doing so they triggered off a movement in which the catholicity of the Church of England was stressed. The best known of its leaders were John Henry Newman and Edward Bouverie Pusey. Adherents of the movement were first referred to as Tractarians or Puseyites but later in the century the term

Ritualist, Anglo-Catholic and High Church were used interchangeably. The tracts and their authors came under attack both from those in the Church of England who did not share their views and from Roman Catholics, for whom the claims to Catholicism were bogus. While the object of the Tractarians was primarily to defend the Church against the encroachments of the State, the tracts opened up a much wider debate about the nature of the Church of England, and for some, notably Newman, the questions raised and the agonised querying they initiated, led them out of the English Church into that of Rome.[122]

After Newman's defection the movement entered a new phase in which the emphasis was less on arguing the theological and intellectual basis of the claims to catholicity of the Church of England. The new direction was pre-eminently concerned with the adoption of the external signs of Catholicism and the revival of Roman Catholic practices which scandalised the majority of Anglicans, who saw in them evidence of a spiritual Fifth Column within the Church. The feeling was heightened by the number of defections to the Church of Rome, many of them well publicised in the press.[123] The practice of auricular confession drew the greatest condemnation from the opponents of the Catholic revival, who saw the whole movement as a betrayal of the Reformation. It is difficult to overestimate the effect of Tractarianism on the Protestant psyche. Typical of the feeling generated was the speech by the Rev. J. Brown, of St Andrew's Scottish Church in Liverpool, to the Protestant Operative Association, on 7th July 1845:

> ... if Puseyism, that Judas Iscariot within the Church, make common cause with Popery, that Pontius Pilate without, then the civil and religious constitution of this mighty empire, like the ship on fire in the storm, can be saved from the wreck and wretchedness of revolution by nothing short of a stupendous moral miracle.[124]

The term 'ritualist' was applied to those who felt that acceptance of the theological arguments concerning the Catholic nature of the Established Church impelled them to adopt Catholic practices, a view not shared by all Tractarians. From 1860 onwards it was this widespread adoption of the external signs of Catholicism that moved the conflict within the Anglican Church from the level of theological debate to the law courts and, increasingly, the mob (see Chapters VII, VIII and IX).

The most bitter Anglican opposition to the Ritualists came from the Evangelicals, who, in the second half of the century, were the most powerful faction within the Church of England.[125] The emotional roots of the Evangelicals were puritanical but the party within the Church of England had been strengthened as a result of the Weslyan upsurge of the late eighteenth century. In the latter half of the nineteenth century Evangelical fervour frequently deteriorated into crude No Popery rhetoric, but it is important to appreciate that the majority of Anglicans were neither Ritualists nor Evangelicals. They could be described as broad-churchmen, people who disliked extremes of any kind and for whom membership of the Church of England was often a sign of patriotism rather than religious conviction. They were on the sidelines of the bitter legal contests that were to take place between Evangelicals and Ritualists in the latter half of the century (see Chapter VII). The contempt for the Tractarians felt by McNeile and those who shared his beliefs probably equalled that which they exhibited towards the Roman Catholic Church: Newman, Pusey and the rest were traitors, more culpable than the poor deluded Roman Catholics.

Simultaneously with the rising level of concern over Tractarianism, Protestant fears were agitated when, in 1845, the issue of the Maynooth grant came to the fore. Conspiracy theory was rife. In Dr Norman's view it was the 'great political controversy of the year'.[126] The Royal College of St Patrick was a Catholic seminary established in 1795 at Maynooth in County Kildare. It was financed by an annual vote of public money by the Irish parliament, and after the Act of Union in 1800 the annual vote of funds was continued by Westminster. The reason for the establishment of Maynooth was to try to obtain the loyalty of Irish Catholics by providing facilities for training priests in Ireland, thus making it less necessary to train abroad, where exiled Irish nationalism might exercise a hostile influence. To McNeile the grant was simply illogical and unchristian. State funds were being used to finance the training of Roman Catholic priests whose function, in his view, was to subvert the British constitution and the Established Church and return England to the Roman fold.

Protestant anger increased when, on 19th March 1845, Peel announced the intention not only to increase the grant but to make it permanent, by contrast with reliance on an annual vote. In a massive resurgence of No Popery, all the old doctrinal, historical and constitutional objections to Roman Catholicism were aired. Nevertheless a Bill was introduced into Parliament on 3rd April 1845 and, supported by Whigs and Radicals, received the royal assent on 30th June. Peel had again split the Tory party. In the debates in the Commons concerning Maynooth, Lord Sandon, Protestant hero of the 1837 Liverpool election, expressed an opinion which suggested that public faith in the matter was pledged to support the grant. It was to prove electorally fatal for him. For McNeile opposition to the Maynooth grant was a Christian duty, and he took the lead in Liverpool in orchestrating an opposition which caused Sandon not to seek re-election in 1847. Not all Tories supported McNeile, and the divisions in the Tory ranks resulted in the defeat of the protectionist candidate in the 1847 parliamentary election.

The debacle originated in McNeile's decision that Sandon was 'unsound'. If Sandon had stood for re-election, the Tories would almost certainly have retained both seats.[127] The conclusion to be drawn from these events is that by the mid 1840s the Liverpool Tories, though in overall control of the council, could not afford to relax their efforts to attract votes, and there were sufficient divisions within their ranks to kindle some hope among the Liberals that their position was not hopeless.

What was the state of Orangeism in Liverpool in the mid 1840s? To some extent the disarray among the Liverpool Conservatives was also present among Liverpool Orangemen, although for different reasons. With regard to organisational structure, the Grand Lodge in London ceased to exist after the adverse report in 1835, and with its demise the Orange Institution ceased to function. The aristocratic support for Orangeism declined as the ultra-Tories, as a political faction, faded into the background of English politics, their defeat marked by the Catholic Emancipation Act of 1829 and the Reform Act of 1832. The political ideals of Orangeism resurfaced, however under the umbrella of the Grand Protestant Confederation, which came into being almost immediately after the publication of the 1835 report. At its first anniversary meeting, in May 1836, many of the aristocratic Tory ultras who had been members of the Orange Order appeared on the platform, as did W. E. Gladstone.[128] However, the focal point of English Orangeism remained in the provinces where it had always been, and Orange lodges continued to function, either individually or as members of loosely organised groups. Speaking of this period, Sibbert states that two organisations survived, 'working on Orange lines'. These were the *Grand Orange Lodge of Liverpool* and the *Grand Protestant Confederation*, under which name there were 'a great many lodges'. Sibbert claims that, for reasons which are not clear, the Liverpool Orangemen did not like the title 'Grand Protestant Confederation' and the two organisations continued to operate separately.[129] In 1840 the Confederation changed its title to the *Grand Protestant Confederation of Loyal Orangemen of Great Britain*. This appears to have been more acceptable to some of the Liverpool Orangemen. On 11th March 1841 the *Liverpool Mercury* reported the first quarterly meeting of the Grand Protestant Society of Loyal Orangemen, lodge No. 148. However, it is clear that many lodges in Liverpool continued to be members of an organisation called the *Loyal Orange Institution*, with a Grand Lodge in Liverpool, and the existence of two bodies claiming authority over individual lodges may have been the reason for the difficulty the authorities had in persuading Orangemen not to hold a 12th July procession in 1841 and 1842.

Attempts to unite the Orange lodges continued, and on 1st July 1844 a meeting took place in Kidderminster between representatives of the Orange Institution of Liverpool and the Confederation.[130] Delegates from Liverpool included Robert Leigh, Leonard Addison, John Payne and Joseph Crisp. The outcome was an amalgamation of the two bodies under the title *Grand Protestant Association of Loyal Orangemen of Great Britain,* and the Earl of Inniskillen was elected Grand Master. Joseph Crisp was elected District Master for Liverpool. On 12th July the Liverpool lodges in the Association attended a church service in Liverpool. McNeile did not attend, and the only councillor present was James Parker. The *Liverpool Standard* wrote:

> We gave in our last a brief notice of the meeting of the Grand Lodge of the Loyal Orange Institution, held in this town, at which a union was happily formed between that Institution and the Protestant Confederation - a very powerful body entertaining the principles of Orangeism but who have hitherto been kept separate from the Order by a few immaterial points of discipline, which from this time will be assimilated. The headquarters of the Confederation have been Birmingham, where their members are very numerous and influential . . .[131]

The report in the *Standard* must be regarded as authoritative, because the Leonard Addison who attended the meeting at Kidderminster was a partner in the firm of Addison & Lee, printers and stationers, who published the *Standard.* The report implies that the Orange Institution continued to exist in Liverpool after 1835 but that the Confederation had been outside the Order. What is significant is that some lodges in Liverpool refused to join the Association and continued under the nomenclature *Orange Institution.* As delegates from Oldham, Manchester and Ashton under Lyne attended the Kidderminster meeting, it is probable they also joined the Association. However, Sibbert makes no reference to Blackburn, Wigan or Halifax, where lodges continued to flourish. At a meeting in Liverpool on 1st July 1845 the first annual general meeting of the amalgamated body took place, attended by 200 delegates from all over Britain. Lord Inniskillen however, sent his apologies. At the meeting new rules for the Association were debated and approved, and the major topic of discussion was the disturbed state of Ireland.[132]

On Monday 13th July 1845 the annual procession to celebrate the battle of the Boyne took place at Newton le Willows because the magistrates in Liverpool had expressed their disapproval. An estimated 800 people left Liverpool in procession, accompanied by a large crowd of 'supporters' and headed by Councillor Richard Harbord, who was now the

Deputy Grand Master of the Loyal Protestant Association. At Newton an estimated 2,000 Orangemen gathered, including Joseph Allday, District Master of Birmingham, and T. J. Ousely of Shrewsbury.[133] Ousely was later to move to Liverpool and become the Deputy Grand Master and the proprietor of the *Liverpool Herald*, an even more strident anti-Catholic paper than the *Standard*. Thus, ten years after the cessation of the Orange Institution, the Orange Order had reorganised, with the centre of activities Liverpool but with splinter groups still remaining outside the Grand Protestant Association of Loyal Orangemen. It is important to realise that many lodges had an ephemeral existence and often it was not clear whether a body of men were operating as an Orange lodge or a benefit society or both. For example, in September 1840 the Grand United Order of Oddfellows held a meeting in the South End and the speakers platform was decorated with Orange and Conservative flags and the toasts were to William III and the Protestant cause.[134] Similarly, the Secretary of the *Liverpool Protestant Benevolent Society* in 1843 was Ambrose Byeford, an Orangeman, later to become Deputy Grand Master.[135]

How big was the Order in Liverpool in terms of the number of lodges and membership? In 1835 there were thirteen warrants in existence in the Liverpool district, although it is not clear from the 1835 report just what geographical area the 'district' covered. There is no doubt that McNeile's activities and the Conservative victories in 1841 encouraged Orangeism. For example, in 1843 new lodges were formed in Liverpool on 3rd March, 25th March, 17th April (No. 36 at Birkenhead) and 17th July (No. 27).[136] In July 1843 the Rev. Joseph Baylee, an Orangeman, claimed there were twenty-two lodges in Liverpool.[137] With regard to support for the Orange Order it is necessary to distinguish between membership of the Order and Orangeism, a set of attitudes and beliefs regarding Catholicism held by many who were not members of a lodge but were 'supporters'. Orangeism was more widespread than membership of Orange lodges. The radical press described *anyone* who held strong Protestant views as an Orangeman, e.g. McNeile, Nolan and Holmes. One way of calculating membership is to take the newspaper estimates of the numbers involved in processions. In 1819 and 1820 the number of processionists was put at ninety, while in 1842 only two or three lodges processed but the crowd of supporters was estimated to be 2,000.[138] In 1843 no procession was held but thirty delegates from Liverpool attended the annual general meeting of the Grand Orange Lodge of England at Wigan. However, two Liverpool lodges went to Birkenhead for a parade and the numbers were said to be 500.[139] In April 1844 the *Standard* claimed there were 3,000 Orangemen in Liverpool, while at the Kidderminster meeting in July 1844 it was claimed that the delegates represented 15,000 members throughout the country. the *Liverpool Courier* put the number at 20,000.[140] No estimate was published in the Liverpool papers concerning membership of the Liverpool lodges at this time. However, it was reported that 'some hundreds of Orangemen, mainly young men' attended the 12th July church service.[141] If it is assumed that there were twenty-five lodges in Liverpool in 1845, with an average membership of 100, then a total of 2,500 Orangemen would still make Liverpool the centre of the English Orange Order.

The social composition of the leadership is more easily established. In 1827 and 1832 the District Master in Liverpool was Amos Studdart, book-binder and stationer. He attended meetings of the English Grand Lodge at Lord Kenyon's and must have been extremely flattered by the experience.[142] Similarly for 1829, Richard Corner was the District Grand Master and he was a marine stores dealer.[143] Leonard Addison, who attended the Kidderminster meeting in 1844, was also a stationer and a printer. Joseph Crisp, who became District Grand Master of the new Association in 1844, was a partner with Daniel Healey, another zealous Protestant, in a firm of clerical and scholastic agents and ecclesiastical auctioneers.[144] Richard Harbord, the Deputy Grand Master of the new Association in 1845, was probably the wealthiest of all of his colleagues, being a warehouse owner in a big way. James Parker, another Orangeman, was a brewer but on a relatively small scale compared with John Bent. Another prominent Orangeman was Ambrose Byeford, who was to become Deputy Grand Master in the 1850s. He was an auctioneer and estate agent.

What is noticeable is the total absence of the more affluent merchants who made up the overwhelming body of Conservative councillors (see Appendix 2). This distancing of the majority of the Conservative middle class from the Order had been and continued to be a cause of resentment among Orangemen. The *Liverpool Standard* of 16th July 1844 provides some evidence of the resentment Orangemen felt at the attitude of Conservative councillors. In a leader it complained bitterly that many Conservatives in Liverpool criticised Orangemen and Orangeism and that the Orange Order in Liverpool was 'hounded'.[145] Richard Harbord and his brother, Surgeon H. G. Harbord, were unusual in their public appearances on Orange platforms and in taking part, on some occasions, in direct action against opponents. In fact Dr Harbord left the Orange Order soon after 1845 disillusioned with sectarianism.[146] It can be assumed that the *Standard* would have maximised publicity concerning any influential support the Orange Order attracted. The *Standard* of 4th July 1843 reported that on 30th June a meeting of Liverpool Orangemen took place to express support for the Irish Orangemen. According to the *Standard*, the meeting was attended by 'hundreds of the most zealous Conservatives in Liverpool' but the names published of the most important people present were only those of Joseph Crisp, Richard Harbord, Messrs Gleave, Albin and Bentley, together with a Mr Jackson, District Grand Master of the Orange Institution. Clearly the Conservative councillors, with the exception of Harbord, had ignored the meeting. However, though they kept their distance, the wealthier Conservatives needed the votes of Orangemen. How *many* Orangemen had the vote is not known, but it is likely they were all registered voters and, if necessary, their rates would be paid by the Conservative Association. Thus they represented a formidable block vote, particularly in North and South Toxteth wards. Probably more significant in terms of working-class social relationships than the number of Orangemen, however, was the spread of Orangeism over the decade 1845-55.

Notes

1   *Albion*, 8th August 1842.

2   D. Fraser, *Urban Politics in Victorian England: the structure of politics in Victorian cities* (1976), introduction.

3   The Corporation of Liverpool owned the land on which the docks were built and were trustees of the dock estates. In 1801 dock revenues were £28,365 and increased to £269,021 in 1851. See T. Baines, *History of the Commerce and Town of Liverpool* (1852), appendix, p. 7). The town dues were a feudal levy on all goods imported and exported through the port. Baines, op. cit., pp. 633-34. Also B. D. White, *A History of the Corporation of Liverpool, 1835-1914* (1951), pp. 12-14.

4   For a full account of the Freeman voter see, E. M. Menzies, 'Freeman voters in Liverpool, 1802-1835', *Transactions of the Historic Society of Lancashire and Cheshire*, Vol. 124 (1972), pp. 85-107. Also F. E. Sanderson, 'The structure of politics in Liverpool, 1780-1807', *Transactions of the Historic Society of Lancashire and Cheshire*, Vol. 127 (1977); pp. 65-89.

5   I. Sellars, 'William Roscoe, the Roscoe circle and radical politics in Liverpool, 1787-1807', *Transactions of the Historic Society of Lancashire and Cheshire*, Vol. 120 (1968), p. 57.

6   *A Report of the Proceedings of a Court of Enquiry into the existing State of the Corporation of Liverpool - before . . . two of His Majesty's Commissioners appointed to Inquire into Municipal Corporations in England and Wales, in the Month of November 1833*, p. 234.

7   Sellars, op. cit., p. 51; Menzies, op. cit., p. 91.

8   Menzies, op. cit., p. 99. At the start of the 1841 election, Samuel Holmes, a Tory builder, was accused of giving his men a holiday to swell the Tory procession and, by implication, to join in the intimidation of Liberal voters. See *Liverpool Mercury*, 3rd July 1841, letter from Holmes to editor.

9   Sellars, op. cit., pp. 56-62.

10   Report S.C. on Orange Lodges, p. xix. Meeting of Grand Lodge at Moston resolved to organise a collection to defray expenses of the prosecutions at Liverpool. On 13th October 1819 a meeting of the Grand Lodge at Moston thanked Lord Kenyon and those lodges which had contributed towards the prosecutions at Liverpool. *The Liverpool Mercury*, 30th July 1819, claimed specifically that the event was organised by Manchester men.

11   *Billinge's Liverpool Advertiser*, 19th July 1819. *The Liverpool Mercury*, 30th July 1819, in its account of the trial at the borough sessions names Woodburne as one of the prosecuting lawyers.

12 John Denvir, a notable Liverpool Irishman, describes how, as a boy, he and his relations and neighbours waited in his home for an attack by ship's carpenters. He refers to carpenters' day. See J. Denvier, *The Life Story of an old Rebel* (1910). The evidence does not support Vincent's view that the carpenters were radical. J. R. Vincent, *Poll books; How the Victorians Voted* (1967), p. 61.

13 *Liverpool Mercury*, 14th July 1820. The Mercury described his speech as one in which 'The genious of grammar was sadly mauled'.

14 On 12th July 1820 an Orange procession took place in Glasgow, involving three lodges (Nos. 56, 83 and 100) and involving some eighty men. A riot occurred when Catholics attacked the parade. *Manchester Guardian*, 21st July 1821. In 1822 an Orange procession in Glasgow resulted in a violent clash with Catholics, 127 people being arrested. *Manchester Guardian*, 27th December 1822.

15 *Liverpool Mercury*, 16th July 1824. In a letter to the Mercury an Irish correspondent suggested the reason why St Patrick's day processions were not attacked was because of the large numbers taking part. The writer referred to Chowbent and Wigan as the centres of Orangeism. *Liverpool Mercury*, 30th July 1824.

16 *Liverpool Mercury*, 14th July 1820. Describing the processionists and their supporters, the not unbiased Mercury wrote, '. . . their class was that of a very inferior dress of society but they were surrounded by a considerable number of friends, whose miserable attire would not have disgraced Falstaff's renowned regiment'.

17 *Liverpool Mercury*, 21st July 1820. The Mercury claimed the Rector of Liverpool refused to preach a sermon for the Orangemen.

18 *Liverpool Mercury*, 16th July 1824. The Mercury criticised the Irish for causing trouble when the Orange lodges had foregone their parade.

19 *Liverpool Mercury*, 3rd April 1828. A correspondent claimed he knew a small boy who was going round the town, signing the petition at every opportunity. See also *Liverpool Mercury*, 10th and 31st April 1828.

20 The scale of the disturbances was such that they received detailed press coverage. See *Liverpool Journal*, 16th and 18th July 1835; *Liverpool Chronicle*, 18th July 1835; *Manchester Guardian*, 18th July 1835; *Liverpool Standard*, 14th and 17th July, 7th August 1835; *Albion*, 13th and 20th July 1835. The account of the riots in his book are based on a careful examination of all these reports and the reports of the trial of prisoners at the assizes.

21 Three years later Orangemen in St Helens, twelve miles from Liverpool, held a procession on 12th July. Irish Catholics from the Green Bank district attacked the Orangemen. The Orangemen regrouped and invaded the Irish streets in Greenbank, breaking windows. *Manchester Guardian*, 18th July 1835.

22 In 1833 the unreformed council consisted of forty-one members of whom thirty-six were Tories. Under the terms of the 1835 Municipal Corporations Act the borough was divided into sixteen political wards.

23 J. Murphy, *The Religious Problem in English Education: the Crucial Experiment* (1959).

24 Murphy, op. cit., pp. 7-8.

25 Murphy, op. cit., chapter 2.

26 Murphy, op. cit., chapter 3.

27 Despite the fact that McNeile is referred to frequently in works on nineteenth-century Liverpool, there is little written about him. The author has had to rely on an intensive search of newspaper reports for the purposes of this book. For some biographical details see *Dublin University Magazine*, Vol. 39, No. 172 (April 1847), pp. 462-71; J. Evans, *Lancashire Authors and Orators* (1850), pp. 182-189; Nicholl W. Robertson, *Life of Ian Maclaren: his Ministry in Liverpool* (1908), pp. 87-8; *Dictionary of National Biography*, pp. 690-1. For obituaries see *Times*, 31st January 1879; *Liberal Review* 1st February 1879; *Porcupine*, 1st February 1879; *Liverpool Mercury*, 29th January 1879; *Liverpool Courier*, 29th January 1879.

28   *Liverpool Standard*, 29th June 1845. This contains an account of an address by McNeile to Orangemen.

29   *Liverpool Mercury*, 30th October 1835. This meeting was chaired by William Hulton. Now that Fletcher was dead, Hulton was the leading ultra Tory in the Bolton area.

30   Ibid.

31   The table has been compiled from the detailed election results published annually in all the Liverpool papers.

32   These were the branches in Toxteth Park, Pitt Street and Great George ward, Vauxhall, Wavertree and St Simon's. Thus some were based on wards, some on districts and others on churches.

33   *Liverpool Courier*, 24th March 1841.

34   *Liverpool Mercury*, 10th November 1837. James was a Welshman. In December 1847, an Irishman was appointed chaplain to the workhouse. A vestry member objected to the number of Irish priest's in Liverpool Anglican churches. He was told 'they fill their churches'. *Liverpool Mercury*, 11th December 1847.

35   Murphy, op. cit., pp. 79-80.

36   *Liverpool Mercury*, 6th October 1838. McNeile gave details of the Fisher Street affair to the annual meeting of the Protestant Association in Liverpool on 5th October 1838.

37   *Liverpool Mercury*, 12th October 1838. This contains a long account of the interviews carried out with the neighbours of the Stephensons and copies of their testaments.

38   C. E. Trevelyan, *The Liverpool Corporation School: No Popery Agitation* (1840).

39   Trevelyan, op. cit., p. 6.

40   *Liverpool Mercury*, 24th April 1849.

41   *Liverpool Standard*, 23rd March 1841; *Liverpool Standard*, 15th June 1841. The theme of the speeches was the duty of Protestants in the forthcoming elections. *Liverpool Standard* 8th June, 30th July, 6th August 1841.

42   *Liverpool Standard*, 26th September 1840.

43   *Liverpool Standard*, 5th February 1841.

44   *Liverpool Mail*, 14th March 1837.

45   *Liverpool Mercury*, 24th March 1837.

46   *Liverpool Mercury*, 16th June 1837.

47   Hugh Stowell was Manchester's leading anti-Catholic at the time. See J. B. Marsden, *Memoirs of the Reverend Hugh Stowell* (1868).

48   *Liverpool Standard*, 30th September 1840.

49   *Liverpool Standard*, 5th December 1843. Leader article on Operative Protestant Associations.

50   *Albion*, 18th March 1844. Leader article claimed McNeile said so at a meeting of the Operative Protestant Association on 11th March.

51   *The Liverpool Standard* gave most coverage to Orange affairs, followed by the *Liverpool Herald*. These two papers were strongly pro-Orange. The *Courier* and the *Mail* were Tory papers but less strident in their Conservatism.

52   *Liverpool Mercury*, 3rd November 1837. Municipal election results and comments.

53   Ibid.

54   *Liverpool Standard*, 5th October 1840. In the 1840 elections Sheppard was nominated as candidate for South Toxteth by Duncan Gibb, a wealthy timber merchant. Gibb praised Sheppard as 'a true churchman'.

55   Murphy, op. cit., p. 52.

56   Charles Tayleur arrived in Liverpool in 1808 from Market Drayton. He made a fortune as a shipowner and merchant and in 1832 went into partnership with Robert Stephenson in setting up the Vulcan Foundry at Newton le Willows. W. H. Tayleur was his eldest son.

57   Rae was the first Conservative councillor in St Peter's since the passing of the 1835 Municipal Corporations Act.

58   H. G. Harbord eventually became disillusioned with the Orange Order and sectarian politics and abandoned the Tory cause.

59   He was described as a 'staunch and consistent supporter of Conservatism' and won by sixty-five votes. Liverpool Standard, 1st November 1842.

60   It was a close contest. Glazebrook was declared the loser by one vote but this was disputed by the Tories. The Attorney General reversed the result. The case gives a good insight into the practical problems of keeping voting lists up to date at that time. See *Manchester Guardian*, 20th January 1844; *Albion*, 22nd January, 11th March and 18th March 1844. Similarly, Samuel Holmes was not an Orangeman. At a meeting of Conservatives held to select Sandon and Cresswell as the candidates for the 1841 election, Holmes made a speech in which the central theme was the crisis in England's affairs. To him the issue was 'whether England is to have an established Church, a Protestant established Church, with its chaste and beautiful and tolerant worship, with a natural recognition of religion, or a free trade in religion . . . Protestantism or Popery?' See *Liverpool Standard*, 15th June 1841.

61   White, op. cit., p. 29.

62   N. Kirk, 'Ethnicity, class and popular Toryism, 1850-1870', in *Hosts, Immigrants and Minorities*, ed. K. Lunn (1980), pp. 64-106. For another view of working men's receptivity to Tory paternalism see R. N. Soffer, 'Attitudes and allegiances in the unskilled north, 1830-1850', *International Review of Social History*, Vol. X, Pt 3 (1965), pp. 429-54. Soffer is mainly concerned with the unskilled workers.

63   Murphy, op. cit., p. 153.

64   Tory councillors in April 1844 took legal advice to see if Liberal magistrates had exceeded their powers in requiring police officers to state whether they were members of a secret society. It was alleged the move was aimed at trying to remove from the bench those Liberal magistrates who had attended a meeting addressed by Daniel O'Connell. See the *Albion*, 29th April 1844.

65   *Liverpool Standard*, 21st June 1841. Price asked Lord Sandon and Cresswell to present any petition to Parliament on the issue of apprenticeships should they be elected.

66   H. J. Dyos and D. H. Aldcroft, *British Transport: an Economic Survey from the Seventeenth Century to the Twentieth* (1969), pp. 238-47, contains a survey of shipping technology. See also J. H. Clapham, 'The last years of the Navigation Acts', in *Essays in Economic History*, ed. E. M. Carus-Wilson Vol. III (1962), p. 177. *Liverpool Standard*, 30th September 1840, report on the launching of what is claimed to be the first ever vessel fitted with iron lower-deck beams, built by Jackson in the South End. 'It is by such practical combinations of wood and iron we may expect to compete.'

67   For a full account of the development of steam navigation on the Mersey see P. L. Cottrell, 'The steamship in the Mersey, 1815-80: investment and ownership', in *Shipping and Trade: Essays in Memory of Ralph Davis*, ed. P. L. Cottrell and D. H. Aldcroft (1981), pp. 137-63. *Liverpool Standard*, 25th September 1835, report on launch of new steam vessel, engines made by G. Forrester of Vauxhall, Liverpool.

68   In a victory speech following the election of G. H. Lawrence in Great George's ward, Samuel Holmes referred to Conservatives who were well known to the tradesmen and mechanics of Liverpool: '. . Well known and respected East and West India merchants . . who built their vessels in our own port-who rigged them with Liverpool spun ropes - and found them with stores, the production of Liverpool mechanics'. See *Liverpool Standard*, November 1841. Clapham, op. cit., pp. 144-78. This article is a useful survey of the events leading up to the abandonment of the Navigation Acts, brought into being to protect British shipping interests.

69   *Liverpool Standard*, 31st July 1840. Statistics of elections and registered voters, 1836 and 1837.

70   Murphy, op. cit., p. 97.

71   *Liverpool Mercury*, 28th July 1837.

72 This account of the day's rioting is based on a detailed examination of press reports. See *Liverpool Mercury,* 28th July 1837; *Liverpool Courier,* 26th July 1837; *Liverpool Mail,* 27th July 1837. For details of claims for damage after the rioting see *Liverpool Courier,* 2nd August 1837.

73 *Liverpool Mail,* 27th July 1837.

74 Ibid.

75 Liverpool Record Office (L.R.O. henceforth), Minutes of Watch Committee 12th June 1841, p. 408. *Liverpool Mail,* 12th June 1841.

76 *Liverpool Standard,* 18th June 1841. The three priests stated, 'We have every confidence that the authorities of the town are ready and able to protect you and your pastors from insult or injury.'

77 Watch Committee Minutes, op. cit. *Liverpool Mail,* 12th June 1841, claimed there were 600 carpenters in the procession.

78 This account of the day's disturbances is taken from the report of the chief constable and press reports. L.R.O., Minutes of Watch Committee, *Head Constable's Report,* 3rd July 1841, p. 421; *Liverpool Mercury,* 2nd July 1841; *Albion,* 8th July 1841; *Liverpool Mail* 3rd July 1841.

79 *Albion,* 8th July 1841. Casement was given bail pending trial at the assizes.

80 *Liverpool Mercury,* 16th July 1841. Meyers had been a flag bearer in a Conservative procession. At the time he was attacked he was on his way to visit another Tory who had been seriously injured. David Shield, an Irishman, was committed for trial at the assizes on a charge of the manslaughter. He was found not guilty.

81 *Albion* 8th July 1841. During the disturbances a body of ship's carpenters attempted to march into Thomas Street in an attempt to attack Irish homes. They were stopped by police. *Liverpool Mail,* 3rd July 1841.

82 *Liverpool Standard,* 5th November 1841.

83 *Liverpool Mail* 25th November 1841. Leader article on Daniel O'Connell.

84 *Liverpool Standard,* 19th March 1841.

85 Ibid.

86 Public Record Office (P.R.O. henceforth) HO 45/249D. Document 4. Report of meeting between Mayor and Magistrates to discuss Orange resolution of 23rd June.

87 P.R.O. HO 45/249D/document 2. Letter from Mayor to Home Secretary, 28th June 1842, concerning meeting between Mayor, magistrates and representatives of the Orange lodges. This meeting took place on 25th June and the council's legal advisers were present.

88 P.R.O., op. cit., letter from Mayor to Home Secretary dated 8th July 1842, expressing the opinion that dissident Orangemen had finally agreed to obey their officials and not to hold a parade. Another letter from J. S. Leigh to the Home Secretary stated that the previous evening a meeting of Orangemen had confirmed the decision not to hold a procession. See also *Liverpool Mercury,* 8th July 1843. This contains a report that on 8th July some Orangemen in Toxteth had decided to hold a procession.

89 P.R.O., op. cit. Request from Whitty to Mayor for elucidation of his powers vis-a-vis processions. The opinion offered made it clear that if a breach of the peace was likely he had the power to disperse the procession.

90 For accounts of the day's rioting see P.R.O., op. cit. *Head Constable's Report* dated 10th July 1842; *Liverpool Herald,* 18th July 1842; *Liverpool Mail,* 14th July 1842; *Albion,* 18th July 1842.

91 *Albion,* 18th July 1842.

92 *Liverpool Mercury,* 15th July 1842.

93 *Liverpool Herald,* 18th July 1842. This edition complains of the attitudes of the authorities towards Orange parades.

94 Whitty had been in charge of the corporation watchmen of the unreformed council. In 1815 the Dock Committee formed a dock police to combat large-scale thieving and in 1833 Mathew Dowling, ex-Metropolitan Police, was head of this body. The day police

were commanded by William Parlour. By 1838 all three bodies had been amalgamated into one. Whitty resigned in December 1843, and was followed by H. Miller.

95 L.R.O. Watch Committee Minutes, 27th April 1844. For the Protestant reaction to this move see *Liverpool Standard,* 30th April, 7th May, 11th June 1844; *Liverpool Mail,* 1844. Ribbonmen were members of an agrarian Irish secret society. The term became generalised among Protestants to mean a member of any Irish secret society. It was later replaced by 'Fenian' as a catch-all phrase.

96 L.R.O., op. cit, Letter from Head Constable to Mayor dated 18th April 1844.

97 *Albion,* 6th May 1844. Proceedings of Town Council.

98 *Liverpool Mail,* 21st September 1844.

99 Parker, councillor for St Anne's, was particularly dependent on votes of Orangemen.

100 L.R.O., Minutes of Watch Committee, 30th November 1844, p. 409. *Report from Head Constable.*

101 L.R.O. Minutes of Watch Committee, 23rd November 1844, The resolution was passed by the magistrates on 18th November 1844. The claim that members of the Watch Committee and councillors generally interfered with the Police, see S.C. on police (1853). Minute of Evidence. T. H. Redin, former Chief Superintendent, 1465-1490.

102 L.R.O., op. cit. The Watch Committee's attention was drawn to the resolution at this meeting on the 23rd November.

103 *Liverpool Mercury,* 23rd September 1842.

104 *Liverpool Mercury,* 9th December 1842.

105 *Liverpool Mercury,* 11th July 1845; *Liverpool Standard,* 8th July 1845; *Liverpool Journal,* 12th July 1845. Seven years later, the problems caused by 'party' funerals resulted in the magistrates asking the Head Constable to produce a report on the issue. In November 1852, the magistrates passed a resolution ordering the Head Constable to stop any such processions. W.C. Minutes, 27th November 1852.

106 J. Murphy, *Liverpool Journal,* 15th January 1842.

107 *Liverpool Courier,* 10th March 1841.

108 *Liverpool Standard,* 14th September 1845.

109 *Albion,* 25th August 1845.

110 *Liverpool Standard,* 30th September 1840.

111 *Albion,* 1st January 1844.

112 *Liverpool Chronicle,* 6th April 1850: This edition contains detailed accounts of the parish of Liverpool.

113 Parker was assiduous in courting the Orange Order, For example, on 29th January 1844 he addressed a meeting of Orangemen on 'The principles of the Church of England', *Albion,* 5th February 1844.

114 *Liverpool Standard,* 20th October 1846. In the course of a long leader on the tactics of the Liverpool Liberals the reference is made to the attacks on Holmes.

115 *Albion,* 19th March 1844, 'Thoughts on the last two councils'.

116 *Liverpool Mercury,* 6th February 1846.

117 *Liverpool Standard,* 20th October 1846, leader.

118 *Liverpool Standard,* 8th July 1845.

119 *Liverpool Mail,* 10th November 1845. See also *Liverpool Mercury,* 14th November 1845; *Albion,* 1st December 1845. The Mail carries a list of the twenty-seven councillors who voted for Hodgson, almost certainly all McNeilites.

120 *Liverpool Standard,* 30th September 1840. Report of a meeting to form a branch of the Protestant Association in Toxteth. In fact Holmes resigned his seat because he had a contract to undertake work on St George's Hall. See *Liverpool Mercury,* 14th November 1845.

121 A knowledge of this movement is crucial for any attempt to understand the controversies which rent the Church of England in the nineteenth century and which brought the issue of enforcing religious discipline into the courts. See G. Faber, *Oxford Apostles* (1954); J. Bentley, *Ritualism and Politics: the attempt to legislate for belief*

(1978). E R. Norman, *Anti-Catholicism in Victorian England* (1968), chapter 5; S. Neill, *Anglicanism* (1958), pp. 253-62.

122 The publicity given to such conversions was a source of great anger among Protestants.

123 On 9th July 1843 the Hon. Rev. George Spencer brother of Earl Spencer, preached a sermon at St Nicholas's Catholic church in Liverpool. He referred to the Tractarians and claimed that in his college there were five ex-Anglicans training for the priesthood. *Manchester Guardian* 19th July 1843.

124 *Liverpool Standard,* 8th July 1845. The tensions within the Liverpool Anglican clergy had surfaced in May 1843 at a meeting held to pass resolutions in support of Sir James Graham's Factory Education Bill. McNeile shared the platform with Archdeacon Campbell. Campbell had defended the Tractarian 'style' but McNeile launched a bitter attack on the 'historical weaknesses' of his clerical brethren. He went on to compare Tractarianism with Pharisaism. After this Campbell declined to share a platform ever again with McNeile. See *Manchester Guardian,* 26th July 1843.

125 E. Jay (ed.), *The Evangelical and Oxford Movements* (1983), p. 3. These essays deal with the theological content of the dispute and are an excellent entry into the controversy. For a study of the social and political aspects of Evangelicalism see I. Bradley, *The Call to Seriousness* (1976). See also Neill op. cit., pp. 234-43.

126 E. R. Norman, 'The Maynooth question of 1845', *Irish Historical Studies* Vol. XV, No. 60, (September 1967), p. 407.

127 For Sandon's reply to Orangemen see *Liverpool Standard,* 11th March 1845. The *Liverpool Standard* of 18th March 1845 carries a copy of McNeile's letter to Sandon. For details of this Conservative quarrel, and the subsequent election fiasco, see the *Liverpool Standard,* 25th March 1845, letter from Sandon dated 15th March. Also *Liverpool Mercury,* 21st March, 18th April, 1845; *Liverpool Standard,* 8th July 1845; *Liverpool Courier,* 18th August 1847. See also leader in *Liverpool Mercury,* 29th June 1847; *Manchester Guardian* 10th and 21st July 1847; *Liverpool Standard,* 3rd August 1847, leader; *Liverpool Courier,* 4th August 1847, Leader; *Liverpool Standard* 3rd August 1847, leader *Liverpool Mail,* 7th August 1847; *Albion,* 16th August 1847, 'Rev. McNeile and the election'. Also *Liverpool Courier,* 11th August 1847.

128 R. M. Sibbert, *Orangeism in Ireland and throughout the Empire* (1939), Vol. 2, p. 259.

129 Sibbert, op. cit., pp. 269-70.

130 Ibid. See also *Liverpool Courier,* 10th July 1844; *Liverpool Standard,* 16th July 1844.

131 *Liverpool Standard,* 16th July 1844.

132 *Liverpool Mercury,* 11th July 1845; *Liverpool Standard,* 8th July 1845. Surprisingly, the *Standard* gave little space to this meeting.

133 *Liverpool Standard,* 15th July 1845. Squire Auty claimed that after 1835 the Orange Order was kept going by J. W. Sylvester, of Atherton, until 1841. in a lodge at Huddersfield. See obituary for Sylvester in *Orange and Protestant Banner,* Vol. IV (January 1857-December 1858), p. 772.

134 *Liverpool Standard,* 22nd September 1840.

135 *Liverpool Standard,* 26th May 1843.

136 *Liverpool Standard,* 20th January, 7th March, 17th April, 26th May 1843. Significantly Mr Squire Auty, an Orange official from Bradford, was a frequent visitor to the Liverpool lodge meetings. See *Liverpool Standard,* 6th February 1844. Auty attended Liverpool meetings of both Orangemen and Protestant Operatives.

137 *Liverpool Standard,* 18th July 1843.

138 *Liverpool Herald,* 14th July 1842.

139 *Liverpool Standard,* 11th, 18th July 1843.

140 *Liverpool Standard,* 30th April 1844; Liverpool Courier, 10th July 1844.

141 *Manchester Guardian* 13th July 1844.

142 Report on S.C. (G.B.), appendix 2. Proceedings of the Grand Lodge, 4th June 1832, List of District Masters.

143 Op. cit., Grand Lodge, 15th June 1829. Reference to Richard Corner.

144 Pigot and Slater, *Liverpool Directory*, 1842, p. 51.

145 For a defence of Orangemen see *Liverpool Standard*, 30th April 1844. 'They entertain principles of devotion to the Constitution and the Established Church of their country.'

146 In December 1843 a free-trade lecture in Toxteth was broken up by a gang of carpenters under Richard Harbord. *Albion*, 15th January 1844. This refers to his leaving the Orange Order. For an obituary of Dr H. G. Harbord see *Liverpool Chronicle*, 15th January 1850.

Chapter III **The Irish famine**
The scale of
Irish immigration,
1847-53

I

The experience of Liverpool during the years of the famine had a traumatic effect on officials of the borough and parish and also on the general
public. In this chapter the events in Liverpool during 1847 will be looked
at, from the point of view of the immigrant Irish themselves and as
regards the consequences for the town and the citizens. In 1847 neither
officials nor townspeople were prepared for what was to happen, and to
this extent the year was unique in Liverpool's history.

The general public first became aware of the horrors of the famine
when, on 24th December 1846, a letter appeared in the *Times* from
Nicholas Cummins, a Cork magistrate. He described the scenes he had
witnessed in Skibbereen, County Cork, on 15th December and his letter
and the subsequent investigations revealed the full extent of the nightmare.[1] The administrative system in Ireland for dealing with 'normal'
poverty was based on the Irish Poor Law Act, 1838. Under its provisions
the country was divided into 138 administrative areas or unions, each
with a workhouse in its geographical centre. The financing of the Union
was the responsibility of the ratepayers but in fact, even before the
famine, many of them could not or would not pay their poor rates and the
numbers seeking relief in some areas could not be accommodated. Yet this
was the system that had to cope with one of the worst famines in history,
and the scale of the problem during the years 1845 to 1849 simply overwhelmed the authorities. In contrast to the English system there was no
right to relief, and in practice it was offered only to the old, the very young
and the sick. The able-bodied destitute had to fend for themselves.[2] In
1846 the Irish began to leave in abnormally high numbers to escape the
nightmare at home, and just a few hours across the sea, served by a fleet
of low-priced steamers, was Liverpool and the English poor law.

II

Before examining the qualitative nature of Liverpool's experience during 1847 it is useful to establish as accurately as possible the scale of the Irish movement into and through the port in the years of the famine and immediately after. We have already noted that in 1841 the Irish-born population was 49,639 and that this number had increased to 83,813 by 1851 (see Table 7). Practically all this increase of 34,174, or 69%, was accounted for by the influx of famine Irish. However, the impact of Irish immigration on the borough at this time must not be judged solely by the size of the resident Irish population. Account must be taken of the number of Irish passing through the port on their way to towns in the interior or transhipping for vessels to America, Canada or Australia. Such transients could spend days, weeks or months in Liverpool, often claiming poor relief and adding to the problems of housing, health and crime.[3] Central government kept no records of the number of Irish immigrants landing at British ports, and local authorities in the ports concerned were left to take whatever measures they felt were necessary. In Liverpool, by December 1846, the number of Irish paupers flooding in was such that Edward Rushton, the stipendiary magistrate, ordered the police to meet the Irish steamers on their arrival at the Clarence dock and count the number coming ashore. The police were asked to try to distinguish between those who were emigrants, those who were transhipping at Liverpool, those who were looking for work and those who were destitute.[4] Despite the normal chaos on the quays this operation would not be as difficult as it might seem, as the passengers had to disembark down gangways, thus facilitating counting. Emigrants usually possessed some luggage and personal belongings, but the paupers often had nothing but the rags on their backs. Emigrants, 'jobbers' and paupers were easily distinguishable from the comparatively few businessmen, civil servants and military personnel who utilised the small amount of cabin accommodation available.

This police counting operation appears to have been carried out over the years 1847 to 1853 inclusive, but unfortunately the information was not released in a systematic way. On 21st April 1849 Rushton wrote to the Home Secretary and explained the desperate situation resulting from Irish immigration. In reference to the year 1847 he stated :

> ... that between the 13th day of January and the 13th day of December 1847, both days inclusive, 296,231 persons landed in this port from Ireland: that of this vast number, about 130,000 emigrated to the United States; that some 50,000 were passengers on business and the remainder were paupers, half naked and starving, landed for the most part during the winter, and becoming immediately on landing, applicants for parochial relief . . .[5]

Thus we have the claim that, of the 296,231 arrivals during 1847, 50,000 (17%) were on business; 130,000 (44%) were emigrants and 116,231 (39%) were paupers. Rushton's claim must be regarded as authoritative, as it was he who had instituted the system of counting arrivals. This should be borne in mind because of the widely quoted statement by Dr Duncan, the Medical Officer of Health, that in the first six months of 1847 296,000 Irish landed at Liverpool, a rate that is not substantiated by the press publication of daily steamer arrivals and the number of passengers disembarking.[6]

For the year 1848 a search of official documents and the local press has failed to reveal any statement of the total number of arrivals from Ireland. Though the press reporting of arrivals, presumably using police statistics, was sporadic during 1848, a reasonable estimate of the annual total can be made using this source[7]. Taking these estimates, the average weekly rate of arrivals from Ireland during 1848 was 4,861, which if maintained over the year would have given an annual total of 252,772. Similarly, the average weekly rate of arrival of paupers was 1,811, which, extrapolated over a full year, would yield a figure of 94,190, or 37% of the total. These projections do not look unreasonable when set against the official (police) statistics for the years 1849 to 1853, provided by the parish authorities for the *1854 Select Committee on Settlement and Poor Removal*, which are reproduced in Table 16 with slight changes in layout.[8] Allowing for the arbitrary classification of pauper (based on their

TABLE 16
The number of Irish poor arriving in Liverpool, 1849-53, distinguishing as far as possible those who remained in Britain from those who emigrated overseas

Year	Deck passengers, emigrants, jobbers	Deck passengers apparently paupers	Total	Paupers as % of total
1849	160,458	80,468	240,923	33
1850	173,236	77,765	251,001	31
1851	215,369	68,134	283,503	24
1852	153,909	78,422	232,331	34
1853	162,299	71,353	233,652	31

Source: Select Committee on Poor Removal, 1854, appendix: 'Irish Poor'.

appearance), the picture is clear enough. Despite fluctuations, the inflow of paupers remained at a relatively high level for at least four years after the crop failure of 1849, as did the flow of emigrants through the port. Over the seven-year period 1847-53, using the estimates for 1848, 586,563 paupers landed at the docks. The number landing in the famine years of 1847-49 was 290,889, and the consequences of this tide of destitution and misery being unloaded into the town turned Liverpool, for a while, into a place under seige.

III

Marshalling the statistical evidence regarding the scale of the pauper immigration during the famine years is a necessary condition for any appreciation of the problem facing the authorities. However, the quantitative evidence is not sufficient, because it gives no indication of the physical condition of the immigrants on their arrival: yet this was a significant factor in the crisis. The problems posed by sheer numbers were compounded by the debilitated condition of many who disembarked at the Clarence dock - and this needs to be taken into account in any attempt to understand the problems of the poor-law officers and of the immigrants themselves. While the starvation in Ireland has been well documented and much written about, conditions on the vessels carrying the victims to Britain have received little attention, yet the experience of the crossing frequently compared in its hardship and nightmarish quality with anything endured in Ireland.[9]

From the 1820s onwards Liverpool was connected with all the main Irish ports by a fleet of relatively fast, cheap steam vessels, mainly paddle-driven but some screw-driven. There was little cabin accommodation and the main trade involved carrying animals below deck. Few vessels had steerage accommodation, so the overwhelming majority of passengers were carried on deck with virtually no shelter from the elements. The result was that they frequently arrived in a state of exhaustion; some died on the way. Exposure to the weather was not the only reason for the frightful condition of so many of them. Another factor was overcrowding, particularly bad on the Liverpool route.[10] John Besnard, the general weighmaster of Cork, told the *Select Committee on Emigrant Ships:*

> I have gone to Liverpool expressly to wait the arrival of Irish steamers and no language at my command can describe the scenes I witnessed there; people were positively prostrated, and scarcely able to walk after they got out of the steamers, and they were seized hold of by those unprincipled runners so well known in Liverpool. In fact, I consider the manner in which these passengers are carried from Irish to English ports is disgraceful, dangerous and inhuman.[11]

The conditions on board the cross-channel ferries were brought before the public by a series of tragedies. The most notorious was the case of the steamer *Londonderry,* which left Sligo for Liverpool on 1st December 1848 with 206 deck passengers. As a result of bad weather, they were forced by the crew to go below deck into a space 18 ft long, 10 ft wide and 7 ft high. Seventy-two died of suffocation.[12] On the night of Thursday 19th April

1849 the steamship *Britannia* left Dublin for Liverpool carrying 414 deck passengers. On its arrival three were dead, having died of exposure.[13] Commenting on this tragedy, the *Liverpool Mercury* referred to 'the human cattle trade'. Despite questions in the House and pressure on the government resulting, in 1849, in a Board of Trade inquiry, nothing happened to impede the traffic during the famine years.[14]

Before the publication of Cummin's letter in the *Times* the people of Liverpool were aware what was happening in Ireland because of the numbers of starving and diseased people arriving at the docks. For the last quarter of 1846 St Thomas's, a dockside parish in the South End, recorded 340 deaths, a considerable increase on the number over the corresponding period in 1845. Commenting, the *Liverpool Journal* stated:

> . . . a considerable portion of the increase arises from the great influx of poor people from Ireland, most of whom are quite destitute when they arrive. Some have been here only a few weeks, others a few days in the town previous to their deaths.[15]

Blanket references to the hardships does little to convey the appalling reality of their experience on arrival in England, yet that experience was to colour the outlook of the immigrant Irish for generations. The texture of a part of this experience can be illustrated by the cases of individuals who arrived at the beginning of the influx.

On 26th November 1846 Luke McCoy was found collapsed in the street and was taken to the police cells for safety but died during the night. The inquest verdict was death from diseased lungs and heart.[16] Michael McGill arrived on the Drogheda steamer, already ill, and, on taking a room in a lodging house, died the same night of congestion of the lungs.[17] On 23rd December 1846 Sarah Burns, an Irishwoman and mother of seven, died after complaining of pains in the head and chest. At the inquest it was revealed that between Sunday and her death on Tuesday all she had eaten was a piece of bread. The coroner and jurymen visited the cellar where she and the children lived and the coroner described it, somewhat inadequately, as deplorable:

> A person could not stand upright in it, the floor was composed of mud; and in that hovel there were seventeen human beings crowded together without even so much as a bit of straw to lie down on. We felt convinced that if they were allowed to remain in their present condition there would be two or three deaths before many days.

Sarah Burns and her children had been surviving in Liverpool by begging and the inquest verdict was 'Died from disease of the lungs accelerated by the want of the common necessities of life.'[18] Three days later a policeman found Martin Finnegan collapsed in the street and unable to speak. He was taken back to the cellar in Lace Street where he 'lived'. His bed was straw on a mud floor, with no covering of any description, and he died during the night. The post-mortem verdict was 'Death from diseases of the lungs combined with want of sufficient food.' Finnegan, his wife and three children had been surviving by begging.[19] In yet another similar case a policeman found a man dying on the footpath. He died in hospital and the post-mortem verdict was 'Death from starvation.' The inquest was held on 26th January 1847; the coroner remarked that it was the seventh case of its kind within the past few weeks, and he feared many more people were on the point of starvation.[20]

Mary Meganey lived in the Vauxhall Road, which ran through the centre of the most notorious Irish settlement. She was found dead in bed, and at the inquest it was revealed she had had only a cup of tea in three days. The post-mortem verdict was 'Death from starvation'.[21] The case of eight-year-old Luke Brothers caused a particular wave of concern among middle-class newspaper readers. The wretched Brothers family had experienced extreme deprivation since arriving in Liverpool and had been continually ill. The parish had allowed the family 3s a week, of which, it was alleged, 1s a week had been kept by the neighbour who collected the relief for the prostrate family. When fit enough the children had gone out begging, but on 8th May 1847 Luke Brothers died and the post-mortem report stated there was not 'the least particle of food in the stomach'. On the mud floor of the room in Banastre Street in which Luke died were five other people, all suffering from typhus.[22] At a public meeting on 12th May it was stated that on that day there had been inquests on two children who had died of starvation, and it was alleged that they had been left by their parents outside the workhouse door, too far gone to hold out any hope of recovery.[23]

These examples are illustrative of the problem facing the authorities from 1846 onwards; not only were the numbers demanding poor relief unprecedented in English experience but the condition of many of them was such that it was a question of whether large-scale death from starvation could be avoided. In judging the response of the Liverpool Board of Guardians, the Select Vestry, it should be borne in mind that they had no legal obligation to provide *continuing* relief to the immigrants. The *Liverpool Mercury*, liberal and sympathetic to the sufferings of the Irish, carried a long leader article on 15th January 1847, criticising the law which threw the burden of relief on the local taxpayer rather than the Irish landlords:

> The fact is; that in the cold and gloom of a severe winter, thousands of hungry and half naked wretches are wandering about, not knowing how to

obtain a sufficiency of the commonest food nor shelter from the piercing cold. The numbers of starving Irish men, women and children - daily landed on our quays is appalling; and the Parish of Liverpool has at present, the painful and most costly task to encounter, of keeping them alive, if possible . . .

IV

What was the administrative and political response in Liverpool to the influx of paupers in 1847? The reaction of the authorities must be seen in the context of the legal and administrative framework within which they had to operate. The Poor Law Amendment Act, 1834, laid down the principles that were to determine the provision of poor relief. In Liverpool the parish was the Union and the Board of Guardians were known as the Select Vestry, consisting of twenty-one ordinary members, elected by the ratepayers; two churchwardens, also elected by the ratepayers; and the two rectors of Liverpool.[24] At the time of the immigration crisis these were the Rev. Jonathan Brookes and the Rev. Augustus Campbell.[25]

Coexisting with the provisions of the 1834 Act was a body of law concerned with settlement and removal. Settlement and poor relief had become linked issues since the passing of the Act of Settlement and Removal in 1662 (13 and 14 Charles II, cap. 12). The validity of a person's claim to poor relief depended on whether or not he or she had acquired the status of being settled in the parish where the claim was made. Settlement status could be achieved in a variety of ways, but the principal means was inheriting settlement from one's father. If a pauper's inherited settlement could not be established, the magistrates would settle for the parish of birth. In situations where claimants could not prove settlement within the parish, they could be forcibly removed to the parish within which they had settlement *assuming this could be established.*[26] The Irish did not have settlement in English parishes, which meant they could be removed back to Ireland if they were forced by circumstances to claim poor relief while in England. English pragmatism, recognising the value of Irish labour gave rise to legislation (17 Geo. II, cap. 5) which enabled any destitute Irish to apply voluntarily to be 'passed' back to Ireland.[27] If the application was granted by the justices, the fare to Ireland was paid by the parish. Thus there were two legally distinct situations that gave rise to an official traffic in Irish paupers back to Ireland at ratepayers' expense. First, there were those who applied for poor relief while in England and were forcibly removed back to Ireland under the provisions of the laws of settlement and removal. Second, there were those who were destitute and wanted to go back and who asked the magistrates to be passed, which, if granted, meant that their fares were paid. The essential difference in the removal, as opposed to the passing, of an

Irishman or woman back to Ireland was voluntary versus forcible removal.[28]

The extent to which the removal laws were invoked varied, depending on local conditions and individual cases, but in Liverpool, before the arrival of the famine Irish, it had been used sparingly because of the widespread use of Irish labour. For example, between 1835 and 1846 inclusive, only 784 removal orders had been taken out in Liverpool, resulting in 477 families, English, Irish and Scots, being removed.[29] In the latter years the ability of parish authorities to remove paupers was lessened by the passage in August 1846 of the *Five Years' Residence Act* (9 and 10 Vict., cap. 66), which introduced the new concept of irremovability. It became illegal to remove paupers who had resided continuously in a parish for five years. This, then, was the legislative framework within which the parish authorities in Liverpool had to deal with a major crisis of poverty and disease. Under the law the Select Vestry were required to relieve all genuine cases of hardship, irrespective of settlement, but the applicants had to accept relief on the terms offered, which might include taking up residence in the workhouse and undertaking work. The parochial authorities had no obligation to provide continuing relief, and after initial assistance had been given they could inquire after the applicants' parish of settlement and, where possible, remove them. Leaving people to die was not an option the Select Vestry even considered, despite the scale of the relief operation. In their reaction to the crisis the comments of the Select Vestry distinguished between the 'settled Irish' and the 'casual' (newly arrived).

By mid November 1846 the vestry realised it was dealing with an unprecedented situation. Applications for relief from newly arrived Irish paupers were so numerous that the relieving officers abandoned any attempt at a thorough investigation of claims and instead simply handed out a bread ration of 6 oz per day. Even by Victorian standards this was a spartan hand-out, and by December the condition of many of the Irish was so bad that soup was added to the diet. By mid December the Select Vestry was distributing to the Irish poor alone 800 rations of bread and 700 quarts of soup daily.[30] The vestry were now thoroughly alarmed because, for example, in the week ending 19th December 1845 the number of casual Irish poor relieved was 888, while for the corresponding week in 1846 the number was 13,471.[31] This presented logistical problems for which the relieving officers were totally unprepared. As the immigrants disembarked at the Clarence dock, if they wanted relief they went to a shed in Fenwick Street. Thousands of paupers crowded the streets around the shed, and the frantic officials simply gave out bread and soup without any attempt to ascertain eligibility, in sharp contrast to the manner in which the settled poor were relieved. The amount of relief depended on the number of children a claimant said he or she had. There was no way in which the officials could check the size of families, and the system was quickly exploited by the settled Irish poor, giving rise to an alarming increase in the instances of relief - as shown in Table 17. Such a rate of increase

TABLE 17
Weekly instances of Irish outdoor relief during January 1847

Week ending	Number
9th	29,437
16th	66,255
23rd	130,795
30th	143,872
Total	370,359

Source: *Liverpool Mercury* and *Manchester Guardian,* January 1847.

could not be explained by the arrival of new Irish claimants over the same period and was prima facie evidence of fraud. The officials appear to have been mesmerised by the sheer numbers until rescue came in the form of Austin, the Assistant Poor Law Commissioner for the Northern Counties. Arriving in Liverpool, he immediately initiated an investigation of the emergency relief system. He noticed that on 16th January the ratio of children to women being relieved was 4·5 : 1. On 23rd January, when there were 23,886 cases of relief, the ratio of children to women was 3·12 : 1. Meanwhile he had recorded the number of Irish paupers arriving from Ireland over the nine-day period 12th January to 22nd January and noticed two things. First, that, among the 7,403 arrivals, the ratio of children to women was 0·66 : 1, a dramatic contrast to that which existed at the Fenwick Street shed. Second, of the arrivals, 1,867 had not claimed any relief, leaving 5,536 individuals who did, yet the claims for relief over the same period increased by 87%. Austin concluded that fraud was taking place in the form of resident Irish poor borrowing children to obtain relief at Fenwick Street. They were confident, he felt, that as a result of the pressure on the relieving officers there was little chance there would be any check on new claims.[32]

Austin presented his findings to the Select Vestry on 26th January 1847 and suggested that the giving of relief at Fenwick Street should cease and that the town should be divided into twelve districts, each with two relieving officers operating from an office. Applicants for relief should first be visited at home in the morning and, if they satisfied the officers, they should visit the officers in the afternoon, when they would be given a ticket of a certain colour, to be taken in exchange for food. The relieving officer in each district should, Austin argued, keep a book in which were entered the details of each claimant, and relief should be available on a day-to-day basis. Given the numbers claiming relief, the normal parochial provision of relieving officers was obviously inadequate, and Austin suggested that twenty-four policemen should be appointed relieving officers. All his recommendations were accepted and the new system came into operation on 2nd February 1847. The effect on the numbers claiming relief was immediate and dramatic. On Monday 1st February the total number of casual Irish claiming relief was 22,348, while on 2nd February, the first day of the new system the total dropped to 4,996.

Why did not the Select Vestry impose an efficient system of distributing relief in the first place? Quite simply, they were overcome by the scale of the immigration and, unlike Austin, few of them had ever experienced the giving of relief at first hand: they relied on the paid officers - and the number of these was too small.[33] The *Manchester Guardian* was watching events closely and warned the Board of Guardians in Manchester to take note of Liverpool's experience.[34] Thus, by February 1847, the Select Vestry had imposed a relatively efficient system of what was essentially famine relief. From the point of view of looking at influences on the sectarian conflict, the significance of the exposure of the fraudulent claims on the part of some Irish paupers was that it gave ammunition to McNeile and his allies.

V

Solving the problem of distributing outdoor relief brought little breathing space to the Select Vestry or the magistrates. The large numbers of immigrants passing through Liverpool, or making it their final destination, precipitated a housing crisis every bit as bad as that revealed by Dr Duncan in 1840. During the famine years the building of homes of the type that would be rented by the lower-income groups came almost to a halt. In this context, this means houses that would let at £12 a year or less. Builders were turning their attention to middle-class housing in the range £25 to £35 per year.[35] However, even the lower-valued houses would have been beyond the means of the Irish paupers, and the options open to them were limited. They were offered space in already overcrowded cellars and courts by existing tenants who wished to make some money from sub-letting; they could illegally occupy empty cellars, and as a last resort there were the cheap lodging houses. Between 13th January and 19th April 1847, inclusive, 131,402 'poor persons, many of them shockingly debilitated, all of them in a most distressful condition and some of them diseased . . .' landed at the port.[36] Frantic for accommodation, many of them smashed down the doors of the cellars emptied by the council under the 1842 Act and took up residence, bringing to a complete halt the council's policy of closing cellars deemed uninhabitable. Even by Liverpool standards the result was squalor on an unparalleled scale. Rushton estimated that early in 1847 27,000 immigrants took over cellars which had been condemned as unfit for human habitation.[37] The police were overwhelmed by the problem in that they simply had not the manpower to evict the squatters, and even if they had, eviction would simply have increased the death rate among the immigrant Irish.

On 22nd April 1847 Rushton was asked whether the Irish pauper immigrants in Liverpool were given outdoor relief. His reply gives some indication of the nature of the immigrant experience:

> Yes, and they lodge in cellars and rooms of the lowest character, fifteen or sixteen in a room. There is no adequate provision for the offices of nature, no one convenience of civilised life; they are sleeping in the clothes which they wear in the day, without beds and without utensils. Their relief consists of baked meat and soup, and this is that state in which many thousands of the Irish people are now abiding in that town.[38]

Duncan, the Medical Officer of Health, gave further evidence of the frantic overcrowding:

> The extent to which the overcrowding of dwellings must be carried at the present time may be judged by the fact which was communicated to me a few days ago, is that an entire family had taken up their residence in an old boiler found on some waste ground in the North End of the town. In different parts of Liverpool fifty or sixty of these destitute people have been found inhabiting a house containing three or four small rooms and in more than one instance, upwards of forty have been found sleeping in one cellar.[39]

There were no political wards in which the Irish had not settled by 1841, but the majority of those coming ashore during the period 1847 to 1849, intending to stay, headed for the established areas of Irish settlement. These were the places where they would find cheap lodging houses, cellars, friends and relatives who would give help and advice on how to survive in a hostile urban environment.

In 1847 concern over the illegal occupation of cellars and the overcrowding of houses was not simply based on humanitarian feelings. Among the more perceptive officials was the realisation that the overcrowding would precipitate and facilitate the spread of contagious diseases. In February 1847 Duncan warned the Health Committee that the number of cases of typhus was increasing, together with other diseases related to dirt and overcrowding. This was particularly the case in the North End. He also wrote to Grey, the Home Secretary, warning him that Liverpool was faced with 'the most severe and desolating epidemic'. The case of Lace Street demonstrated the situation in Vauxhall. Its population was almost entirely Irish and it contained many cheap lodging houses, prime breeding grounds of disease. Between 1st January and 31st March 1847, inclusive, 181 people died in this street, not counting residents who died in hospital. This was out of a population of 1,400 (living in 109 houses), and this number of deaths exceeded the combined totals for the Abercromby and Rodney wards, which together had a population of 20,000.[40] The mortality in Lace Street is not surprising, given that the water company turned the supply on only three times a week in a situation in which many people had no utensils for storing water.[41] The registrar of the Great Howard Street registration district in the North End wrote in his quarterly report for the period ending 31st March 1847:

> The return shows a great increase in the mortality of this district, which is without doubt solely attributable to the many thousands of Irish paupers who have landed here within the last three months, bring with them a malignant fever, which is very appropriately called 'the Irish fever' and many hundreds of them were suffering from diarrhoea and dysentry when they arrived, which will account for so many deaths from those causes. Everything which humanity could devise and money carry out for their cases has been adopted by the Select Vestry but so many thousands of Irish are continually pouring in, and their habits are so disgustingly filthy, that little can be done as yet to stay the great mortality among them. Perhaps there is not a parallel case to Liverpool for the last two months in the history of the country.[42]

The language this official uses is interesting on two counts. Firstly, it publicised the view that the typhus epidemic was in some way an 'Irish disease', a view bound to encourage anti-Irish zealots. Second, the words 'disgustingly filthy' applied to the immigrants, without reference to the conditions under which they travelled to England or lived when here, strengthened the already prevalent view that such was the normal condition of the Irish in Britain. The *Times* in a leader of 2nd April 1847 complained :

> Ireland is pouring into the cities, and even into the villages of this island, a fetid mass of famine, nakedness and dirt and fever. Liverpool, whose proximity to Ireland has already procured for it the unhappy distinction of being the most unhealthy town in this island, seems destined to become one mass of disease.

The official statistics illustrate clearly the severity of the epidemic and its progress. During April 654 paupers were buried in the workhouse cemetery alone, compared with an *annual* average over the previous twelve years of 1,357. On 5th April the *Times* gave its readers more details:

> ... The dead are taken by relatives to the Workhouse cemetery at all hours
> of the day, sometimes at night, in coffins, sometimes nailed, sometimes not,
> and if the gates happen to be closed, they are put over the walls ...

Obviously, the usual hospital facilities of the borough were totally insufficient, and the authorities rented three large sheds to house fever victims.
The intention was that, by removing sick people from the overcrowded
cellars and houses, the spread of the epidemic would be slowed down.
However, no sooner was someone taken to the fever sheds than their place
was taken by newly arrived immigrants, and the environment into which
they entered is exemplified by the case described at a meeting of the Select
Vestry on 9th May 1847:

> ... among a certain number of individuals, in Bent Street, it was reported
> that four were lying down in one bed with fever, that twenty-four grown-up
> young men and their sisters were sleeping in a filthy state in one room and
> that fourteen persons were sleeping in another filthy place. Twenty-six
> people were found huddled together in a room elsewhere and eight had died
> of fever in one house.[43]

At about the same time Duncan warned the Health Committee that
typhus was spreading outside the Irish areas and appearing among the
English and the middle classes. Again, he appeared to blame the Irish for
spreading typhus when he quoted the case of a well-to-do woman who had
died of the disease:

> I understand that this death has been pretty clearly traced to the Irish immi-
> grants, the contagion being supposed to have been caught at the Catholic
> chapel in Grosvenor Street.[44]

The epidemic was also taking a heavy toll of those whose duties brought
them into contact with the typhus victims, in particular priests, relieving
officers, doctors and nurses.

Catholic priests especially were at risk because of the extraordinary
devotion they displayed to their parishioners, visiting them in conditions
which were beyond the comprehension of middle-class Liverpool. Given
the shortage of medical staff, the priests were frequently the only people
to visit chronically sick people. For example, in Webster's Court, in
Vauxhall, a whole family were down with typhus, lying on a bed of straw,
unattended by nurse or doctor. The mother had only enough strength to
push the corpse of her baby off the straw, where it was found by Father
Newsham of St Anthony's. He was the only visitor the family had. In the
same court a house had thirteen fever victims, some dying, and no medical
man had visited them from Sunday till Thursday. Father Newsham was
again the only visitor. In some cases small children were unattended

because the family as a whole was ill. In one case in Father Newsham's parish all the family were down with typhus and a small child burned to death trying to make a hot drink on an open fire.[45] The priests were also called upon by the police to help persuade the Irish not to keep infected corpses in order to have a wake. In his report of 13th March 1847 Duncan stated:

> I would like to draw the attention of the Health Committee to the objection-able custom of retaining the bodies of the dead, especially those who have died of infectious fevers, in the sleeping rooms of the living - on Sunday last, a man died of typhus in a small room in Thomas Street in which seven or eight other inmates slept, two of whom were also ill with fever. Their friends objected to the burial taking place before Sunday (tomorrow) and in the meantime the other occupants continued to sleep in the same room with the dead body . . . I myself have seen, last week, the body of a child who had died of smallpox lying in a cellar where fifteen individuals slept.[46]

Such examples could be multiplied many times. In Addison Street, in Vauxhall, the mother of several dead children refused to allow their bodies to be moved, so Rushton told the police to seek the help of the Catholic priest.[47] In another case a man appeared before Rushton complaining that a neighbour in his court had died in a fever shed and the relatives were bringing the corpse back for a wake. The neighbours were terrified that they would catch typhus, so the police were sent to stop the wake taking place.[48]

The fever sheds proved inadequate to house all those who contracted typhus. The *Sheffield Iris* received a report from its correspondent in Liverpool who recorded an instance in which four fever sufferers had been refused admission to the sheds on 12th May, as they were full up, and so had to remain outside, where one died on the footpath during the night. It was alleged that a policeman had had to guard the corpse to stop the rats devouring it.[49] In another incident the police found two men dying of fever in the street and, as the hospitals and sheds were full up, they were placed in the bridewell, incredibly, among the prisoners.[50] In despair, the Select Vestry again approached the government for help; the result was an offer of tents to house typhus victims, which was not taken up, and the offer of two vessels to stand in the Mersey as lazarrettos, which was accepted.[51] By August 1847 the epidemic had reached its peak and early in 1848 the typhus had almost played itself out. The cost, in terms of human suffering and money, had been high, and despite the efforts of the Select Vestry some observers outside Liverpool were critical of the amount of poverty and degradation in the town. In November 1847 the Registrar General launched an extraordinary attack in his official report for the third quarter of the year:

> . . . Liverpool, created in haste by commerce - by men too intent on immedi-
> ate gains - reared without any tender regard for flesh and blood, and flour-
> ishing while the working population was rotting in cellars, has been severely
> taught a lesson that a portion of the population - whether in cellars or on
> distant shores - cannot suffer without involving the whole community in
> calamity. In itself, one of the unhealthiest towns in the Kingdom, Liverpool
> has for a year, been the hospital and cemetery of Ireland.[52]

This remarkably plain speaking touched a raw nerve of the editor of the
Liverpool Mail, who ran a long leader on 'this monstrous piece of absurd-
ity'. Ignoring all the previous reports on Liverpool's housing and sanitation, the *Mail* argued, amazingly, that the health of the English in
Liverpool compared well with any other town. This was not even true of
the middle classes. Duncan's report for 1847 puts events into perspective.
During that year 17,280 people died in Liverpool parish (21,129 in the
borough). This general mortality was 100% up on the average of the
immediately preceding years. Of these deaths in the parish, 5,239 were
due to typhus and 2,236 to dysentry and diarrhoea, a total of 7,475, or 43%
of deaths from all causes. Of the deaths attributed to the epidemic, 3,785,
or 51%, occurred in the wards with the densest concentration of Irish,
Vauxhall, Scotland and Exchange. Quite apart from those who died,
Duncan estimated that 100,000 suffered from contracting the diseases,
and typhus alone, in his view, left at least 1,200 widows and 4,000 orphans.
Surveying the whole year, he wrote:

> During that calamitous season we had to deplore the loss of many
> respectable and useful citizens. Among them may be enumerated the Roman
> Catholic clergymen, a Missionary Minister to the poor, ten medical practi-
> tioners, a number of relieving officers and others whose duties brought them
> into contact with Irish paupers and many hundreds of English residents in
> comfortable circumstances, most of whom might have been alive had
> Liverpool not been converted for a while into 'a City of Plague' by the immi-
> grant Irish who inundated the lower districts.[53]

In fact ten Catholic priests died of typhus during the year and this demonstration of self-sacrifice did a great deal to elevate the standing of the
Catholic clergy in the town, and not only among Catholics. Rushton,
addressing a meeting of disgruntled ratepayers complaining about Irish
immigrants, referred to 'the pestilential hovels that the Catholic priests go
down to perish and the brave overseers contract the disease'.[54] The interesting question is the total lack of casualties among the Anglican clergy,
given the undeniable fact that the non-Catholic working class also
suffered and died. The only Protestant clergyman to die was the Rev. John
Johns, of the Domestic Mission. The remoteness of many of the Anglican
clergy from the events of 1847 is illustrated by the Rev. Augustus

Campbell, chairman of the Select Vestry. In 1854, when told that ten Catholic priests had died in 1847, replied he did not think so, he thought the number was about six.[55] Today, in the middle of the council flats in Toxteth, there is still a memorial to the ten priests outside St Patrick's Church.

VI

During 1847, though the Select Vestry and the magistrates had been concerned primarily to fend off large-scale starvation and to control the typhus epidemic, they were also politically active. In this respect they had three strategic objectives. First, and most immediate, they petitioned the government for financial assistance to help with the cost of poor relief and medical assistance. They were turned down flat in December 1846 and May 1847.[56] They also wanted action to stop the Irish paupers coming to Britain. This too was turned down in December 1846. The second attack on the problem was to petition for a change in the law, giving the Irish the legal right to poor relief in Ireland. It was believed in Liverpool that, if the paupers could obtain such relief, fewer would cross to Britain. If successful this move would, it was hoped, reduce the future burden on the Liverpool ratepayers. However, it was to prove a misconceived view of the realities of the situation. The campaign was successful, and the *Poor Relief (Ireland) Bill* was introduced into Parliament in March and became law on 8th June 1847. However, the paupers continued to arrive in huge numbers. Though the Irish Poor Law Unions now had to provide relief for the destitute, many could not afford to do so, and even when it was provided the diet was inferior to that to be had in British workhouses and gaols.[57] However, at the time this was not obvious, and with the passing of the Act the Select Vestry and ratepayers were jubilant.

Simultaneous with the campaign for a right to relief in Ireland was a demand for a change in the law regarding removal. Under the *Poor Removal Act of 1845* (8 and 9 Vic., cap. 117) any person who applied for relief who did not have settlement could be summoned to appear before the magistrates, who could, if they saw fit, order his or her removal. However, the system was not meant to cope with the large numbers of paupers who descended on Liverpool in 1846 and was impossible to implement. The police had not the manpower to seek out and deliver summonses on such a scale. Finding a particular Irishman in Liverpool's slums was almost impossible, and even when a summons was delivered, if the person chose not to answer it, the police had not the men to seek him or her out and make an arrest. With the passing of the *Five Years' Residence Act* in 1846 Rushton stopped trying to apply the laws regarding removal.[58] Thus, in 1847, the authorities in Liverpool, together with those in Glasgow, Bristol, Newport, Manchester, Salford and other places, campaigned for a change in the law, to make it easier to remove Irish paupers.

This objective was related to the demand for the provision of relief in Ireland, for if the Irish immigrants could obtain relief in Ireland *and* if it was easy to ship them back under the law, then Liverpool could clear its cellars, reduce the rate burden and control disease more easily. Again the campaign was successful, and on 21st June 1847 the Poor Law Removal Act (10 and 11 Vic., cap 33) became law. Under the provisions of this Act the need to issue a summons was dispensed with. A relieving officer simply had to prove that a pauper had been a recipient of relief, and could then take the person before two magistrates. On ascertaining that the pauper had been born in Ireland and did not have settlement, a warrant would be made out and the person taken direct to the Irish steamer and put aboard, the master taking responsibility for him during the passage. Thus by June 1847 the authorities in Liverpool could plan the clearing of the illegally occupied cellars and the removal of Irish paupers. However, they quickly learned the lesson that passing laws and implementing them are two quite separate matters. The regulations governing the removal of paupers to Ireland laid down that they be carried below deck in bad weather. This provision, if adhered to, would have brought the system to a halt, because few vessels on the Liverpool-Ireland route at the time had steerage accommodation, so the paupers could only be carried on deck. Again there simply were not enough vessels to carry the numbers who, in principle, should be removed, estimated at 40,000 by Rushton.[59] More significantly, when the Act came into operation many of the immigrant Irish stopped claiming relief in order to avoid removal. For example, during the week ending 16th July 1847 the number of Irish paupers claiming relief was 3,411. The following week the number had dropped to 1,658.[60] The *Manchester Guardian* of 24th July 1847, commenting on the preparations in Liverpool to implement the new law, told its readers:

> Arrangements for removing the Irish in Vulcan Street are almost complete. A large warehouse has been rented. At the moment nearly 100 voluntary applications a day, but the majority are unwilling to go back and are leaving town - partially convalescent patients have scaled the walls of the fever sheds and disappeared.

Many did not leave Liverpool and survived by begging, already a problem in the town, and again the law was impotent under the pressure of events. Begging was illegal under the Vagrancy Act but any attempt to impose the law caused even more problems. Thus when an Irishwoman was brought before Rushton on a begging charge he gave her a prison sentence, but the overseer of the workhouse objected because he would have had to take her six children into the workhouse and provide a nurse. Rushton reversed his decision, letting the woman off with the statement, 'If this is to be the process, there is an end to the Vagrancy Act in Liverpool.' When asked if the Vagrancy Act was of no use to him, he replied, 'It is a dead letter in the whole place, we are choked out.'[61] Even where a prison sentence could be imposed the prison was overfull, and when it wasn't, for most beggars, prison was not a deterrent anyway, because it offered more comfort than they were used to.

As can be seen from the statistics in Table 16, the new legislation did not stop the influx of famine Irish, and resort to the 1847 Poor Removal Act was limited. For most towns the cost of transporting paupers to Liverpool or other ports was prohibitive, quite apart from paying the steamer fare. Even Manchester, with serious problems arising from Irish immigration, made little use of the law. To remove a pauper from Manchester to Ireland, in 1854, cost 10s 10½d. Of this the train fare to Liverpool cost 2s 7½d.[62] This is probably the main explanation of the fact that in 1847 15,000 Irish were removed from Liverpool whereas the corresponding figure for Manchester was 286. Over the eight years 1846-53 inclusive the total number removed from Liverpool was 72,781, while for Manchester the figure was 4,732. It was simply easier and cheaper for Liverpool to remove Irish paupers than it was for most other places.[63]

In practice Irish pauperism continued to be a problem for Liverpool, and not surprisingly the rate burden resulting from Irish immigration became an issue early in 1847. On 17th January the *Liverpool Mercury* carried the comment:

> Liverpool is at this moment, bearing a burden which belongs neither to itself not the country; nor even to England but to the United Kingdom and that burden will bring bitter distress upon hundreds of struggling tradesmen and small householders.

It was just such groups that provided the Orange Order and the Tory party with many members. At a meeting of the Select Vestry on 26th January 1847 it was claimed that many people living in houses of a value less than £15 per year were having difficulty in paying the poor rate.[64] On 29th January the chairman of the Select Vestry wrote to the Home Secretary yet again, pointing out Liverpool's difficulties, and told Sir George Grey that:

> The position of the Select Vestry is, therefore, very painful to them, they know that it is their duty, as Christian men, to relieve real destitution and prevent the probability of starvation; but while they own this duty to the casual Irish poor, they feel they owe a higher duty to their own settled poor and that they are under very serious moral and legal obligations to their own ratepayers, as trustees of the parochial funds . . . Many of the rate payers may be pauperised by the increase in rates . . . the working classes are becoming exasperated at the supposed preference of Irish to English poor.[65]

Before any rate increases consequent upon the influx of destitute Irish, the lower-income householders in Liverpool were experiencing difficulties in paying their rates. William Rathbone told a public meeting in January 1844 that, as a magistrate, he had just had 130 cases brought before him of ship's carpenters, ropemakers, sailmakers and bricklayers who could not pay. From such men were recruited the members of the Protestant Operative Association. One man told Rathbone in court that he was being asked to support the poor but had not had a day's work in four months.[66] The condition of the operatives had not improved by 1847. On 29th April the *Liverpool Times* carried a leader article attacking the Irish landowners and complained that:

> . . . Liverpool people already support their own poor and ought not, therefore, be called up to support the poor of the Irish squirearchy . . .

On 12th May a large meeting of ratepayers was held, including some of the more important businessmen in the borough. The mayor and Rushton attended, together with Campbell, chairman of the Select Vestry. One speaker claimed that a person present had paid £2,000 in poor rates over the last three weeks. Another speaker suggested the parish should meet the Irish boats, give the immigrants bread, soup and a railway ticket to London, so that people in the metropolis should have a taste of the problem, something, he argued, that would be more effective than petitions. However, Rushton urged the meeting to bear the burden 'in a manner becoming Christian men'.[67] Campbell certainly believed that the poor rates were a burden on the less well-off and later quoted the case:

> I would cite for instance, the example which is frequently cited to prove the injustice of the poor law altogether, the case of the industrious labouring man who, instead of marrying at eighteen or twenty, when he has hardly fee money to pay the marriage fees and buy the marriage ring, waits perhaps until he is thirty, works hard in the meantime and saves money to buy or rent a £15 a year house; it is very hard to make that man pay 5s rates instead of 2s 6d because Irish labour is valuable to Liverpool . . .[68]

VII

The typhus epidemic was almost over by February 1848, although the misery on the streets continued to be reported and the Poor Law Commissioners were sufficiently concerned to write to the Select Vestry in March over the number of cases of death from starvation.[69] On 10th December 1848 an Irish family landed at Liverpool from Dumfries, where a cholera outbreak was raging. The family moved into an unregistered lodging house, and within days three of its members had died of cholera. On 16th December an Irish girl died of the disease in an overcrowded house in Back Portland Street and was quickly followed by her father and brother. By May 1849 the cholera cases had reached epidemic proportions, and during August 1849 572 deaths occurred in one week. October witnessed a decline in the number of new cases, but over the whole year 5,245 people died of cholera, and again it was the Irish districts, particularly Vauxhall and Exchange, which suffered most. However, unlike the 1847 epidemic the better-off wards of Rodney and Abercromby incurred increased losses. The situation in 1849 is seen in perspective when it is noted that in the country as a whole there were 53,000 deaths from cholera, so that deaths in Liverpool alone accounted for over 10%. By comparison, deaths in Manchester numbered less than 1,000.[70]

The reading public could not fail to be aware of the continuing desperate condition of the Irish immigrants as the press continued to report inquest verdicts. For example, John Dobbins came ashore from the Dublin steamer, destitute and depressed. He took a room in a lodging house and committed suicide by throwing himself out of the window. Patrick Burns died of exposure as a result of sleeping outdoors.[71] In Ben Johnson Street an unknown Irishman took a room and died the same day. He said he had walked a long way before catching the steamer to Liverpool. At the coroner's inquest it was revealed that his stomach was completely empty. Nancy McDermott's case is of interest in terms of the light it sheds on the influence and effects of the removal laws. In 1847 she had been removed to Ireland by the Select Vestry; however, difficult as life in Liverpool was, she preferred it to Ireland, for she returned to Liverpool. She could not apply for relief because, as she told friends, she was frightened of being sent back, so she lived by begging. She died in Toxteth and the inquest verdict was starvation.[72] In January 1849 Ellen Kane and her five children, aged between nine months and ten years, arrived from Ireland. They crossed the Mersey and squatted in an empty house in Oak Street, an Irish area of Birkenhead. On Sunday 28th January 1849 Inspector McNeill of the Birkenhead police was called to the house, where he found Ellen Kane and the nine-month-old baby both dead. The remaining children had had nothing to eat since Saturday morning. At the inquest the jury returned a verdict of 'death from starvation' and accused Father Browne, the local Catholic priest, of a lack of human consideration, saying that he might have saved mother and baby. The verdict triggered off a heated correspondence in the Liverpool press when it became known that one of the jury was an Orangeman.[73] As the year went by the Liverpool public were shocked by horror piled upon horror, and two events in particular received extensive coverage. On 28th March a frightened boy ran to a policeman and said there had been a murder. On arrival at 20 Leveson Street the constable found the bodies of Ann Henrickson, the pregnant wife of a sea captain, her two sons and a servant girl. All had been brutally battered to death. A young Irishman, Maurice Gleeson, was arrested, tried and found guilty. On 15th September 1849 he was hanged outside Kirkdale prison in front of an estimated 30,000.[74] The incident had nothing to do with immigration or the Irish influx but, as in other similar cases, it stirred up feelings against the countrymen of the miscreant.[75] This is still the case with respect to similar incidents in all countries with immigrant groups who are resented by some portion of the indigenous population. In the Leveson case the *Liverpool Mail,* in the course of a long leader about the murder, launched into another tirade against Irish immigration:

> . . . the labourers of England are fast sinking to the condition of Irish peasants and paupers. Our workhouses are full and so are our gaols, and an enormously large portion of our population are fluctuating between one and the other . . . We submit that the state of Ireland is intimately connected with the state of poverty and crime in England. Every Assize Calendar and every list of criminals in the quarter sessions prove this . . ."[76]

The case of Patrick Culkin was perhaps more shocking. For those few Irish immigrants who were from the professional classes, life in the cellars of Liverpool must have been doubly unbearable. Culkin had been a schoolmaster before coming to Liverpool, where he resided in No. 1 Court, off the notorious Oriel Street. For two years he and his family had survived on the poor relief given to 'casual Irish'. On 1st August 1849 his eight-year-old daughter died of cholera and the next day his wife died. The same day the relieving officer came to the cellar and found Culkin in bed with the corpse of his wife while that of the child was laid out on a table. The officer told him that the corpses must be moved, as they were diseased, and the prospect of a pauper funeral seemed to upset the schoolmaster. When the officer came back next day to remove the bodies he found that Culkin had cut the throats of his two remaining children and had unsuccessfully tried to kill himself.[77]

Similar scenes of suffering and degradation were repeated elsewhere in the country, and not only among the Irish.[78] But the Irish were the poorest of the poor, and in Liverpool it was the scale of the problem that added an extra dimension to the experience. Writing nearly thirty years later, Gerard Manley Hopkins, Jesuit and poet, described his feelings about the town, where he served for a short time as a priest at St Francis Xavier's. He expressed the view that, compared with the Glasgow Irish, the Liverpool Irish displayed an undying hostility towards their host town.[79] John Denvir, the well known Liverpool Irishman who lived through the experience, wrote:

> Young as I was, I shall never forget the days of the Famine, for Liverpool,
> more so than any other place outside of Ireland, felt its effects. It was the
> main artery through which the fleeing people poured to escape what seemed
> a doomed land. Many thousands could get no further and the condition of the
> already overcrowded parts of the town in which our people lived became
> terrible, for the wretched people brought with them the dreaded famine fever
> and Liverpool became a plague stricken city . . . It will not be wondered at
> that one who says these things, even though he was only a boy, should feel it
> a duty stronger than life itself to reverse the system of misgovernment which
> was responsible.[80]

Denvir became a prominent member of the Irish Republican Brotherhood
in Liverpool. A sense of grievance among the Irish in Britain could easily
be inflamed by the sight of an Orange fife-and-drum band, flying flags
depicting Protestant victories. However, before returning to this theme,
we must examine the evidence of resentment among the indigenous population concerning Irish immigrants and immigration.

Notes

1   The Irish potato crop in 1845, 1846 and 1848 was a total failure. In 1847 the crop was
     good but a shortage of seed had resulted in a greatly reduced acreage. In 1849 the crop
     was a partial failure but, coming on top of the run of bad crops, it was a disaster for
     Ireland. For a graphic account of the famine and the relief operation see Cecil
     Woodham Smith, *The Great Hunger* (1962). Also R. D. Edwards and T. W. Williams,
     The Great Famine (1956).
2   For a detailed account of an Irish workhouse during the famine years see Sean Beattie,
     'Workhouse and famine: Inishowen', Journal of the Donegal History Society Vol. XIII,
     No. 4 (1980), pp. 145-9.
3   For an account of the experiences of Irish emigrants in Liverpool awaiting ships for
     America see Terry Coleman, *Passage to America* (1974), chapter 5.
4   B.P.P. (Commons), *Select Committee on Settlement and Poor Removal* (1847),. Minutes
     of Evidence E. Rushton, q. 4370.
5   B.P.P. (Commons), *Select Committee on Poor Removal* (1854), Minutes of Evidence,
     Rev. A. Campbell, Rector of Liverpool, q. 4954. Rushton's letter is reproduced in its
     entirety.
6   Liverpool, Medical Officer's Health Report (1847), p. 5. The Liverpool papers reported
     the daily arrivals of steamships from Irish ports, giving the total number of passengers
     broken down into emigrants, jobbers and paupers. These figures must have been
     obtained from the police office but the reporting was not systematic so that there are
     gaps in the figures obtained from the press.
7   These statistics were obtained from an examination of weekly statistics in the
     Manchester Guardian during 1848.
8   B.P.P. (Commons), *Select Committee on Poor Removal* (1854). This report was submit-
     ted to the House of Commons on 27th April 1854. J. B. Lloyd, the mayor of Liverpool,
     stated that he could not vouch for its precise accuracy but it had been compiled by the
     police and was the best information available.
9   For a detailed account of conditions on the cross-channel ferries see F. Neal, 'Liverpool,
     the famine Irish and the steamship companies', *Immigrants and Minorities*, Vol. 5, No.
     1 (March 1985), pp. 28-61.

10　The primary purpose for which the steamers operated was the carrying of animals and cargoes. Animals were considered a more valuable cargo than people. See Neal, op. cit.

11　B.P.P. (Commons), *Select Committee on Emigrant Ships* (1854), Evidence of J. Besnard, q. 4896-7. See also the evidence of S. Redmond, q. 1537-41.

12　Times, 8th December 1848. This edition carries a long leader article on the Londonderry tragedy. Also Neal, op. cit., pp. 42-3.

13　*Liverpool Mercury,* 21st April 1849; *Albion,* 23rd April 1849.

14　On 26th April 1849 Labouchere, President of the Board of Trade, faced questions in the House concerning the conditions on board the Irish steamers. Essentially, his reply was that the government could not interfere with the passenger trade from Ireland. In a compromise he asked Captain Denham of the Board of Trade to investigate the matter. Denham reported in June 1849, but nothing happened subsequently. See *Hansard,* Vol. 104, 26th April 1849.

15　*Liverpool Journal,* 6th February 1847.

16　*Liverpool Mercury,* 27th November, 1846.

17　*Liverpool Mercury,* 20th November 1846.

18　*Liverpool Mail,* 26th December 1846.

19　*Liverpool Mail,* 26th December 1846.

20　*Manchester Guardian,* 27th January 1847.

21　*Liverpool Mercury,* 22nd January 1847.

22　*Liverpool Albion,* 10th May 1847. *Manchester Guardian,* 15th May 1847.

23　*Manchester Guardian,* 15th May 1847.

24　For a history of the Select Vestry see S. Kelly, 'The Select Vestry of Liverpool and the Administration of the Poor Law, 1821-71', unpublished M.A. thesis (Liverpool).

25　Under a local Act of 1842 (5 and 6 Vict., cap. 88) the Board of Guardians became known as the Select Vestry. The parish of Liverpool was not identical to the borough of Liverpool. The latter consisted of the parish, parts of the 'out towns' of Toxteth and Kirkdale and parts of West Derby and Everton. At the time of the 1841 census the population of the parish was 223,000 while that of the borough was 296,000.

26　For a background to the English poor-law system see G. Taylor, *The Problem of Poverty* 1660-1834 (1969); M. E. Rose *The Relief of Poverty,* 18341914 (1973); also Settlement, removal and the poor law', in *The New Poor Law in the Nineteenth Century,* ed. D. Fraser (1976).

27　B.P.P. (Commons), *Report on the Law of Settlement and Removal of the Poor* (1854). Letter from George Goode to the Poor Law Board

28　B.P.P. (Commons), *Select Committee on Settlement and Poor Removal* (1847). Minutes of Evidence, E. Rushton, q. 4385-7.

29　Rushton, ibid., q. 4336.

30　*Manchester Guardian* 13th February 1847. In January 1847, the *Mercury* claimed the parish was paying out £300-£400 per week on vagrants compared with £11 the previous year. *Liverpool Mercury,* 29th January 1847.

31　B.P.P. (Commons), 1847, Famine Papers, Correspondence, p. 435.

32　*Manchester Guardian,* 13th February 1847. This carries a long report of Austin's investigation. See also *Liverpool Mercury,* 28th January 1847, for a report of the meeting of the Select Vestry at which Austin alleges that people were borrowing children in order to make bogus claims for relief.

33　Rushton, op. cit., q. 4504.

34　*Manchester Guardian,* 13th February 1847.

35　For an analysis of the housing stock in Liverpool in the first half of the nineteenth century see J. H. Treble, 'Liverpool working class housing, 1801-1851', in *The History of Working Class Housing,* ed. S. D. Chapman (1971).

36　Rushton, op. cit., q. 4370.

37　*Liverpool Mercury,* 19th May 1847, also *Liverpool Chronicle,* 15th May 1847. Rushton made this claim at a meeting of ratepayers held on 12th May 1847.

38   E. Rushton, *S.C. on Settlement and Poor Removal* (1847), q. 4422.

39   Quoted in Treble, op. cit., p. 208.

40   L.R.O. Minutes of Health Committee, 5th April 1847, Duncan's report.

41   *Liverpool Journal*, 6th March 1847.

42   *Times*, 4th May 1847. See also *Manchester Guardian*, 15th May 1847.

43   *Liverpool Mercury*, 12th May 1847.

44   L.R.O. Minutes of Health Committee, 17th May 1847.

45   *Liverpool Journal*, 13th March 1847.

46   L.R.O. Minutes of Health Committee, 15th March 1847.

47   *Liverpool Journal*, 13th March 1847.

48   *Liverpool Courier,* 16th June 1847.

49   *Sheffield Iris,* 13th May 1847.

50   *Liverpool Chronicle,* 15th May 1847.

51   The desperation of the Liverpool authorities can be gauged by noting the possible courses of action suggested to the Select Vestry to cope with the problem. Some of the doctors proposed the building of a fever hospital for 5,000 patients outside the town. Someone else suggested using Hilbre island on the Dee as a isolation hospital. Austin, the Poor Law Commissioner, asked if the industrial schools at Kirkdale could be converted into a hospital because the Manchester Board of Guardians had agreed to take the children into their homes in Swinton. See *Liverpool Courier,* 16th June 1847.

52   *Liverpool Mail*, 6th November 1847, also *Liverpool Albion,* 1st November 1847.

53   L.R.O. Medical Officer's Health Reports, 1847-50, p. 18.

54   *Liverpool Chronicle,* 15th May 1847.

55   B.P.P., Select Committee on Poor Removal (1854). Minutes of Evidence, A. Campbell, q. 4954.

56   The Select Vestry petitioned Grey, the Home Secretary, on 24th December 1846. He replied on the 28th, refusing any help, while recognising Liverpool's problems. B.P.P. (Commons), Relief of Distress in Ireland (1847), Vol. 6. On 7th May 1847 Sir George repeated in the House of Commons that there could be no provision of central funds for Liverpool.

57   For a detailed discussion on the relative merits of the diets in English and Irish workhouses see A. Campbell, op. cit., q. 4982-92. Campbell describes the workhouse stew as 'scouse'.

58   For Rushton's views on the impracticality of working the law see B.P.P. (Commons), 1847, *Evidence to Select Committee in Settlement and Poor Removal,* q. 4379-80.

59   Rushton, op. cit., q. 4380.

60   *Liverpool Chronicle,* 7th August 1847. Report on meeting of Select Vestry.

61   Rushton, op. cit., q. 4370 and q. 4376-8.

62   B.P.P. (Commons) (1854), *Report of the Select Committee on Poor Removal,* appendix 5, table F.

63   B.P.P. (Commons) (1854), *Minutes of Evidence, Select Committee Report on Poor Removal,* Rev. A. Campbell, q. 5026. For Manchester figures see J. Harrop, q. 6230.

64   In 1847, out of 40,000 rated properties, rates were collected on only 8,000. The rest were excused. S.C. op. cit., Minutes of Evidence, M. D. Lowndes, q. 4616-19.

65   *Liverpool Mercury.* 29th January 1847, contains a copy of the letter in full.

66   *Albion*, 22nd January 1844. Rathbone was addressing and anti-monopoly meeting.

67   *Liverpool Chronicle,* 15th May 1847.

68   Campbell, op. cit., q. 5009.

69   *Liverpool Mercury*, 17th March 1848, 'Select Vestry'.

70   L.R.O. Medical Officer on Health's Reports, 1847-50, pp. 25-33.

71   *Liverpool Albion,* 2nd April 1849.

72   *Liverpool Standard,* 8th May 1849.

73   *Liverpool Albion*, 29th January 1849; *Liverpool Mercury,* 30th January 1849; *Liverpool Mercury,* 9th February 1849.

74 *Liverpool Mail*, 7th April 1849.

75 In the case of a triple murder at Mirfield in May 1847 two Irishmen were arrested and tried for the killings. *The Manchester Guardian* of 22nd May 1847 reported that 'among the mass, the feeling experienced is one of deep indignation and which has manifested itself in a most unwise manner. Because the two parties apprehended are Irishmen, so strong a feeling has been excited against the race that in parts of the neighbourhood, breaches of the peace are apprehended in the shape of endeavours to drive the Irish out.'

76 *Liverpool Mail*, 7th April 1849.

77 *Liverpool Albion*, 6th August 1849; *Liverpool Mercury*, 7th August 1849; *Liverpool Albion*, 13th and 16th August 1849.

78 For cases of English dying of starvation see *Times*, 3rd March 1847 (case in Bolton); 12th March 1847 (case in Stepney); *Manchester Guardian*, 12th May 1847 (case in Todmorden). No doubt a thorough search of the press would reveal others.

79 Quoted by P. J. Waller in *Sectarianism and Democracy: a political and social history of Liverpool 1868-1939* (1981), pp. 24-5.

80 John Denvir, *The Life Story of an odd Rebel* (1910), reprinted 1972.

Chapter IV **Immigration and anti-Irish feeling**

In May 1847 the mayor and Edward Rushton had to face an angry meeting of the principal ratepayers, protesting about the burden of immigration on Liverpool, and by the end of 1847 sympathy for the destitute Irish had largely subsided.[1] It was to be expected that the experience of the famine years would provoke some heightening of anti-Irish feeling, and when it came it was in the guise of increased sectarian bitterness. In trying to account for this backlash, which appeared in 1850, three specific issues seem relevant to any explanation: the widespread sense of grievance over the cost of supporting the Irish poor; the relatively high proportion of Irish-born people reported in the borough's criminal statistics, and the fear of rebellion among the Irish community in Liverpool - the English perception of Irish 'disloyalty'.

I

A charge commonly levelled by Protestant extremists and their supporters, together with religiously neutral members of the business community, was that the influx had imposed a large, permanent and unjust burden on the ratepayers.[2] This sense of injustice manifested itself in numerous petitions to the Home Secretary, the House of Commons and the House of Lords. In Parliament, Lords Brougham, Sandon, Campbell and Morpeth pressed the case for special treatment continually but not effectively.[3] The Select Vestry financed poor relief by imposing a poor rate, so that the relation between the number of Irish receiving relief and the rates to be paid was a fairly direct one. Unfortunately the rate books of the vestry for this period have not survived, so we must rely on scattered sources of evidence regarding the charges made by the opponents of Irish immigration.

There are a number of difficulties involved in interpreting the evidence. First, a distinction is not always drawn between relief expenditure on the settled Irish (those with five years' continuous residence in the parish) and the casual Irish, those without settlement. The distinction is of some importance in that those Irish who had settlement had probably contributed their labour to the local economy during all, or some part of, their time in Liverpool, thus, in the view of some ratepayers, earning the right to relief, quite apart from their legal entitlement. By contrast, the casual Irish were unlikely to have jobs, being newly arrived from Ireland or having drifted into Liverpool from other English parishes. It was this category of Irish that provoked the greatest outcry. A second problem arises because the statistics published in the press and elsewhere do not always make clear whether they refer to *instances* of relief or the *number* of individuals, i.e. a person receiving relief on each of six days would be recorded as six instances. For example, the number of cases of relief given to the casual Irish in Liverpool for the six days ended 12th June 1847 was 55,385.[4] But it is not clear how many *individuals* this figure represented. One solution is simply to take the average of the daily totals and assume it refers to individuals, so that for the period mentioned above the result is 9,231. A third difficulty in assessing the cost of Irish immigration is the fact that in addition to the provision of basic relief in the form of cash, bread, soup and clothing the Select Vestry incurred special costs associated with the crisis. These were the result of hiring extra doctors, nurses, relieving officers, three fever sheds in 1847, fitting out the lazarrettoes on the Mersey and paying their crews. The cost of sending Irish paupers back to Ireland increased rapidly after the change, in June 1847, of the law regarding removal, while the cost of running the borough gaol rose because of the increased number of Irish prisoners. There is no one set of accounts available that makes it possible to measure accurately the cost to Liverpool of the Irish famine. The most complete set of statistics, presented to the 1854 *Select Committee on Poor Removal,* refer only to the provision of basic necessities (food and clothing) during each *financial* year from 1844 to 1854.[5] Thus a further complication arises because the statements of many witnesses regarding the cost of Irish immigration do not make it clear whether they are referring to the calendar year or the financial year, so cross-referencing is almost impossible. Keeping such problems in mind, it *is* possible to make some estimates of the financial burden on ratepayers during and after the crisis.

The economic base of poor rate income was the ratable value of property in the parish, which in 1847 was £1,021,898, representing 40,000 dwellings. In practice 32,000 properties - mainly those with a rental of less than £10 a year-were exempt because of the poverty of the ratepayers concerned. This had the result that only 72% of the potential rate income was collected.[6] During the financial year 1846/47 the rate was 2s 1d in the £, and by 22nd April 1847 the new rate had not yet been fixed because of the Select Vestry's difficulties in guessing what was going to happen to the volume of Irish immigration. A 3s rate was contemplated, but Rushton felt this would be insufficient; in fact there were two rate increases during 1847, each of 1s, bringing the rate to 4s 1d.[7] An increase of 2s in the £ represented a considerable additional burden on the more prosperous labourers and tradesmen who provided the grass-roots support for the Tories. For example, on a house assessed at £15 per annum, the additional rate payment was 30s, the equivalent of a week's wages. The magnitude of the cost of providing basic relief in the form of food and clothing is demonstrated by the statistics produced by the Select Vestry in 1854. During the financial year ended March 1845, immediately preceding the famine crisis, the amount spent on the relief of Irish paupers was £2,916, 9% of the total expenditure on paupers. In the year ending March 1847 the expenditure on Irish paupers was £25,926, 40% of a greater absolute amount. The total expenditure on this type of relief for both Irish and non-Irish increased from £31,282 in the financial year 1845/6 to £65,282 in 1847/48, more than double. However, within this aggregate amount, expenditure on the Irish poor rose from £2,916 to £25,926, an increase of 889%.

Even more significant was the fact that, within this overall rise, outdoor relief showed the greatest increase. This form of relief was particularly attractive to the Irish, who in general disliked the workhouse. In principle the giving of outdoor relief was supposed to be discouraged. The reason for this large-scale outdoor relief increase, however, was the lack of workhouse accommodation on a sufficient scale. In the year 1845/46 the expenditure of £648 on Irish outdoor relief represented 3% of the total outdoor relief incurred by the Select Vestry. During the financial year 1847/48 spending of £20,750 on Irish outdoor relief accounted for 49% of this category of expenditure. Campbell claimed that the total cost of the Irish poor to the Liverpool ratepayers during 1847 was £70,000, the product of a 2s rate.[8] The difference between the figures of £25,926 and the £70,000 claimed by Campbell was the additional costs referred to earlier. However, this expenditure total is not an index of Irish deprivation, because many Irish did not ask for relief, in order to avoid the risk of removal. They survived on begging, private charity and the help of friends and relatives. It is clear that the famine in Ireland resulted in a large and permanent increase in spending on Irish destitution in Liverpool, and the hope of many that poor relief would quickly return to the pre-famine level proved illusory.

A charge which had less justification was that of over-generosity in the treatment of Irish paupers. A rough indication of the adequacy of the relief may be obtained by calculating the expenditure per head on the basis of the Select Vestry statistics. For the worst year, ending March 1848, the *per capita* relief was 21·76*d*, compared with 16·96*d* per head for English paupers. However, in all other years the figure for Irish relief dropped below 1*s*, less than the English relief per head by about 2*d*. Judged even by contemporary standards, this was barely survival level. The *relatively* high rate of outdoor relief for 1847 probably reflects the fact that the extreme deprivation of many of the immigrants necessitated more spending on them.[9] It seems reasonable to conclude that the level of assistance was not over-generous, even by the standards of those leaving famine-ridden Ireland. Campbell admitted as much:

> To say the honest truth, I do not think from what I have seen, that our outdoor relief is of a very splendid nature; I do not think we give anything very attractive in the way of food to paupers out of doors; I do not think it ought to be any great attraction to them . . .[10]

Campbell, speaking in 1854, was replying to questions suggesting that Liverpool was creating its own Irish pauper problem by offering outdoor relief on a large scale. If, suggested the critics, the destitute Irish, undeterred by the possibility of removal, could obtain relief only by going into the workhouse, then applications for relief would decline. This was true, but the simple fact was that the parish workhouse would only take 2,000 people, and that after spending £160,000 on extensions.[11] The parish did not want the expense of building another workhouse and, quite simply, it was hoped-wrongly, as it turned out - that the Irish immigration problem would go away. As a basis for comparison Rushton stated in 1847 that an 'infirm' individual received about 1*s* 6*d*, while a married man with three children would probably receive 3*s*. This confirms the spartan nature of poor law provision.[12]

As both chairman of the Select Vestry and as rector, Campbell tried to balance the interests of the ratepayers against the need to fulfill both Christian and legal responsibility towards the poor. The business community in the port certainly benefited from the large pool of unemployed Irish to the extent that Irish labour was widely used, and the presence of so many people looking for work could not fail to influence the wage levels paid to labourers. Campbell himself was absolutely clear on this issue and, speaking of Irish labour, he expressed the view:

> It is extremely valuable; I think it very difficult to ascertain what that value is, I think any estimate of that sort would be fanciful but I am inclined to place a very high value upon it indeed; we would not do without it, either in town or country. In the present state of the labour market, English labour would be almost unpurchasable if it were not for the competition of Irish labour.

He went on to refer to the 'screw of Irish competition' but then added:

> . . . but with the highest appreciation of its value, I think it may be bought too dear; and in the first place I would hazard the opinion (perhaps it too may be erroneous) that a great majority of the ratepayers of Liverpool only profit indirectly by the value of Irish labour, [13]

Whether or not Campbell's view of the effects on wage levels was accurate is not the issue. He *believed* it kept certain wage levels lower than they would otherwise have been, and this belief was shared by many others. A correspondent to the *Liverpool Albion,* writing in January 1849 on behalf of the Operative Porters' Association complained that experienced dockers were being thrown out of work by employers taking on inexperienced Irish at 1s 6d to 2s a day.[14] For the Liverpool businessman a finely balanced calculation was involved in any attempt to decide whether the increased rate burden was compensated for by the availability of a large labour force. However, there was no doubt that the expense, real or imagined, of relieving the immigrants was a source of great resentment.[15] The issue was aired frequently in the national and local press. On 1st February 1847 the *Times* ran a leader on Irish immigration into Liverpool and declared that 'the property of even that rich city threatens to sink under so unequal a load'. Typical of much local press comment was the leader article carried by the *Liverpool Times* on 20th April 1847, in which the whole matter of Irish poor relief was discussed:

> . . . the question at issue is not whether the Irish poor should be supported by the rates upon property but merely whether they should be supported by rates levied on the absentee landlords of Ireland or on that of the heavily taxed merchants and tradesmen of Liverpool, Glasgow, Manchester, Bolton and every other town and village within the reach of the outcast victims of Irish landlordism . . .

So, it seemed, the burden was falling on business and property. The *London Times,* returning to the attack on Irish landlords, widened the range of those who, in its view, bore the yoke of Irish poverty:

> The present question is, the whole question virtually, is whether every English working man is always to carry an Irish family on his shoulders, as he does at the present moment. Do the working men of England choose to have it so?[16]

Such sentiments appealed to those anti-Catholics who were willing to use any weapon that came to hand. It is a short step from resentment based on a perceived economic grievance arising from the presence of a minority alien group to racism. The gradation is a continuum, moving imperceptibly from hostile comment, to scurrilous opinions, to outright attacks on the characteristics of the race. Typical of the scurrilous was the rejoinder in the *Liverpool Mail* to the Registrar General's attack on the commercial classes of the town:

> That the scum of Ireland come to Liverpool and die in thousands is true. But whose fault is that? Misgovernment in Ireland - idleness on the part of the peasantry and ignorance and extravagance on the part of the gentry . . . The people that come here are not labourers . . . they are beggars and paupers. They never were labourers. They never did an honest day's work in their lives. They lived by begging, as the Roman Catholic prelate *regrets* to say they cannot do now, for the potato crop has failed and when they arrive here, begging is their profession, the workhouse their retreat, the four-penny loaf per day a certainty and medical aid, port wine soup, a coffin and a christian burial . . .[17]

Despite the *Mail's* attack on McNeile and Orangeism, its stance was determinedly anti-Catholic. Significantly, though it had a relatively large rate burden, the outcry over Irish immigration was more muted in Manchester and almost totally lacked the religious and racial overtones of much of the public comment in Liverpool. Yet it would be unwise to conclude that rabid anti-Catholicism was the exclusive preserve of Liverpool's clerics and Orangemen; the riots in Stockport in 1852, for example, were to show that such was not the case. In Liverpool, however, the pressure of Irish immigration was much greater than the number of paupers seeking poor relief; the huge numbers of Irish passing through the port, and an economic base characterised by casual, unskilled work were major problems. The crucial difference between Liverpool and Manchester was the extent and ferocity of Liverpool Orangeism.

II

Criminal statistics regarding minority ethnic groups are frequently a potent catalyst with regard to underlying prejudices in the host community. This is particularly the case given the unwillingness of the majority of people to submit such figures to any kind of analytical scrutiny. The issues raised by such statistics, or the behaviour implied, touch deep-seated emotions and fears and add to the basic difficulties of interpreting any kind of criminal statistics.

The most frequently heard charge against the Irish as a group, in Liverpool and other towns, was that they accounted for a disproportionately high number of the cases appearing in the various criminal categories recorded by the police.[18] This pattern was well established in the public mind long before the famine influx. In 1836 William Parlour,

Superintendent of the Liverpool police, claimed that one-third of all people taken into custody were Irish, while in his estimate not more than 25% of the population of the town was Irish.[19] Assuming the figures are accurate, a number of points need to be made. First, even if at the time the Irish population was 25% of the total, it was almost certainly approaching a third of the working-class population, so that the numbers would represent the relative proportion of Irish in the population most likely to be involved in law-breaking. Second, many of the people arrested and designated English would be the children of Irish-born persons and so almost certainly Catholic; hence the proportions of Catholics in the various categories would be higher than those referring to Irish. For the Protestant extremists it was the Catholicity of law-breakers that provided grist to their particular mill. In 1836 Fr Vincent Glover, parish priest of St Peters in Seel Street, claimed that nearly 55% of all the prisoners in the Kirkdale House of Correction were Irish.[20]

Thus, on the eve of the influx of famine Irish, the profile of the Irish as relatively more prone to criminal behaviour than the host population was well established. In the rhetoric of the sectarian conflict, it was an easy move from Irish to Catholic. On 21st April 1848, while Liverpool was struggling with the problems of the famine Irish, Edward Rushton, in his capacity as stipendiary magistrate, wrote to the Home Secretary, Sir George Grey. In the course of a long account of the burdens borne by Liverpool as a direct result of the Irish immigration, he went on to say :

> I believe I have in my former letters to you, stated my conviction that the presence of this miserable population would materially affect the health and character of our own labouring classes, my worst anticipations have been realised. I am unfortunately enabled by the results of my daily experience, to show you how much of the health of the people has suffered and am able, by exact details, to show you how greatly the Irish misery has increased crime in Liverpool . . .[21]

Rushton showed that, of persons appearing before the magistrates in 1848, the Irish accounted for 40%. Again, it must be repeated that as a proportion of the labouring population the Irish probably made up 33% to 40%, so that the figures would not justify the charge that they were over-represented in the statistics. In the same letter Rushton made his thinking on the issue clear:

> . . . now the Irish form but one fourth of the population yet they give nearly half the criminals. The truth is, that gaols, such as the borough gaol of Liverpool, afford the wretched and unfortunate Irish better food, shelter and raiment, and more cleanliness than it is to be feared many of them ever experienced elsewhere, and hence it constantly happens that Irish vagrants who

have offered to them the choice of being sent to Ireland or to gaol, in a great majority of cases desire to go to prison; the fact being that the English gaols are excellent winter quarters for starving Irish paupers and in consequence the Liverpool gaol, which ought never to contain more than 500 prisoners, now has 1100 within its walls. The cost of all this to the people of Liverpool, both in the augmentation of parochial and legal charges, is absolutely enormous. It cannot be surprising that the people of this place who find the rates for the relief of the poor daily augmenting cannot be satisfied under the pressure they sustain . . .

If avoidance of starvation was undoubtedly the motive behind much Irish mendicity, it was equally true that there was a well established tradition of professional begging. James Shaw, agent of the District Provident Society at Liverpool in 1836, expressed the opinion that:

The Irish are more addicted to begging than the English and there are more imposters among the Irish than the people of any other country. They sometimes hire bad cellars for the express purpose of being visited there, which they make look very miserable and live in another part of the town . . . I have never known cases of this kind among the English.[22]

Not only did they borrow rooms, they borrowed children. In one case a policeman visited a cellar in the Vauxhall district, following up an enquiry. In a windowless back cellar he found a pile of straw occupied by a large dog and a skeletal, three-year-old child. A neighbour later claimed that the mother hired it out to professional beggars.[23] There is no reason to believe that such practices were exclusively Irish or Liverpudlian. For example, *The Times* of 3rd January 1849 reported a case in Westminster in which a professional beggar borrowed a child at a rate of 9*d* per day. However, the Liverpool press frequently reported cases in the magistrates' court involving professional beggars. Typical was a case in February 1849 when a group so described were brought before the bench and, of the fifty, forty-eight were Irish. Given the option of being shipped back to Ireland or going to gaol, the majority chose prison.[24]

A matter of concern to the authorities was the high level of juvenile crime, and children arrested for begging frequently stated that they were sent out by their parents. In 1836 Superintendent Parlour expressed the opinion that a large proportion of juvenile thieves were Irish, having progressed from begging.[25] Press reporting of professional begging was at its height during the famine years, but the tradition of begging became an established and continuing fact of Liverpool life. Rushton's actions and opinions while stipendiary magistrate leave no doubt regarding his sympathy for the immigrants and his hostility to the Orange Order. By any account, he was to be regarded as liberal in outlook, humane in disposition and anathema to the ultra Tories. Yet even he expressed concern that the Irish would drag the English working class down:

> It would be out of place to more than state the amount of evil which the inhabitants of Liverpool have to bear, arising out of the unfortunate state of Ireland. I do not therefore attempt to offer any opinion about the matter, but I do most anxiously represent to you the great danger, moral as well as physical, which cannot but be generated by allowing the continued unchecked immigration of the miserable Irish people into such towns as Liverpool. The inhabitants feel the pecuniary cost as a severe evil, but they also feel and fear other events which may permanently deteriorate the condition, the habits, and the morals of the labouring masses of their own countrymen.[26]

Thus, from one who could be regarded as a champion of the rights of the Irish and of Catholics, we have the view that not only did they impose an unjust financial cost on the people of Liverpool, but they threatened the health and moral well-being of the indigenous working class. It is easy to see the ammunition this placed in the hands of anti-Catholics, particularly when it became clear that what might be termed the criminal profile of the Irish during the extraordinary circumstances of the famine influx proved to be of a more permanent nature.[27]

There was general agreement among those closest to the immigrants that drink was a major factor in their involvement with the police. Unimportant in organised crime, they were particularly prominent in crimes of violent assault.[28] During the years 1840 to 1850 the dock system was being expanded rapidly. The impressive Albert Dock was opened in 1845, and throughout the rest of the decade docks in the North End were being completed. In 1846, on the eve of the famine, Mathew Dowling, the Head Constable, told a select committee that there was widespread violence and drunkenness in the North End among the Irish and his men were frequently in great physical danger.[29] This is significant because, as we shall see, Vauxhall was the flashpoint in police-immigrant relations, and Irish spokesmen frequently accused Dowling and the police in Vauxhall of being Orangemen, anti-Irish and anti-Catholic. Subsequent events supported this view, but even allowing for the bad feeling in the North End, drunkenness was usually the main cause of involvement with the police. It was one thing for the police in Sheffield or Bradford to be called to a disturbance in some 'Little Ireland'; in Liverpool they might be faced with trying to arrest a man in a street where several hundred hostile compatriots lived.

From the point of view of sectarian conflict the significance of the Irish/Catholic crime statistics is that they not only reinforced the prejudices of the extreme Protestants, they also influenced the neutrals.

In 1848 the Liberal *Liverpool Mercury* launched an extraordinary attack on the Irish character following the fear of an outbreak of rebellion among the Liverpool Irish (see pp. 115-21):

> It is not to be forgotten too, that much, very much of Irish misery lies quite beyond the reach of any 'remedial measures' of a government, being seated in the character of the Irish people. No government, except by a very indirect and gradual process can change the idiosyncrasies and habitudes of a nation, and convert a slothful, improvident and reckless race into an industrious thrifty and peaceful people ... We may see of what stuff the 'finest peasantry in the world' are made of by visiting the Irish quarter in any of the large towns of England or America. There is a taint of inferiority in the character of the pure Celt which has more to do with his present degradation than Saxon domination ...

To remove any doubt about the racial nature of this piece, the article went on to claim that the Scots Irish of Ulster were superior to the pure Irish.[30] This was stuff to delight the most ardent Orangeman. On 15th September 1849 Maurice Gleeson, the Leveson Street murderer, an Irishman, was hanged in public outside Kirkdale prison. The whole incident and subsequent trial brought anti-Irish feelings to the surface, and the *Liverpool Mail,* in the course of a long leader article, launched into yet another tirade, claiming that Irish immigration and the crime level were intimately linked.[31] As a supporter of the Protestant and Tory cause, the views of the *Mail's* leader writer were less than impartial but, again, the significance of the article was that it was part of a regular outpouring of fanatical anti-Irish, anti-Catholic copy in several Liverpool papers, which could not avoid inflaming opinion, particularly at the level of the public bar and the beer shop. It was here and in the crowded courts and cellars that the poison drained to, often with fatal results. This flood of venom was no passing fad. For example, on 17th November 1855 the *Liverpool Herald*, replacing the *Standard* as the town's foremost Orange newspaper, printed a long article entitled 'The curse of Liverpool'. It deserves extensive quotation because of the insight it gives into the loathing with which the Protestant extremists regarded the Irish Catholics and it presents yet another example of the constant reference to Irish criminality:

> Let a stranger to Liverpool be taken through the streets that branch off from the Vauxhall Road, Marylebone, Whitechapel and the North End of the docks, and he will witness such a scene of filth and vice, as we defy any person to parallel in any part of the world. The numberless whiskey shops crowded with drunken half clad women, some with infants in their arms, from early dawn till midnight - thousands of children in rags, with their features scarcely to be distinguished in consequence of the cakes of dirt upon them, the stench of filth in every direction; men and women fighting, the most horrible execrations and obscenity, with oaths and curses that make the

heart shudder; all these things would lead the spectator to suppose he was in a land of savages where God was unknown and man was uncared for. And who are these wretches? Not English but Irish papists. It is remarkable and no less remarkable than true, that the lower order of Irish papists are the filthiest beings in the habitable globe, they abound in dirt and vermin and have no care for anything but self gratification that would degrade the brute creation . . . Look at our police reports, three fourths of the crime perpetrated in this large town is by Irish papists. They are the very dregs of society, steeped to the very lips in all manner of vice, from murder to pocket picking and yet the citizens of Liverpool are taxed to maintain the band of ruffians and their families in time of national distress . . .

III

During 1848 when the authorities were still struggling with the immediate consequences of the flood of Irish immigration, the nation was swept by a mood of apprehension on the part of the newly enfranchised middle class, who, in the towns and cities, were the new ruling elite. The cause of their concern was the belief that a mood of rebellion was taking hold among the unemployed, the Chartists and the Irish. Not surprisingly, in towns with a large Irish population this concern was greatest because of the expectation that any trouble in Ireland would spread on to their streets. The expectation of trouble reflected a fairly widespread belief that the Irish were ungrateful on two counts. They were ungrateful for the poor relief they received in England from the Unions and the plethora of private charities that collected for the famine victims. The contemporary press contains many accounts of attempted fraud on the Unions, and in Liverpool Austin's uncovering of large-scale frauds in January 1847 seemed to provide concrete evidence.[32] Second, the Irish were considered 'disloyal' in that constantly simmering rebellion in Ireland and the desire of many of them to be free of British rule offended many British loyalists.[33] Simultaneously, though the means the Chartists sought in 1848 remained at least nominally constitutional i.e. another monster petition backed up by mass public opinion, the issue of physical force entered their considerations at the same time that Irish nationalists, free of O'Connell's influence, were pondering the same option. Thus in spring 1848 the overthrow of the French monarchy and the setting up of a republic, severe economic distress at home, a rising tide of militant Irish nationalism, and Chartist confrontations with the police, all induced an almost neurotic response from the authorities. For a brief spell Chartists and Irish nationalists seemed likely to join forces.[34] In fact there is little evidence that the Chartists had any significant following in Liverpool. For example, in 1842 the number of signatures for the National Petition numbered only 23,000, compared with 99,680 in Manchester, a town with a smaller population.

In Liverpool the magistrates were more sensitive to events in Ireland. In 1846 the *Young Ireland* movement set up the *Irish Confederation* in which they were joined by William O'Brien, and when O'Connell died in 1947 the Young Irelanders became the dominant force in nationalist politics. Thus there were Repealers and Confederates in the nationalist movement, and frequently in the press the two terms were used synonymously. In 1848 John Mitchell left the Repeal Association and joined the Confederates and started a newspaper, the *United Irishman,* in the pages of which he advocated armed insurrection, the overthrow of the landlord system and the setting up of a republic. It is generally accepted that in 1848 the authorities in Britain were concerned at what appeared to be a twin threat to law and order.[35] In Liverpool it was the Confederate clubs which engaged the attention of the politically minded Irish of whom the leaders were Terence Bellow McManus, Dr Lawrence Reynolds, George Smith, Dr O'Donnell, Dr Murphy and Patrick O'Hanlon.[36] This essentially middle-class 'leadership and the Confederates' subsequent failure to launch any large-scale demonstrations in Liverpool, of all places, suggest that their support was limited and tepid. In June 1848 the Confederates in Liverpool claimed they had forty clubs, each with a membership of 100, but this is almost certainly untrue.[37] *The Liverpool Journal* of 5th August 1848, in an article on the clubs in Liverpool, could name only fourteen. However, in the fevered atmosphere of 1848 the authorities took no chances, whether the trouble was expected from the Irish, the unemployed or the Chartists. The police, under Dowling's command, operated a system of surveillance over all potential troublemakers with such success that there was no chance of the authorities being taken by surprise.[38]

However, initially, it was concern over the possibility of rioting on the part of the unemployed that occupied the attention of the magistrates, although the source of the numerous posters appearing on walls in the town may have been Chartist or Confederate. On 1st March 1848 a poster appeared inviting attendance at a meeting to discuss the 'Revolution in France' and reminding the 'Men of Liverpool' that:

> . . . the citizens of Paris have achieved their objective viz: a Republican government . . . Resist to your utmost any increase in your national expenditure (rather insist on a reduction). Be suspicious of any increase in our army and navy; beware that it is not wanted for evil purposes; should any attempt be made, rise up to a man . . .[39]

It is not clear precisely who in Liverpool was to 'rise up to a man', nor where their arms were to come from, but despite the emptiness of the injunction such placards helped to fuel the apprehension over social unrest. However, Rushton was more immediately concerned about the growing numbers of unemployed gathering on the Exchange flags hoping to be taken on by employers. He told the Home Secretary that the men were excited by the news of riots in Glasgow and that 'responsible' people in the town were apprehensive.[40] He was sufficiently concerned to send for troops 'as quickly as possible'.[41] In addition 424 special constables were sworn in, of whom '326 were gentlemen and the remainder were in the employ of the dock company'. At a meeting of unemployed dock porters on 11th March, called to discuss the cost of living, there were more than 500 constables and a company of the 60th Rifles present. The forces of law and order exceeded the number attending the meeting several times over and, not surprisingly, it passed off quietly.[42] This massive show of force was clearly intended to be intimidatory and in that it was successful. It was concern over how the Irish might react to events in Ireland which troubled Rushton most, however, on 8th March he told the Home Secretary that he was worried about St Patrick's day and the Irish parade.[43] Two days later the mayor told Sir George, 'let's get the 17th of March over with', and on 15th March the Home Secretary was informed that 3,455 special constables had been sworn in and '. . . unless there is trouble in Ireland, we should be able to cope with anything . . . I think the Irish will wait and see if Mr O'Brien and his party come to anything . . .'[44] The Roman Catholic clergy in Liverpool, and indeed elsewhere, were not enthusiastic about St Patrick's day parades. Father William Parker of St Patrick's in the South End was particularly hostile to the whole idea of repealing the union with Britain. On one occasion he kicked over a table put inside the church to collect signatures in support of the restoration of the Irish parliament.[45] In 1847 Dr Brown, bishop of the Lancashire district, had a letter read out in all Roman Catholic churches, strongly deprecating any St Patrick's day procession.[46] The mayor had taken the opportunity of appealing to him to try and dissuade the Irish societies from parading, and on 15th March 1848 employers of Irish labour in the town were also asked to persuade their men not to turn out on 17th March.[47]

Meanwhile the atmosphere of crisis grew, fed by rumour, unsubstantiated reports and anonymous letters. For example, on 15th March Dowling received an official letter from Dublin Castle stating that :

> Information is received that the Repealers of Manchester and Liverpool, in conjunction with the Chartists entertain the idea of setting fire to these towns on the 17th.

The Irish police also said that Mitchell was due in Liverpool to address the Confederate clubs and suggested that he should be put under surveillance and his speeches recorded.[48] At the same time the mayor of Liverpool received an anonymous letter from Glasgow, claiming that on St Patrick's day a rebellion would take place in Ireland, and simultaneously the Irish, *low* English and Scots would rise up in Liverpool, Manchester and Glasgow.[49] Just how much notice was taken of such alarms it is not possible to judge, but the massive show of force on the part of the authorities indicated an unwillingness to take chances. In the event St Patrick's day passed off even more quietly than usual hardly surprising, given the 3,455 special constables, the entire police force, members of the county police, a troop of the 11th Hussars, a company of the 60th Rifles, and the 52nd regiment. Even the local pensioners were on call. On St Patrick's day two leading Confederates, Meagher and Doherty, had arrived in Liverpool to address the Confederate clubs but were under observation as soon as they disembarked at Clarence Dock. Rushton told the Home Secretary that they represented no danger but repeated his fear that if there was trouble in Ireland it would have consequences in Liverpool.[50]

Following St Patrick's day several Chartist meetings took place on the approach of the Kennington Common meeting. On 26th and 31st March meetings were held. The latter was called to sympathise with the French republic. It was addressed by Mathew Sommers, who told the audience, 'This night, as an Irishman, I offer you the hand of fraternity. Let us swear this night to one common cause of the Charter of England and the repeal of the Union.'[51] In an editorial of 11th April the liberal *Liverpool Mercury* called the 'physical force' Chartists at the National Convention 'knaves and simpletons'. At another Chartist meeting in the Music Hall on 14th April Dr Lawrence Reynolds, Mathew Sommers and other Irish speakers used inflammatory and bellicose language. Reynolds told the listeners he was going to open an ironmonger's shop at 14 Vauxhall Road and would sell 'good short swords, at 6½d each'.[52] It was all empty talk, and the Irish were furious over a leader in the *Liverpool Journal* of 8th April in which Michael Whitty - Catholic and Irish - mocked the pretensions of 'physical force' Chartists and Repealers.[53] There were no large Chartist meetings in Liverpool and the magistrates did not record any concern over Chartist activities in the town.

Police surveillance of the Confederates and Chartists was complete, and at a meeting of a Confederate club on 27th June 1848 the police recorded the proceedings in full despite the claim, made at the meeting, that it was 'no good the police trying to infiltrate'.[54] Present were McManus, Dr Reynolds and Laffan. The language used at the meeting was violent and calculated to alarm those outsiders to whom it was reported. Reynolds begged every man present to purchase arms and 'never mind the police or military', they were quite able to overcome them. McManus told the meeting, 'it was no foolish thing they were about . . . they would have to contend with disciplined troops . . . it was no trifling thing to deluge a country in blood'. Laffan claimed that in three months they would have an organised force 'fit to meet any quantity of soldiers the government could spare'.[55] The boasts were ludicrous, for there is no evidence that at any time the members of the Confederate clubs in Liverpool were drilling and training in the use of arms. No one named times and places at which drilling took place. The kind of language used at this and similar meetings was either a deliberate ploy to raise morale or indulgence in the grossest self-deception. The only hard evidence regarding the arms available to the Repealers and Confederates was that produced when two men were arrested on 24th July for carrying pikes.[56] There is no doubt the police were harassing Irish nationalists and Chartists. In April Dr Reynolds had opened a foundry in Leeds Street where pikes, swords and other weapons were produced and sold from a shop he had purchased, as promised.[57] This was a legitimate business but his activities were closely monitored by the police. On one occasion he complained to Rushton about the behaviour of the police when entering his premises, and an officer was reprimanded. Another Irishman made an official complaint about damage to his workshop on the part of policemen who carried out a search.[58] One of the men arrested on 24th July was found to be connected with Reynolds and admitted he was exporting 100 pikes to Waterford. There was nothing illegitimate in such a business transaction.

A week later, two Irishmen were arrested, also carrying pikes, and a search of their homes revealed one gun and a letter concerning the movements of Repealers in other towns.[59] Though the pikes hardly added up to an arsenal adequate for mounting rebellion, they increased the sense of threat. Commenting in court on this latter case, Rushton said:

> . . . the case required great consideration. Intelligence given to the magistrates, and this discovery tended to confirm it, that in this town there was an organisation for open, serious armed rebellion . . .[60]

This edginess on the part of the magistrates in towns with a large Irish population was the result of events in Ireland, where, on 21st July, the government suspended Habeus Corpus. Unsubstantiated claims proliferated. A correspondent to the *Liverpool Mercury* of 21st July wrote:

> . . . there is at this moment, a rapid and dangerous club organisation going forward in Liverpool and other large places. The real motives of the originators of this scheme, though not publicly avowed, may easily be guessed at. It can be nothing less than the destruction of the lives and property of the middle and higher classes of our townsmen: it may be much more. We have seen the imminent danger in which the Parisians have been placed in consequence of a very similarly organised conspiracy.

On 25th July the *Mercury* carried a long leader on the threat of civil disorder among the town's Irish and repeated a claim that there were fifty clubs, each with a membership of 100. By this time the decision had been made to increase the regular police force by 500 men, and in addition, 2,000 regular troops were stationed in the borough. An incredible 20,000 special constables had been sworn in to assist the police and army should disturbances break out. Pressure was put on an estimated 500 Irish dockers to sign on as special constables, but they refused and were promptly sacked.[61] Despite this huge show of force there was something approaching panic when, on 28th July, a printed report was circulated claiming that rebellion had broken out in Ireland, around Thurles, and that British troops had refused to obey orders. The mayor telegraphed Sir George Grey for confirmation and was told the Home Office knew nothing of it. When passengers arriving on the Irish steamers also expressed ignorance, it was realised that the rumour was a hoax.[62] With regard to local Confederate leaders, the discovery of the pikes led the magistrates to take action against Reynolds, misleadingly termed the 'Chartist ironmonger', and McManus. Reynolds had left Liverpool and was believed to be in Birmingham.

In fact there was no serious trouble with the Irish in Britain during 1848, the Year of Revolution, but the tensions raised by the expectation of an uprising did little to endear the Irish to many English people, particularly when the emergency measures added to the rate bill. The *Mercury* was probably voicing the views of many English, and certainly the Orangemen, when it wrote:

> It is an ascertained fact that 75 per cent of the poor rates are expended upon the Irish inhabitants and persons of Irish extraction, and we have no doubt whatever that they participate in the benefits of the public charities in the same enormous proportion. Yet Irish clubs are organising here to threaten Liverpool.[63]

The authorities in Liverpool and Manchester were determined to demonstrate their unwillingness to tolerate the threat of insurrection, and the Liverpool Confederates were tried at the Lancashire assizes in December 1848 on charges of treason and felony; nine received prison sentences, Mathew Sommers, Robert Hopper, Francis O'Donnell and George Smythe each receiving two years. The Manchester prisoners were found guilty of charges of conspiracy and unlawful assembly and received lighter sentences.[64] It is doubtful whether anything other than a very small proportion of the Irish in Liverpool were politically active; most were more concerned with survival. However, the atmosphere of crisis lasted throughout most of 1848, and the fears thus stirred were easily translated into anti-

Irish prejudice and anti-Catholicism. This was not confined to Liverpool or any particular class. For example, *The Times* of 26th July 1848, in the course of a long leader complaining about Ireland and its problems, commented:

> taking all things into account, we do not hesitate to say that every hard-working man in this country carries a whole Irish family on his back. He does not receive what he ought to receive for his labour and the difference goes to maintain the said Irish family, which is doing nothing but sitting idle at home, basking in the sun, telling stories, plotting, rebelling, wishing death to every Saxon and laying everything that happens at the Saxon's door.

In 1848 the police in Liverpool were reacting to the rhythm of events in Ireland rather than the noises coming from Chartists. Significantly, though the Irish in Liverpool failed to rise up in rebellion at the behest of Repealers and Confederates, they were to demonstrate a much fiercer reaction to any insults or assaults on their Church and religion. In most towns with an Irish Catholic population of any size, militant Protestants were wary of direct conflict. In Liverpool the strength of Orangeism was to become such that conflict was welcomed.

Notes

1   B.P.P. *Select Committee on Settlement and Poor Removal* (1847), Minutes of Evidence, E. Rushton, q. 4418. Rushton stated that the labouring classes had shown great kindness to the immigrants but they might become uneasy if disease broke out.

2   The chairman of the Select Vestry claimed as early as January 1847 that 'the working classes are becoming exasperated at the supposed preference of Irish to English poor'. See *Liverpool Mercury*, 29th January 1847. Charities were concerned that relief money sent to Ireland might be misused. See *Liverpool Mercury*, 22nd January 1847. At a meeting of the Select Vestry on 22nd December 1846 Archdeacon Campbell implied that some relief money would be used to buy guns in Ireland.

3   In reply to questions from Sir Bernard Hall regarding the government's attitude towards Liverpool's immigrant problem, Sir George Grey promised to send tents. See parliamentary reports, *Times*, 8th May 1847. On Monday 1st February 1847 Lord Brougham presented a petition to the House of Lords from Liverpool. *The Times* was scathing in its comments on his poor performance; 2nd February 1847; also 23rd March, 8th May 1847.

4   *Liverpool Courier*, 16th June 1847.

5   B.P.P. *Select Committee on Poor Removal* (1854), appendix 'Return of the number of Irish paupers relieved in the parish of Liverpool'.

6   *S.C. on Settlement and Poor Removal* (1847), Minutes of Evidence, E. Rushton, qq. 4328-9; M. Lowndes, qq. 4578 and 4617-9; Lowndes was a Liverpool solicitor.

7   Ibid., E. Rushton, qq. 4328-32.

8   *S.C. on Poor Removal* (1854), Minutes of Evidence, A. Campbell, qq. 4951 and 4592. Campbell claimed that in 1847 alone outdoor relief to the Irish cost £20,750. He did not make clear whether this referred to casual or settled Irish or both.

9   The problem during 1847 was simply one of keeping the immigrants alive. See *Times*, 2nd April 1847, leader. Rushton, as early as 1843, stated in court that parish relief was so inadequate, begging was necessary. *Liverpool Standard*, 4th April 1843.

10   *S.C. on Poor Removal* (1854), Minutes of Evidence, A. Campbell, q. 5208.

11   Ibid., qq. 5206-9.

12   Op. cit., E. Rushton, q. 4602.

13   Op. cit., A. Campbell, qq. 5007-9.

14   *Liverpool Albion*, 22nd January 1849. Rushton disagreed with this view. See *S.C. on Settlement and Removal* (1847), Minutes of Evidence, E. Rushton, q. 4443; also Lowndes, M.D., q. 4459.

15   A meeting of ratepayers on 12th May 1847 was the most obvious sign of discontent but the press carried numerous articles articulating anger over the rate bill attributable to the casual Irish pauper relief. The Tory press in particular were most vociferous (*Liverpool Mail, Courier and Standard*). For reports of the meeting of ratepayers see *Liverpool Chronicle*, 15th May 1847; *Liverpool Mercury*, 19th May 1847.

16   *Times*, 6th May 1847.

17   *Liverpool Mail*, 6th November 1847.

18   A number of local studies of Irish immigrants reflect this phenomenon. R. Swift, 'Crime and ethnicity: the Irish in Wolverhampton', West Midlands Studies, 13 (1980), pp. 1-5; T. Dillon, 'The Irish in Leeds, 1851-61', *Publications of the Thoresby Society, Miscellany*, Vol. 16, Pt I (1974), pp. 1-27; C. Richardson, 'Irish settlement in mid-nineteenth century Bradford', *Yorkshire Bulletin of Economic and Social Research*, Vol. 20 (1968), pp. 41-57.

19   B.P.P. *Report on the State of the Irish Poor in Great Britain* (1836), appendix G, No. 11, *State of the Irish Poor in Liverpool*, Evidence of William Parlour, p. 22.

20   *Report on the State of the Irish Poor in Great Britain* (1836), appendix G, No. 11, Evidence of Fr Vincent Glover, p. 22.

21   *S.C. on Poor Removal* (1854), Minutes of Evidence, A. Campbell, qq. 49524. Rushton's letter is reproduced in full.

22   *State of the Irish Poor in Great Britain* (1836), appendix G, No. 11, Evidence of James Shaw, pp. 14-15; Fr Thomas Fisher, p. 23. In 1853 the Rev T. Carter, chaplain to the borough gaol, commented that the Irish children in Liverpool were very precocious, particularly those from Dublin. *S.C. on Criminal and Destitute Children* (1853), Minutes of Evidence.

23   The house was in Gascoigne Street. *Manchester Guardian*, 21st July 1847.

24   *Liverpool Mercury*, 20th February 1849.

25   W. Parlour, op. cit., p. 20.

26   A. Campbell, op. cit., q. 4954. Campbell gave Rushton's letter in full.

27   Fr James Nugent, Catholic chaplain at the borough gaol, stated in 1877, 'Owing to the tide of immigration from Ireland, Liverpool is an exceptional case as regards Catholic crime'. *S.C. on Intemperance* (1877), q. 4036.

28   *State of Irish Poor in Great Britain*, appendix G, No. 11, Evidence of W. Parlour, M. J. Whitty, Fr V. Glover, Fr F. Murphy.

29   B.P.P. *Select Committee on Railway Labourers* (1846), Minutes of Evidence; M. M. G. Dowling, qq. 3056-7.

30   *Liverpool Mercury*, 1st August 1848, leader. This view of the Irish was widespread and long lasting. The report for the 1871 census in Scotland, after commenting on the numbers of Irish in Scotland, stated 'This very high proportion of the Irish race in Scotland has undoubtedly produced deleterious results, lowered greatly the moral tone of the lower classes . . .' Census Report (Scotland), 1871.

31   *Liverpool Mail*, 7th April 1849. The most virulent anti-Catholic papers in Liverpool were, in descending order of fanaticism, the *Standard*, the *Herald*, the *Courier* and the *Mail*.

32   The examples of attempted fraud are too numerous to mention. For examples, see *Manchester Guardian*, 13th February 1847. It was reported that able-bodied Irish in Newport were refusing to work in the Poor Law Union. In Liverpool an Irishman asking to be passed to Ireland was found to have 5s 6d hidden in his shoes: *Liverpool*

Mercury, 11th May 1847; an Irishwoman applying for relief in Liverpool was found to have seven soup tickets in her pockets: *Liverpool Albion*, 15th March 1847. At a meeting of the Select Vestry on 6th July 1847 it was reported hundreds of persons in receipt of good wages were claiming relief: *Manchester Guardian*, 7th July 1847.

33 In 1868 the parish priest of St Marie's Roman Catholic church in Sheffield found it necessary to state in public that Irish Catholics in England were 'loyal' subjects of Queen Victoria. This followed the arrest of James Quigley, a Fenian organiser in Sheffield: *Sheffield Times*, 18th January 1868.

34 For an account of Irish involvement in English radicalism see D. Thompson, 'Ireland and the Irish in English radicalism', in *The Chartist Experience: Studies in Working Class Radicalism and Culture*, 1830-1860, J. Epstein and D. Thompson (1982). For an examination of events in Liverpool in 1848 see W. J. Lowe, 'The Chartists and the Irish Confederates: Lancashire, 1848', in *Irish Historical Studies*, XXIV, No. 94 (November 1984). I have examined the Home Office files concerning events in Liverpool at this time and differ from Dr Lowe's conclusion in that I rate the threat of the Liverpool Confederates as less than he implies.

35 Economic distress was widespread in Liverpool at this time. P.R.O. HO 45/ 2410, Mayor to Home Office, 8th March 1848.

36 J. Denvir, *The Irish in Britain* (1892), chapters 16 and 19. Denvir gives a general description of the activities of the Irish nationalists in Liverpool at the time.

37 P.R.O., HO 45/2410. A letter from mayor to Secretary of State, 28th June 1848. Horsfall gave details of police notes taken at a meeting held in a schoolroom in Liverpool on 27th June, attended mainly by 'lower Irish'.

38 P.R.O., HO 45/2-110A. Rushton to Home Office, 15th March 1848. Dowling warned Chartists they were being watched.

39 P.R.O., HO 45/2410A. Letter from Rushton to Secretary of State, 5th March 1848.

40 P.R.O., HO 45/2410A. Rushton to Home Office, 8th March 1848.

41 Ibid.

42 P.R.O., HO 45/2410A. Horsfall to Secretary of State, 10th and 12th March 1848.

43 P.R.O., HO 45/2410. Rushton to Home Secretary, 8th March 1848.

44 P.R.O., HO 45/2410A. Rushton to Secretary of State, 15th March 1848. Rushton told Sir George Grey, 'I think the Irish will wait to see if Mr O'Brien and his party come to anything'.

45 For a detailed reference to the circumstances surrounding the incident, see *Liverpool Journal*, 27th March 1847.

46 Leaders of the Liverpool Hibernian societies were under the impression that they had been given permission by Dr Brown, bishop of the Lancashire district, to process to St Anthony's in Scotland Road. There appears to have been some dispute over what was agreed, and the clergy's condemnation of the small procession of 170 persons produced strains within the Liverpool Catholic community. For the Hibernians' version of events see *Liverpool Journal*, 27th March 1847. See also *Liverpool Journal*, 6th March 1847. For details of police preparations for the 1848 St Patrick's day see *Liverpool Mercury*, 21st March 1848. This also covers the full letter of appreciation of the mayor's preparations for trouble from the middle classes.

47 P.R.O., HO 45/2410A. Mayor to Sir George Grey, 15th March 1848.

48 P.R.O., HO 45/2410A. D. McGregor, Dublin Castle, to Dowling, Head Constable of Liverpool, 15th March 1848.

49 P.R.O. HO 45/24i0A. Anonymous from Glasgow to mayor of Liverpool, 15th March 1848.

50 P.R.O., HO 45/2410A. Rushton to Secretary of State, 17th March 1848. For an account of a meeting of repealers in Liverpool see *Liverpool Journal*, 8th April 1848.

51 *Liverpool Mercury*, 4th April 1848.

52 *Liverpool Mercury*, 18th April 1848.

53 Whitty was the ex-Head Constable.

54   P.R.O., HO 45/2410A. Mayor to Secretary of State, 28th June 1848. The meeting took place at the Circus Street schoolroom. It was claimed the first Confederate club formed in Liverpool was the Daniel Club and that its members were armed.

55   Ibid.

56   For a full account of the seizure of the pikes see *Liverpool Mercury,* 25th and 28th July 1848. The men arrested were James O'Brien, Henry McCavat Henry Banner and James Cuddy. These were men of no standing in Liverpool, indicative of the lack of political or organisational 'weight'. Eventually the Liverpool Confederates were arrested and put on trial at the December assizes. Nine received prison sentences. See Lowe, op. cit.

57   Reynolds was a medical doctor, trained in Dublin. He disappeared from Liverpool in 1848, went to Birmingham and finished up in America. See Lowe, op. cit.

58   It is clear that the Liverpool police, under Dowling, were harassing the Irish Confederates as a deliberate policy to unnerve them. Dowling sent for the secretary of the Confederates and told him that their activities were known and watched. P.R.O., HO 45/2410A. Rushton to Secretary of State, 15th March 1848. The complaints about the police were revealed in the hearing before Rushton at the Liverpool magistrates' court. *Liverpool Mercury,* 28th July 1848.

59   *Liverpool Mercury,* 28th July 1848.

60   Ibid.

61   *Liverpool Mercury,* 1st August 1848, leader. The day following their sacking some of the dockers asked for their jobs back, agreeing to help in the defence of the town. However they were told their cases would be considered.

62   So much alarm had been created by the false report that the mayor had to have a placard on walls throughout the town stating the 'alarming intelligence' was untrue. See *Liverpool Mercury,* 28th July 1848, leader.

63   *Liverpool Mercury*, 21st July 1848. 64 Lowe, op. cit.

64   Lowe, *op. cit.*

Chapter V **Resurgence of No Popery politics**

I

Despite the virulence of anti-Catholicism, the mass of people in Liverpool were estranged from religion. Middle-class Anglicans were fond of extolling the glories of the Established Church and the constitution, under which 'Free-born Englishmen' enjoyed peace and liberty. The state of Anglicanism in Liverpool was revealed by Canon Abraham Hume of St Stephen's, Byrom Street, in February 1850.[1] His parish, together with the adjacent ecclesiastical district of Vauxhall, bore the brunt of the Irish invasion, and the conditions under which most of his parishioners lived were, as we have seen, appalling. In February 1850 he published *Missions at Home: a Clergyman's Account of a Portion of the Town of Liverpool*, a detailed account of the state of religious observance in the ecclesiastical districts of Vauxhall and St Stephen's.[2]

The situation he revealed concerning the provision of accommodation for worship brought no comfort to Anglicans. In the borough there was church accommodation for 57,522, or 17% of the population. The two ecclesiastical districts, with a joint population of 24,000, were under the care of one clergyman. In Vauxhall, population 13,028, there was church accommodation for 100 people, while in St Stephen's, population 10,662, there was a church that would hold about 500, but none of the latter seats were free to the public. For the middle-class Anglicans who never visited the slums the facts revealed about the numbers of Catholics were even more unnerving. In Vauxhall there were 2,894 families of whom 1,142 were Catholic. Hume estimated that in the town as a whole 33% of the labouring classes were Catholic, which meant that the proportion in the lower part of the parish was even greater.[3]

The publication of these simple facts was unpalatable to the town's Anglican establishment but the estimates of church attendance produced by Hume were equally unpleasant. In the lower part of the parish attendances represented 5·4% of the population, while in the more respectable upper part it was only 19%. As some people attended church more than once, the proportion of *individuals* attending was correspondingly less. In a group of streets in Vauxhall, with a population of 5,850, Hume found that no one attended church. Thus, though church accommodation was inadequate for the number of potential churchgoers, it was more than adequate to meet the needs of the few who did attend. Commenting on this state of affairs Hume said:

> There are thousands of these nominal Churchmen in town who have never been within either Church or Chapel in the whole course of their lives, except at their baptism. Hundreds, probably thousands, even among the adult population, have never been baptised. There are hundreds of others who would never be baptised but that the burial clubs require it . . . Thousands never saw a catechism, do not know the number of commandments, never read a chapter of Scriptures, know nothing of any creed, do not utter a prayer.[4]

Hume's pioneering work was confirmed in its general conclusions when, as a result of government action, a national religious census was carried out. This was the 1851 *Official Census of Religious Worship*. It aimed at establishing how many people attended divine worship. An enumeration of attendances was carried out on Sunday 30th March 1851.[5] Attendances would not be easily translated into individuals, and so there was strong opposition among Anglicans on the grounds that the results could be used for propaganda purposes.[6] Parliamentary defenders of the Establishment feared that it would reveal the Church of England as by no means the Church which most Englishmen attended, a fact that could be used by its enemies.

According to Horace Mann, director of the census, fewer than 10% of people living in the large towns (with a population above 10,000) attended church. It was revealed that in Liverpool on census day Anglicans represented 40·7% of all attendances; Nonconformists 26·8% and Roman Catholics 32·5%. Given the habit of multiple attendance among the Nonconformists, it is clear that the number of individual Roman Catholics attending church far exceeded that of Nonconformists (including Methodists) and was much nearer that of the Anglicans than the figures suggest. Also, the Irish immigrants had less church accommodation to meet their needs; had more churches been available to them, attendance among Catholics would undoubtedly have been higher.[7] Whatever misgivings were felt about the manner in which the census was carried out, the results were an accurate reflection of the situation, i.e. the majority of people did not attend church at all, and of those who did a large proportion were not members of the Church of England.

Another survey, of religious attendance in Liverpool, was published in February 1853.[8] The main findings are summarised in Table 18.

TABLE 18
Church attendance in Liverpool - on a Sunday in 1853

Denomination	Seat room	Average Attendance	Proportion of attendances working-class (%)
Church of England	63,760	35,526	45
Dissenters	54,594	28,843	60
Roman Catholic	15,300	43,380	90

Source: *Liverpool Mercury*, 25th February 1853.

Despite the fact that the town had been long considered an Anglican stronghold, the Church had clearly made little impact on the bulk of the working-class population. The class structure of attendance was revealed by the fact that 90% of Catholic worshippers were designated 'working-class' in contrast to 45% of Anglicans.

In 1855 the *Mercury* published the results of yet another survey of church attendance in Liverpool which once again revealed that the Established Church could not fill its pews. There were 63,009 seats available, while attendance on the Sunday of the survey was 44,842. Roman Catholic seatings were 15,900 and attendance was 46,130. The *Catholic Institute Magazine*, commenting on the survey, said:

> This is an attendance of more than one out of every two, and the only wonder is that the ratio is so high when we consider the thousands of homeless, moneyless, raimentless, foodless creatures that call the Catholic church their mother in Liverpool. We fill our accommodation three times over. And if anybody doubts it, let him pass a Sunday morning in St Anthony's or St Patrick's, or indeed in any Catholic Church in the town and he will witness such a sight as 'not all the King's men' could realise on behalf of the Protestants.[9]

This choice of language is of interest because it clearly reveals the self-perception of Catholic priests regarding their integral place in the life of the Irish Catholics and the role of the Church as defender of its flock. It also reflected the confidence of the Catholic clergy in the belief that they fulfilled a role denied to Protestant clergymen. The same article made a scathing attack on the Liverpool Church of England Scripture Readers who carried on a 'missionary' campaign among the town's Catholics:

> . . . but as for sending their spiritual labourers into our fields it is simply insanity at a moment when their own vineyard is thus deserted, weedy, fruitless and unprofitable . . . were they to join us in our common crusade against

dishonesty, indecency, drunkenness and vice in general, Liverpool would not be the sinkhole of sinfulness and immorality that it is.

Such sentiments, expressed by Catholics, infuriated Anglicans all the more so because they were based on fact.

Further insights into the reality of life in the working-class areas are given by the various reports of those clergymen who, unlike McNeile, were in close contact with the slum dwellers. In October 1840 the Rev. J. R. Connors of St Simon's, an Anglican church off Dale Street in the town centre, wrote that in Peter Street, in his district, of 379 adults, 319 never went to any church at all. The Sabbath was completely ignored and 'the extent to which drunkenness is carried on is beyond conception'. The bulk of the population in St Simon's district were Irish Catholic and the Anglican church workers were frequently attacked; 'my reader has had the clothes torn off his back'.[10] In 1850 the Rev. F. Bishop of the Unitarian Liverpool Domestic Mission described visits to cellars in which the inhabitants had hardly any furniture, the walls were oozing with slime, and drunkenness was rife. In many instances he had had to fight the revulsion he experienced when faced with the stink and vermin. His experiences made him angry with Anglicans spending money on theological controversy instead of bath houses.[11] An Anglican minister described the continual violence due to drunkenness. One Monday morning he came upon two drunken women fighting in the street, clothes ripped off their backs, heads matted in blood. In another instance he came upon two men, stripped to the waist, fighting in the street and cheered on by a large crowd. Soon after, in another street, he passed *forty* drunken women. He visited women beaten up by drunken husbands and was in despair that the Church had so little influence.[12] However, though the Protestant labourers were indifferent to the claims of the established Church, the claims of Orangeism struck a much more responsive nerve.

II

In March 1850 the Liverpool magistrates were once again having their nerve tested over the issue of processions. Both the Roman Catholic clergy and the magistrates had expressed disapproval of any public processions but, like the Orangemen, there was no unanimity of opinion among the Irish and some members of the Hibernian Societies were determined to have a St Patrick's day march. *The Mercury* asked the Irish to forgo their parade and pointed out that the Orangemen had announced, 'with an audacity which could scarcely be exceeded in Northern Ireland', that if the authorities would not stop the St Patrick's day processions, they would.[13] Despite these entreaties, some Irish did hold a parade on 18th March, without interference from police or Orangemen. A Liverpool correspondent wrote in the *Tablet* that those in the procession were a 'miserable minority' of the Irish residents and blamed the turn-out on publicans touting business.[14]

The annual general meeting of the Loyal Orange Institution of Great Britain was held on 1st July 1850 at the Wavertree Coffee House.[15] The Orangemen were once more divided over the issue at a 12th July parade but the growth in their numbers meant it was even more difficult for the officers of the lodges to impose their will, and many Orangemen were angry that the Irish had held a St Patrick's day parade. In the event a 12th July procession was held, but only a few lodges took part. The route taken on this occasion avoided the streets where the Irish were numerous, and though the procession passed off fairly quietly, some of those in the procession were armed, and pistols were fired in the air whenever any Catholic establishment was within earshot.[16] Despite the absence of trouble, the power of the magistrates concerning processions became a matter of dispute. In a leader article of 2nd August 1850 the *Liverpool Chronicle* wrote:

> We believe no step whatever was taken to prevent this procession by the magistrates, and we are not aware that any precaution were taken against disturbance. It is undoubtedly strange that large bodies of men should walk armed through the streets, and that firearms should be discharged in the very face of the strongest police force in England and yet no persons be called to account for it.

The matter took on a more serious aspect, however, because of an affray at the house of an Orangeman after the procession was over.[17] Henry Wright, a beer seller, lived in Chadwick Street, off Great Howard Street in the North End. After the procession some Orangemen went to Wright's house, and it was alleged by the Irish in the locality that Wright himself had taken part in the procession. This belief, together with the presence of the Orangemen, caused a mob to gather and launch a furious attack on the house with rocks and stones, attempting to force their way into the building. Police officers eventually persuaded the Irish to retire and a police squad was left around the house. The following day the neighbourhood was still disturbed, and by the evening Wright told the police that he feared another attack. The Irish again attacked the house, driving the policemen away. Fortunately, they had been driven back only fifty yards when reinforcements arrived; during this time gunshots rang out, and three of the crowd were injured, one of them, John Sangster, aged nineteen years, receiving serious wounds. The shots came from a window on the middle floor of Wright's house; a policeman went in, and found a carbine and a blunderbuss, both loaded. Wright was arrested and brought before the stipendiary magistrate the next day. Despite contradictions in the evidence, Rushton remanded Wright without bail, and in this decision he seems to have been influenced by the fact that the shots were fired while policemen were guarding the house and a belief that in some way they were colluding with Wright.[18]

Sangster died of his injuries and the affair poisoned social relationships between working class Protestant and Catholics even further. For example, in the days following the shooting a man was attacked and injured in Chadwick Street because he was seen *talking* to an Orangeman.[19] Wright, aged twenty-six, was remanded to stand trial at the next South Lancashire assizes, charged with having 'shot at and wounded John Sangster, thereby causing his death'.[20] The *Liverpool Chronicle*, in a leader article commenting on the Orange procession, stated that the magistrates took no steps whatsoever to stop it:

> Why are not these party processions put down? Why should the scenes of blood and riot that disgrace Ireland and are illegal there, be permitted in England? The magistrates declare their hands are tied. *Why not* procure a local act to meet such cases?[21]

Such views and questions were repeated throughout the town. The Party Processions Act applied only to Ireland, though the circumstances in Liverpool reflected many Irish situations.[22] In fact the magistrates did have the power to ban processions under the local improvement Act of 1842, and the lack of action on their part seem strange if one assumes they really wanted to stop such events. The alternative assumption is that they did not wish to ban the procession, a view widely held by Catholics and Liberals and which, for many, was vindicated the following July.[23]

III

The Chadwick Street shootings caused a lot of comment and discussion, and it had hardly died down when, on 29th September 1850, the Pope issued a Bull restoring the Roman Catholic hierarchy in England and Wales.[24] It produced an upsurge of anti-Catholic feeling in middle-class England. Because of the Irish immigration in the first half of the nineteenth century, English Catholics felt the need for a proper diocesan system of organisation to administer to the spiritual requirements of the tens of thousands of urban Catholics. The very influx of Irish Catholics that increased the desire for a formal diocesan system was the same phenomenon that disturbed many English Protestants and, among the Catholic population, increased the pressure on the English Roman Catholic clergy and laymen for an approach to Rome to restore the Hierarchy. It is probable that the Pope was influenced in his move by the fact that encouraging noises regarding a restoration had been coming from Westminster, including Lord John Russell himself.[25]

Given the indifference to religion on the greater part of the Protestant working classes, the issue was not likely to provoke a reaction, but the affair triggered off a wave of middle-class indignation that found an outlet in meetings throughout the country protesting at 'papal aggression'.[26] To ultra-Protestants the restoration of the Hierarchy was simply another hammer blow in the constant chipping away of the base of the Constitution. Catholic Emancipation, the Maynooth grant, Puseyism in the Church of England, were all part of the same conspiracy, aided and abetted by soppy Liberalism, too naive or stupid to see the real intentions of the Church of Rome. Typical of Protestant feelings at this time was the leader in the *Liverpool Standard* of 29th October 1850:

> There can be no mistake now as to the nature of the struggle upon which we are entering with this apostate power. From the lips of its high priest, the feeble and insensate Pio Nono, we have it now distinctly proclaimed that Rome scoffs at the authority of the Protestant Sovereign of the British Empire, and is resolved to treat her dominions as if they were a fief under its absolute control. The insolent edict has gone forth which is to elect amongst us a hierarchy owning allegiance both temporal and spiritual, not to a constitutional queen but to a foreign potentate. Our soil and the population attached to it, have been parcelled out by the Pope to these his nominees whose fabricated title, and dignities are henceforth to flout those enjoyed by the Archbishops and Bishops of our National church and aristocracy.

This was the view of events retold at hundreds of meetings held throughout Britain. Liverpool Orangemen were particularly incensed by the fact that, because Liverpool parish was in the diocese of Chester, the first named Bishop of Liverpool was a Roman Catholic. In Liverpool, McNeile led others in organising a series of meetings but here the issue died a quiet death. However, in other places the protests quickly turned to violence, and where Irish Catholics were a minority they were subject to physical violence. For example, Mold in North Wales had an Irish Catholic population estimated to be 300, almost entirely famine Irish. On 2nd November a Protestant mob took to the streets, burning effigies of the Pope and attacked the homes of Catholics, destroying furniture and beating several people up. In addition, there was an attack on the room where the consecrated host was kept. Father Scully, the parish priest, claimed that on the preceeding Sunday the Anglican vicar had preached a violently anti-Catholic sermon.[27] By contrast, in Birkenhead, where there were relatively large numbers of Irish, the Catholics went on to the offensive.

In November 1850 a group of Protestant ratepayers of Birkenhead requisitioned the magistrates, asking for a meeting to address Her Majesty on the issue of Papal aggression.[28] As in Liverpool, this initiative was in complete contrast to the lack of action on the part of the 'lower orders'. On Saturday 25th November placards appeared throughout Birkenhead saying that the magistrates, in compliance with a requisition, were to hold a meeting of ratepayers on Wednesday 27th November, in the town hall, despite the fact that the town hall could only hold about 200 people, roughly ten per cent of ratepayers. At the Catholic services held in Birkenhead next day, Father Browne, the parish priest, let it be known that he would be attending and urged any of his parishioners who went to behave peaceably. His parishioners were mainly Irish Catholics, many of them drawn from the estimated 1,000 to 2,000 labourers working on the docks. Not many of them would have been ratepayers, and because of this fact the Tory press later accused Browne of exhorting his parishioners to turn up to intimidate those who went to the meeting. Certainly in Birkenhead there was an expectation that there would be some opposition to the proposed meeting, and on 26th November the Watch Committee asked Liverpool for thirty policemen; the request was granted and the men were put on standy-by.[29] The meeting was fixed for 1.00 p.m. but by ten o'clock the crowds were armed with bludgeons and exhibiting an aggressive mood. The Birkenhead police force of twenty men was obviously incapable of controlling such a crowd if trouble broke out, and word was sent to Liverpool for reinforcements, which arrived at about 12.30 p.m. They consisted of thirty constables under Superintendent Ride, and they met with considerable opposition in clearing a way to the main entrance of the town hall. They drove back the men at the front of the crowd, but these were prevented from retreating by the crowd behind. Father Browne, the parish priest at St Werburgh's Catholic church, subsequently said that at this apparent reluctance to move Liverpool police attacked the crowd savagely and drove them down the side streets. A cry went up among the Irish for more help, and shortly afterwards their numbers were greatly increased by men armed with iron rails, pokers, wooden staves and large stones.

Just before the meeting started, Edward Bretherton, a Catholic lawyer, and Father Browne secured entry and asked to see the requisition to the magistrates in order to make up their mind whether or not the meeting was legal. The requisition was provided, and on perusing it Bretherton declared the meeting illegal. While Bretherton, Browne and the magistrates were discussing the issue in a side room, the Irish launched a fierce attack on the building, using stones as ammunition. Superintendent Ride, with eleven Liverpool men, charged the crowd but were easily beaten back, three of the officers receiving serious head wounds. 'It was,' said Superintendent ride, 'the most furious attack I have witnessed.' He and his party had to take refuge inside the building and became cut off from the main body of police, while the fury of the crowd outside increased. By now the Irish were in complete control of the area round the town hall, and the magistrates, by now extremely frightened, suggested that the Riot Act be read, but it was quickly decided that an appeal from Father Browne might be more useful. Browne jumped up into the frame of a shattered window and held up his hand. There was general agreement that the effect was instantaneous. The hail of stones ceased immediately. This is of interest because it is yet another example of the frequency and success with which Catholic priests were called upon by the law enforcement agencies to help control Irish Catholics on the rampage.

At about 2.30 p.m. a further fifty Liverpool police arrived under Head Constable Dowling and took up positions around the town hall, but as the situation was still threatening, with crowds of Irish in the streets, the magistrates decided to send for the military, and a detachment of the 52nd Regiment arrived later in the day. By evening all was quiet. On Wednesday night and Thursday morning the infirmary was busy treating Irishmen, the injuries being mainly bruises, cut heads, black eyes and facial injuries. The Liverpool police suffered twenty-one men injured, two seriously. The riot created great bitterness among the Irish Catholic community in Birkenhead, Liverpool and elsewhere in England. A particular cause of concern was the fact that it was the magistrates who had called a meeting on what was regarded as an anti-Catholic issue, and the Irish were further incensed at what they claimed was the brutality of the Liverpool police in dispersing the crowd in front of the town hall. The Catholic community regarded the magistrates as Orangemen, or at least Orange sympathisers, who had called a provocative meeting and then dealt with the Irish rioters in court. Six Irishmen were sent to the Chester assizes for trial.[30]

IV

By 1851 the borough police were the largest force outside London, numbering 806 officers and men, a ratio of one policeman to every 464 persons. Mathew Dowling, appointed Head Constable in 1845, had inherited an efficient force from Michael Whitty, but by 1851 there was growing concern about the morale of the force and the manner in which it was being run.[31] Dowling was unlucky in the sense that, soon after taking over, the borough was subjected to the considerable strain of the large-scale Irish immigration. This was on top of the problems of policing the largest town in the country outside London and the largest seaport in the empire. Thus by 1850, despite its size, the borough police force was fully extended and Dowling himself suffering from the strain. It was against this background that the police force again became embroiled in the sectarian feud.

On 4th July 1851 the Home Secretary, Sir George Grey, received a letter from a Liverpool Irishman, Arthur McEvoy. McEvoy pleaded with

Sir George to use his influence to stop a planned Orange procession in Liverpool. McEvoy claimed that lodges were coming from Ireland and all over England, and that if the procession went ahead there would be bloodshed. He also claimed that guns were being stored in a house in Chadwick Street. It was the same street that was the scene of the shootings the year before.[32] On 5th July Sir George sent a copy of McEvoy's letter to Liverpool and asked the mayor for his views. John Bent, the brewer, was mayor and, by virtue of his office, chief magistrate, and he asked Dowling to comment on McEvoy's claims. Dowling replied that he had been aware for some time that an Orange procession was planned for Monday 14th July and claimed that after making extensive enquiries he was convinced there was no truth in McEvoy's claim that lodges were coming from Ireland. The 'leading members' of the lodges were against the procession, and of those lodges that were marching, their officers had issued instructions that firearms were not to be carried and expulsions from the Order would follow 'any and every breach of this rule'. In any case, before St Patrick's day or 12th July there were always exaggerated rumours of trouble. McEvoy, he said, was a leading member of a Roman Catholic society and a troublemaker.[33]

Dowling's reply seems unduly complacent. The Chadwick Street killing of John Sangster, a Catholic, and the Birkenhead riot would seem to have been reasonable grounds for expecting trouble: The enormous increase in the number of Irish in the town and the aggressive nature of local Protestantism made the borough a likely flashpoint. Whatever the reasons for Dowling's complacency, the extent of his mis-judgement of the consequences of the procession is revealed in the last paragraph of his letter to the mayor:

> However these party processions may be condemned I have in this case no reason to apprehend any riot or violence. I shall of course take measures to secure the peace of this town on Monday if any circumstances should arise to menace it.[34]

The mayor was uneasy about the Head Constable's judgement, and he called a meeting of the magistrates to discuss the chances of dissuading the Orangemen from their procession.[35] Dowling was called in front of them and repeated his view that there was no danger, so the question of whether to ban the procession was put to the vote. Nine were against and six voted for; thus only fifteen magistrates were present out of a list of forty-one. The mayor sent a copy of the Head Constable's letter to the Home Secretary, a move that could be seen as cover for himself should things go wrong.[36]

On Monday morning, 14th July 1851, the first Orange lodges began to gather at the monument at the top of London Road.[37] Despite Dowling's assurances to the magistrates, lodges came from Shropshire, the rest of Lancashire and Ireland, and there were difficulties in getting them all to the assembly point on time. At 10.00 a.m., while the Orangemen waited, a large number of Irish labourers, estimated between 500 and 1,000, advanced up Shaw's Brow and London Road. Carrying large stones and staves, they launched an attack on the Orangemen. At first the Orangemen did not fight back because they were outnumbered, and they were driven away from the monument, but as their numbers increased with the arrival of more lodges a group of them armed with cutlasses charged the Catholics, who scattered. Incredibly, no police had been present when the lodges assembled, an indication either of slack policing or of an arrogant assumption that the Catholics would not dare attack such a large gathering. In the general *mêlée* pistols were fired by the Orangemen, adding to the general panic and confusion. The Orangemen's repulse of the labourers and the eventual arrival of a large body of police meant that enough order was restored for the procession to form up and start. At this point, there would seem to have been enough evidence of disorder to have justified stopping the procession on the charge of riotous assembly or behaviour likely to lead to a breach of the peace, and the absence of police action may reflect the fact that Dowling felt he could not stop the Orangemen without provoking a riot which the police could not hope to control.

There were an estimated two to three thousand in the procession itself, which was preceded by a large crowd of young men, many armed with staves. It was the largest turn-out that Orangemen had staged in England and it meant that the Irish Catholics would not find it as easy to attack, as in previous years. Prominent in the procession were four or five bands, and many carts decorated with Crowns and Bibles. There were a large number of new flags and banners; even the anti-Orange *Mercury* admitted it was a brilliant display. After the first attack word had been sent to Dowling, who ordered reserves of police to stand by at each police station, then took a body of 150 men to walk *behind* the procession, an action that was seen by Catholics as police protection. Further reserves were ordered to stay in London Road in readiness for trouble when the procession ended and the lodges marched off to their respective premises, this being the time when they were in most danger of Irish attack. Such precautions were even more necessary when it became know that dockers were leaving ships and heading into the town centre to join the attacks on the procession. When the Orangemen reached St James's Market in the South End a large crowd of Irish Catholics had gathered, and at one point, according to a Catholic observer, some Orangemen left the procession in

Pitt Street and beat several Irishmen to the ground whilst the police looked on. The same person claimed that when Orangemen in the procession fired pistols in the air the police cheered.[38] On the procession reaching St Anne Street, the Irish attacked and once again were beaten off by the Orangemen and their followers. However, in Richmond Row the procession was broken by another assault and several people were injured, one Irishman being seriously wounded. Eventually, despite continual clashes, the procession returned to the monument in London Road, where the dispersal was accompanied by a good deal of confusion. The parade had attracted large numbers of young followers, not members of the Orange Order but in a highly excitable state and spoiling for a fight.

By 2.00 p.m., with the lodges dispersed, the trouble was by no means over. A lodge marching through Duncan Street and Pitt Street was attacked by dockers, and its members were only saved from a serious beating by the arrival of the police. By early afternoon the Catholic areas along the docks were seething with rumours about the fighting in the town and large crowds of people were blocking the traffic in Byrom Street, Scotland Road and Fontenoy Street. Shopkeepers put up the shutters and the police were sent in to clear the streets to keep traffic moving. The crowds were in an ugly mood and attacked anyone who was thought to be a Protestant or unwise enough to wear anything that seemed Orange in colour. The Wheatsheaf public house in Scotland Road was the meeting place of an Orange lodge, and was also used as a Tory ward room during elections. It was also a notorious trouble spot. In the early afternoon a large group of dockers at the North End left work prematurely and, joined by women and children, made their way to Scotland Road, where they attacked Orange lodge members marching to the Wheatsheaf. A fierce fight broke out. At first there were no police present, then three policemen arrived, one of them a P.c. Green. Just as they arrived two shots rang out and John Malley, an Irish labourer involved in the fighting, fell wounded. He died two days later. The second shot wounded a fourteen-year-old boy. The whole area remained disturbed until late at night and a large body of police were stationed around the Wheatsheaf to protect it from further attack. At the end of the afternoon seventy people, remarkably enough all Irish, had been arrested and taken into custody; many people had been injured and three people had been shot, the borough had been subjected to widespread disturbances and religious feelings were once again inflamed. Significantly, in the eyes of many, no Orangemen were charged.

Later in the day an incident witnessed by few people brought to the forefront of public debate the question of the impartiality of the police. At 10.30 p.m. P.c. Green finished duty and returned to his house in No. 6 Court, Penryhn Street, just off Scotland Road. He had been one of the three policemen near the Wheatsheaf when Malley was shot. He asked his wife to go out and get him a jug of ale. When she left the house he heard her call his name. On rushing to the door he saw a man pulling her hair and knocked him down with his fist. Two more men joined in the attack on Green and he was stabbed six times. A man named Jones put a sword-stick into Green's hands, who chased the three men, finally cornering one of them, Patrick Shea, an Irishman. With the assistance of another constable Shea was arrested, by which time Green was in a state of collapse. During the fight Jones was also stabbed and died the following day, 15th July.

The events of 14th July raised a storm which exceeded any reaction to clashes in the past, and in the weeks immediately following the procession of 14th July there was a great deal of press comment. The *Manchester Examiner* of 16th July 1851 commented:

> The Loyal Protestants of Liverpool as they style themselves par excellence, must be either besottedly fond of self-exultation, or else callously indifferent to the woes of human kind, if they can regard with any complacency their achievement of last Monday. A street procession with ever so many banners and trumpets is a poor set-off against a hundred shattered limbs and a thousand embittered hearts . . . and how can the fiery declaimers of the pulpit and platform who have been stimulating the fanatical fury of half taught zealots against the disciples of a different faith, acquit themselves of some share in this calamitous result? We do not know that the Rev Dr McNeile or the Rev Canon Stowell or any other renown Boanerges of the Protestant Ascendancy, directly sanctioned the vexatious parade that tempted the Irish and Catholic labourers to this lamentable outrage. But sure we are, that the spirit which induced the members of the Orange Lodges, in spite of all reason, prudence and charity, to blazon their religious animosities before the eyes of the world, was learnt of such teachers. It is the practical fruit of those frantic paroxysms of excitement into which, by the influence of example, sympathy and oratorical mesmerism, multitudes of their audiences have been goaded . . .

This view of McNeile's role in promoting sectarian violence was widely held. In fact McNeile made no comment on the day's happenings, either immediately afterwards or, as far as can be ascertained, ever. The magistrates were also singled out for criticism. The Tory press placed the blame for the violence squarely onto the Irish, in terms of overt racialism. The *Liverpool Mail* of 19th July 1851 commented:

> It appears that scenes which formerly distinguished Ireland have been translated to the streets of Liverpool and that peaceable and well behaved men of sober and industrious habit, cannot hold a holiday or walk in procession from clubroom to clubroom in the sight of their families and friends, without running the risk of having their brains knocked out by ferocious Papists, who, as lumpers or barrow men, work in the docks . . . Popery has so completely polluted their mental faculties, and debased the physical and moral

habits of the Irish peasant that it is impossible to ameliorate his condition as a social animal. He does not think as the Englishman, or Scotsman and Welshman does, because he is so saturated with traditional falsehoods . . . a parcel of besotted and ignorant Irishmen must not be allowed to interfere with the liberty of the English subject.

The *Mail* was articulating an opinion held by many Protestants, that Orange processions and meetings were peaceful affairs and the actions of an alien minority (Irish Catholics) were aimed at restricting Englishmen's liberties. There was general agreement that the procession of 14th July had been accompanied by an unacceptable degree of violence and that such a situation must not be allowed to recur. In particular there was growing criticism of Dowling's handling of the police arrangements and of the magistrates' inertia in not stopping the procession. The press had been aware of McEvoy's letter to the Home Secretary and of correspondence between the Home Office and the magistrates, but no details were known publicly. Similarly the Watch Committee had no detailed knowledge of what had passed between the Liverpool magistrates and London, again demonstrating the lack of co-operation between the magistrates and the Watch Committee.

The central question was why the procession had been allowed. At 8.00 p.m. on the night of the procession the mayor had sent a communication to the Home Secretary, stating that there had been no organised breach of the peace.[39] This was an odd claim after the events of the day and suggests that the mayor had been shut in his office with no direct knowledge of what was happening and was fed misleading reports by the police. He enclosed a copy of a low-key report of the day's disturbances with no mention from Dowling of the shooting of Malley in Scotland Road. This means either that Dowling himself did not know of the incident, hours after it had happened, or he knew and chose not to tell the mayor. This point was later commented on officially by the magistrates. The Home Secretary was unhappy, and on 15th July a letter was sent to the mayor of Liverpool which the magistrates took to reflect adversely on the way they handled the whole issue of the procession.[40] On 19th July the mayor wrote again to Sir George Grey, regretting the implied criticism of their conduct and in defence argued that Dowling had dispelled any fears of disturbance when they had interviewed him.[41] The mayor's letter refers clearly to the fact that the Liverpool magistrates had previously appealed to the Home Office for help on the issue of processions after the shootings in Chadwick Street and it had not been forthcoming.

On 26th July the Watch Committee received from the Head Constable a full report concerning the procession, in which Dowling mentioned the letter from McEvoy to the Home Secretary and repeated his claim that there was no substance to the allegations in McEvoy's letter.[42] Dowling went on to give an account of the happenings on 14th July which was at odds with the newspaper reports. The Watch Committee as well as the magistrates were now very concerned over the whole affair, and passed a resolution critical of the policing of the procession and of Dowling.[43] In addition to this resolution the Watch Committee passed another, yet again banning police membership of any 'political' party or society. The reason for the resolution was that the inquest on the two dead men raised once again the question of whether or not the police force was pro-Orange. The resolution is noteworthy because, as we saw in Chapter II, the Watch Committee had laid down in 1842 that Orangemen must either leave the Order or leave the police. Thus it appears that, despite the efforts of past Watch Committees, there was still a suspicion that the borough police contained many Orangemen and the resolution was another attempt to assuage public opinion. Catholic opinion was unconvinced, and, commenting on the day's happenings, the *Catholic Standard* said:

> It is also well known that a report was industriously circulated amongst the dock labourers or Catholic party to this effect:- that it was the intention of the Orangemen to burn Cardinal Wiseman and the Holy Virgin in effigy. This rumour, no doubt, was put in motion with a view of inflaming the fiery passion of the Catholics. Still higher to excite those inflammable passions, a large body of Orangemen reached the Clarence Dock from Belfast. These men openly boasted their intention of clearing the town of 'Romanists' on the following day. They exhibited firearms in the public houses where they visited for refreshment.[44]

True or false, the Catholics of Liverpool believed such claims, including the accusation that 70% of the police were Orangemen, and typical of the rumours were the charges in an anonymous letter received by the Home Secretary on 21st July 1851, claiming that Dowling, most of the police and the majority of magistrates were Orangemen.[45]

The inquest on John Malley took place on Tuesday 22nd July 1851 before the borough coroner and a special jury. The case is of some importance because the outcome convinced many Irish Catholics that they could not expect justice in a town where Orangeism was so strong. What appears to have happened is that at about 2.00 p.m. an Orange lodge marched down Scotland Road and entered the Wheatsheaf.[46] A crowd gathered outside, throwing missiles and generally adopting a hostile attitude. At no time, according to the various witnesses, were any policemen in the vicinity. While the mob was still outside the public house the yard gate opened and a group of men ran out, some of them roughnecks but at least two respectably dressed. Most had sticks and swords. What is not in dispute is that the Irish scattered before this onslaught but the evidence was at odds concerning Malley's role in the fighting. There was general agreement that he ran towards Byrom Street and was pursued by a tall, powerfully built man. The witnesses agreed that this man was loading his pistol as he ran, that he deliberately shot Malley in the back and then returned to the Wheatsheaf yard. A crucial discrepancy in the evidence was that four independent witnesses claimed the killer wore a dark coat and white trousers whilst three others denied it. When the Orangemen had come out of the Wheatsheaf to clear the Irish, three policemen had appeared, and significantly one of them was P.c. Thomas Green. According to several witnesses, the policemen intervened in a fight taking place between Malley and a group of Orangemen just before Malley ran off and was shot. Particularly important, a witness gave evidence that the police beat him with their sticks before he ran away and P.c. 124 (Green) was the most active assailant. If true, this would explain the subsequent assault on Green, but most incredible of all, the policemen present did not arrest the man who shot Malley. This simple fact convinced Catholics that the police concerned were Orangemen.

At the renewed inquest on 25th July Inspector Bates said he had arrested Thomas Weaver, a brick moulder. Weaver appeared in the dock, a tall, strongly built man of about thirty years of age. One witness stated that he was outside the Wheatsheaf on 14th July and saw Weaver shoot Malley. He had no doubts, because he had once lived in the same street as Weaver and knew him by sight; he claimed Weaver was in the Orange procession and had come out of the Wheatsheaf with the group who chased Malley. He said the police laid about Malley with their sticks before he ran off and that he was only two yards from him when he fell down wounded. When asked why he had not told the police he replied that it was not necessary because a policeman had witnessed the whole incident. Two other witnesses positively identified Weaver and said he wore white trousers. Other witnesses, who did not identify him, also said the killer wore white trousers, but Weaver's employer and some workmates testified that he had been at work in nearby brickfields at the time of the killing. The jury were out about forty-five minutes and returned a verdict of 'Manslaughter against some person unknown'. Weaver was cheered out of the court by his friends but the Irish were quite unconvinced that justice had been done. Malley had been pursued and shot down in cold blood, on that there was no disagreement.[47] Even if there was conflicting evidence about the *identity* of the killer, there was no doubt it was murder, in contrast to the verdict of manslaughter. Even more astonishing was the fact that three policemen had been present at the killing: in Irish eyes they must be shielding the murderer.

On the same day as Malley's inquest, an inquest was held on William

Jones, who died of stab wounds received during the attack on P.c. Green. The deputy coroner said that it was evident one of the three Irishmen arrested had stabbed the deceased but which one it was had not been established. After retiring for a few minutes the jury returned a verdict of 'Wilful murder against some person/persons unknown'.[48] It contrasts with that in Malley's case, where there was general agreement among the witnesses at the inquest that the man who shot him did so deliberately. On 26th July 1851 the *Liverpool Journal,* a pro-Catholic paper, contained a letter critical of the magistrates and commenting on the inquest into Malley's death:

> A man has been shot in the open day, in the public street, not when resisting or offering violence but when attempting to escape from it. A man pursues him and deliberately shoots him. His previous offence may have been provoking; he may have been and possibly was, there for the purpose of outraging the peace but it is monstrous that, after the disturbance had endured in Scotland Road, according to Mr Smith, formerly connected with the police, for three years, a ruffian could pursue a man, murder him and yet escape the detection of the officers of justice, then and there on the ground. Not one shot, but two were fired, one man was killed and another is wounded and no one is apprehended by constabulary . . . The magistrates owe it to themselves to make a prompt enquiry into this disgraceful affair.

On 29th July Patrick Shea appeared before the stipendiary magistrate on a charge of stabbing P.c. Thomas Green. A great stir occurred when Mr Yates, a Catholic lawyer defending Shea, asked P.c. Green if he was an Orangeman and Green admitted he was. It was also established that Jones was an Orangeman. Yates then asked whether or not Green knew of any other police officers who were members of the Order and referred to the killing of John Malley, at which Green had been present. There is little doubt that Yates and other members of the Catholic Defence Association were convinced that the police and the Orangemen at the Wheatsheaf were in collusion, but Yates was ruled out of order and Patrick Shea was sent for trial at the assizes.[49] Yates's attempt to raise the issue at the inquest is to be seen as part of a long-term campaign against the police in the North End.

The revelation at the inquest that Green was a member of the Orange Order could not be ignored, and as part of the political' backwash from the events of 14th July even the Watch Committee, with its Tory majority, felt action was needed. On 31st July the new stipendiary magistrate, J. B. Mansfield, wrote asking the Watch Committee to investigate the possibility that other members of the police force were also Orangemen.[50] After discussing the letter the committee passed three more resolutions banning policemen from membership of party or political societies.[51] At a meeting of the committee on 9th August 1851 the full correspondence between the Home Secretary and the mayor concerning the procession was read, and P.c. Green was dismissed because of his membership of the Order.[52]

V

Dowling's reputation suffered severely from his handling of the procession. Both inside and outside the town council criticisms continued regarding the general inefficiency of the police and their allegedly pro-Orange sympathies, particularly in the North End. The death of Edward Rushton in April 1851 had been followed by the appointment of J. B. Mansfield as stipendiary and he was quickly given the opportunity to demonstrate that he was equally determined to deal with any sectarian bias in the force. The Watch Committee was under increasing pressure to do likewise and on 13th December 1851 passed yet another resolution requiring the Head Constable to establish which men were members of 'party societies' and report back.[53] On 27th December 1851 the council set up a sub-committee charged with reporting on whether or not there was substance in the allegations of anti-Irish attitudes in the borough police.[54]

Dowling was not without friends on the council but even among them there seems to have been the view that he had to go. After discussions with him the Watch Committee, on 31st January 1852, minuted the view that he was worn out by his length of service in the borough police and unanimously passed a resolution that he be awarded a pension of £300 per annum on his resignation.[55] At a meeting of the full town council on 4th February the committee's resolution was put forward for approval, including the recommended pension, and this gave the opposition the chance they were waiting for. The Liberals and their supporters took the opportunity of opening up the whole matter of policing. They moved an amendment to the Watch Committee's resolution. This required that the matter be referred back to the committee for further consideration and for it to enquire and report upon the present arrangements concerning the police force generally and 'any alterations which may beneficially be made'.[56] The implications were clear, and it was strongly opposed by Dowling's supporters, but it went to the vote and was carried by twenty-five votes to twenty-four, a result which meant that some Tories had voted with the opposition. Thus the issue of policing had come into the political arena and the battle lines were drawn.

When assessing the behaviour of the police towards the immigrants it is important to understand the context. The problems posed by sectarian clashes were considerable, and were additional to the difficulties of policing areas in which the immigrant Irish gathered in their tens of thousands. The difficulties were particularly acute in the North End where a dangerous hostility to the police had developed among the Irish Catholics. Dowling's view of the problems was quite clear. In 1846 he gave evidence to the Select Committee on Railway Labourers.[57] During his examination he was asked about the behaviour of the labourers working on the dock extensions in Liverpool, about 4,000 in number. In reply he stated, 'A great many of them are Irish, and they are the most reckless, violent set of people that can be imagined.' In reply to further questioning, he went on to say:

> They assist each other, and attack the authorities, whoever they may be; they keep the neighbourhood where they reside, which is the North part of the town of Liverpool, in a constant state of uproar and confusion on Saturday nights, Sundays and Mondays and generally a part of Tuesday.[58]

Sir Thomas Ackland asked whether the Irish offered resistance to the police.

> Yes frequently, great violence; some of my men on several occasions have been nearly killed by them; they make the most violent attacks . . . even if a man commits a disturbance in a house, it is folly for the police, singly, two or three of them, to attempt to take him in the neighbourhood; there must be a considerable force. I recollect one case where they had a fight amongst themselves in a court at the North End of the town, and one of my men was near, went to see what was the matter; they immediately turned from each other upon him and got him down; in fact they were in the act of butchering him; they were hacking him with their spades and had injured him seriously.[59]

Dowling was not exaggerating the risks his men faced. In 1845 a policeman was killed on duty.[60] In 1847 Rushton commented that with regard to Irish assaults the police were in danger of their lives.[61] In May 1850, in a fight between police and navvies in the North End, the police had to take refuge in a public house until reinforcements came.[62] In January 1851 they had taken a severe beating when they clashed with off-duty soldiers in Liverpool town centre. Many of the troops were Irish and the police were routed, many being seriously injured. The riot was brought under control only when troops and officers of the regiment involved were brought into town to arrest the ringleaders.[63] In 1853 P.c. Sunderland was killed in a fight in Scotland Road, while two years later Sergeant Tinker was killed by a hammer blow when intervening in an Irish fight in Vauxhall.[64] It is against this background that police actions must be judged. It is not surprising that the police gained a reputation for being unnecessarily harsh in their dealings with the Irish, who, in turn, were convinced the police were prejudiced.

Events on the streets, however, overtook the local politicians' deliberations and led to a speedy conclusion of the debate about Dowling's future. On Monday evening, 23rd February 1852, Dr Cahill, a famous Catholic preacher, was addressing the congregation of Holy Cross Chapel, just off Great Crosshall Street (see Fig. 3). An estimated 900 Irishmen, women and children were in attendance when, during the service, a beam supporting a packed balcony cracked with a noise like a pistol shot. Panic ensued and people began rushing for the doors.[65] At about 9.30 p.m. on the same night, P.c. Boardman, a young officer, was walking up Great Crosshall Street, near the junction with Marybone, and saw two people who were singing rebel songs. He went over and told them to stop singing. As he was walking away two men and a woman approached him and said that Orangemen had got into Holy Cross Chapel and were killing people. Without checking the story, Boardman ran to the Vauxhall bridewell and told Sergeant Tomlinson. Tomlinson, with two constables, accompanied Boardman back to Holy Cross. Going along Marybone, a difficult area to police, Boardman said it was not safe to go without more men, so Tomlinson sent him back for assistance while he and the two other police-men went on. Outside the church there was a crowd of Irish, and he asked what was happening, as people were still running out of the church. While he was being told of the beam cracking, reinforcements arrived, under Sergeant Wilson, knocking their sticks on the walls, a technique used to intimidate people. At this point the evidence of the witnesses is confused regarding the sequence of events, but what was indisputable was that some police used their sticks to beat the crowd and a number of Catholics received injuries, mainly head wounds. Even Sergeant Tomlinson in his subsequent evidence was critical of some of the police.

The incident caused an uproar in the press and the town generally, and was seen as yet another example of the anti-Irish leanings of the police in the North End. Charges of assault were brought against Tomlinson and other officers, and on Friday 27th February 1852 the mag-istrates investigated them.[66] It seems highly probable that the speed with which the stipendiary magistrate moved was due to the continuing rever-berations from the events of seven months before and anxiety to restore confidence in the law enforcement authorities. J. B. Aspinall, a Catholic lawyer, conducted the prosecution. He stated that the objection of bringing the charges before the magistrates was to draw attention to the state of the police force, for it was, he said, the impression of the inhabi-tants of the neighbourhood that the police operating from the Vauxhall Road bridewell were strongly anti-Irish. Further, it was the general impression that the police force was unduly filled by men belonging to societies of a particular description, an allusion to the Orange lodges. A large number of witnesses testified to individual acts of assault, many of them carrying bandages on their heads. Several claimed they heard the police making anti-Irish remarks, and during the giving of evidence it was claimed the police had knocked a blind man senseless. Though the attack on the Catholics caused concern, the evidence of Sergeant Tomlinson created a sensation.[67] On the morning after the fracas, Tuesday 24th February he entered in the report book an account of the events of Monday night which stated that some of the police had attacked the people outside Holy Cross chapel. This version was subsequently torn out and a second entered which gave a less damaging account of the police's behaviour. This revelation was admitted by Dowling. The whole of the evidence implied that Superintendent Towerson (subsequently revealed to be an Orangeman) ordered the report to be changed, and Dowling, a sick man, concurred. The day the report was altered was also the day Dowling heard that there was to be a magistrates' investigation, and one conclusion to be drawn is that, knowing the magistrates would want to examine the book, he was happy to substitute a report that put his men in a better light. He admitted that he had not told the stipendiary magistrate that the report to be sent to him was not the original. Dowling gave his evidence in a vague manner and at one time had to be taken out of court, suffering from an overdose of laudanum.[68]

In summing up, the prosecuting attorney, Mr Aspinall, said the evidence they had heard fully justified his opening remarks concerning the partisan feeling that pervaded the force. However, he argued, the original charge of attacking the crowd outside Holy Cross paled into insignificance against the revelations of gross irregularity. Aspinall argued there would be little doubt the report was altered *after* Dowling knew there was to be an investigation into the affair and the stipendiary magistrate gave the judgement of the bench. He said the inquiry had opened up a much larger subject of investigation and went on:

> It is true there are persons belonging to these objectionable associations in the force. I have endeavoured to remedy this, and my efforts, though hitherto unsuccessful, shall not be relaxed, for it is of utmost importance that the police should be believed by the whole population to be impartial protectors of the public, though as long as these parties remain in the police force, of course, that opinion cannot be maintained.[69]

He blamed the police for using their sticks indiscriminately but his main criticisms were reserved for the manner in which Dowling and Towerson had given their evidence regarding the report book.[70]

The Holy Cross affair had completely changed the situation regarding Dowling's possible retirement and pension, in so far as his part in removing Tomlinson's report set his future in jeopardy. In the ensuing flurry of meetings the ill feeling between the Watch and the magistrates came to the surface. On 3rd March Dowling submitted his resignation, but it was not accepted, pending the result of the magistrates' investigation into the report book affair. However, it was agreed to give him a pension of £200, thus embarrassing the magistrates.[71] The Watch Committee should have consulted the magistrates first out of courtesy, but legally they were within their rights. The main criticism of the committee was that it seemed more concerned with protecting Dowling than with the serious offence he had committed. On 4th March the magistrates dismissed him and Towerson. On 6th March the Watch Committee met, and a letter from the mayor was read, giving an account of the magistrates' actions. The Watch Committee passed resolutions dismissing Dowling and Towerson from the force with loss of pension rights.[72]

There was a lot of sympathy for Dowling, and in the public debate about the dismissal constant reference was made to his ill health: the claim was made that he was worn out in the service of the town.[73] The *Liverpool Mail* bitterly criticised the magistrates' action in dismissing a man with twenty years' service but the majority of his supporters realised that Dowling could not be rewarded for committing a criminal act. Equally, he had left the police force in a bad way - undisciplined, violent and distrusted by a significant proportion of the population. *The Liverpool Chronicle,* in a leader on 6th March, stated:

> . . . The police force of this town is, it is clear, in an unsatisfactory state, utterly disorganised, without subordination or discipline, filled with the members and confederates of secret and illegal societies, and altogether disgraceful to a community which pays so dearly for its services.

The *Chronicle* blamed successive Watch Committees, who had left the running of the police to the Head Constable, meeting only once a week instead of every day as formerly. Even John Tobin, chairman of the committee and a leading member of the group supporting Dowling, admitted that:

> . . . Mr Dowling's health was fast failing him, that he was unfitted for the discharge of the responsible duties of his office, the inevitable result of which had been most conducive to the want of discipline in the police force.[74]

The whole affair had one important effect. Control of the police force was tightened up, and the Irish Catholic community felt the incident vindicated their view, though it should be remembered that many Irish immigrants were willing to believe almost anything about the police. Dowling was a tragic figure. A man of some intellectual capacity, he was ruined. He was given a job looking after a weighing machine on the docks; within eighteen months he was dead. Towerson became a publican.

Notes

1   Hume, A., *Missions at Home or, A Clergyman's Account of a Portion of the Town of Liverpool* (1850). See also *Liverpool Mercury*, 12th February 1850. The *Mercury* analysed the results of Hume's survey.

2   In 1699 the new parish of Liverpool was divided into a number of ecclesiastical districts. Each district had a church but the concept of a parish with a resident priest did not exist. People went to whichever church suited their likes and visiting and other 'parish' responsibilities were not generally undertaken. For a treatment of the ecclesiastical districts in Liverpool see J. Klapas, 'The Religious Geography of Victorian Liverpool', unpublished M.A., Liverpool (1977), p. 21. See also R. B. Walker, 'Religious changes in Liverpool in the nineteenth century', *Journal of Ecclesiastical History*, Vol. XIX, No. 2, (October 1968), pp. 195-211.

3   Hume, op. cit., p. 8. Dr Duncan made a similar statement in 1840. See B.P.P. *Select Committee on Health of Towns* (1840), Minutes of Evidence, q. 2537.

4   Hume, op. cit., p. 12.

5   This census was surrounded by controversy arising mainly from the concern of Anglican activists that the Church of England would be shown to be in a poor condition vis-a-vis its influence on the mass of the population. See W. S. F. Pickering, 'The 1851 religious census - a useless experiment?', *British Journal of Sociology* Vol. 18 (1967), pp. 382-407; K. S. Inglis, 'Patterns of religious worship in 1851', *Journal of Ecclesiastical History*, Vol. II, No. 1 (1960), pp. 74-85· B. Coleman, 'Religion in the Victorian city', *History Today* (August 1980), pp. 25-31.

6   Pickering, op. cit.

7   In 1852 the Roman Catholics had thirteen places of worship in Liverpool, with seating for 15,300, and the average Sunday attendances were 43,380. See *Liverpool Mercury*, 25th February 1853, 'Religious statistics of Liverpool'. This was the result of the survey carried out by Mr Caulderwood and Nathaniel Caine.

8   *Liverpool Mercury*, 25th February 1853. In this edition Nathaniel Caine published an up-to-date table of seatings and attendances. In 1854 Caine had written to the press a hostile letter concerning the so-called 'Irish clique' of Anglican clergymen in Liverpool. See *Liverpool Mercury*, 25th April 1854. Hence his survey was regarded as anti-Anglican.

9   *Catholic Institute Magazine*, No. 2, Vol. 1 (November 1855), *Liverpool Mercury* October 1855.

10   *Liverpool Standard*, 3rd November 1840.

11   *Liverpool Mercury*, 18th January 1850. This edition contains a long account of Bishop's report.

12   *Liverpool Standard and General Commercial Advertiser*, 8th November 1853, 'The monster vice of Liverpool, as depicted by a clergyman'. The priest was arguing for less concern with theological dispute and more controls over the number of public houses and beer shops.

13   *Liverpool Mercury*, 15th March 1850; *Liverpool Chronicle*, 13th July 1850.

14   *Liverpool Mercury*, 26th March 1850; carried a report on the Tablet article.

15   *Liverpool Chronicle*, 7th July 1850.

16   *Manchester Guardian*, 13th July 1850.

17   This incident was widely reported in the press. See *Liverpool Chronicle*, 13th July 1850; *Liverpool Mercury* 16th July 1850; *Liverpool Times*, 18th July 1850; *Manchester Guardian*, 18th July 1850. *Liverpool Standard*, 16th July 1850. For the inquest on John Sangster see *Liverpool Mail*, 10th August 1850.

18   This view appears to be based on the fact that two policemen were placed on guard at Wright's house.

19   *Liverpool Mercury*, 16th July 1850; *Liverpool Standard*, 16th July 1850.

20   *Manchester Guardian*, 17th August 1850. In evidence at the trial it was alleged that Wright shouted at the crowd, 'Come on, you bloody Papists, and we will blow your brains out'.

21 *Liverpool Chronicle,* 3rd August 1850.

22 2 and 3 William IV. This Act banned party processions in Ireland for five years, It was then renewed for a further five years.

23 In fact four months later the Irish Catholic community on Merseyside was accusing the Birkenhead magistrates of being anti-Catholic by calling a meeting of ratepayers to protest against the restoration of the Hierarchy.

24 For an account of the restoration of the Hierarchy and the outcry, see E. R. Norman, *Anti-Catholicism in Victorian England* (1968); also C. A, Beck (ed.), *English Catholics, 1850-1950* (1950). In Liverpool the Tory press frequently referred to the Catholic bishops of Liverpool as 'sham bishops'. For example, on 8th January 1859, the *Liverpool Herald* carried a piece headed 'The sham Bishop of Liverpool'. The article referred to Dr Goss, the successor to Dr Browne, the first Catholic Bishop of Liverpool.

25 J. B. Conacher, *The Peelites and the Party System* (1972), pp. 75-83.

26 Norman, op. cit.; Beck, op. cit.

27 *Liverpool Mercury,* October 1850. Letter from Fr Scully, parish priest at Mold.

28 The meeting was accompanied by rioting which received widespread press coverage. See *Liverpool Chronicle,* 30th November 1850; *Liverpool Mercury,* 3rd December 1850. Fr. Browne, a priest at St Werburgh's Catholic church in Birkenhead came in for heavy criticisms and allegations that he urged the Irish to attack the town hall where the meeting was held. He defended himself vigorously in the press. See *Liverpool Mercury,* 29th November 1856; *Liverpool Chronicle,* 30th November 1850.

29 L.R.O. Watch Committee Minutes, 30th November 1850.

30 P.R.O. HQ 45/05/3472 S.R. Letters from Bretherton to Home Department dated 25th March, 10th and 16th April 1851, Eleven years later a more serious riot was to occur in Birkenhead and the magistrates were to be accused of being too 'soft' with the rioters. See F. Neal, 'The Birkenhead Garibaldi riots of 1862', *Transactions of the Historic Society of Lancashire and Cheshire,* Vol. 131 (1982), pp. 87-111.

31 Whitty resigned in 1844 to return to a career in journalism. Initially a Mr Miller was appointed to replace Whitty but he resigned in under a year and Dowling was given the job. For criticism of the running of the police force before the crisis years of 1851-53 see *Liverpool Mercury,* 22nd February, 21st March and 25th April 1848.

32 P.R.O. HO 45/347M.

33 P.R.O. HO 4513472. Dowling to mayor, 7th July 1851.

34 Ibid.

35 The mayor and chief magistrate was John Bent, the Tory brewer.

36 P.R.O. HO/45/3472. Mayor to Home Secretary, 14th July 1851.

37 For accounts of the day's disturbances see *Liverpool Mercury,* 15th July 1851; *Manchester Guardian,* 16th July 1851; *Liverpool Courier,* 16th July 1851; *Liverpool Chronicle,* 19th July 1851; *Catholic Standard,* 19th and 26th July 1851, Vol. IV, No. 93; *Tablet,* 19th and 26th July 1851; *Orange and Blue Banner,* No. 8, Vol. 1 (August 1851), pp. 157-9.

38 *Catholic Standard,* Vol. IV, No. 94 (26th July 1851), p. 5.

39 P.R.O. HO 45/3472. Mayor to Sir George Grey, 14th July 1851.

40 P.R.O. HO 45/3472. Mayor to Home Secretary, 19th July 1851. HO 45/ 3472. Dowling to mayor, 14th July 1851.

41 P.R.O. HO 45(3472. Mayor to Home Secretary, 19th July 1851. See also *Liverpool Chronicle,* 26th July 1851, 'Meeting of magistrates'.

42 L.R.O. Watch Committee Minutes, 26th July 1851.

43 Ibid.

44 *Catholic Standard,* Vol. IV, No. 94 (26 July 1851).

45 P.R.O. HO 45/3472. Letter dated 19th July 1851.

46 Traditionally, and up to the present day, an Orange lodge is most at risk of attack when it leaves the main procession, and in the case of the Wheatsheaf it was near the Vauxhall area, with its dense concentration of Irish Catholics. Two Orange Lodges

used the Wheatsheaf as a meeting place. At the inquest on John Malley further details emerged about the fighting around the Wheatsheaf. See *Liverpool Journal*, 26th July 1851; *Liverpool Mercury*, 25th July, 1st August 1851; *Liverpool Mail*, 26th July 1851, *Liverpool Albion*, 21st July 1851.

47   For the Catholic community the issue was rapidly becoming one of a lack of confidence in the police force. Commenting on the Orange procession, the *Catholic Standard* of 19th July 1851 stated, 'If the magistrates, police and Orangemen of Liverpool escape with impunity, Lord John Russell and Lord Clarendon must allow they behaved infamously to Lord Roden' (re. Dolly's Brae).

48   No one was ever charged with the murder of Jones.

49   Shea was discharged because of the impossibility of proving which of the three attackers stabbed P.c. Green.

50   L.R.O. Watch Committee, Minutes, 30th August 1851.

51   Ibid.

52   L.R.O. Watch Committee Minutes, 9th August 1851.

53   L.R.O. Watch Committee Minutes, 13th December 1851. Unfortunately, a copy of this report which was in the Liverpool Record Office has been misplaced and cannot be found.

54   The press reflected a growing concern over the state of the borough police and its possible infiltration by Orangemen, particularly among the senior ranks. A related concern was the antagonism between the stipendiary magistrate and the lay magistrates. See *Liverpool Journal*, 19th July 1851; *Liverpool Chronicle*, 26th July 1851; *Liverpool Journal*, 26th July 1851; *Liverpool Times*, 6th November 1851; *Liverpool Chronicle*, 20th December 1851.

55   L.R.O. Watch Committee Minutes, 31st January 1852.

56   L.R.O. Watch Committee Minutes, 4th February 1852.

57   *Select Committee on Railway Labourers* (1846). Minutes of Evidence, M. M. G. Dowling, q. 3056-7.

58   Ibid.

59   Ibid., q. 3066-7.

60   *Liverpool Mercury*, 4th April 1845. Two men were charged in connection with the policeman's death.

61   *Liverpool Standard*, 3rd August 1847.

62   *Liverpool Chronicle*, 25th May 1850. Weeks earlier police had been assaulted by a mob in Marybone which was trying to rescue arrested men. See *Liverpool Chronicle*, 4th May 185·.

63   The ill will arose from the fact that it was alleged by the soldiers that some of their comrades had been beaten by the police. See P.R.O. H 145/OS/3472/8, Commander of Northern Area to Home Office, 5th July 1851. *Catholic Standard*, 5th July 1851.

64   *Liverpool Mercury*, 8th November 1853.. P.c. Sunderland died of stab wounds. Thomas Copeland was convicted of the crime and transported for twenty years. *Manchester Guardian*, 30th June 1855.

65   The Holy Cross incident received wide coverage. See *Liverpool Mail*, 28th February 1852; *Liverpool Journal*, 28th February 1852; *Liverpool Mercury*, 2nd March 1852 contains a particularly detailed account of the incident and court case; *Tablet*, 6th March 1852.

66   Rushton had died in 1851 and Mansfield was the new stipendiary magistrate.

67   This account of events is put together from the newspaper reports referred to above.

68   During all the discussions in the press and in the meetings of the town council and Watch Committee, there were frequent references to the fact that Dowling had been a very sick man over the preceding eighteen months. See *Liverpool Chronicle*, 6th March 1852, 'Town council proceedings'; also 24th January 1852.

69   *Liverpool Mail*, 28th February 1852.

70   Ibid.

71   At a meeting of the Watch Committee on 3rd March 1852 supporters of Dowling tried to pass a motion offering him a reduced pension of £200. This was defeated by a vote of thirty-six to fourteen. A second motion, to give him a pension of £150 p.a., was also defeated, by twenty-eight to eight. L.R.O. Watch Committee Minutes, 3rd March 1852. At a meeting of the Watch Committee on 4th March a letter of resignation was received from Dowling. It was not accepted, as the committee wanted to await the outcome of the magistrates' investigations. At a meeting on 6th March Towerson and Dowling were dismissed. L.R.O. Watch Committee Minutes, 6th March 1852.

72   *Liverpool Chronicle,* 6th March 1852, 'Town council proceedings'.

73   Dowling's sympathisers collected £900 and bought him an annuity which gave him £100 p.a. His salary as Head Constable had been £750. See *Liverpool Mail,* 6th March 1852. This contains a detailed defence of Dowling and the view that he had been badly treated. Also *Liverpool Standard,* 9th March 1852.

74   The morale of the force can be gauged by the fact that between 4th May 1852 and 3rd May 1853 161 officers were dismissed and 153 resigned. See Watch Committee Minutes, May 1853, p. 148.

Chapter VI **Heightened religious tension,** 1852

During the years of the famine, local politicians had been concerned not only with the immediate consequences of the influx of Irish but also with a number of economic and social issues which cut across party allegiances- in particular, the question of rating warehouses; whether the council should own warehouses in competition with the private sector; the exten- sion of the dock system, including the magnificent Albert dock, and con- troversy over the proposed abandonment of the Navigation laws. All engaged the time and energy of the borough councillors.[1] However, the most time-consuming matter of all was the need to provide Liverpool with a source of fresh water. The division of opinion was between those who favoured sinking wells and those who supported an ambitious and costly plan to build a reservoir at Rivington Pike, on the moors above Bolton, and pipe the water to Liverpool.[2] At the same time municipal pride was manifest in the building of the huge neo-classical St George's Hall, opened in 1852. Over the years 1847 to 1852 these preoccupations and achieve- ments, together with typhus and cholera epidemics, tended to shove the sectarian issue to the side, but the restoration of the Hierarchy and the shootings in 1850, the 1851 July disturbances and the Holy Cross affair in 1852 demonstrated that on the streets sectarian tension remained near the surface.

I

National politics brought No Popery back again as an election slogan in 1852. Lord John Russell needed the Peelites if his government was to survive but he had been unsuccessful in attempts to get them into gov- ernment. By January the obvious difficulties of the Russell administration made it seem likely a dissolution was near and hence an election.[3] It was this belief that caused the Liverpool Constitutional Association to seek candidates for a parliamentary contest, as the sitting members, Cardwell and Walmsley, were totally unacceptable to the Conservatives because of their support for free trade. On 10th January the Constitutional Association wrote to Lord John Manners, asking him to become a candidate at the next election. He declined, pointing out that, while opposed to any further concessions to the Roman Catholic Church, he would not oppose the existing Maynooth grant.[4] Still under the impression that they had little time to obtain satisfactory candidates, the Association asked McNeile's advice. After asking for time to think about it, McNeile set his views out in a letter on 4th February (see Appendix 4). Of the four names given to him, all were unwilling to oppose the existing arrangement concerning Maynooth and on that score all were not an ideal choice for sound Protestants. However, two of them, Manners and Sir Stratford Canning, were protectionists and on that basis they should be chosen, expressing the view that they 'would be a vast improvement on our present representation'. McNeile's dilemma was that he had opposed Manners in 1847 on the ground that he was a Tractarian and at the same time had hounded Lord Sandon out of Liverpool because of his support for Maynooth. Now he was recommending Manners, a Tractarian, who would not vote against the Maynooth grant. This left McNeile open to attack from the Liberals and their press allies, who would accuse him of expediency, and from Protestants, who would feel betrayed. His letter is a carefully worded justification of a decision which he knew would be attacked from all sides. After a lengthy reiteration of where he stood on the Protestant issue and the logic behind his decision, he stated:

> I am quite alive to the outcry which some persons of high and sincere Christian feelings will make against all this, as the tone and strain of an unworthy expediency. But I take the liberty to differ from these well meaning and zealous friends, and to request them to consider whether we may not lawfully attempt to ameliorate what we see and confess we cannot cure; whether we may not do *something* for our country, although England is not and cannot be made Utopia; or whether we must *practically play the game of our opponents*, because we cannot accomplish what in every respect we would prefer ourselves.[5]

Thus, in McNeile's view, not to have any candidates because they were in some way deficient in adhering to the purest Protestant principles would give the opposition free entry to Parliament and bring about more undesirable national policies. Given the premise that free-trade and pro-Catholic candidates should be kept out of Parliament, his logic was impeccable, but he was a hostage to his own extravagant condemnations of Maynooth and Tractarianism. When his decision became public, it seemed to many, allies and enemies, that the Lion of St Judes was retiring from the holy war.

Lord John Russell resigned on 20th February 1852 and Lord Derby formed an administration which was protectionist in policy. This development removed the threat of an immediate election and coincided with a storm of controversy in the press over McNeile's support of Manners. He was bitterly attacked in the Tory *Liverpool Courier,* while the Liberal press had a field day. The *Liverpool Chronicle* of 13th March claimed that while the restoration of the Hierarchy had given McNeile a 'temporary elevation', his actions over Manners had irretrievably damaged his standing as the Conservative leader. However, the *Liverpool Standard,* the Orange newspaper, threw all its support behind McNeile, but, like him, revealing a pragmatism totally at odds with its previous uninhabited attacks on Maynooth and Tractarianism.[6] While this furore continued, the Constitutional Association decided to invite Forbes Mackenzie, an outsider, and Charles Turner, a Liverpool councillor and chairman of the dock trustees, to stand. Both accepted. Thus there were four candidates, Edward Cardwell, the Peelite, Thomas Birch, the Liberal, Mackenzie and Turner. Mackenzie had revealed himself a good committee man during his fourteen years as an M.P. but his performance in the House was undistinguished and he knew little of shipping and commerce.[7] On arrival in Liverpool, he quickly set about proving his Protestant credentials. This was a necessary step, as the *Liverpool Standard* made clear, in a leader on 13th April 1852, that *the* political issue was Popery, 'Protestant ascendancy or Roman Catholic ascendancy'. On 4th June Mackenzie addressed the Conservatives of the Lime Street and St Anne's Ward and stated his intention of voting against the Maynooth grant. On 28th June he addressed a meeting of Orange lodges. He was asked outright whether he would oppose any legislation to outlaw the Order. He replied that he would. Would he vote against any Bill aimed at suppressing Orange processions? In an ambiguous answer he said he was sure the processions would not cause breaches of the peace, totally ignoring events over the previous two years.[8]

While the Conservatives were in disarray, the Liberals were experiencing their own difficulties. During the uproar over the restoration of the Hierarchy, Lord John Russell's government had introduced the Ecclesiastical Titles Bill into Parliament, which became law in July 1852. It prevented the Roman Catholic Church adopting the names of any of the ancient Anglican dioceses for any Catholic diocese. A highly controversial measure, implying that Protestantism needed legal protection against Roman Catholicism, it seemed to be against the spirit of the 1829 Emancipation Act. Russell's move angered the Peelites and put back further any chance of a Liberal-Peelite alliance.[9] The Act must be seen as a diversionary tactic on the part of a weak government trying to hang on to the Protestant vote at a time when no other great issues diverted attention. Sir Thomas Birch, the successful Liberal candidate in the 1847 Liverpool election, voted for it, and this produced a hostile reaction in the Catholic community. In March 1852 Catholics in the various wards met to discuss election tactics, and though they did not yet have enough votes to put up their own candidate they could influence the outcome of an electoral contest. At these March meetings it was decided to oppose anyone who had shown hostility towards Roman Catholicism. On 22nd March, at a meeting of the Catholic Registration Committee, a resolution was passed attacking the Liberals decision to adopt Sir Thomas as their candidate at the next election.[10] This development presented William Rathbone and his colleagues with a dilemma. If they ditched Birch they would be accused of giving way to Papist pressure. If he was retained, the Catholics would vote against him. However, Richard Sheil, a prominent Roman Catholic member of the Catholic Registration Committee, made it clear to Rathbone that Birch was totally unacceptable. At this Birch was dropped and replaced as a candidate by Joseph Christopher Ewart.[11] The Liberals had no choice; they had become almost as dependent on the Catholic vote as the Conservatives were on the Orange vote. The weak Derby administration finally went to the polls in July 1852, Parliament being dissolved on the 2nd.

Nomination day, 6th July, was accompanied by a great deal of drunkenness and some skirmishing between Orangemen and Irish. The four candidates were Cardwell (Peelite), Mackenzie (Conservative), Turner (Conservative) and Ewart (Liberal). McKenzie's nomination speech was an attack on the allegedly pro-Catholic sympathies of Lord John Russell's administration and on 'papal aggression'. Then, with the Orange lodges in mind, he claimed that carpenters, riggers, sailmakers, coopers and others had been hurt by free-trade policies. Surprisingly, Turner declared himself to be a 'Protestant free-trader' but covered himself by launching an attack on the Liberals for dropping Birch as a result of Catholic pressure, and he went on to urge action to counter Catholic political influence.[12] By contrast, Cardwell and Ewart confined themselves to the issue of free trade. The election took place on 6th July and McKenzie and Turner were both returned, obtaining 57% of the votes. It is clear that the issue for the electorate was religion, not economics. The *Manchester Guardian* voiced Liberal frustration at the result in the course of a long leader. It attacked the Liverpool electorate for rejecting a man of Cardwell's talents in favour of McKenzie, and gave McNeile the credit for a Tory victory based on hatred of the Irish.[13] Even allowing for the *Guardian's* partisan stance it is difficult to disagree with the central thrust of its argument, that Irish immigration had produced a reaction which had been exploited for political purposes and that McNeile was the central figure in the campaign. Certainly this was the view held by thinking people outside the borough. However, the *Guardian* was underestimating the opposition to free-trade policies in a town totally dependent on trade and shipping. Also, it is by no means clear what part McNeile played in the detailed organisation of the Conservative Party in Liverpool. He frequently denied that he was involved in party politics. For example, in March 1852, during the controversy over his support for Lord John Manners, he denied any active participation in party politics. He saw his role as preaching sermons on political issues concerned with maintaining the Protestant constitution of Britain. This, by implication, could involve urging voters to register in order to support sound Protestants. He claimed his only overtly political act was to record his vote.[14] It is difficult to believe that this disclaimer was not a display of false modesty on McNeile's part. Though the 1841 elections were the high point of his political success, he continued to exercise great influence through his charismatic preaching, letter writing and disputations. In particular, he was held in high regard by Orangemen.

Despite the religious polemics of the election, more important in its influence on working-class relationships was action on the streets. The 1852 general election posed the first big test for the resolve of Major Greig, the new Head Constable, who could not help but be sensitive to the criticisms of the behaviour and efficiency of the police following the Dowling affair. Though he would initiate new procedures aimed at removing irregularities, he had little control over events on the streets, and it was the day-to-day experience of the ordinary policemen that coloured their view of how to behave. Given the amount of violence they had to contend with, it would not be surprising if they developed prejudices, and in 1852, despite Greig's determination to wipe the slate clean, they became once again embroiled in accusations of anti-Irish behaviour. In assessing these claims it is important to appreciate the environment in which the ordinary constable had to work. Examples have already been given of behaviour towards the police, and similar incidents were a continuing feature of the policeman's lot. For example, on 9th February 1852 two policemen, Slaney and Brown, arrested a man in Vauxhall Road for stealing bacon. They were attacked by a mob and severely beaten. In May a constable was attacked by two Irishmen while he was arresting a third. The two men themselves had been arrested by the constable on a previous occasion and were obviously out for revenge. They chased him into a public house, where he shut the doors. Joined by a crowd, they battered them down and beat him up.[15] It was against this background that Greig was trying to achieve an improvement in police morale and in public esteem, an effort that received a severe setback on election day 1852.

Fortunately for Greig, the Orange lodges had decided not to hold a 12th July procession, 'out of respect to the Protestant government of Lord Derby'.[16] However, on election day some individual lodges held parades. In the South End a lodge parade was attacked, and when the police intervened they were stoned by Irish crowds in Jordan Street, New Bird Street and St James's Street.[17] In the North End, Irish were stoning cabs and coaches carrying anyone sporting Conservative colours. These disturbances kept the police at full stretch, but in the North End the police themselves became involved. Some carpenters wearing Orange colours had caused a disturbance in Grosvenor Street: a group of police arrived and chased a number of Irishmen into their homes. Four constables chased a man into the house of Margaret Baines, a Catholic. One policeman was claimed to have shouted at the man, 'Paddy go into your house or I'll put your eye out with my stick'. It was subsequently alleged that Margaret Baines was beaten and kicked in the stomach by P.c. Slaney, the same man who himself had been beaten up months before. In addition to the attack on Margaret Baines, her mother and a man were also beaten up. Margaret Baines was heavily pregnant and died.[18] Three policemen were arrested including Slaney, who was picked out at an identity parade. On 12th July he was committed on a charge of wilful murder. An incident indicative of the attitude of many Catholics occurred during the inquest on Margaret Baines. An Irishman was caught trying to pass a note to a juror. It said the aggrieved parties would find it hard to obtain justice, as they were Catholics.[19]

The death of Margaret Baines greatly increased Greig's difficulties in rehabilitating the police. It was therefore essential for him to deal firmly with the problem of Orange processions. Though the lodges had abandoned their 12th July parade, some lodges belonging to the Orange Institution were determined to march on 12th August in celebration of the battle of Augherim, and placarded the walls of the town announcing their intention.[20] Greig acted immediately. He informed the magistrates that any such parade would lead to a breach of the peace. His view was based not only on common sense but also on a number of police reports that the level of sectarian incidents was rising. For example, Thomas Blathers was arrested on 25th July, drunk, carrying a pistol and threatening to shoot 'every Papist he could find'.[21] On 8th August a man named Green was arrested and charged with shooting Timothy Dalton with intent to kill. Green said he did this after himself being assaulted by Dalton during an argument over religion. On 9th August another shooting occurred over religious differences.[22] Faced with this evidence, the mayor, Thomas Littledale, a sound Protestant, acted decisively. Greig was told no procession must be allowed, and meanwhile the Attorney General was consulted concerning the charge to be brought should anyone be arrested for trying to do so. On 12th August groups of Orangemen tried to form a procession and were immediately arrested, brought before the magistrates and committed to the assizes on a charge of unlawful assembly and released on bail. At the assizes, on the advice of the judge, they pleaded guilty. It was made clear by Lord Chief Justice Campbell that, rather than punish them, he wished to spell out the law regarding such processions as they had planned, and when he had done so they were discharged. All fifteen prisoners were drawn from the Protestant working class; no prominent Conservatives or members of the middle class were involved, illustrating yet again the distance between the middle-class Protestants in general and the Orange Order.[23]

The significance of the affair was that it brought to an end the tradition of Orange processions round the streets. From 1852 onwards, processions would in future have to be held over the borough boundary to be legal. Even more important, it was tangible evidence to Catholics that the authorities were not the instrument of the Orange Order, a charge frequently heard in Catholic circles. It could be argued that events reflected the particular social structure of the town at the time, and that they held no relevance to the study of contemporary working-class attitudes elsewhere. However, such a view cannot be sustained. There was widespread antagonism towards Irish Catholics and it needed little encouragement to come to the surface. In Stockport in June 1852 two days of clashes between Irish and English resulted in two deaths, while in July the same year rioting between English and Irish occurred in Wigan.[24] Such outbreaks were not confined to elections or 12th July processions. For example, in November 1852 a Protestant mob, celebrating Guy Fawkes night, attacked the Catholic church of St John's at Gravesend. It was alleged that the crowd smashed the windows, burned tar on the church gate, threw fireworks and threatened to kill the priest. The magistrates had been warned of trouble but sent only six policemen. Four rioters were arrested, two acquitted and two fined 10s each. In a bitter attack on the authorities' lack of concern, the *Tablet* compared the incident to a mini-Stockport riot:

> We have not forgotten Stockport yet, and the hours and days when a poor, helpless Catholic population were at the mercy of a ruffianly mob, their houses sacked and their churches desecrated. The contemptuous indifference, the insulting sarcasms even, with which the just, the liberal, the kind Protestant party received the news of the Stockport riots, showed these were no mere isolated instances of popular madnesses; they were examples of what may occur any moment, while the temper of the Protestant people remains in its present condition.[25]

The *Tablet* went on to claim that there was no justice for Catholics in England and that they had to suffer continual insults and injury without any expectation of fair play. This was undoubtedly an extreme interpretation but, equally, there is no doubt that for much of the century Catholics were subject to a non-stop stream of abuse, and the Irish in particular were frequently at the receiving end of violence where they were in a small minority.

II

The question to be posed is, how different was mid-nineteenth-century Liverpool from other English towns in terms of the scale and ferocity of sectarian conflict, if it was different at all? Also, to what extent was antagnoism a part of the normal experience of working-class people outside the institutionalised conflict situations such as elections, the 12th July processions and Guy Fawkes' night? The lack of written records makes it difficult to form a first-hand account of relations between neighbours or workpeople, but using police court reports and the published accounts of those clergymen who went among the slums of the port, a reasonable picture can be drawn of the extent and nature of the bitterness generated by the religious polemics. It is a reasonable assumption that the reported cases of conflict were only the tip of the iceberg. Many squabbles and fights between neighbours or workmen were unreported. Strains within mixed marriages were experienced but frequently not publicised. Many brawls in public houses were over before the police arrived but the bitterness would be carried on to the workplace or courts and streets. Given these considerations, there is little doubt that by the end of the 1850s the working class in Liverpool was divided in a way that was unique in England. The following examples are not meant to be exhaustive. They are given in the belief that to assert that the theological conflict poisoned working-class relationships is not a hypothesis that can be tested in any meaningful way. All that can be done is to quote evidence to support it. It is certain that a more detailed examination of press reporting of cases would reveal many more instances of conflict.

The schools campaign had raised the level of religious dispute and after 1841 increasing instances were reported of people challenging members of the opposition to a fight. These incidents, nasty as many of them were, did not impinge on the middle classes, whose anti-Catholicism was, in general, more subtle. However, they were the very substance from which the working-class divisions were created and, at the same time, reflected those divisions. The details of each occurrence were rapidly transmitted verbally, embellished and used to sharpen mutual prejudices. Fighting was not confined to men. In July 1844 a disturbance in

Grosvenor Street was caused when a woman challenged an Orangeman to a fight.[26] In November 1847 one Mary Kelly led an Irish mob in an attack on a chapel in Bishpam Street, in which the congregation were stoned and the windows broken. Kelly said in court she 'would die for her religion'.[27] Frequently the origins of a dispute had nothing to do with religion, but religious labels became handy excuses for attacking someone. In May 1848 two small boys were fighting outside a butcher's shop, and the wife of the butcher called the police, with the result that the two boys were arrested. This aroused a good deal of hostility and a threatening crowd gathered outside the shop. Parker Unsworth, the butcher, asked the crowd to move on but they refused. One man was shouting at the butcher and called him an 'Orange bastard'. On this the butcher, who was alleged to have called him an 'Irish scoundrel', ran out with a knife and stabbed a John Clarke who had been attempting to persuade the aggressive spectators to move. Clarke died almost immediately.[28] In another incident soon after, a gang of Irishmen went round public houses looking for Orangemen. At one where the publican was believed to be an Orangeman, he was attacked with pokers and severely injured.[29] Bryan Sheils, his wife and eleven-year-old son were Catholics and rented rooms from the McConvilles. McConville was a Catholic but his wife was a Protestant. Following the 1850 Orange processions, Mrs McConville boasted to the Sheilses that she was an Orangewoman before asking for the rent. This led to a row and Sheils attacked her. In return McConville attacked the Shielses with a hammer. In court it was claimed the bad feeling had arisen over arguments about the Orange procession.[30] Many incidents arose from what to outsiders appeared quite trivial issues. In October 1850 Bryan Murphy, an elderly Irishman who earned a living playing the flute, went into the Plough Vaults in Scotland Road to see if anyone wanted him to play. A group of Protestants asked him to play *Boyne Waters,* an Orange tune. Murphy refused on the grounds that he might be in trouble if it got around that he played Orange tunes. The Protestants took the flute from him, broke it into pieces and then assaulted the old man.[31] In November 1850 a drunk was put into the cells in the Vauxhall bridewell. Already in there was a Catholic Irishman. The drunk started to sing *Boyne Water,* which so incensed the Catholic that he attacked him savagely, using his iron-tipped boots to such effect that the drunk was rushed to the infirmary.[32] In December 1850 the police were called to a domestic row in Toxteth and found a drunken man, a Protestant, beating his Catholic wife. They had had a row over the restoration of the Hierarchy and she had tried to burn his Bible.[33] The Rev. Francis Bishop was in charge of the Liverpool Town Mission and had first-hand experience of life in the slums. In his report for 1849 part of it was headed 'The evils of sectarianism'. He directly charged

No Popery orators with the blame for much of the bitterness in working-class life:

> I have seen the 'evangelical' Protestant husband and Catholic wife, giving loose to their passionate bigotry in actual personal conflict with each other; I have heard the Pharasaic and unfeeling man taunt his dying wife with her attachment to 'Popery'. I have known homes to be broken up from the same cause, husband and wife to be separated, and the most unseemly contests carried on respecting the division of the children; and of feuds and ill blood between neighbours, springing from the roots of bitterness - I am constantly seeing instances.[34]

While Bishop was correct in blaming McNeile and his colleagues for cultivating sectarian attitudes in the minds of working-class Protestants, it must be borne in mind that the Roman Catholic clergy were equally intransigent. This was clearly demonstrated in their attitude towards the Industrial Ragged Schools. These were run by the Church of England and had as their objective 'to rescue young persons from a state of present destitution and incipient vice and thus prevent them becoming confirmed criminals'.[35] They provided a rudimentary education for a small number of children and had been operating in Liverpool since 1846. The Roman Catholic clergy believed they were run by 'blanket and soup' Protestants, that is, people out to convert Roman Catholics by offers of food and clothing. In February 1852 Fr Noble, of Holy Cross Church in Vauxhall, preached a sermon expressing the desire to bring England back to the 'faith of her forefathers'. The very title of the sermon confirmed Protestant opinions about the conspiratorial designs of the Roman Church. In the course of the sermon he denounced Ragged Schools as a medium for proselytising Catholic children.[36] His opposition had been dramatically displayed when on 4th December 1850 he had gone to the Ragged School in Soho Street and demanded that the Rev. W. Wolsey bring out all Catholic children, accusing Wolsey of being a souper. Wolsey refused and Noble left to return with a crowd of several hundred Catholics. He ordered the parents of children at the school to withdraw them. After they had done so, it was claimed, Fr Noble had addressed the crowd and told them that, after that night, any parent who sent children there would be denied the last rites on their deathbed.[37] It is difficult to imagine a more potent threat to the Irish Catholic. It is clear, the working class were subject to fierce religious indoctrination from both sides.

Many public house brawls were triggered off by religious arguments. In March 1852 the police were called to a fight in a public house in Lime Street. By the time they arrived, all the windows had been broken and they found the combatants were two women who subsequently vowed in court that they would fight for their religion.[38] Francis Bishop, in his report for 1853, deplored the effect of Orange parades on the people in the slums. He told of touring the back streets and courts on the night after the 1853 procession and finding drunken prostitutes fighting outside a brothel, ostensibly over religion. He then witnessed the results of a public house brawl which had started over the relative merits of Henry VIII and the Pope, in which one man had his leg broken. He was particularly alarmed to observe small children playing 'Catholics and Protestants', holding mock processions which were then 'attacked'.[39] The possibilities for conflict were apparently infinite and difficult for the police to prevent, assuming they wished to. In May 1852 an Anglican clergyman decided to given an open-air sermon in Banastre Street in the North End, primarily a Catholic area. He was threatened by a crowd, and when the police intervened they were attacked.[40] Two weeks later, Orangemen in Toxteth gathered to bury a brother Orangeman. While the Orangemen were at the cemetery, crowds of Irish gathered in the streets near the deceased's home, armed with stones and sticks, ready to attack the mourners. On being told of this threat, more Protestants joined the funeral procession, and on reaching Albert Street a clash occurred during which the Irish were beaten off.[41] Such attacks on funerals particularly incensed working-class Protestants. In the same area, two weeks later, an Orangeman chastised a boy for throwing mud. The boy was a Catholic and a group of women remonstrated with the man. Within minutes Protestants from surrounding streets, including carpenters, went to protect their co-religionist, only to be met by hundreds of Irish. A riot took place and the police drove the Irish into their houses, but not before several people were injured.[42] Soon after, Joseph Wright, a Protestant, was involved in an argument over religion and was attacked by women using pokers, then shot by William Roberts, a Catholic.[43] A week later the congregation at St Bartholomew's Anglican church were alarmed when, during the evening service, the windows were broken by stones thrown by an Irish mob and by six pistol shots. The church normally needed police protection, being in a predominantly Irish area.[44] Such incidents were a continuing feature of Liverpool life throughout the rest of the 1850s and were not simply a reflection of short-term, heightened religious tension over the years 1850-52. Press reports of court cases reveal the same picture over the whole decade. Thus in 1855 a drunk in Scotland Road was arrested wielding a knife and shouting, 'To hell with the priests and the Pope.' The arrest saved him from attack by a hostile crowd.[45] A steward from a ship in dock was arrested for drunkeness. He had been standing in the street singing Boyne Water and cursing the Pope.[46] Such a simple incident could quickly cause a disturbance. Anglican churches continued to be at risk. In July 1858 a group of Orangemen were allowed to use St Matthew's schoolroom for a tea party which attracted an angry Irish crowd who launched such a fierce attack that the police had to seal off the surrounding streets while they gained control. During the riot a policeman had his skull fractured.[47]

Against this background of continued social disharmony any larger-scale outbreak of lawlessness was correspondingly more damaging in its influence in confirming stereotypes. The so called 'bread riots' of 1855 illustrate this.[48] About the middle of January 1855 an easterly wind started to blow off the west coast of England and continued until the end of February. It had the startling consequence that the majority of inward-bound ships were kept out of the port of Liverpool. The *Liverpool Mail* in a leader on 17th February wrote:

> When it is remembered what vast numbers of our poorer fellow townsmen are dependent for their daily bread upon casual employment at the docks, it will be evident that a state of things as that which now exists, *in which scarcely six ships arrive in as many days,* must of necessity be attended with severe and extensive destitution.

Large numbers of dockers and porters were thrown out of work because of the lack of shipping, and the *Liverpool Albion* of 19th February estimated that between 15,000 and 20,000 dockers, porters and other casual workers had been made unemployed. However, the suffering caused by the lack of ships due to the wind was nothing compared with the distress resulting from the coldest winter in living memory. On both sides of the Mersey the situation of poor people was desperate, and suffering from starvation and cold was widespread. The District Provident Society, between 1st and 23rd February, distributed 16,153 loaves and 9,081 soup tickets. Of the total number of persons relieved by the society during this period, the numbers in the various national groups were: 1,830 English, 7,496 Irish, 143 Welsh, 68 Scots, 46 Aliens. Many Irish could not seek poor relief because they did not have settlement and so were forced to go to the charities for help. Despite this, such statistics helped fuel resentment against the Irish. The large contributions of private charity during the crisis exceeded any previous philanthropic efforts on behalf of the poor. Further, it was complementary to the relief provided by the parochial authorities, who were having difficulty in coping with the numbers of destitute families. By 13th February the number of families seeking relief from the parish was 700 above the figure normal for that time of the year, and it continued to increase. Given the intensity of the deprivations suffered by the working classes of the town and the length of time over which the deprivations had to be endured, it is hardly surprising that trouble erupted. When this happened, the outrage of the press was all the greater because of the considerable charitable efforts of the better-off citizens.

Early on Monday 19th February 1855 a large mob gathered in St

Paul's Square, in the Scotland Road district, where it had been announced previously that relief would be dispersed out of a fund raised by the merchants of the town. At 10.00 a.m. approximately the crowd went on the rampage, and started to attack shops and bakeries over an area that eventually included Scotland Road, Vauxhall Road, Tithebarn Street, Paddington, Brownlow Hill, Great Homer Street, Great Howard Street and Bootle. The initial mob broke up into smaller gangs and simultaneously attacked premises where food and provisions were known to be available. The rioting was confined almost entirely to the North End and involved both men and women. The crowds took food, oatmeal and in several instances money from the tills. In one incident, men threw bread and sacks of flour into the streets, where women were waiting to take them away. At shops where resistance was offered, doors, windows and shutters were smashed. The number of gangs meant that the police initially had great difficulty in getting the situation under control, for on their appearance the gangs would simply run off into the warren of courts and streets of the teeming slums in the Scotland Road-Vauxhall Road area. At the South End there was a lot of excitement as the rumours of the rioting in the North End circulated but there was no trouble.

The authorities were thoroughly alarmed and the mayor and magistrates met for a whole day, swearing in 200 special constables in each of the North and South police divisions. They were armed with staves and went on patrol with the regular police, whilst the Royal Lancashire Artillery Militia were armed and kept on stand-by at Seel Street police station. In fact it appears that the hard core of rioters numbered about 1,000, a much smaller number than the police had had to deal with on many previous occassions. The difficulty this time in controlling events was simply the spread of incidents throughout the North End.

Over the three days of disturbances 106 people were arrested, eighty-three of whom were Irish.[49] The sentences handed out went up to three months hard labour in some cases; several prisoners were remanded for trial at the quarter sessions. Mansfield, the stipendiary, commented on the seriousness of the offences, for which, he stated, there was no excuse, particularly as the inhabitants of Liverpool had subscribed liberally for the relief of the poor.

In fact there had been little injury to people and property, only one policeman had been hurt; the real damage was that the incidents were seen in the eyes of many as the kind of behaviour to be expected of the Irish. It did not follow that because the arrested men were almost entirely Irish so were most of those involved. It could have reflected police prejudice; however, even allowing for some prejudice, it is probable that most rioters were Irish, given that the crowds involved were mainly in the

Vauxhall area. Commenting on the events at the magistrates' court, the *Liverpool Mail* of 24th February exonerated the 'honest working men' from any blame and went on to attack the Irish :

> Of nearly 60 prisoners who had been taken into custody by the police for actual participation in the riots, the whole, with the exception of two, are described as 'belonging to the lowest and most vicious class of the Irish population of the town' the class which, according to the police returns, gives us 45 per cent of our thieves and 44 per cent of the disorderly prostitutes who infest our streets - whose haunts are scenes of debauchery and profligacy of the most debasing kind.

After making the point that not all the Liverpool Irish participated in the events of 19th, 20th and 21st February, the *Mail* commented:

> If Irish paupers are to be absolutely irremovable by law - all property in Liverpool must gradually deteriorate in value-while our local burdens our expenditure not only for pauperism but for crime - just continually increase, for Irish poverty of the lowest grade seems inseparable from habitual criminality.

This outraged reaction from a Tory newspaper typified the view of many people and added fuel to the feelings of the Protestant working class. In the Tory *Liverpool Courier* of 21st February a letter was printed from a cotton porter. He claimed that relief from the Temporary Relief Fund was not going to the deserving unemployed:

> There can be no mistake as to the characters in general applying. Truth compels me to say that 90 out of 100 are Irish of the lowest and most degraded class, assisted by the idle and disaffected of the town - beggars by profession - people who would not work were it offered to them.

Whether it was true or not was not the issue. Protestants *believed* it to be true.

The leader writer in the same issue, commenting on the letter, suggested that the malcontents should be sent to the Crimea as the 'Black Brigade'. It did not take long for religion to enter into the recriminations. In the *Tablet* a correspondent from Liverpool wrote a long letter about the riots. He referred to the extreme poverty in Ireland and the fortitude with which it had been borne. This was contrasted to the behaviour of the Liverpool population. In Ireland, the writer claimed, the Catholic Church provided the moral teaching and succour which gave the Irish their discipline, whereas in Liverpool no such discipline existed.

> . . . in a short season of a few weeks distress, which compared to what had subsisted in Ireland for years, was opulence itself - in that short season of mitigated trial there have been more civil confusions and convulsions in the one city of Liverpool than in this poor country during the long years of the most

dire calamity that desolated a portion of this earth. And yet is Liverpool the glory and boast of Protestant England, the daughter of the Protestant creed and the fruit of Protestant progress, it is a Protestant city . . . oh, if Liverpool were a Catholic city, what glorious creations of beneficence would not Catholic charity rise up in every quarter, to relieve, to instruct, to console.[50]

The writer's view of events was, to say the least, exaggerated. Certainly the majority of people arrested for being involved in the riots were Irish, and the letter implied that the riots were the fruits of Protestantism. The *Courier* printed the following reply:

It was the Irish, by universal consent, who created and carried forward the late riots in Liverpool. The scum of Irish Popery, abundantly thrown into that great city from Dublin, is the very element that is and has been for half a century, demoralising that and all our large cities. The argument, therefore tells the other way. This influx of semi-savages brings all the turbulence and disorder of Popish Ireland with it.[51]

Soon after the disturbances the weather improved and the wind changed. The resumption of work helped to relegate the events quickly to history, but the prejudices concerning the Irish had been once more confirmed in many minds.

Frequently there were short bursts of intense sectarian confrontation which unpredictably blew up out of nothing but raised feelings of intense bitterness and hatred. A good example was the incidents in the Old Swan district in 1858. In May a procession took place around the grounds of the Roman Catholic church of St Oswald's at Old Swan, now a district of Liverpool but at that time just over the borough boundary. About 150 children took part, carrying banners and, according to some Protestants, a representation of the bleeding heart of Jesus. The procession had attracted the attention of Protestant groups and a disturbance took place. On Saturday 11th June Father Bennett, the parish priest at St Oswald's, heard that Orangemen were coming from Liverpool to carry out a revenge attack on the church on Sunday 12th June.[52] Hence a number of parishioners were inside the grounds on Sunday to defend the building if need be. On the Sunday a group of preachers arrived from Liverpool and started to preach near the top of Edge Lane, not far from St Oswald's. The county police, aware that feeling was running high, had brought seventy constables. By arrangement with the borough police, a further reserve of Liverpool police were on stand-by at Prescot Street police station.

The crowd around the preachers grew to about 2,000 and, according to police evidence, a disturbance seemed highly likely. The police requested Israel Argyle, the principal preacher, to stop, but he refused. The police moved in and arrested him and another man, James Peat; the two were escorted towards the Old Swan bridewell. They were followed by a crowd of hostile Protestants, and the procession of police, prisoners and Protestant supporters had to pass St Oswald's, where the Catholic 'defenders' were waiting. They started to shout slogans and throw stones at the Catholics, who responded in kind, and a general fight broke out. Father Bennett was trying to restrain his parishioners when a Protestant ran at him with a piece of wood, and the excitement was heightened even more when someone fired a pistol. Eventually the police obtained order and their procession, with two additional prisoners, went to the bridewell, which was immediately surrounded by the Protestant crowd, who, however, did not attack. Israel Argyle had a preachers's licence and his occupation was that of newspaper seller, whilst his companion in misfortune, James Peat, was a fitter. Next day they were brought before the county magistrates and charged with creating a riot. As in the case of all such affairs, crowds were attracted in the hope of seeing more trouble, so that the following Sunday, 19th June, crowds of sightseers gathered around St Oswald's in the hope that more Protestants would come up from Liverpool. The county police, in anticipation of further trouble, drafted in 100 policemen but the day passed without incident and the Old Swan district was spared further visits from street preachers.[53]

However, during the same period street preaching by scripture readers caused a series of minor incidents. There were forty to fifty scripture readers in Liverpool, organised under Anglican auspices to visit the poor in their homes and to instruct them on spiritual affairs. Each reader was under the control of the Anglican minister in whose area he operated. In addition to house-to-house visiting, some of the scripture readers held open-air preaching sessions, and in June 1858 they seem to have become increasingly involved in brawls. A popular site for the preachers was the old Islington market at the south end of St George's Hall. On Sunday 12th June 1858 George Berry, a scripture reader, was arrested, together with John Clancy and James Welsh, all charged with fighting at an open-air preaching session.[54] The following Sunday there was another disturbance at the same spot, where a large crowd had gathered to listen to the preachers. Michael Gallagher and William Highton were charged with fighting. Their case is of interest because it demonstrates the flimsiness of the grounds needed to start a sectarian dispute. It appears that Highton turned up at the meeting with a marigold in his buttonhole. The colour of the flower was suspiciously close to Orange, and seems to have provoked Gallagher. Mansfield told Highton he ought to have known better than to go to a religious meeting in Liverpool wearing party colours.[55] The following week, on Sunday 26th June, a preacher, the Rev. W. B. Keer, was attacked by a Catholic mob with stones and sticks and received a beating before the police arrived. The next Sunday he brought a large force of Protestant bodyguards and got through his address without interference.[56] On Sunday 31st there was another fight in the old Islington Market sector during a preaching session.[57]

Lastly an incident in 1859 clearly reflected the fact that, long after the peak of his political triumphs, McNeile was still firmly established as a hero in the minds of working-class Protestants, most of whom had never met or spoken to him. In January 1859 Cardinal Wiseman was in Liverpool to give a lecture at the Philharmonic Hall. The meeting was well publicised, and in case of trouble a body of police were stationed around the building. A Protestant crowd had gathered, and afterwards owing to misunderstanding on the part of the police, the coach carrying the Cardinal set off unguarded and was attacked by a stone-throwing mob. A seventeen-year-old Protestant labourer was arrested and on appearing in court told the magistrates he and the others had turned up at the meeting because they had heard McNeile was going to debate with Wiseman. They all wanted to cheer McNeile.[58]

III

In the decade following the restoration of the Hierarchy the English Orange Order was split by internal divisions, reflecting no deep differences of principle but merely personality clashes. Despite these differences, the membership increased during the 1850s but inability to attract the middle-class Protestant remained a problem for the Order's leaders.

The fundamental divide within the ranks of English Orangemen was between those who gave their allegiance to the Grand Protestant Association of Loyal Orangemen, and those, mainly in Liverpool, who had refused to join the Association in 1844 and belonged to the Loyal Orange Institution, with its Grand Lodge in Liverpool. The driving force behind the Association was Mr Squire Auty of Bradford. Born in Dewsbury into a humble family in 1812, Auty became a successful businessman and councillor in Bradford who quickly identified with the Anglican Tory tradition and became a vigorous defender of the Church of England.[59] Precisely when he became an Orangeman is not known, but on 30th January 1844 he appeared on a platform in Liverpool together with Irish and English Orangemen.[60] In 1851 Auty began publishing a monthly newspaper devoted almost entirely to the affairs of English Orangemen. It was called at first *The Orange and Blue Banner,* later changed to *The Orange* and *Protestant Banner,* and it was produced regularly until it collapsed from lack of support in 1869.[61] The role of the journal was not only to give news of Orange lodge affairs. It also contained a continual stream of articles attacking Roman Catholicism on every conceivable basis. Few had any scholarly content and were characteristic of the type of anti-Catholic writings indulged in by the less well educated opponents of the Church. This newspaper is the greatest source of information regarding the affairs of English Orangemen during the years of its publication.

Auty was an indefatigable traveller, turning up at Orange meetings all over the country, and was mainly responsible for initiating changes in the Association's organisation. As had always been the case, the strength of the Order in the 1850s was in Lancashire and West Yorkshire; Grand Lodge meetings in London were inconvenient and irrelevant now that the ultra-Tory aristocracy had abandoned Orangeism. In August 1851 a Grand Lodge of the Association was held at Rochdale and the decision was made to adopt a system of provincial grand lodges, four for England, one for Scotland and one for Wales.[62] On 21st November the first meeting of the North West Provincial Grand Lodge took place, in Liverpool.[63] The meeting is of interest on a number of counts. Firstly, neither McNeile or any councillor attended the meeting. Second, Ambrose Byeford, the Liverpool estate agent, was described as a Provincial Grand Master, as was J. T. Ousely of Shrewsbury.[64] Ousely was a newspaper proprietor, owner of the *Shropshire Conservative,* which adopted a hard-line Tory and Protestant stance. He subsequently became the proprietor of the *Liverpool Herald,* the main organ of extreme Protestant views in the town. Both Byeford and Ousely appear to have been determined to acquire power within the Orange movement, and so the results of the first Grand Lodge of the North West Province must have disappointed them. Of the sixty members and visitors present, the Liverpool contingent numbered sixteen. In the voting for officers Ousely was beaten for the office of Provincial Grand Master by William Jones, ex-mayor of Oldham, and Ambrose Byeford also failed to be elected as a Provincial Deputy Grand Master, this office going to T. H. Redhead of Manchester. Neither was voted on to the Grand Committee, on which there was only one Liverpool man.[65] This removal from office seems to have been the signal for Byeford and Ousely to leave the Association and throw in their lot with the Institution.

At the annual Grand Lodge meeting of the Loyal Orange Institution of Great Britain, held in Liverpool on 1st July 1853, Ousely was described as the Grand Master and Byeford as the Grand Secretary. The other officers were obscure figures not warranting a mention in any Liverpool directory. At this meeting Ousely announced that the Institution Lodges were going to amalgamate with the Irish lodges.

Despite the fact that his claim had no basis in reality, the announcement infuriated Auty and the Association members, but it was typical of the exaggerated and unreal claims made at the time by all Orangemen regarding their status and influence.[66] The defection of Byeford and Ousely to the Institution probably reflected not only personal pique at not being elected to the Provincial Grand Committee of the Association but also a genuine belief that Liverpool Orangeism was in the forefront of the battle against Catholicism. Hence they should, in their view, have carried corresponding influence in the Orange Order. In 1855 the Shropshire connection with the Orange Institution was emphasised when Richard Burton, High Sheriff of Shropshire, was elected to the office of Grand Master 'of the Orange lodges of England and Ireland'.[67] This inclusion of the Irish lodges in the Institution's title was absurd. The Irish lodges were members of the Association, under the Earl of Inniskillen. Butler Lloyd, mayor of Shrewsbury, was the Deputy Grand Master of the Institution while Ousely was the Provincial Grand Master. However, in the competition for membership among the Liverpool Orangemen, the Institution was far more successful than the Association. In 1856 the situation was as shown in Table 19. Of fifty-five lodges in the Liverpool Order, forty-seven belonged

TABLE 19
The number of Lodges in the Orange Association and Institution - Liverpool, 1856

Orange Order	No.
Association	
Duke of York and High Stowell district	8
Institution	
North district	25
South district	12
Duke of York district	5
St Pauls district	5
Total	55

Source: *Orange and Protestant Banner,* III, March 1956, p. 321.

to the Institution. In fact there were some lodges with Irish warrants unattached to either organisation, making a total of seventy lodges in Liverpool. However, even within the Institution there was feuding and at the annual Grand Lodge of the Loyal Orange Institution, held on 1st July 1857, every member of the Shrewsbury district was expelled 'for non-compliance with the rules of the Order'. Ousely was elected Grand Master for the fifth time.[68] Auty expressed the opinion that these squabbles went over the heads of the rank-and-file membership and simply reflected the personal ambitions of a few men.[69]

These upheavals in the English Orange Order were of little

consequence to the great mass of respectable middle-class Conservative voters. It continued to be the case that at election times, municipal or parliamentary, the Orange vote was sought. In Liverpool particularly, the Orange vote remained important. For example, in the 1856 municipal elections, members of No. 3 lodge voted for John Buck Lloyd, the Conservative candidate in the Lime Street ward.[70] Outside these events, Orangemen continued to be kept at arm's length. The reason for this aloofness on the part of the middle class remained what it had always been, the fact that Orange lodge membership was drawn overwhelmingly from the lower orders of Victorian society. This was a matter of continuing concern to the more reflective members of both the Association and the Institution; typical of this concern was the correspondence in the *Orange and Protestant Banner.* In May 1861 a correspondent argued that numbers of 'respectable' persons were put off Orangeism because of the fact that lodge meetings were held mainly in public houses:

> There are numbers of persons in the upper ranks sir, who would join the Association willingly except for this, but who could never be persuaded to frequent a public house and sit there among the fumes of gin and tobacco. Secondly, the necessity of 'doing something for the good of the house' is an insuperable obstacle to ever doing any business effectively. I have seen lodges opened by a prayer, for the sake of form, the dues taken, and the lodge closed almost immediately; and then the drinking begins, which went on for a much longer time than the transactions of the lodges.[71]

Though the need to get away from the public house was generally accepted among the more thoughtful, the membership of the Order was too poor to finance the building of lodge meeting places.[72] In addition, the drinking had a popular appeal to many. The relatively low social status of Orangemen in Liverpool is revealed by the positions of the officers of the lodges. In 1853 some Orange lodges tried to hold a parade despite the ban on processions. Their leaders were arrested. Among them were a Mr Goodfellow, boot and shoe maker, Mr Higgs, ironmonger, Mr Carter, hairdresser, and Mr Brown, foreman in an iron foundry.[73] In 1857, when J. T. Ousely was elected Grand Master, Oxley Ellam was made Grand Treasurer. Ellam was a publican.[74] In 1856 Richard Pugh was the District Master of the Institution's North District in Liverpool. He was a bookkeeper. David Rea, Master of the South district, was a bookseller; Samuel Darch, Master of the Duke of York district, was a warehouseman, while John Everett, Master of St Paul's district, was a ropemaker.[75] In 1859 Charles Chalk, a publican, was the Grand Treasurer and a George de Bentley the Grand Master. De Bentley was a shadowy figure. In reports of the 1859 12th July procession he was described as Mr De Bentley. Later he used the title 'Captain' and eventually described himself as Major De

Bentley. At no time is he listed in the Liverpool directories, and his enemies attacked him in the press because no such name appeared in the army list and it was alleged he was an Irishman of no social standing whose real name was Corry.[76] These were not the men with whom the merchant princes, shipowners and wealthy businessmen socialised.

Apart from the working-class membership another reason for the reluctance of the more educated Protestants to join Orange lodges was the lack of any coherent, intellectual content to support the Orange defence of the Church and constitution. The sheer crudity and ferocity of the anti-Catholicism were repellent to more delicate spirits. Much Orange rhetoric consisted of the repetition of slogans and references to such abstract concepts as the 'good old cause' and 'sound Protestants'. It was lacking in the analysis characteristic of McNeile's anti-Catholic sermons and devoid of theological scholarship. Even some clergymen who were also Orangemen indulged in the most incredible arguments. The Rev. Samuel Fenton, an Orangeman, of St Mary's, Wavertree, in the course of an address to an Orange gathering in 1851, claimed that every time Popery had been encouraged disaster overtook England: following Catholic emancipation in 1829 the country had experienced a cholera epidemic; after the restoration of the Hierarchy in 1850, 14,000 British soldiers had been slaughtered in the Khyber Pass.[77]

For the less educated working men the Orange lodge offered conviviality, companionship, colour in its ceremonies and, more practically, funeral and benefit club facilities. These had been discouraged in the early days of Lord Kenyon and Blennerhasset, but they continued to be an important feature. Not everyone liked this. The correspondent to the *Orange and Protestant Banner* quoted earlier claimed that dealing with funeral and benefit matters took up most of the time of many lodge meetings and, combined with drinking, left little to discussion of the defence of Protestantism.[78] It is fairly certain that these non-religious aspects of membership were, for a substantial minority, the more important. In Liverpool for example, the Orange Association and Institution gave relief to members who fell on hard times, not only Liverpool men but Orangemen from all over the country while they were in Liverpool.[79]

Lastly, what happened to the size of the Liverpool Orange fraternity over the years 1850-60? The brief answer is it increased both in terms of those who joined the Orange lodges and in terms of the number of Protestants who espoused 'Orangeism', a set of anti-Catholic attitudes indulged without formal membership. It had been estimated that in the fatal 12th July procession of 1851 there had been 2,000 marchers. In 1854 the number was estimated at 1,300-1,400. The *Liverpool Chronicle*, describing the event, wrote:

The men who walked appeared to be of the lower class of carpenters, ropers, etc., followed throughout their routine by the lowest rabble. We are informed that the numbers belonging to the lodges in Toxteth Park have lately considerably increased.[80]

The point about the followers of the processions is important in the context of 'sectarian' violence. The banning of processions within the borough in 1852 had resulted in the 12th July procession becoming an outing into the nearby countryside for the town's slum dwellers, greatly increasing the appeal of the day. The heavy drinking which characterised the outings meant that the potential for fighting after the march back to the borough boundaries was considerable, and the Irish were always waiting. In 1859 the pro-Orange *Herald* estimated that 20,000 followed the procession.[81] It was this decade that witnessed the establishment of 12th July as a holiday celebration in the working-class Protestant calendar in Liverpool. Though Orange lodges flourished in Manchester and the rest of Lancashire, nowhere else had the music, songs and attitudes of Irish Orangeism taken root to anything like the same extent. The Orange Institution was almost entirely a Liverpool affair. At the Grand Lodge of the Institution, held in July 1860, of the thirty-four officials who attended, twenty-eight were from Liverpool.[82]

Notes

1 The warehouse issue was particularly volatile, as many councillors, on both sides of the political divide, were warehouse owners. It was also a long-running controversy. David Hodgson, the Orangeman, argued in the council in 1843 that for the Corporation to use public money to purchase warehouses in competition with the private sector was an invasion of private rights. See council meeting report, *Liverpool Standard*, 7th November 1843. With regard to the Navigation Laws the Liverpool shipowners were accused by the *Times* of wanting free trade in everything but shipping (8 April 1852).

2 For a full treatment of this dispute see B. D. White, A History of the Corporation of Liverpool (1951), chapters 5 and 6.

3 Russell failed to persuade the Peelites to support his administration and one reason was the behaviour of the government in bringing in the Ecclesiastical Titles Bill. See R. Stewart, *The Foundation of the Conservative Party*, 1830-1867 (1978), chapter 12.

4 *Liverpool Standard*, 2nd March 1852. Copy of a letter from Manners to Lawrence Peel, dated 13th January 1852.

5 *Liverpool Standard*, 2nd March 1852. Letter from McNeile to Constitutional Association dated 6th February 1852. For a fuller self-justification of his actions, see *Liverpool Mail*, 20th March 1852. This edition carries a long letter from McNeile to the citizens of Liverpool, covering the events of the preceding weeks.

6 *Liverpool Standard*, 9th March 1852, see also *Liverpool Mail*, 6th March 1852.

7 For a comment on McKenzie's candidature see *Times*, 8th April 1852, leader.

8 *Liverpool Journal* 5th June 1852, 'Lime Street and St Anne's Ward meetings last night'; *Liverpool Standard*, 29th June 1852, 'Messrs. Turner's and Mackenzie's addresses to the Orangemen'.

9 The Ecclesiastical Titles Act was never invoked. The appointment of Dr Browne as the first Bishop of Liverpool infuriated Protestants, who for a long time referred to him as the 'sham bishop'.

10   *Liverpool Chronicle*, 27th March 1852. See also *Tablet*, 13th March 1852. The *Liverpool Albion* of 22nd March 1852 attacked the Catholics' decision to oppose Birch and support Forbes Mackenzie.

11   Ewart was a politically inexperienced free-trade candidate. In an election speech he bombarded the audience with statistics concerning free trade, ignoring all religious issues. See *Liverpool Journal*, 5th June 1852, 'Great free trade meeting last night'.

12   For an account of the nomination day speeches see *Manchester Guardian*, 7th July 1852. See also *Liverpool Albion*, 12th July 1852.

13   *Manchester Guardian*, 14th July 1852.

14   *Liverpool Standard*, 2nd March 1852. Letter, McNeile to Constitutional Association.

15   *Liverpool Standard*, 24th February 1852; Liverpool Journal, 1st May 1852.

16   *Liverpool Standard*, 6th July 1852.

17   *Liverpool Albion*, 12th July 1852; *Liverpool Mail*, 10th July 1852; *Liverpool Standard*, 13th July 1852.

18   This incident and the consequent court case received widespread press coverage. See *Liverpool Journal*, 10th July 1852; *Manchester Guardian*, 19th July 1852; *Liverpool Albion*, 12th July 1852.

19   *Liverpool Albion*, 12th July 1852.

20   *Liverpool Mail*, 14th August 1852. P.R.O. HO 45/4085F, Deputy Mayor to Home Office, 10th August 1852. In this letter John Holmes told of the placards and referred to the deaths which occurred after the 1851 Orange processions. Greig had expressed the view that a procession would lead to a breach of the peace. See also *Times*, 13th August 1852; *Liverpool Journal*, 14th August 1852.

21   P.R.O. HO 45/4085C. Report of Head Constable to magistrates. Extracts from police log books.

22   Ibid.

23   *Liverpool Mail*, 14th and 21st August 1852; *Liverpool Albion*, 16th August 1852; *Times*, 16th August 1852. For the case at the assizes see *Liverpool Journal*, 28th August 1852; *Manchester Guardian*, 25th August 1852; *Liverpool Albion*, 23rd August 1852; *Liverpool Mercury*, 24th August 1852.

24   For a full account of the Stockport riots see P. Millwood, 'The Stockport riots of 1852: a study of anti-Catholic and anti-Irish sentiment', in R. Swift and S. Gilley (eds.) *The Irish in the Victorian City* (1985), pp, 207-24. For a detailed account of the Wigan riots and the consequent court cases see *Wigan Times*, 16th July; 27th August 1852.

25   *Tablet*, 13th and 20th November 1852.

26   *Liverpool Courier*, 17th July 1844.

27   *Liverpool Albion*, 8th November 1847.

28   *Liverpool Mercury*, 30th May 1848.

29   *Liverpool Mercury*, 9th June 1848.

30   *Manchester Guardian*, 20th July 1850.

31   *Liverpool Chronicle*, 26th October 1850.

32   *Liverpool Chronicle*, 16th November 1850.

33   *Liverpool Mercury*, 6th December 1850.

34   *Liverpool Mercury*, 15th January 1850. This edition carries a long account of Bishop's report.

35   *Liverpool Standard*, 24th February 1852. Annual general meeting of Industrial Ragged Schools.

36   *Liverpool Journal* 21st February 1852. Catholic authorities were obsessed by the idea that Catholics were being tempted by money, food and clothing. A Liverpool correspondent of the *Tablet* claimed Irish emigrants were given money to emigrate by Protestants and when they arrived on board ship at Birkenhead they were forbidden to attend mass and were compelled to attend Protestant services; *Tablet*, 14th February 1852. For an account of Ragged Schools see *Liverpool Journal*, 20th February 1847. For friction with Roman Catholics over Ragged Schools see *Liverpool Standard*, 22nd February 1853.

37 *Liverpool Mail*,13th December 1850.

38 *Liverpool Standard*, 9th March 1852.

39 *Annual Report of Town Mission for 1853*. The section of the report referred to is reproduced in *Liverpool Chronicle*, 29th April 1854. Commenting on the Irish Protestant clergy, the Chronicle remarked that the difference between them and the English was 'very marked'.

40 *Liverpool Standard*, 11th and 18th May 1852; *Liverpool Mail*, 22nd May 1852.

41 *Liverpool Mail*, 19th June 1852.

42 *Sheffield Times*, 16th July 1852.

43 *Liverpool Times*, 12th August 1852.

44 *Liverpool Mail*, 28th August 1852. The *Tablet* of 13th November 1852 carried a letter from a Liverpool correspondent, claiming that the Sisters of Mercy were 'insulted and harrassed'.

45 *Liverpool Herald*, 27th October 1855.

46 *Liverpool Mercury*, 7th August 1857.

47 *Manchester Guardian*, 13th July 1858; *Liverpool Mercury*, 14th July 1858; *Liverpool Mail*, 17th July 1858. During the same week a Catholic was kicked and beaten in a row over 'party songs'; see *Liverpool Mercury*, 21st July 1858.

48 These riots received widespread press coverage. The following account is taken from: *Liverpool Courier*, 21st February 1855; *Liverpool Albion*, 26th February 1855; *Liverpool Courier*, 28th February 1855; *Liverpool Mail*, 17th February 1855; *Liverpool Albion*, 19th February 1855.

49 For the official list of all those arrested, with names and nationalities see *S.C. on Poor Removal* (1854), appendix 1. Letter from Campbell to chairman of S.C., written on 15th March 1855. He gave statistics of arrests during the rioting, to support his contention made to the committee in 1854, that the Irish were a burden on Liverpool.

50 *Tablet*, 24th February 1855.

51 *Liverpool Courier*, 14th February 1855.

52 *Liverpool Mercury*, 14th, 16th and 20th June 1859.

53 Dr Goss, Catholic Bishop of Liverpool, thanked the police for their efforts to protect St Oswald's and appealed to Catholics to avoid provocation from Protestants; *Liverpool Albion*, 20th June 1859.

54 *Liverpool Mercury*, 16th June 1859.

55 *Liverpool Mercury*, 21st June 1859.

56 *Liverpool Mercury*, 30th June 1859.

57 *Liverpool Mercury*, 2nd August 1859.

58 *Liverpool Mercury*, 29th January 1859.

59 J. T. Ward, 'Squire Auty (1812-1879)', *Bradford Antiquary*, New Series, Part XLII (November 1964), pp, 103-123. This article contains little information on Auty's activities as an Orangeman.

60 *Liverpool Standard*, 6th February 1844. Councillors James Parker and Henry G. Harboard were also present at this meeting.

61 A complete collection of the editions of this journal is deposited at Bradford City Library, Local History Section.

62 *Orange and Blue Banner*, No. 9 (September 1851), p. 179.

63 *Orange and Blue Banner*, No. 12 (December 1851), p. 249.

64 Ibid.

65 Ibid.

66 *Orange and Protestant Banner*, Vol. 2 (January 1853), pp. 187-90; in this article Auty reviews the claims of the Institution to be the 'true' Order. He described the *Shropshire Conservative* as the organ of the Liverpool Party.

67 *Liverpool Courier*, 18th July 1855, 'Twelfth of July in Liverpool'; *Orange and Protestant Banner*, Vol. III (August 1855), p. 169. For a further reference to the Shrewsbury Orangemen see *Orange and Protestant Banner*, Vol. III (August 1855), pp. 207-9.

68   *Liverpool Herald* 18th July 1857.

69   *Orange and Protestant Banner,* Vol. II (January 1853-December 1854), p. 188.

70   *Liverpool Herald* 8th November 1856.

71   *Orange and Protestant Banner,* Vol. VI (June 1861), pp. 145-47.

72   Op. cit. p. 107.

73   P.R.O. HO 45/5128U. Samuel Holmes, mayor, to Home Office. Holmes sent a copy of the Head Constable's report on the day's events. See also *Liverpool Mercury,* 15th July 1853. The lodges attempting the illegal procession belonged to the Association.

74   *Liverpool Herald,* 18th July 1857.

75   *Orange and Protestant Banner,* Vol. III (March 1856), pp. 321-2.

76   In fact at an Orange Institution lodge meeting in January 1859 he was described as Captain De Bentley. See *Liverpool Herald,* 15th January 1859. In February 1859 an Orangeman wrote to the *Liverpool Herald,* referring to differences of opinion among members of the Institution as to whether or not De Bentley had ever had a commission. The writer offered £5 to anyone who could produce evidence that he had. *Liverpool Herald,* 19th February 1859; the *Liverpool Mail,* though still Tory in politics and anti-Catholic in outlook, was by now anti-Orange. On 19th March 1859 it carried a long article attacking the social standing of 'these sham Grands' and analysing De Bentley's pretensions in some detail.

77   *Orange and Blue Banner,* Vol. III (March 1851), p. 41-2. Fenton was addressing a meeting of Wigan Orangemen on 17th March 1851. During his speech he claimed he would have been a bishop but for the animosity shown towards Orangemen.

78   *Orange and Protestant Banner,* Vol. VI (June 1861), p. 146.

79   In February 1856 an Orangeman from Barnsley wrote to the *Orange and Protestant Banner,* claiming he had not received help from Liverpool Orangemen when down on his luck in Liverpool. This triggered off a correspondence. In particular see *Orange and Protestant Banner,* Vol. III (March 1856), pp. 320-1. At the annual general meeting of the Orange Association to be held at Stockport in July 1857, a scheme of Life Assurance for members, was to be discussed. See *Liverpool Standard,* 20th June 1857.

80   *Liverpool Chronicle,* 15th July 1854. The Chronicle claimed there were between eight and ten bands of music.

81   *Liverpool Herald,* 16th July 1859.

82   *Liverpool Herald,* 14th July 1860. This contains a list of all the names of those attending. The non-Liverpool attenders were from the Isle of Man, Bacup and Whitehaven.

Chapter VII **Mounting pressure:**
Home Rule,
Irish nationalism
and Ritualism

I

Despite their distaste for Orangeism, the Liverpool Tories needed the Orange vote more than ever following the municipal elections of 1858. For the first time since the 1835 elections, Liberal councillors were in a majority, numbering twenty-six as against twenty-two Tories, although the Conservatives retained overall control because of their aldermen, fifteen as opposed to one Liberal.[1] This dramatic decline in Tory support at the polls had more to do with the warehouse and water controversies than any upsurge in Liberal sentiments. However, by 1860 the Liberals had developed a more effective leadership consisting of J. R. Jeffrey, elected in the Lime Street ward in 1856, Robertson Gladstone, the ex-Tory, William Rathbone and Joseph Robinson, a group sneeringly referred to as the 'Board of Directors' by the *Liverpool Herald*.[2] Throughout the 1860s a better organised and better led radical party forced the Tories to fight hard to retain control over municipal affairs. At the same time there was a discernible drop in the quantity and decibels of the clerical No Popery haranguings. McNeile, though still a popular preacher and Protestant figurehead, was a fading force, seemingly having lost some of his appetite for controversy. He was soon to be offered the deanship of Ripon cathedral, far removed from the turbulence of Liverpool life.[3] Politically he was also a has-been, as memories of the Corporation School campaign faded and new men came to the fore in the Conservative Party. In the 1860s the most important of these was Edward Whitely.

These changes did not however, result in any lowering of sectarian passions, and even among the non-Orange Protestant middle class there remained a widespread antipathy to Irish Catholics. However, it was working-class insecurities which were assiduously fanned by Orange leaders, in particular by Ouseley, in the pages of the *Herald*. Typical was a long article on 7th November 1857, in which it was claimed that the number of Catholics working in the docks equalled the number of Protestants and that the 'Irish sepoys' were employed on better terms while Protestants were discriminated against. The growing confidence of the Catholic community was itself a promise of conflict. It had still not achieved political power anywhere near commensurate with its numbers, and in the fight to advance its claims to a say in local affairs, particularly as they affected Catholics, it was met with an undiminished degree of hostility. In 1853 David Powell, a Catholic corn merchant, challenged William Nicholson, a Tory, in the Vauxhall ward municipal election and lost by only fifteen votes.[4] In 1857 J. C. Corbally, a Catholic, won the seat in Vauxhall, beating the Tory by fifty-six votes in a low turn-out. The Liberals assiduously courted the Catholic vote but the increasingly tactical nature of Catholic voting was revealed during the same elections in the Scotland ward, where Fr Newsham urged Catholics to vote for James Crellin, the Tory candidate, against William Liversedge, the Liberal. Newsham's motive was the view that Crellin had been supportive of Catholics in the Select Vestry controversy over the education of children in the Industrial Schools.[5] As Crellin won by five votes, the power of the relatively small Catholic electorate was obvious. By 1863 there were three Catholic councillors, Michael Whitty, the former Head Constable, J. V. Yates and Richard Sheil, and as this trio, aided by the Liberals, spearheaded the campaign for Catholic rights they met ubiquitous opposition. All departments of local administration became a battleground in the religious conflict. For example, in January 1859, at a meeting of the Toxteth Park guardians called to appoint a relieving officer, a member of the committee accused an applicant of being an Orangeman. This provoked a bitter row as to whether an applicant need reveal whether or not he was an Orangeman.[6] At the same time the Workhouse Committee became involved in a dispute concerning a female Roman Catholic visitor to Catholic pauper children. She was accused of trying to convert a Protestant girl by telling her she was damned for changing her religion.[7] In this, as in all such disputes, the arguments only served to remind Catholics that they were tolerated, not accepted.

Catholics were concerned not only with securing council seats but with securing admission to any municipal or parish office which offered the opportunity of furthering Catholic interests. The Select Vestry was the Liverpool equivalent of the Poor Law Guardians, and because a large proportion of the inmates of the Industrial Schools and the borough workhouse were Catholic, vestry seats were important to Catholics. Whitty had been a member of the Select Vestry since 1852 when, in 1862, he clashed with other members over a request for the provision of a priest to minister to the needs of Catholic children at the Kirkdale Industrial School. Of the

795 children 451 were Catholics, and all of the pupils were the children of prostitutes and criminals. Whitty wanted a priest to give the Catholic children religious instruction, but the request was thrown out on the grounds that the vestry did not have the authority to pay for one.[8] This kind of opposition embittered Catholics, who interpreted it as anti-Catholic bigotry rather than administrative red tape. In 1863 the Liberals held the same number of council seats as the Conservatives, twenty-four, and during the 1863/64 council session Father James Nugent was appointed Catholic chaplain at the borough gaol, a move seen by the hard-line Protestants as a further concession to Popery.[9] The award of a grant of £1,500 towards the fitting out of a ship as a Catholic reformatory also angered Protestants.[10] During this session of the council a motion was proposed, inviting Garibaldi to visit Liverpool. The three Catholic councillors, Whitty, Yates and Shiel, stood up and opposed the motion on the grounds that any such invitation would be an insult to Catholics.[11]

This evidence of Catholic muscle-flexing was intolerable not only to Orangemen but to a wide spectrum of Protestant opinion, and such incidents increased in number. In March 1864 a tremendous row broke out over allegations concerning Fr Wilson, a young priest who visited Catholic paupers in the workhouse. A Protestant woman was dying and asked for a priest in order to be received into the Catholic Church. This was a very sensitive issue, as Protestant critics of the Catholic clergy were ever vigilant for evidence of Catholic proselytising. The nurse consulted a doctor and Fr Wilson was sent for; the woman became a Catholic, dying soon afterwards. The Select Vestry, with the exception of Whitty and four others, were furious and the nurse was sacked on the ground that she should have sent for the governor of the workhouse. Subsequently the Vestry criticised Fr Wilson and threatened to bar him from visiting Catholic paupers.[12] The Catholic grievance, other than the imputations of improper behaviour on the part of Fr Wilson, was that Anglican clergy who visited the workhouse were paid by ratepayers, including Catholics, but the Catholic clergy received nothing while undertaking the same duties. Whitty argued, to no avail, for all clergymen to be paid for administering to the paupers. In 1865 John Laird, the Birkenhead shipbuilder and M.P., financed the purchase of a site for a new hospital. On the management committee no Roman Catholics were elected and Fr Brundrit, the parish priest, told Catholics not to vote for Laird.[13]

There is a temptation to assume that such rows were pinpricks, of no significance in explaining sectarian violence. This would be wrong. To the sincere Protestant, Roman Catholicism was evil, and it was immoral to support the system in any way, while to the Roman Catholic exclusion from the benefits of civil administration were a manifestation of bigotry and anti-Irish feeling. This struggle for a share in municipal power was as bitter as the struggle for parliamentary representation. For example, in April 1868 Catholics in Liverpool, supported by the Liberals, mounted a sustained campaign to secure the election of a Mr Martin, a Catholic, to the Select Vestry. His opponent, supported by the Orange lodges, was Mr Ball. At the time, of twenty-eight Vestry members, only one, Michael Whitty, was a Catholic. On 27th April Martin was declared the winner, and several streets in the North End were decorated in green as several thousand Irish Catholics celebrated. An effigy of Ball was burned in the street, and when the police moved in to restore order, inevitably, they were attacked.[14] This particular event raised sectarian passions in the North End. On 9th May an argument started outside a public house over religion and a Catholic killed a Protestant in the ensuing fight.[15] At the same time a man appeared in court charged with cutting off his father-in-law's nose after an argument in which the Catholic father-in-law called his Protestant son-in-law an Orange dog.[16]

To some extent, such incidents reflected the general level of anti-Irish/anti-Catholic feeling in the country at large throughout the 1860s, erupting in frequent outbreaks of inter-communal violence. In 1859 Baron de Camin, a noted anti-Catholic lecturer, gave some lectures in Wigan which resulted in serious disturbances during which Irish homes were attacked and damaged.[17] In October 1862 the Birkenhead Irish were involved in even more serious rioting following the publication of notices advertising a meeting of a debating society to discuss Garibaldi and his campaign in Italy. The Birkenhead riots followed disturbances in London over the same issue and needed a considerable force, including Liverpool police, soldiers and special constables, to restore order. The sentences on the Irish rioters who were subsequently charged, including transportation, angered Irish Catholics throughout the country.[18] In December 1862 the death of an Englishman following a fracas with an Irishman triggered off disturbances in Chesterfield in which Irish homes were attacked and Irish workers chased out of the local ironworks.[19]

A more potent source of anti-Irish feeling was the shooting of Sergeant Brett, a Manchester policeman, in September 1867, during an attempt by Irish Republicans to rescue some of their comrades being taken to court in a police van.[20] The Irish Republican Brotherhood was formed in 1858, to organise an armed struggle against British rule in Ireland, and contained within its ranks many Irish Americans. In the 1860s the activities of the Irish Republicans were a matter of some concern in Liverpool, Manchester and London, with their large Irish populations. Major Grieg was successful in smashing the Fenian organisation in Liverpool using the well established method of paid informers.

The rumours concerning Fenian activities in Liverpool confirmed Orange beliefs about the inherent disloyalty of Irish Catholics, despite the efforts of Whitty, Shiel and Yates to distance Catholics from any association or sympathy with treasonable activities. In February 1867 a Fenian attack on Chester Castle was planned, but frustrated by the efforts of Corydon, the informer.[21] However, the very fact of an attempt on an arsenal inflamed Orange tempers and scared the authorities. To the Orangemen it justified everything they had stood for, the need to defend the nation against Irish rebels, a far cry from Fletcher's desire to defend the country against trade unionists. In September 1867 Sergeant Brett was killed in Manchester when an attempt was made to rescue Colonel Thomas J. Kelly and Captain Timothy Deasy, Irish Americans and members of the I.R.B. Five Irishmen were arrested and, after an emotional trial, were found guilty of murder. Following appeals, three men, Allen, O'Brien and Larkin, were hanged on 23rd November 1867 - the 'Manchester Martyrs'. The hangings caused great anger and bitterness among the Irish in Britain, and in many towns funeral processions were planned.[22]

In Liverpool it was known by 9th December that a Fenian procession was planned, and on 10th December leaders of the Orange lodges went to see the mayor, Edward Whitely, a Conservative and Orange sympathiser. The Orangemen told Whitely that if a funeral procession took place they would hold a counter-demonstration.[23] Clearly, in these circumstances, the authorities would be faced with the probability of serious rioting. Whitely told the Home Secretary, 'Liverpool is a very exceptional place owing to the Orange element prevailing to a large extent.'[24] The Catholic clergy held a meeting, dissociating Catholics from the murder of Sergeant Brett, and Bishop Goss signed a proclamation asking Catholics to avoid any processions. The joint appeal of magistrates and clergy seemed to work, because on 13th December a notice appeared in the local press calling the procession off. What particularly infuriated the Liberals was that a deputation from the Conservative Working Men's Association visited the mayor to thank him and the magistrates for securing the safety of the town and were followed by a delegation from the Loyal Orange Institution, which also thanked the magistrates and the Chief Constable. In return, Edward Whitely *thanked* the Orangemen profusely.[25]

What the Orangemen had done was call off a counter-demonstration that would have inevitably led to riots. They could have safely left the threat of an Irish procession to the police and troops, and their threatened counter-demonstration was mischievous. This fulsome praise from Whitely angered Catholics and Liberals. In a flood of euphoria the Orange leaders issued a press release, inviting people to join a vigilante force.[26]

The *Porcupine* launched a vitriolic attack on the Orangemen, accusing them of lacking any political ideas at all and of having only one concern, to attack Irishmen, a view shared by most Liberals and Catholics.[27] However, the Orange psyche needed such a crisis situation. The Order had been founded to defend Ireland against rebels. The English Orangemen, inheriting the same rhetoric, historic lessons and imagery, had no such organised physical threat to face up to them. Their enemy had been the Roman 'conspiracy', which did not offer many tangible opportunities for physical combat. The 1848 scare over Chartists and the Confederates had been a damp squib. The Fenians, however, were a foe worthy of Orange steel, and in their mind it justified the existence of the Orange Institution. The events certainly hardened attitudes on both sides. The Tory *Liverpool Courier* published a letter on 10th December 1867, from a cotton porter, referring to Irish Catholics:

> They come here to seek employment, and by their competing with their English fellow labourers, tend materially to reduce the daily chance of obtaining work. The cry of 'Ireland for the Irish' is to them familiar. Let them beware of arousing a counter cry of 'England for the English' from the English working men and labourers and being met, as was once the case, with the notice 'No Irish need apply'.

It is certain that the Fenian scare contributed to the outbursts of anti-Irish feeling in May the following year, when there was serious rioting at Ashton under Lyne, with less serious disturbances in Oldham, Manchester and Preston following anti-Catholic lectures by William Murphy.[28]

II

While Liverpool's Catholics were fighting to extend their political influence, changes were also taking place within both the local Conservative Party and the Orange Order. On 3rd January 1848 the Tories had abandoned the old *Conservative Association*, the central Tory body in the town, and adopted a new set of rules under the title of the *Liverpool Constitutional Association*. Henry Buckmaster was appointed as a paid, full-time secretary. More significant was one of the passages in the new regulations, enunciating the new principles:

> To vindicate the principles of the British Constitution, as generally held by William Pitt and George Canning, securing for commerce, agriculture, manufacturers, shipping and railways, due encouragement, thereby procuring for the artisan, the peasant, the operative and the merchant seaman, that fair reward for his labour which Englishmen have been used to enjoy.

Later in the document a statement referred to defending the Church and its 'rights and liberties'.[29] Thus the new Tory party was out to secure the allegiance of the working class. In the manner of most human endeavours the renewed enthusiasm seems to have been short-lived. For in May 1859 the Conservatives in the Everton and Kirkdale ward were complaining of the lack of organisation and apathy. They set up a ward *Conservative Association,* aimed at encouraging voter registration and improving organisation-in effect, replicating the work of the Protestant Association in the 1840s.[30]

Quite apart from the problem of apathy, the Conservative leaders also had a dilemma in their pursuit of the Orange vote. Though respectable Orangemen consistently argued that they held no enmity towards individual Roman Catholics, they had little control over their wilder members and none at all over non-members who were Orange 'sympathisers', particularly on 12th July. Typical of the spontaneous eruptions of violence was the riot in St Helens on 12th July 1867.[31] Three train-loads of Liverpool Orangemen went to St Helens to hold a procession with the St Helens lodges. Large numbers of Irish attacked the parade, and it was only with considerable difficulty that the police restored order. On the way back to Liverpool the trains stopped at Widnes and the Orangemen waved their flags out of the carriage windows and sang party songs. Some Irish gathered and jeered the Liverpool men, one of whom produced a pistol and shot an Irishwoman. Commenting on the affair, the Tory *Liverpool Mail* accused the Liverpool Orangemen of being more blood-thirsty than their Irish counterparts.[32] It was no part of Conservative strategy to be associated with street disorders, so the Tories needed to distance themselves from Orangeism without losing the support of Orangemen. A further difficulty was that most Orangemen regarded themselves as Protestant first and Conservative second, and successive Tory administrations had offended ultra-Protestants by their lack of zeal in pursuing 'sound Protestant' policies. Maynooth still received government money and concessions were still made to Catholics, and in addition the more reflective Orangemen realised the middle-class Conservatives despised Orangeism. Orange mistrust of the Conservatives was clearly articulated by the *Liverpool Herald* on 15th December 1865 when it argued, with reference to Protestant interests:

> Mere party associations of Conservatives, or tories, cannot be depended upon with such unbounded confidence, as men who act under a religious obliga-tion ... There is a higher and nobler aim in the Orange Institution than sup-porting a mere section for political purposes and the great men of old England have only to inform themselves of the real nature of the Orange Order, to at once acknowledge its superiority to all other institutions.

Clearly, no political party could commit itself to a programme in which the Church and Constitution were the issues to determine all policies.

In an effort to separate itself from the Orange Order and yet secure Orange votes, the *Liverpool Working Men's Conservative Association* was formed in 1867. Exclusively Protestant, it was an integral part of the Tory machine, and by 1872 it had twelve branches in the town, with a membership that included many Orangemen. The L.W.M.C.A. branches were represented on all committees of the Constitutional Association and became the medium through which Edward Whitely and later, and more importantly, A. B. Forwood and Archibald Salvidge pioneered a Tory working-class 'democracy'. This process has been brilliantly described and analysed by Waller.[33] Forwood became the leader of the Liverpool Tories in 1880 when Whitely entered Parliament, and he continued Whitely's policy of wooing the Protestant working class by flattery. As Waller points out, 'The skilled seducers of the uneducated were not radicals or politically conscious working men-mahdis in clogs - but the traditional ruling class, to whom they habitually deferred in matters of state.'[34] However, despite the success of the L.W.M.C.A. in capturing working-class votes, the Orange Order still needed to be courted, if for no other reason than that during the last quarter of the nineteenth century the Liverpool Orangemen increased in numbers.

III

Throughout the 1860s the squabbles between the Institution and the Association had continued, and as a whole the Orange Order failed to attract any political figures of standing. The only one of any consequence who associated himself in Parliament with the Orangemen was George Hammond Whalley.[35] The speeches of the 12th July rallies are a good indicator of Orange concerns at the time. In 1862 Maynooth and grants to Catholics were still the main topic, together with an attack on Pope Hennessy's Bill to introduce paid Catholic chaplains in prisons. Tractarians also came in for criticism as part of an attack on the Roman conspiracy. In 1864 the speeches on 12th July attacked those who were trying to disestablish the Church of Ireland. In 1868 the speeches were again hostile to Tractarianism and the use of State funds to assist Roman Catholic Institutions. A call was made not to vote for anyone who would not pledge himself to 'maintain the Church of England and the Church of Ireland' nor oppose grants to the Roman Catholic Church. A Liverpool Orangeman, R. Louis Cloquet, proposed that Lord Sandon and W. S. Graves, Liverpool members of Parliament, should be written to, to establish whether they were prepared to vote against any further concessions to Rome and to oppose any attacks on the Church of Ireland.[36] These preoccupations on the part of the Orange leaders illustrate the minefield trodden by Liverpool politicians when pronouncing on matters of national concern.

The scope for political banana skins was infinite, any policy statement that involved the Church or the establishment could be an own-goal. National education, temperance, Ireland, even foreign policy (Garibaldi, the Eastern question), all needed thoughtful comment.

This became more the case after 1876 when the Orange Institution and the Association finally amalgamated. On Tuesday 4th of July a meeting took place at the Cannon Street Hotel, London, between delegates from both the Orange Institution and the Association. The result was a union of the two bodies, to be called the Loyal Orange Institution of England. The existing Grand Masters were Edward Harper of the Orange Institution and Booth Mason from Ashton under Lyne, representing the Association. Also present at this meeting was the Earl of Inniskillen, 'Grand Master of the Imperial Grand Orange Council of the Universe'. New rules were drawn up and it was agreed that existing warrants were to be exchanged for new ones issued by the new body. Lord Arthur Hill Trevor, M.P., was to be the Grand Master of the new English body but no other person of standing was present, except Inniskillen.[37] In November a Grand Lodge meeting of the new body took place in Liverpool for the first time, chaired by Trevor, and new rules were approved. Significantly, Whitely and Forwood both attended, and Forwood told the Orangemen that he saw before him a body of hard workers for the Conservative cause, to whom the town 'owed very much for Liverpool's proud position in Conservatism'. He adroitly attacked the Liberals for supporting Home Rule.[38]

The increased strength of the Orange Order was dramatically illustrated on the occasion of the 12th July celebration in 1876. The new Institution held the parade in Liverpool, marching from the borough boundary to Lord Derby's estate at Knowsley. The number of lodges on parade was estimated to be 160, consisting of 7,000 to 8,000 Orangemen, accompanied by a crowd of 'supporters' said to be between 60,000 and 80,000.[39] This was the biggest Orange turn-out in English history, and was a demonstration of voting power which no local politician could ignore. However, during the speeches from the platform at Knowsley, George Ferguson, an Orangeman, criticised those public men who 'only courted Orangemen at election time'.[40] The increase in numbers was no temporary phenomenon. It is possible to obtain a much clearer picture of Liverpool Orangeism in 1885. In that year the Loyal Orange Institution published a 'handy guide' to the lodges of the Liverpool province, which was divided into fourteen districts, of which eight were in Liverpool and one each in Wallasey, Birkenhead, St Helens, Southport, Ashton in Makerfield and Warrington.[41] Within this organisational structure there were seventy-eight lodges in Liverpool, three in Wallasey, five in Birkenhead, three in

Southport, five in Warrington, four in St Helens and five in Ashton making a total of 103 lodges. If it is assumed the average lodge membership was 100, there were nearly 8,000 lodge members in Liverpool alone. Because the guide lists the names and addresses of the officials, provincial, district and lodges, it is possible to identify their occupations in many cases, using the Liverpool directories. Of the eighty-seven officials listed, it has proved possible to trace fifty-six, and the results confirm unambiguously the previous generalisations that the membership was almost entirely working-class. In 1885 the Provincial Grand Master was J. W. Ballard, who made iron and tin trunks. John Lang, the Provincial Grand Treasurer, was a poor-law relieving officer and Harry Thomas, Provincial Grand Secretary, was a plumber. Thomas was soon to become Provincial Grand Master. Of the remaining district and lodge masters, the men were drawn almost exclusively from the ranks of tradesmen, including plasterers, shipwrights, plumbers, joiners, boilermakers, porters etc. (see Appendix 5). These were the men, many newly enfranchised in 1867, with whom the Tory power brokers had to do business.

Any explanation of the increased strength of Liverpool Orangeism must look beyond the obvious attractions of social activities, benefit and burial clubs, quasi-religious ceremonies and Tory flattery. These activities alone are not sufficient to account for the revival. What gave Liverpool Orangemen a *raison d'être* absent in Bradford, Dewsbury, Barnsley, Oldham and other towns where Orange lodges existed, was the baleful shadow of Ireland, which always lay across Liverpool. The Irish Orange Order came into being as a result of a perceived and real threat to Protestants. The Liverpool Orangemen shared to some extent that sense of threat, if only vicariously, or at least had an understanding of the feelings and emotions of Irish Protestants. By 1871 the Irishborn population of Liverpool had fallen to 76,761, but this was still more than twice the combined Irish populations of Manchester and Salford. Also, the *Liverpool Irish* population was much bigger, and increasing, and this large ethnic group identified strongly with Ireland. In November 1875 Lawrence Connelly won a seat on the council, campaigning on an Irish ticket. Following the 1877 municipal elections, there were five Irish nationalist councillors. In 1879 Parnell addressed a nationalist meeting in Liverpool attended by an estimated 20,000. In 1885 T. P. O'Connor was elected M.P. for the Scotland division, the only election of an Irish nationalist in a seat outside Ireland. By 1890 there were reputed to be seventeen branches of the Irish Nationalist Connection in Liverpool, with 10,000 members.[42] Faced with a huge Irish Catholic population and an active and high-profile nationalist political movement, Liverpool Orangemen felt some of the pressures endured by their Irish brethren. The Fenian activities in Liverpool during the 1860s strengthened this Anglo-Irish solidarity, as did an abortive attempt to blow up the town hall in 1883. For this James McGrath was sentenced to penal servitude for life and James McKevitt received fifteen years.[43]

The passing of a Bill in 1869, disestablishing the Church of Ireland, had been a particularly bitter pill for Orangemen to swallow. If the Church of Ireland was disestablished, why not the Church of England? The affair increased Orange detestation of Liberals in general, and Gladstone in particular, an enmity nurtured from 1880 onwards by the Home Rule campaign and exacerbated by the activities of Irish nationalists in Liverpool. The by-election of 1880 demonstrated the need for Tory nursing of the Orange vote. Lord Ramsay was the Liberal candidate, opposed by Edward Whitely. The campaign centred on Home Rule and there were probably 10,000 Irish votes in Liverpool. Whitely won in an 80% turn-out but his majority was only 2,221.[44]

The Home Rule election campaign of 1886 brought tempers to the surface and demonstrated the impossibility of Orange and Tory politicians controlling events on the streets. Months before the July 1886 election, the Nelson True Blues drum-and-flute band was parading the streets when it stopped outside a public house and went in for a drink. A fight started, and when the police arrived they received a beating from the bandsmen and a hostile crowd.[45] On Friday 2nd July, at the end of polling in the election, an Orange band marched from Toxteth to Lime Street, accompanied by a large crowd, for no apparent reason. In Lime Street the police turned it back, and in Toxteth a police squad lined up to stop the by now large parade, from passing St Patrick's church. They failed and the church was stoned with many windows broken. Irish retaliation was swift, and Protestant churches in Toxteth received similar treatment. On Saturday and Sunday 3rd and 4th July, Protestant and Catholic mobs fought in the streets of Toxteth; on the Saturday eighty persons were treated at the Southern Infirmary for injuries.[46] On Monday 5th July, in Catholic Addison Street, Catholics and Orangemen fought a pitched battle, men climbing on the roofs to throw slates.[47] At the same time, also in the North End, the inhabitants of Bostock Street (Orange) fought with persons from the neighbouring (Catholic) Kew Street. Again men took to the roofs for ammunition.[48] While this battle was in progress a Protestant mob attacked four Catholic houses in Downe Street, battering doors down and throwing furniture into the streets. At No. 21 the man of the house hid in the cellar, as it was assumed the gang were after him. Instead they beat up his wife. It was alleged the men were shouting, 'If you want Home Rule, we'll give it to you.' There was no evidence given subsequently in court that they were Orangemen, but they used Orange slogans.[49] In the

South End an old woman led an estimated 150 men and boys from Catholic Norfolk Street to stone the Anglican school in St James's Place while three Irishmen broke into the workshop of an Orange shoemaker and stabbed him.[50] The general air of excitement in working-class areas continued because of the forthcoming 12th July. Catholics in the North End burned effigies of William and Mary and in Blenheim Street a clash occurred between Orangemen and Catholics.[51] The continual parading of Orange drums and fifes made it difficult to restore order.

In the council chamber Dr Commins, an Irish nationalist, complained that the police were not doing enough to stamp out street disorder, but Nott-Bower, the Chief Constable, was facing an almost impossible situation. Violence could break out anywhere, and he told the council he would need 200 extra men to guarantee no trouble. With regard to Orange bands, he claimed he had no legal powers to ban them.[52] The middle-class council members lived away from the innercity streets and regarded the disturbances as a nuisance rather than a problem to be tackled with urgency. Toxteth Orangemen held a meeting on 8th July to discuss street disorders. It was denied that Orange bands were responsible for triggering off the disorder and suggested that, if the police could not maintain order, then Orangemen should form a vigilante group and 'put down all lawlessness'.[53] Thus by 1885 working-class Liverpool was more divided than in the 1840s, when McNeile was at the height of his popularity. Nott-Bower wrote of this time in Liverpool:

> Liverpool was peculiarly situated as regards the Irish question. A large district of the town was quite as Irish as any district in Dublin and 'Nationalists' and 'Orangemen' were as strongly represented and as antagonistic as in Belfast.[54]

The striking feature of the period is that there was no Orange or Protestant leader of stature to impose discipline and order on the streets, in particular to control the activities of Orange bands. The Catholic hierarchy in Liverpool had tried to stop Catholics indulging in street warfare by means of pastoral letters, although not even Catholic priests could always countermand the influence of hot summer days, boredom and drink.[55]

IV

In July 1886 a drunken labourer broke up a procession at St John's church shouting 'No Popery, I'll have none of it.'[56] It is unlikely that his action was a considered response to the apparent impotence of Anglican bishops to discipline Ritualist priests, but the impotence was real enough. By 1850 the actions of Ritualist clergy were becoming a disruptive element in the life of the Church. A major problem facing the bishops was that the beliefs of the Church are contained in the thirty-nine articles while the ceremonies and rites are laid down in the Prayer Book rubrics. In both cases the wording is sufficiently vague to allow many interpretations of what is acceptable. This was the core of the dispute between Ritualists and Evangelicals.[57]

In 1859 the Ritualist church of St George in the East was attacked several times by mobs incensed by relatively mild ceremonial innovations.[58] Roman Catholics observed the increasingly physical opposition to Ritualism and the *Tablet* had no illusions about its significance. In a leader on 1st October 1859 it declared:

> Excessive ritualism is but another name for the Catholic religion, and the Catholic religion is that which this mob undertakes to fight against . . . the real object aimed at is the Catholic Church. The old instinct lives on in the people and if their suborners thought it worthwhile, they would get up a No Popery cry and revive the ancient savage laws. At present they are training their troops and for that purpose they have set up excessive ritualism as a target for the musketry.

This was an accurate forecast of events to take place in Liverpool nearly fifty years later. A feature of this phase of Ritualism in the Church of England was that it attracted a large number of well-to-do and aristocratic adherents, imparting a class dimension to the conflict. The class overtones in the religious dispute were constantly surfacing. The *Liverpool Mail* of 31st July 1869 gave an account of a meeting of the Everton C.W.M.A. The speakers attacked some lords over their behaviour regarding the Irish Church Bill:

> It was very evident that they could not trust the sacred interests of Protestantism to the Lords, aristocracy or the upper middle class. They must depend on the conservative working men of England for the maintenance of the glorious constitution of the church and state.

This class dimension was emphasised because of the fact that Ritualist churches, particularly in London, attracted large numbers of young men, and this factor, together with the setting up of monastic-type establishments, brought forth the accusation that Tractarians were effeminate, if not homosexual.[59] Characteristic of such insinuations was the article in the *Liverpool Herald* of 15th December 1855, which attacked the Ritualist practice of believing that the bread used at communion became the actual body of Christ and so was broken:

> What sane man could for a moment conceive such a blasphemy as that of giving man the power to break his Creator? Yet such is the means resorted to by professed ministers of the Church of England; nice young men from Oxford, with their womanish soft speech and grave assumption of piety, creeping amongst our homes with feline gentleness and insinuating their Popish poison with all the craft of accomplished Jesuits.

The rapid spread of Ritualism after 1850 resulted in the warring factions each forming its own pressure group to further its cause. In 1850 Ritualist clergy in Liverpool had formed an English Church Union branch, to protect their interests, particularly in organising the defence of priests brought before the ecclesiastical courts on charges concerning Church discipline.[60] In 1865 the Evangelicals formed the Church Association, with the object of bringing prosecutions against Ritualists and providing the finance to do so. In 1867 this alarming state of affairs resulted in a Royal Commission being set up to examine the state of Church law and to see if any changes were needed. The 'Ritual' Commission was thought necessary because the challenge to both ecclesiastical and State authority by the Ritualists was causing great concern inside and outside the Church of England. The commission was chaired by the Archbishop of Canterbury, and by 1870 it had produced four reports. These contained no recommendations for changes in the law and an important conclusion that the Ornaments Rubric in the Prayer Book should not be altered. The work of the commission had one significant consequence in that it increased the level of public awareness of the conflict in the national Church.[61] Meanwhile the Church Association began its policy of instituting proceedings against prominent Ritualist clergy who simply ignored the decisions of the courts. Victorian public opinion was, on the one hand, scandalised at the contempt shown to the courts by the dissentient priests but, on the other, it was troubled at the attempts to enforce belief by law. There was something distasteful in hounding clerics who in most cases were well liked and devoted priests. Moreover it saw the clash leading to the breakup of the 'consensus' religion which was a unique characteristic of the Church of England. If either of the protagonists, Ritualists or Evangelicals, left the Church of England that would further reduce its claim to be the *national* Church and lead Parliament to look more closely at the question of disestablishment. The mass of practising Anglicans, who were suspicious of both parties, were emotionally committed to the idea of an Established Church and so wanted an end of the conflict. The bishops found recourse to the courts distasteful but their efforts at persuading Ritualists to modify their behaviour were largely ignored. To many observers the Ritualist clergy seemed to welcome martyrdom.

In Liverpool the process of stirring up local feeling against Ritualism had begun in 1850 with McNeile but in 1867 the campaign began in earnest. On 7th July the Church of England Working Men's Society held a meeting at Birkenhead to protest against Ritualism and express support for Lord Shaftesbury's Clerical Vestment Bill.[62] The notorious William Murphy was to visit Birkenhead to give one of his anti-Catholic lectures and threats had been made to kill him. The anti-Ritualist meeting, on being told this, burst into song:

> And shall this Murphy die?
> And must this Murphy die?
> Then thirty thousand Liverpool boys
> Will know the reason why.

Later the same week the Liverpool Working Men's Church Association held an anti-Ritualist meeting at which it was alleged that the career of Hugh McNeile had suffered because of his stand against Romanism.[63] Confrontation commenced in July 1869 when St Margaret's, in Toxteth, was consecrated. In the week following the consecration a number of services were held that were blatantly Ritualistic, and among the visiting priests were a number of prominent Ritualists including Fathers MacKonochie and Lord F. G. Godolphin-Osborne. During these services, mobs gathered outside the church, abusing the congregation as they arrived. Some Orangemen got inside and on several occasions tried to rush the clergymen, who were saved from assault by a strong police presence, while in the struggles with the mob outside one policeman received head injuries.[64] A leader of one of the mobs was arrested, charged and found guilty of 'brawling in church' for which the magistrates imposed a 20s fine. Local opinion was antagonised when the Rev. Lord Godolphin-Osborne wrote to the local press complaining at the smallness of the fine and criticising the magistrates. This drew an angry response from the *Porcupine,* which declared:

> Surely a nobleman and a gentleman, not to speak of a christian minister, would be satisfied with this punishment of an excited, ignorant man, who doubtless believes (as thousands of sincere, well educated people do) that ultra ritualism closely approximates to Popery, and that clergymen ought to set an example in obeying - not defying-the laws of the land.[65]

Porcupine was simply reiterating the constantly expressed criticism of many citizens, even the religiously uncommitted, that the Ritualists were bringing the law into disrepute. The *Liverpool Mail,* with its long-established Tractarian sympathies, was even more concerned at the importation of a new source of religious violence:

> Is Liverpool to become a second Belfast? Are such low and brutalised localities as Sandy Row and Pound Street to be, in a figure, transferred to the respectably conducted suburbs of our Princess Park Road? . . . These roughs and monsters and cowards, who molest ladies and clergymen dare not molest Roman Catholic worshippers; they know full well that the Irish navvies would retaliate terribly.[66]

Liverpool had long possessed many features of Belfast life. What was upsetting the *Mail* was the fact that such behaviour had intruded upon the quiet streets of middle-class Liverpool.

In the country at large the behaviour of MacKonochie, Purchas and others increased the pressure within the Church of England to strengthen the hand of the bishops in dealing with recalcitrant clergy. In May 1873 the Church Association presented the two archbishops with a petition signed by 60,000 laymen, protesting against 'Romish' practices in the Church of England and appealing to the archbishops to refuse to ordain, license or present to benefices any clergymen who espoused Ritualist practices. In the same month 483 Ritualist clergymen petitioned the Convocation of the Church of England, asking for approval of the training of confessors. It is difficult to think of an issue that would infuriate Evangelicals more. Auricular confession was in their eyes the most odious of Ritualist practices, giving the priest access to the innermost thoughts of their womenfolk.[67] In the heat of the conflict both Evangelical and Ritualists adopted unreasoning attitudes. In the case of the Ritualists this was highlighted by their refusal to accept the direction of their bishops on the matter of ritual and ceremony and their ignoring of the judgements of the ecclesiastical courts. This behaviour was at odds with the Tractarian view that the bishops were the apostolic successors of Peter. Against this background Archbishop Tait initiated political action, culminating in the *Public Worship Regulation Act* of 1874, aimed at increasing the power of the bishops.

It is hardly surprising that these scandals within the established Church should have inflamed the Evangelicals in Liverpool. After all, in their eyes Ritualism was Popery by the back door. Until 1880 Liverpool was in the diocese of Chester. In 1878 the *Additional Bishoprics Act* provided for the creation of several new dioceses, including Liverpool, where the local Conservative Party was prominent in raising the funds necessary to sustain a bishop. In particular they wanted an Evangelical appointed, so that when the Conservatives lost the general election of February 1880 local opinion was alarmed that the replacement of Disraeli by Gladstone as Prime Minister could result in a High Churchman being appointed the first Bishop of Liverpool.[68] Gladstone was well known to be a High Churchman, so the Liverpool M.P. Lord Sandon made representations to Disraeli stating that his parliamentary seat depended on Liverpool getting an Evangelical bishop. In his last day in office Disraeli secured the appointment of J. C. Ryle, acknowledged by many to be the leader of the Evangelical party within the Church, an appointment that initially delighted Liverpool Protestants.[69] On 19th April 1880 Liverpool became both a city and a diocese, and Ryle was consecrated Bishop of Liverpool on 11th June 1880 at York Minster.

Protestants assumed that Ryle would take a firm line with Ritualist clergy in the new diocese. Much to their anger, Ryle consecrated St Agnes, a city church, on 21st January 1885, where the clergy appointed were known to be Ritualists. In his defence Ryle argued that he could not refuse to consecrate in anticipation that the services would be illegal. The Liverpool branch of the Church Association was numerically strong and influential, and it was determined to force Ryle to use his authority to discipline the Ritualists. Still smarting over the St Agnes affair, Dr James Hakes, the leading member of the local Church Association, turned his attention yet again to St Margeret's, Prince's Park. On 29th January he formally complained to Ryle about twelve 'illegal' practices carried on at St Margaret's, where the vicar was the Rev. Bell-Cox, a popular and hardworking priest. Under the Public Worship Act Ryle could have vetoed Hake's request for a suit before the provincial court in York, but, though Ryle was reluctant to allow proceedings against Bell-Cox, equally he believed strongly in the right of a citizen to bring complaints before the courts of the land. In an attempt to defuse the situation Ryle visited Bell-Cox, who refused to modify the forms of worship at St Margaret's. Reluctantly Ryle allowed Hakes to bring a suit before the provincial court, which met on 31st July 1885. Like many Ritualists before him, Bell-Cox refused to recognise the jurisdiction of the court and did not make an appearance, On 11th December 1885 he was found guilty of contempt and suspended from his priestly office for six months, an action that provoked an outcry in the press, in which Ryle came in for much personal criticism both from inside and outside the Church.

After his period of suspension Bell-Cox resumed his duties and Ryle hoped that the Church Association would leave well alone, but Hakes was after blood and took up the issue again in the courts. On 4th May 1887 Bell-Cox was arrested by a sheriff's officer, acting under a warrant issued by the Court of Arches, on a charge of contumacy and taken to Walton gaol. Again, there was widespread condemnation and Ryle became the centre of much of press criticism.[70] Bell-Cox was in prison for only seventeen days and then released on a writ of Habeus Corpus, ceded on a technicality. Hakes appealed and the court decided in his favour but Bell-Cox successfully took his case to the House of Lords, so life at St Margaret's went on much as usual, further increasing the bitterness felt by the Evangelicals.[71] While the Bell-Cox case captured national attention, it was followed by a more sensational one arising from the Church Association's suit against Bishop King of Lincoln. Despite the interest in King's trial, however, the controversy was running out of steam in the nation at large. As Marsh points out, '1874 was the last year of English history in which, for a whole session, Parliament was preoccupied with the condition of the Established Church.'[72]

Thus the last four decades of the nineteenth century witnessed a bitter struggle within the Church of England, in which the courts were used in an attempt to curb the spread of Catholic doctrine and practices. In the end the Evangelicals failed; in the nation as a whole it simply was not an issue of great importance. It was frustration resulting from this failure that gave birth to a more working-class response in Liverpool, which substituted direct action for legal procedures. Up to this point the campaign had been an internal affair within the Anglican community and had not involved any conflict, intellectual or physical, with the Roman Catholics. This changed with the arrival in Liverpool in 1888 of George Wise. He was to usher in the beginning of a period of bitter street conflict between the Orange and Green. As the *Tablet* had forecast thirty years before, the real target was Roman Catholicism.

Notes

1   For a table giving a complete breakdown of the political composition of Liverpool town council over the period 1835-67 see D. Fraser, *Urban Politics in Victorian England: the Structure of Politics in Victorian Cities* (1976), table 10, p. 137. This work also gives an overview of Liverpool local politics over the same period, pp. 133-42.

2   Following the Conservative triumphs in the 1864 municipal election, the *Liverpool Standard* gave the 'Board of Directors' the credit for winning a third Catholic seat on the council. *Liverpool Herald*, 5th November 1864.

3   In 1868 McNeile became Dean of Ripon.

4   Commenting on Powell's campaign, the *Liverpool Standard* claimed that Nicholson's supporters had been threatened with physical violence. It alleged a publican hired to provide a dinner for Powell's supporters, called it off because of the fear of violence. *Liverpool Standard*, 1st November 1853.

5   See election results and comments, *Liverpool Herald*, 7th November 1857.

6   *Liverpool Herald*, 8th January 1859, 'Meeting of Toxteth Park Board of Guardians'.

7   For reports of the Workhouse Committee meetings at which this case was discussed see *Liverpool Herald*, 8th January 1859.

8   *Porcupine*, 12th July 1862, p. 117.

9   Commenting on this appointment, the *Liverpool Herald* of 14th May 1864 stated with reference to the Select Vestry and Workhouse Committee, 'Those men have appointed a Popish priest to Walton gaol for the purpose of teaching popery, while popery itself has been the root of the evil which sent the Romanists to prison . . .'

10   *Liverpool Herald*, 5th November 1864, referring to this move, accused the Liberals of buying Catholic votes. For a history of Liverpool reformatory ships see J. Rimmer, *Yesterday's Naughty Children* (1986).

11   *Liverpool Herald*, op. cit. 'The three Romish councillors stood up in their midst [council] as three champions of Italian slavery, three brigands of Pio Nono.'

12   *Liverpool Herald*, 19th March 1864.

13   *Liverpool Mail*, 1st July 1865.

14   *Daily Courier*, 28th April 1868. *Liverpool Chronicle*, 25th April 1868, leader. *Daily Post*, 24th April 1868. Martin polled 9,115 votes against Ball's 8,842.

15   *Manchester Guardian*, 11th May 1868. At the Liverpool summer assizes Edward Bailey, aged twenty-six years, was charged with the murder of Arthur Brock. Found guilty of manslaughter and sentenced to penal servitude for life. See *Manchester Guardian*, 21st August 1868.

16 *Daily Courier,* 28th April 1868. When the younger man was called an 'Orange dog' he replied, 'I'll give you an Orange mark.'

17 For a full account of these riots see *Manchester Guardian,* 1st and 2nd July 1859.

18 F. Neal, 'The Birkenhead Garibaldi riots of 1862', *Transactions of the Historic Society of Lancashire and Cheshire,* Vol. 131 (1982), pp. 87-111.

19 *Sheffield Daily Telegraph,* 2nd, 4th, 6th, 8th, 9th, 11th, 12th, 16th December 1862.

20 For a full account of this event and its consequences see P. Rose, *The Manchester Martyrs: a Fenian Tragedy* (1970).

21 W. J. Lowe, 'Lancashire Fenianism, 1864-71', *Transactions of the Historic Society of Lancashire and Cheshire,* Vol. 126 (1976), pp. 156-85.

22 Rose, op. cit., chapter 3.

23 P.R.O. HO 45/9472/A199903. Whitely to Gaythorne Hardy.

24 Ibid.

25 *Liverpool Albion,* 23rd December 1867.

26 Ibid.

27 *Porcupine,* 15th February 1868, p. 455.

28 For an account of Murphy's career see N. L. Arnstein, 'The Murphy riots: a Victorian dilemma', *Victorian Studies,* September 1975, pp. 51-71. For the Ashton riots see *Manchester Guardian,* 12th and 22nd May 1868; *Times,* 18th May 1868.

29 *Liverpool Standard,* 4th January 1848. This edition contains a copy of the principles agreed at a meeting of the late Conservative Association on the previous day.

30 *Liverpool Herald,* 7th May 1859. It was decided to appoint a paid official in the Everton and Kirkdale ward. *The Herald* strongly criticised the apathy and lack of organisation among Conservatives.

31 *Liverpool Mail,* 20th July 1867.

32 Ibid.

33 P. Waller, *Sectarianism and Democracy: a Political and Social History of Liverpool, 1868-1939* (1981), chapters 3 and 4.

34 Ibid., p. 44.

35 *Porcupine,* 19th July 1862, p. 124. Porcupine claimed that the procession through the Welsh countryside after leaving Ruabon was a drunken rabble. For alternative accounts see *Daily Post,* 18th July 1862, *Liverpool Herald,* 19th July 1862.

36 *Liverpool Mercury,* 13th July 1868.

37 *Liverpool Mail,* 8th July 1876.

38 *Liverpool Mail,* 4th November 1876.

39 *Liverpool Mail,* 15th July 1876.

40 *Liverpool Mail,* 15th July 1876. The *Mail* commented that it had to be admitted that the behaviour of Orangemen in former times had put people off joining the Institution but it felt that such an attitude was no longer justified.

41 Bodleian Library, 247911.g.1, *A Handy Guide to the Various Lodges of the Province of Liverpool* (1885).

42 B. O'Connell, 'The Irish Nationalist Party in Liverpool, 1873-1922', unpublished M.A. thesis, Liverpool (1971).

43 The trial took place at the Liverpool assizes in August 1881.

44 Waller, op. cit., p. 34.

45 *Liverpool Weekly Albion,* 10th April 1886.

46 *Liverpool Daily Post,* 5th July 1886; *Liverpool Mercury,* 6th July 1886.

47 *Liverpool Courier,* 6th July 1886.

48 *Liverpool Courier,* 9th and 13th July 1886. *Liverpool Mercury,* 8th July 1886.

49 *Liverpool Mercury,* 9th July 1886; *Liverpool Courier,* 9th July 1886.

50 *Liverpool Courier,* 13th July 1886.

51 *Liverpool Weekly Albion,* 17th July 1886.

52 For local political comment and reports of council debates on the issue see *Liverpool Courier,* 8th and 9th July 1886.

53 *Liverpool Mercury*, 9th July 1886.

54 Nott-Bower, *Fifty-two Years a Policeman* (1926), p. 57.

55 The Catholic Bishop of Liverpool frequently issued pastoral letters imploring Catholics to ignore provocations and not to retaliate. For example, on 9th July 1869 a pastoral letter was read asking Catholics to stay away from public houses on 12th July and to avoid any counter-demonstrations, 'which may only lead to bloodshed'. P.R.O. A 19903/6.

56 *Liverpool Courier*, 5th July 1886.

57 Ecclesiastical law is a rather specialised area of legal practice. I am indebted to Brian Doyle of Salford University for expert help in identifying sources. See R. J. Walker, *The English Legal System*, 5th ed (1980), pp. 68-72 and 2067. Also Garth E. Moore, *An Introduction to English Canon Law* (1967), chapter 14.

58 These occurred in October and November 1859 and resulted in persons being charged before the consistory court with 'brawling in church'. See *Times*, 19th October 1859. Such disturbances in London were not new. In 1850 mobs attacked St Barnabas's, a Ritualist church. *Times*, 19th November 1850.

59 D. Hilliard, 'UnEnglish and unmanly: Anglo-Catholicism and homosexuality', *Victorian Studies*, winter 1982, pp. 181-209. Hilliard surveys the evidence available to sustain the charge.

60 *Liverpool Standard*, 12th November 1850. St Martin's branch of the Liverpool Church Union met on 30th October 1850 and issued a copy of a resolution emphasising the view that the Church of England was, in their view, the Apostolic Church of the land. On 6th November 1850 the Liverpool Church Union issued a resolution condemning the Papal bull restoring the Hierarchy.

61 The best book dealing with this particular phase of Anglican history is J. Bentley, *Ritualism and Politics in Victorian Britain: an Attempt to Legislate for Belief* (1978). Also, P. T. Marsh, *The Victorian Church in Decline: Archbishop Tait and the Church of England, 1868-1882* (1969), chapters 5 and 7. E. R. Norman, *Anti-Catholicism in Victorian England* (1968).

62 In 1850 McNeile had addressed the Protestant Operatives' Association in Toxteth on the evils of Tractarianism. *Liverpool Mercury*, 3rd December 1850. For account of Birkenhead meeting see *Liverpool Albion*, 8th July 1867. In fact Edward Harper, Grand Master of the Orange Institution, had addressed a large meeting in Liverpool in February 1864, called specifically to rally opposition to tractarianism; *Liverpool Herald*, 31st January 1863.

63 *Liverpool Albion*, 15th July 1867.

64 For an account of the opening ceremony at St Margaret's see *Liverpool Albion*, 19th July 1869, and *Liverpool Mail*, 24th July 1869.

65 *Porcupine*, 7th August 1869.

66 *Liverpool Mail*, 24th July 1869.

67 *Liverpool Courier*, 7th February 1844. Readers are given a long account of auricular confession as early as July 1844 in a report of a speech by McNeile to the Protestant Reformation Society. For an account of the system of patronage in the hands of Prime Ministers, see D. W. R. Bahlman, 'Politics and Church patronage in the Victorian age', *Victorian Studies*, spring 1979, pp. 253-96.

68 P. Toon and M. Smout, *John Charles Ryles, Evangelical Bishop* (1976), chapter 3.

69 Toon and Smout, op. cit., pp. 87-90.

70 *Manchester Guardian*, 6th and 10th May 1887 (long leader on the case),

71 It was estimated there were at least thirty Ritualist clergy in the Liverpool diocese by 1897. Toon and Smout, op. cit., p. 90.

72 Marsh, op. cit., p. 158.

Chapter VIII George Wise, John Kensit and the anti-Ritualist campaign, 1900-03

I

By 1886 the sectarian geography of Liverpool was established. It had not been the result of streets becoming Catholic in terms of their inhabitants; rather, certain streets were becoming Orange. By the end of the century the most partisan Orange area was the Everton district, running north of Netherfield Road. Great Homer Street was generally regarded as the real border between Catholic and Protestant Liverpool. However, throughout the inner city, whole streets were recognisably Orange, revealing their allegiance by their decorations on 12th July. This staking out of territory increased the dangers of riots arising from drum-and-fife bands asserting their right to march anywhere they pleased. The squalor of the town appeared just as horrific in 1883 as it had in 1843, and its criminal profile was unchanged, with drunkenness, prostitution and violence matters of considerable public concern.[1] The national outcry over the brutal murder of Richard Morgan in 1874 had brought no discernible change, and inter-communal violence appears to have been on the increase. By 1877 many Orange leaders were worried over the trouble that seemed inevitably associated with 12th July processions, no matter what precautions they took. It is difficult to see how Orange officials *could* control what happened on the streets, given that many 'followers' were not members of the Order. Forty-two years after the arrival of McNeile a whole generation of working-class Protestants had been reared on a diet of anti-Catholicism and anti-Irish rhetoric, the consequences of which could not be switched off by middle-class expressions of concern.

Examples have already been given of the so-called 'religious rows' which led to killings. These did not disappear during the last quarter of the nineteenth century and the absence of large-scale disturbances did not mean that all was well. For example, in 1877 many Orange leaders decided not to take part in the 12th July parade, which was to go to a rally in

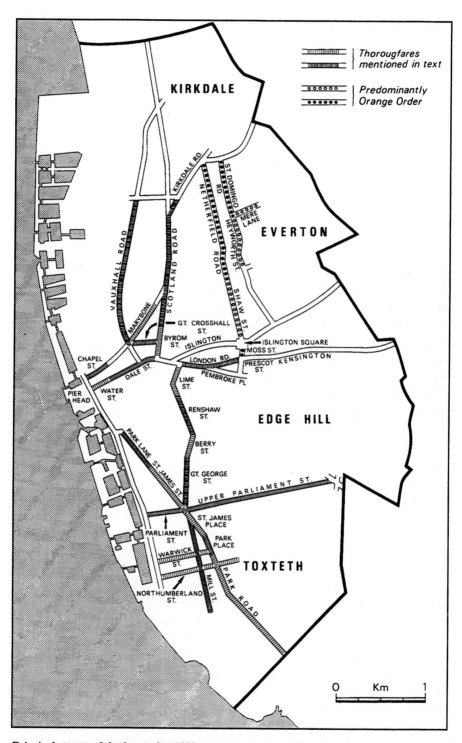

Principal streets of the inner city, 1903

Litherland, just over the northern boundary. No local politician attended, although Whitely and Forwood covered themselves by sending letters of apology. In neighbouring Bootle several thousand Irish labourers attempted to march into Liverpool to attack Orange streets off Scotland Road such as Bostock Street. They were stopped by the police and, frustrated, returned to Bootle, where they attacked the county police.[2] The same day effigies of the Pope were burned in Orange streets while the Catholics reciprocated by incinerating William and Mary.[3] The next year Orange leaders again avoided the 12th procession but events away from the main proceedings illustrated the volatility of the atmosphere. In Tindall Street James Canning, a Protestant, remonstrated with some children singing songs about William of Orange outside his windows. A Catholic named Sharkey rushed from a house opposite, carrying a knife and shouting, 'I'll have the heart's blood of an Orangeman.' Canning knocked him down and struck another man with a poker. The man died, and the coroner's jury returned a verdict of murder. It requires little imagination to appreciate the effect of Catholic-Protestant relations.[4] In another instance, in a public house, an Orangeman held an orange lily in his teeth for a joke, and was stabbed.[5] In Litherland an outbreak of 'national animosity resulted in four Irishmen beating one Robert Bradshaw to death, for which they each received six years' penal servitude on a manslaughter charge.[6] Presiding at the assizes at which all these cases came before him, Lord Chief Justice Cockburn commented, 'It is sad to find in Liverpool so many cases in which brutal and ferocious violence is used without regard to personal safety or life.'[7] On 12th July 1880 some Orangemen and women returned home to Beresford Street after the 12th July outing and stood in the street singing 'God Save the Queen'. In parts of Liverpool this was regarded as a provocation, and some Catholic youths began to stone the group. The police arrested the offenders but then an Orange woman began to fight with a Catholic woman. The Catholic's husband rushed out and stabbed the Orange woman, and when the latter's husband went to her defence he was fatally stabbed. Robert Foulkes, the Catholic, was sentenced to twenty years penal servitude.[8] Away from the council chamber, the political meeting and the church hall, this was the reality of the No Popery agitation, and the 1886 Home Rule disturbances had provided ample warning about inter-communal relationships which politicians and preachers ignored.

Ritualism became *the* political issue for Conservatives in 1898 because the majority of Protestant artisans who were members of the Working Men's Conservative Association put the suppression of Ritualism above Home Rule as their main objective, overriding any concern about Liverpool's appalling poverty. The reasons were complex and can only be guessed at. Ritualism, by 1890, had become a term of general abuse among Protestant working men. It could refer to a church service in which two candles burned on the altar. Equally it could refer to a church where a full sung mass was celebrated by priests wearing elaborate vestments, using incense and accompanied by altar boys. Lurking near the surface of hatred of Ritualism was the hatred of Roman Catholicism, close behind was the identification of Catholicism with the Irish. From this standpoint the Irish were responsible for most of Liverpool's crime, slums, drunkenness and, of course, for keeping wages down. After taking over as Conservative leader in 1880 A. B. Forwood had led the Conservatives to flirt with policies designed to deal with municipal social problems such as sanitation, housing and drunkenness, but by 1890 he had abandoned such concerns: they simply were not vote-catchers.[9] Forwood turned to other, wider issues, of which Home Rule seemed a vote-winner. In 1893, in a speech to Conservatives, Forwood indulged in anti-Irish rhetoric that was unchanged in style and content from speeches made in the heady days of McNeile's triumphs fifty years before. In the course of his address he referred to the Liberals and their Irish nationalist supporters and said that he objected to Liverpool being controlled by men who:

> . . . regarded the English as foreigners in Ireland, and whose countrymen in Liverpool were certainly foreign in many of their ways to the ideas and principles of his hearers. The influx of Irish into Liverpool brought poverty, disease, dirt and misery; drunkenness and crime, in addition to a disturbance of the labour market, the cost to ratepayers of an enormous sum of money.[10]

Such sentiments expressed by Conservatives were nothing new, but in the circumstances prevailing in Liverpool after 1886 they were extremely inflammatory. The activities of Irish nationalists had added another dimension to inter-communal antagonisms, one result of which was that the effort to establish territorial rights on the streets was exacerbated. For example, during the first week of July 1889 the Irish National League organised a meeting in Everton of a new branch. Everton was considered by Orangemen to be their territory, which looked down on the crowded Catholic areas alongside the Mersey. Large hostile crowds gathered outside the meeting hall, and when the Irish dispersed several were beaten up. In order to establish that they could hold a peaceful meeting anywhere in Liverpool, the nationalists announced another meeting at the same venue the following Sunday. This was the week leading up to the 12th July celebrations. The meeting took place and again an Orange crowd gathered. On police advice the nationalists left the meeting in a body for safety but the exodus turned into a parade, running fights took place and some police were injured. Ominously, at the time, two parades of nationalists from other areas were heading for Everton to help their colleagues.[11] However, for the members of the L.W.M.C.A. preserving the union with Ireland was secondary to ridding the Church of Ritualists.

Forwood died in October 1898, enabling Archibald Tutton Salvidge to fill a vacuum in Liverpool Conservatism. Salvidge was thirty-five years old and a director of Bent's Brewery. His power base was the L.W.M.C.A., of which he became vice-chairman in 1888 and chairman in 1892. The members were dissatisfied with the performance of Conservative Ministers and members of Parliament over the issue of Church discipline and, by association, the Liverpool Constitutional Association did not have their undivided loyalty. The patrician members of the latter, as ship-owners, merchants, brokers and suchlike, had wider horizons than Church issues and as long as they could escape with lip service to anti-Ritualism their relations with the L.W.M.C.A. were tolerable. However, those Liverpool politicians who wished to secure their base had to adopt a more positive anti-Ritualist, pro-Protestant stance, and of these oppor-tunists the more prominent were David McIver, Charles McArthur, W. W. Rutherford and Robert Houston. Salvidge, as chairman of the L.W.M.C.A., was the leading political figure in the anti-Ritualist campaign, and from 1898 onwards more of the upper echelons of Liverpool Conservatism joined the Orange Order. W. W. Rutherford became Grand Master of England in 1912. As long as the anti-Ritualist campaign was a matter of *political* campaigning it was something that most councillors and M.P.s could live with. In Liverpool, however, it was inevitable that the campaign would deteriorate into violence of a scale and intensity that splintered local Conservatism and resulted in the emergence of a 'Protestant' party. This proved not to be fatal to the Tories because of the weakness of the Liberal opposition.

II

George Wise was born in Bermondsey, London, in 1855. He received little formal education but even as a young man evinced a great interest in religion.[12] At twenty-one years of age he was so influenced by a pamphlet written by J. C. Ryle that he was received into the Church of England. At the time he was working in an office and spending all his spare time as a lecturer for the Christian Evidence Guild in the East End. For a short period his activities took him to America, where he was exposed to the peculiarly American brand of Evangelicism, a path trodden much later by Ian Paisley. In 1888 he moved to Liverpool at the invitation of a group of Evangelicals. For a man of his strong evangelical views Liverpool must have been an irresistible attraction. His mentor, Ryle, was now Bishop of Liverpool; Protestantism was bolstered by a revived Orange Order, and he was aware of the reputation of Liverpool Protestantism. Of his first ten years in Liverpool little is known, except that he displayed immense energy in undertaking a large number of lecturing engagements.

In many ways Wise was the opposite of McNeile. Hugh McNeile was tall, slim and handsome. Wise was short, stocky and nondescript. McNeile was wealthy, Wise relatively poor. McNeile was a scholar and theologian. Wise, though intelligent, was not an intellectual; his motives and speeches were visceral, eventually too crude even for some of his friends. McNeile was never a pastoral priest: his mission was preaching, mainly to the middle class. Wise became very much identified with the Protestant working class. McNeile was a married man, with five children, Wise a bachelor. What they had in common was that they were both politicians and ferocious anti-Catholics. In 1891 Wise gave up his Christian Evidence work and J. A. Bramley-Moore became his patron. Bramley-Moore was one of the old Tories from the days of McNeile and had always been identified with sound Protestant policies.[13] The absence of diaries or other personal correspondence, and only a small number of printed speeches, make it difficult to evaluate Wise, the man, and his motives. What is clear is that he was intelligent, possessed of energy and political acumen and would have made his mark in whatever career he had chosen. Fate had deposited him in Liverpool at a time of intense nation-wide Protestant activity aimed at fighting Ritualism, and societies were springing up like mushrooms. Among the more important were the Protestant Alliance (1889), the National Protestant League (1890), the Churchman's Council and the Layman's League (1898), the Imperial Protestant Federation (1898) and the British Protestant Union, formed by Wise himself in 1898, the aims of which were to fight 'Romanism, Ritualism and Infidelity'.[14] In the world of Protestant activists this was a period of intense excitement, equalling the furore over 'papal aggression' in 1850 but it was a world still inhabited by a small minority of the population. Only in Liverpool were the issues of political significance.

Initially, following his arrival in Liverpool, Wise did not indulge in the anti-Catholic diatribes which later were to become his hallmark. However, the foundation of the British Protestant Union heralded a significant shift in his objectives. In 1897 he hit the headlines in the local press by giving a series of lectures in reply to the criticisms of a Fr Donnelly regarding a pamphlet entitled *The Claims of the Church of Rome*. The same year he attended a service at St Thomas's, in Warwick Street, in the South End, long a target for anti-Ritualists. Here he made a public protest about the nature of the services held there.[15] His methods began to attract attention. In another case he became involved in a controversy with the Rev. John Wakeford, Vicar of St Margaret's, Anfield, over the issue of prayers to the dead, and followed it with an attack on

Bishop Ryle for his lack of action over Ritualism in the Liverpool diocese. Ryle, who had found the Bell-Cox case distressing, had taken no action to stem illegal practices and many who were not admirers of Wise admitted the validity of his arguments. The *Liverpool Review* finished a long editorial about 'Brawling Mr Wise' and his activities at St Agnes's Church:

> It is indeed trifling with the facts to contend that there is no disobedience and no illegality in the diocese of the Bishop of Liverpool. We have here in full blast all those ritualistic practices in which Cardinal Vaughan sees the elements of the movement that is to lead the English Church to Rome, namely auricular confession, prayers and offices for the dead, belief in purgatory, and invocation of the Blessed Virgin and the Saints: 'the very doctrines', chuckles the Cardinal, 'stamped in the thirty nine articles as fond fables and blasphemous deceits'. Thus out of the very mouth of Rome are the Catholic revivalists condemned and to Brawling (but unavoidable) Mr Wise's protests, the Bishop of Liverpool, who has sworn at his consecration 'to correct and punish the disobedient', the Bishop of Liverpool says nothing.[16]

Those who dismissed Wise as a vulgar hooligan were mistaken. He was a shrewd strategist and opportunist, with a well developed political sense. The *Layman's League* in Liverpool, under the leadership of Austin Taylor, a son of Archdeacon Taylor, had brought about the promotion of a Church Discipline Bill. Wise, Taylor and Salvidge formed an alliance aimed at securing the passage of the Bill. The objective was to discipline Ritualist priests by removing the bishop's veto on laymen bringing suits, and to substitute deprivation of a living for imprisonment, the latter having disgusted public opinion. Unavoidably Liverpool M.P.s had to declare their hand regarding this Bill, support of which was demanded by Protestant extremists as the price of their votes. In 1899 David McIver (Kirkdale), Charles McArthur (Exchange), W. F. Lawerence (Abercromby) and Robert Houston (West Toxteth) declared their support. The other three were equivocal.[17]

The significant feature of Wise's activities from 1901 onwards, compared with his previous activities, was that he became increasingly anti-Catholic in his speeches, and diverting from Ritualism, a purely internal Anglican affair, he launched a 'Protestant Crusade' which led to clashes with Roman Catholics. Why this occurred is not known. Perhaps it was frustration, the Church Discipline Bill having failed in 1899. More probably it was disappointment with the lack of action on the part of the new Bishop of Liverpool, Chevasse, appointed in 1900. Ryle had been a disappointment to the anti-Ritualists, and now their expectations regarding the new bishop appeared equally futile.

The improved weather and lengthening nights meant that April 1901 ushered in the marching season, by now a tradition among Orangemen. On 7th April Wise and a group of followers met at St George's Hall and marched in procession to St Catherine's Church, Grove Street, to protest against Ritualist practices. Wise did not disrupt the service but on leaving he attempted to hold a meeting near by. A body of police moved the Wiseites on, The protestors held a meeting on some nearby open ground, where Wise addressed his followers. He said they had given Bishop Chevasse a year to tackle the problem of Ritualism and urged his listeners not to give a penny towards the proposed cathedral until they had been assured it would not be used for Ritualistic services. He and his supporters tried to form a procession but, significantly, the police dispersed them.[18]

This was the first of a number of moves on the part of the police to stop Wise's processions, and such action was to be bitterly resented by Wise and his followers. The process of winding up Protestant passions began in earnest. On 21st April Orangemen marched to St Silas's Church and the procession was accompanied by five drum-and-fife bands. It needs to be understood that the beat of the Orange drums was, and is, a potent element in stirring up the passions of both friends and enemies. In the sermon the Rev. Joseph McKinney, an Irish clergyman, displayed a paranoid obsession with the threat of subversion from within, preaching against any attempt to change the coronation oath.[19] The even warmer weather and longer nights of May witnessed a dramatic increase in the activity on the streets. On 15th May Wise held a meeting in Islington Square. This was a popular venue for public meetings, but it was next to St Francis Xavier's Catholic Church and a strongly Catholic area, and so was not an ideal spot for holding the type of meetings Wise had in mind. The title of his lecture on this occasion was 'The Jesuits and the Coronation Oath'. Probably because most Catholics were not aware of the meeting it passed off fairly quietly, but the next night Wise returned and this time there were large numbers of Catholics present. During the lectures Wise asked whether Catholics drank holy water and his supporters yelled back, 'No, they drink whiskey.' He waved a crucifix round his head and put rosary beads around his neck. The Catholics in the crowd were infuriated and, sweeping his supporters aside, they knocked him off his stand and only swift action on the part of the police saved him from serious injury. In an ugly situation Wise and his supporters received a police escort away from the square.[20]

On 19th May Wise kept the temperature up at a meeting held well away from any crowded Catholic area, A large number of Protestants attended and Catholic intervention was restricted to stone-throwing and some individual fights in the crowd. The language Wise was reported to have used was to be of crucial significance in future court cases. He referred to a procession of the Blessed Blood in Belgium and told his hearers that, for all the Catholics knew, it could be duck's blood, words guaranteed to anger Catholics. Wise went on to challenge 'Red necks' to show that what he said was untrue, language that in Liverpool was gratuitously insulting.[21] Before ending the meeting Wise asked his supporters to attend another the following Saturday, 25th May, in Islington Square. It was to have started at 8.00 p.m. but the time was brought forward to 7.30 and Wise is alleged to have told the crowd, 'The sooner we get at them the better.' Policemen in the crowd passed this information back to the Chief Constable. On 22nd May a meeting was held in Everton and once again the subject was 'The Jesuits and the Coronation Oath'.[22] At the meeting Wise read out a letter purporting to warn him that when he next spoke in Islington Square the Catholics would be ready with sticks and stones: He addressed the crowd to the effect that they could use sticks and stones just as well. He urged them as 'Britishers' to attend the meeting and protect him. The use of the term is an example of Wise's frequent innuendo that the Catholics were alien, i.e. Irish. He alleged that the police had refused to offer protection and this subtle invitation to indulge in violent confrontation with the Catholics at no time involved him in actually urging his followers to carry arms. Thus the scene was set for a confrontation between the campaigners and Catholics on 25th May, the issue of Ritualism seemingly forgotten.

At this juncture Leonard Dunning, Assistant Head Constable, entered the lists with Wise for the first of many conflicts. The Head Constable, Nott-Bower, was away and Dunning was in charge; on the basis of information received he was convinced that if the meeting in Islington Square took place there would be a serious breach of the peace. To make matters worse, an advertisement, placed by Wise, appeared in the *Liverpool Evening Express* on Friday 24th stating:

> Protestantism and Free Speech. Do not allow the Romanists to triumph, but maintain your liberties. Support Mr George Wise on Saturday next, at 7.30 pm in Islington Square.

Wise had adroitly turned the affair into a defence of the principle of free speech but the notice convinced Dunning that he had to take action, and on the morning of Saturday 24th May Wise was summoned to appear before the stipendiary magistrate, W. J. Stewart.[23] Like Dunning, Stewart was to have bitter cause to remember George Wise. Wise was brought before him to 'show cause why he should not be bound over to keep the peace and be of good behaviour'. W. W. Rutherford defended Wise.[24] The argument of the defence was basically that Wise was exercising the right of free speech and that it was the Catholics who were causing the disturbances. Rutherford argued that there was no evidence that Wise had done anything to provoke a breach of the peace. If Catholics kept away there would be no problem. The police case was that Wise's speeches at the meeting of the previous week were a clear invitation to his followers to use violence. The stipendiary rejected Rutherford's arguments and Wise agreed to change the venue to the plateau outside St George's Hall. The prosecution withdrew the summons. Wise's pugnacious nature was demonstrated by the fact that, even though he agreed to abandon his meeting, he immediately planned a march that took him *past* Islington Square at the same time, just to see if the 'other side' were there. If they weren't, then, he said, his supporters would carry on past. He did not say what would happen if the Catholics were waiting.[25]

All these events had been followed by the public at large, and the knowledge that Wise planned a demonstration of some sort ensured that the crowds would be out on the night of Saturday 25th. By 7.30 p.m. several thousands of people were milling around St George's Hall, the majority of them Catholics, and the police, anticipating trouble, had fifty men on duty. Wise arrived at Lime Street on a tram, and a gang of Catholics rushed him, but the police were ready and he was escorted to the steps of St George's Hall. The senior police officer present pleaded with him to leave the area but he insisted on two minutes to say something. He thanked the police for their efforts and asked his followers to sing the national anthem, but by then the noise from the Catholics drowned all else. The total identification in Liverpool of Catholics with Ireland was clearly illustrated. They were singing 'Faith of our fathers' and 'God save Ireland' and calling for cheers for the Pope. Wise abandoned all attempt to speak and the police escorted him to Central Station, during which time several desperate attempts were made by the Catholics to get at him and several policemen received injuries. Fights broke out on St George's plateau and, to add to the chaos and excitement, an Orange drum-and-fife band marched towards St George's Hall and immediately drew the attacks of the Irish, who were then dispersed by the police.[26]

Wise again appeared before Stewart and was ordered to enter into a recognisance in the sum of £100, with two sureties of £50 each, to keep the peace and be of good behaviour during the next twelve months or in default go to prison. Wise agreed but immediately set about organising an appeal. Stewart, the stipendiary, became the focal point of Wise's criticism, he was held up to be an anti-Protestant who was trying to stop Protestants exercising their right of free speech. In particular, it became known that the stipendiary attended St Luke's (Ritualist) Church in Southport, and this, in the view of Wise and his supporters, meant that he could not administer justice impartially. The appeal was heard in the King's Bench Division in November 1901 and the judges all found in the magistrate's favour. The essential question was whether the natural consequences of Wise's language concerning Catholics would, in a place like

Liverpool, lead to a breach of the peace. The conclusion was that it would.[27] It is not clear what Wise's objectives were during his 1901 campaign. Only *national* action would have brought about parliamentary changes to the law regarding the Church of England. In his Liverpool rallies Wise was preaching to the converted, many of whom would not have had votes. What is clear is that he had become the centre of attention, obtaining press coverage, negotiating with policemen, courted by local politicians, as well as experiencing the heady thrill of addressing adulatory crowds. It seems more than probable that his inflated ego was dented somewhat the following year when the formidable Kensits arrived in town.

III

Wise's 1901 campaign of meetings and the subsequent court case had the effect of establishing him as a Protestant folk hero while at the same time casting Leonard Dunning and W. J. Stewart as villains. By the end of 1901 Captain Nott Bower had left Liverpool to take up the post of Commissioner of the Metropolitan Police and Dunning became Head Constable. It was with no enthusiasm at all that the Liverpool police heard that John Kensit and his son were to undertake an anti-Ritualist campaign in the city, commencing in August 1902.[28] Kensit senior was a man of the same stamp as Wise, a Londoner who at an early age was inordinately interested in religion. As a boy he was a member of the choir of St Lawrence Jewry, a High Church in the East End of London, and the experience seems to have triggered off an intense dislike of High Church practices and beliefs. He attended a course of lectures in London, organised by the Rev. Dr Maguire, which convinced him of the errors of Ritualism. At seventeen years of age he organised open-air preaching in the East End and undertook the printing of leaflets to offset what he considered to be the unwholesome literature circulating among the working class. In 1889 he founded the *Protestant Truth Society,* and in 1898 began his campaign against Ritualism. He had started by writing to the bishops in whose dioceses there were High Church parishes, but because of their reluctance to prosecute he adopted a policy of direct action. On Good Friday 1898 Kensit, his wife and son, together with some friends, attended St Cuthbert's in Kensington, where the service of the Adoration of the Cross was being held. At a particular point in the service, when members of the congregation were asked to kiss a crucifix, Kensit shouted 'In God's name I denounce this idolatry in the Church of England.' Such dramatic intervention caused uproar, and the police were called. Kensit was charged with brawling in church. The charge was dismissed but he and his followers achieved national press coverage. Kensit subsequently admitted *he* did not like the methods he used but, in view of the bishops' inaction, felt he had no choice.[29] To assist him in his crusade against Ritualism he formed an organisation known as the Wycliffe Preachers and led protests throughout the country, including one at the consecration of Dr Winnington-Ingram as Bishop of London.[30] Why the Kensits chose to launch an anti-Ritualist campaign in Liverpool is not clear. Ritualism was not as prevalent as in many other dioceses, and, as the *Liverpool Review* said, 'Liverpool is favoured by the residence here of the one, only and irrepressible George Wise and therefore Mr Kensit is a superfluity.'[31] It is fairly certain that Wise did not invite him.

The *Liverpool Courier* of 30th July 1902 carried an article explaining the itinerary of the Wycliffe Preachers in their forthcoming campaign. From 1st August to 15th September there were to be meetings throughout Liverpool on the issue of Ritualism and the Anglican churches picked out for special attention were St Margaret's, Anfield, and St John's, Tuebrook.[32] The clergymen behind the invitation to the Kensits were probably G. Musgrave-Brown, vicar of St Clement's, Toxteth, and J. W. Baker, Orangeman and vicar of St Ambrose's, Everton. The campaign ran into trouble before it started, in that the organisers had wanted to book St George's Hall for a meeting in September but the town council had refused, an action which resulted in claims that the council was anti-Protestant. In retrospect, an indoor meeting might have resulted in less disorder. Until 29th August all the meetings had passed off without serious trouble. On Friday night, 29th August, John Kensit, junior, held a meeting in Islington Square. The subject was the 'Ritualistic Conspiracy in the Church of England'. He spoke of the various organisations of the Anglo-Catholics and made the claim that thirty-four clergymen in the diocese of Liverpool were Ritualists. He made references and used language that were bound to inflame any Roman Catholics within hearing. Kensit did make it clear early on that he was concerned with Ritualism in the Church of England, but most Catholics were convinced that the campaign was intent on insulting their faith. The Irish in the crowd kept up a constant hissing and singing of 'The Boys of Wexford' and only the large police presence prevented violence.[33] Concerned over the way events were moving, H. P. Lane, the Assistant Chief Constable, wrote asking Kensit to abandon a meeting in Islington Square to be held on 30th and 31st August. Kensit refused :

> I think it will be a danger to the future welfare of the city were we to do otherwise for then mob rule having been successful in one direction it would be tried in others . . . our fight is for a principle which we cannot very well surrender. More especially so since we give no reasonable cause for the opponents behaviour.[34]

The *Liverpool Review* saw Kensit's reply as 'a distinct challenge thrown down to riotously disposed individuals-a truculent invitation to disorder'.[35]

On Saturday 30th August, Kensit junior and about 900 followers assembled in Edge Hill and marched to Islington Square. They carried flags and banners, the banner leading the procession bearing the words 'Kensit's Wycliffe Preachers. The word is truth. We protest against the idolatrous Mass and the God dishonoured in our schools'. When the procession reached Islington Square a crowd of several thousand were waiting, many of them Catholics. The police, expecting trouble, had placed their men in the crowd, and held reserves in the nearby Alexander Hall. As soon as Kensit arrived the Catholics attacked and the flag-bearers were knocked to the ground. The police intervened, calling out their reserves, and quickly cleared the square, but not before several vicious fights had occurred. The Kensitites regrouped and, under a heavy police escort, marched away accompanied by an Orange drum-and-fife band.[36]

The general public were becoming worried over the confrontations, which were following the pattern of the year before, and the issue of police policy regarding such meetings was to the forefront of most discussion. *The Liverpool Review* of 6th September asked why the police did not stop the meetings and the familiar debate opened up concerning the freedom of speech. The *Review* commented:

> A man's religious convictions are usually very dear to him and it cannot be wondered at that people whose mental training has not been carried far enough to enable them to meet abuse with argument or with the silent contempt it deserves, now and then break out in physical violence. The less educated a man is, the more likely he is to resent attacks on his religion by means of the reverse of gentle, and we contend that such people, to whatever side they belong, have a right to demand that, when using the streets for perfectly legitimate purposes they shall not be subjected to any temptation to disturbance.

The Kensitites, naturally, saw the issue in a different light, as the reply to Lane's letter showed. They were exercising their right of free speech. The Catholics who attacked them were breaking the law.

The temperature of the debate rose after a meeting held by Kensit outside St George's Hall on Sunday 7th September. Despite a large police presence, a group of Catholics tried to reach the speakers and fights broke out. Two men were arrested and charged with assault. On Monday morning, 8th September, they appeared before Stewart but the surprise was that Kensit was also summoned to appear as a result of H. P. Lane laying information to the effect that if more meetings were held, they would lead to a breach of the peace.[37] Thus the nettle was being grasped. Kensit was defended by a lawyer from London, John Othen. He immediately revealed his strategy by alleging that Stewart's views on the issue of Protestant meetings and processions had been expressed on previous occasions and revealed bias on the bench. Because of this he asked that the case be tried in another court and heard by another magistrate. This attack on his impartiality stung, and Stewart refused Othen's request. Evidence was given by the police concerning Kensit's words in Islington Square on 30th August which, they alleged, were inflammatory. Stewart accepted the police evidence and passed the sentence that, in the sum of £200 and two bails of £100 each, Kensit should undertake to keep the peace and abstain from holding meetings for twelve months, or in default, suffer three months' imprisonment. Kensit chose to go to prison, with the words 'as long as I have breath, I shall continue to oppose error'.[38] He was taken to Walton gaol, whose inmates were predominantly Irish Catholic. The reaction to his imprisonment was immediate and widespread. The press was inundated with letters of protest and the question of meetings and free speech was debated from every conceivable viewpoint. The local press coverage, particularly in the *Courier*, was enormous, far exceeding the space allotted to George Wise in 1901. Protestant organisations rallied to Kensit's support and protest meetings were held throughout the city. Orange lodges and the W.M.C.A. passed resolutions condemning the imprisonment and a campaign was mounted for his release which quickly became a nation-wide effort on the part of Evangelical churchmen. Stewart, the stipendiary, was vilified as an enemy of Protestantism and John Kensit, junior, became the hero of evangelical England.

IV

There can be little doubt that the attention Kensit received was not to the liking of such a strong personality as Wise. And Kensit had chosen to go to prison, upstaging Wise. Commenting, the *Review* expressed the opinion that when in a similar situation Wise had exercised the greater discretion. 'Whether Mr Wise was short of courage, we do not know.'[39] Wise must have been aware of the innuendoes and he needed to get back on centre stage. In fact, on the very day of Kensit's meeting at St George's Hall, Wise and Arthur Trew, a veteran battler from Belfast, had led a large procession of Orangemen from Islington Square to Seaforth, north of the city, where Wise had already held meetings that had ended in disorder due to a large Catholic opposition. Again, there was no obvious reason for such a parade other than to assert territorial rights; again, a large police presence was needed to keep Catholics and Orangemen apart.[40]

On the night of 9th September Wise held a meeting at the St Domingo Pit in Everton, where an estimated eight to ten thousand supporters had gathered. They marched to Islington Square, causing a great deal of unrest on the streets and stretching the resources of the police yet again; the inhabitants were experiencing a growing sense of drama.[41] Events were moving with the inevitability of a Greek tragedy. Though Kensit's imprisonment gave Wise the opportunity to regain the initiative the imprisoned Kensit was still the centre of attention as the protest meetings continued. On the evening of 11th September a protest meeting was held at the Hope Hall and John Kensit, senior, travelled up from London to address it and take over the protest campaign. The whole weight of the Conservative-Orange machine was thrown into the campaign to secure the release of Kensit, junior, and the press attacks on Stewart's professional integrity intensified. The tenor of Protestant protests was that Englishmen exercising their right of free speech in opposition to illegal practices in the national Church was being intimidated by Irish Catholics and harassed by a Ritualist magistrate and a vindictive chief constable. On 13th and 14th September there were three more large demonstrations over Kensit's imprisonment, involving parades and fife-and-drum bands.[42] On 15th September Frank Cable, a London preacher, held a meeting at St Domingo Pit, whilst John Kensit, senior, held a meeting at Hope Hall. At the same time Catholics were holding a protest meeting in Islington Square, so the city police were fully stretched. Typical of the problems facing them was the experience of Inspector Foulkes. He was at Islington Square when he received word that several thousand Protestants from the St Domingo meeting were marching from Everton to Kensit's meeting at Hope Hall and that they would pass by Shaw Street, near the Catholic meeting in Islington Square. Such a situation could well result in a major riot and Foulkes had not enough men to cope. They lined up across Shaw Street, and when the Protestant procession approached Frank Cable was asked to halt it and move back. The Protestants were in no mood for compromise. At the same time the Catholics had left Islington Square and were approaching from the rear. Thus the police were in the middle of two large and truculent crowds, Foulkes hit on a brilliant idea. He shouted in a loud voice, 'Put on the hoses.' In fact there were no water hoses available, but the bluff worked and both crowds retreated.[43] The next evening, 16th September, Wise and Cable held a meeting in Islington Square and a crowd of Catholic women converged on it, singing 'The Boys of Wexford' and 'God bless Ireland'. The police immediately dispersed them, arresting the ringleaders. Wise and his supporters then marched from Islington to St Domingo Pit, where, in spite of the rain, he addressed a large crowd in a markedly anti-Catholic spirit. It was at this meeting that he announced that he was to form a bodyguard of 100 young men to act as defenders of Protestant truth, in effect a personal bodyguard.[44] So far the campaign had been confined to Liverpool but on 16th September a meeting was held at the Queen's Hall, Birkenhead, which passed off relatively quietly.[45]

On Sunday 21st September the crusade held an afternoon meeting in Birkenhead, followed by a procession headed by a drum-and-fife band. The same evening they held another procession and marched to the Queen's Hall, where a large crowd of Catholics were waiting. While the meeting was in progress the crowd outside, estimated at 3,000, began to sing Irish hymns and kept up a barrage of noise. Bored with waiting for the meeting to end, elements in the crowd began to stone the hall, breaking the windows. At the same time gangs of Irishmen were circling in case the speakers tried to leave by a side door, and when the speakers eventually emerged the crowd rushed them. It was a dangerous situation and the police drew their truncheons. The infuriated crowd began stoning them and the speakers, and running battles took place all the way to the ferry boat. Many of the Birkenhead police were injured by missiles, and they had to board the ferry with the Kensitites as a number of Irishmen had also boarded the vessel. On the Liverpool shore the Kensitites had to be escorted through the city until they were on safe territory. Meanwhile, in Birkenhead, fights had broken out around the Queen's Hall during which a policeman was badly beaten up.[46]

While Kensit, senior, was holding his meeting in Birkenhead, George Wise was leading a procession from Islington Square to Soho Street, a matter of a quarter of a mile. The object was to attend a harvest festival service. A large crowd of Catholics had gathered near Islington Square and attempted to attack the Wiseites. The police managed to hold them back, but when the procession reached Soho Street the Catholics made a determined attack and eleven were arrested before the crowd were dispersed.[47] The next day, 22nd September, the Kensit crusade held another meeting at the Queen's Hall in Birkenhead. The numbers attending were few, hardly surprising in view of the previous day's disturbances. There was a massive police turn-out and all streets leading to the hall were blocked off. On 23rd September both Wise and Kensit held further meetings attended by large crowds and necessitating police protection.[48]

The Wycliffe campaign in Birkenhead was scheduled to finish on 25th September with a meeting at Claughton Music Hall at which John Kensit, senior, would be the main speaker. Up till then he had not attended any meetings in Birkenhead and the campaign had been in the hands of Louis Ewart and J. Major Thompson. The police were expecting trouble after the events of the preceding week and special steps were taken to prevent disturbance. The meeting itself passed off quietly and while it was in progress the police arranged with R. Moss, the secretary of the Birkenhead campaign, for Kensit, his wife and Ewart to leave by a side door and take a tram to Hamilton Square station, where they could catch a Liverpool train.

The party and eight policemen duly boarded the tram, which drove at speed through the crowds. At the station the police alighted but Kensit and his friends stayed on as far as the ferry landing stage. The police were taken completely by surprise. With an element of farce, four of them chased after the tram and managed to scramble aboard. At the landing stage there was a short walk down to the ferry. A group of youths were waiting, not obviously hostile, but as Kensit walked past a two-foot iron file was thrown which struck him over the eye. He collapsed and a doctor was called. The file weighed 2 lb and had inflicted a serious wound. By the time a doctor arrived an unfriendly crowd had gathered, and it was decided to take Kensit to the Royal Infirmary.[49] No one had seen who threw the chisel. The police believed no one had recognised John Kensit, so the missile was probably meant for Ewart, who was bitterly disliked by local Catholics. Understandably Protestant opinion was outraged by the attack and it swept John Kensit junior and George Wise out of the head-lines.

The Home Office was writing to Leonard Dunning concerning events in Liverpool. In his reply, after outlining the events of 1901 and more recent happenings, Dunning made clear his view as to where the blame lay:

> In conclusion I may say that though we have some 100,000 Irish Roman Catholics and a great number of Orangemen here, we have for years been free from party disturbances until recent angry feelings were stirred up, first by Wise and then by Kensit.[50]·

The Protestant campaign was beginning to provoke a Catholic reaction. On 1st October handbills were circulated urging Catholics 'to protest against the insults hurled at their religion and to march on the place of meeting'.[51] This was a reference to St Domingo Pit, where Wise was to hold yet another meeting on 3rd October. As president of the Protestant Union Wise had called the meeting to protest against the Roman Catholic religion and he called upon Protestants *in their thousands* to attend. Dunning realised that if the Catholics attempted to get to St Domingo Pit - in the heart of Protestant Everton - there would be a riot. On 3rd October he sent a large body of police to the Catholic assembly point. Those who were there, according to Dunning, were 'of the lower orders and had no leaders of any merit'.[52] They were working themselves up singing 'God bless Ireland' and waving green flags. When they attempted to march in procession to Everton the police intervened and fighting started which resulted in Irishmen being arrested. Later in the day, in an even more alarming development, an estimated 8,000 Catholics tried again to march to St Domingo Pit and once again the police dispersed them, using some degree of force. Whilst this later clash was in progress Wise was holding his meeting at the pit. Dunning felt that the language Wise used at the meeting was provocative in the extreme.[53]

On Saturday 4th and 5th October Wise held two more meetings and a parade. On 5th October a crowd of Catholics tried to attack a meeting in Liverpool.[54] The events of the weekend convinced Dunning that he had to take action, and on the 6th he had Joseph Harrington and George Wise arrested. Harrington was a Catholic, who had organised the attempted march on St Domingo on the 3rd. The pair were summoned to show why they should not be ordered to find sureties to keep the peace and be of good behaviour.[55] The summonses were heard on 8th October. In explaining his actions to the Home Office Dunning was unequivocal in allocating blame:

> I am in hopes that the prosecution of one of each side may have a quietening effect but I fear that it will be some time before the bad feeling on both sides, for which Wise and the Kensits are all to blame, will die out.

In a report to the Watch Committee, which met on 6th October, Dunning said that Wise's language and the conduct of his meetings led him to believe it right to make another application to have him bound over.[56]

Meanwhile permission was granted for Kensit junior to visit his father in hospital, as he did on the afternoon of 7th October, accompanied by a warder. At six o'clock on the morning of the 8th, John Kensit died, in the presence of his wife, two daughters, Louis Ewart, the regional leader of the Wycliffe Preachers, the Rev. Musgrave Brown and Miss Dodman, the fiancée of John Kensit, junior.[57] John Kensit junior was released from prison unconditionally. The death of Kensit received immediate and widespread publicity, and as far as the extreme Protestants were concerned they had their first martyr of the new century. The event represented a climax to the events of 1902. The precise cause of Kensit's death was to be a matter of some controversy but most people immed-iately put it down to the attack on 25th September. He was buried at Hampstead cemetery on Saturday 11th October and his funeral was turned into a monster Protestant demonstration.[58]

Meanwhile public tension and a general air of hysteria in Liverpool were maintained by the appearance in court of George Wise and by the forthcoming court appearance of John McKeever, a nineteen-year-old youth arrested for the attack on Kensit senior. On the day John Kensit died Wise appeared in court with a Roman Catholic, Joseph Harrington.

He was represented by F. E. Smith, the future Lord Birkenhead and sympathiser with the cause of Ulster Protestants. The case against Wise involved police evidence about his meetings in September and October and the language used on those occasions. Smith tried to get police witnesses to say that the disturbances were caused by Roman Catholics but without success. In another attempt he asked P.c. Hughes whether Wise's meetings should have been held in Roman Catholic areas, to which Hughes replied, 'Where will you get any place in Liverpool without Roman Catholic residents?' In the end Wise consented to be of good behaviour and was bound over for six months. It is highly probable that he agreed to this because the open-air preaching and marching season was over and nothing was to be lost. The Treasury Solicitor took over the prosecution of McKeever in view of the importance of the case. Though injured in Birkenhead, Kensit had died in Liverpool, but Dunning, Stewart and the town clerk were against the trial being held in Liverpool, on the grounds that a jury might be biased against McKeever and also on account of the probable cost. They feared too that the trial might inflame sectarian animosities.[59] They were overruled and the trial began on 8th December 1902. F. E. Smith was one of the prosecuting counsel. The essential issue was whether Kensit had died as a direct result of the injury received in Birkenhead and, if so, whether McKeever had thrown the missile. Contrary medical evidence and eye witnesses resulted in his acquittal, and he was cheered from the court.[60]

V

With the approach of spring Wise began to plan his new open air preaching season. On 27th February 1903 he notified the town clerk of his intention to hold a Protestant demonstration at the St Domingo Pit on 8th April. This date was just outside the six-month period for which he had been bound over in October 1902. Wise pointed out that the space was corporation property and in a pronounced Protestant district, and he urged the council to allocate the site for the open-air meetings. In view of the events of the last two years, the council were understandably sensitive over the issue of open-air meetings. It was recognised that there were some advantages in confining meetings to specified sites, as other cities had already done. In particular they would be easier to police. (Better still, in their opinion, that contentious issues should be debated inside closed doors.) However, it was clear that no Catholics would ever be able to use St Domingo Pit for a meeting. In effect it would be a council-provided Protestant meeting place. On 4th March the council set up a special committee to investigate the possibility of allocating certain sites for public meetings. Dunning was hostile to the idea of the proposed Protestant demonstration, John Kensit's death was still fresh in mind, and sectarian feelings were still high. His fears were expressed in a special report for the Watch Committee.[61] He summarised Wise's activities over the previous two years and expressed the view that the proposed meeting at St Domingo Pit on 8th April would lead to a breach of the peace. He gave examples of Wise's language used on several occasions. By any standards they were ill considered, to say the least. In one instance, referring to Catholic priests, he is alleged to have said:

> They waste their lives with harlots, they rob the poor to feed their own children; they are incarnate devils. The Saint ought to know what they are. I don't. Your Mass is gambled away. They live upon you and you know it. No man likes whiskey more than them. The monks in monastaries were living lives of devils. The Monks and Nuns live together in impurity.

There was more of the same. (Wise subsequently defended himself on the grounds that he was quoting St Catherine of Siena.)[62] Dunning also stated that if the meeting went ahead, about half the city police force would have to be withdrawn from other duties or the force would have to be increased by about 200 men. He added:

> Comparison has been made between the city [Liverpool] and London, but everybody who knows the two places must recognise the fact that a Protestant lecturer may talk his fill in the latter place and nobody but his followers will listen, while here he cannot do it on the fringe of a definite Roman Catholic quarter without danger to the public peace.[63]

The Watch Committee met on 23rd March and a copy of Dunning's report was presented to them. On 26th March the special committee on open spaces met for the first time but Dunning had already acted on 14th March by laying information asking that Wise be summoned to show 'why he should not be ordered to find sufficient sureties to keep the peace towards all his Majesty's subjects and be of good behaviour during the next twelve months'.[64] Wise appeared in court on 20th March and it was ordered that before 8th April next he enter into a recognisance in the sum of £100, with two different sureties in the sum of £50 each and to keep the peace for twelve months. In default, he would go to prison for two months as a First Division offender.[65] Thus Stewart had given Wise the opportunity to think over his position, no doubt wishing to appear fair. However, it also gave time for the build up of tension, which Wise was expert at orchestrating. The local press was inundated with letters concerning 'free speech' and the myriad Protestant organisations passed resolutions condemning the summons. Many of the resolutions called for action on the part of the mayor, W. W. Rutherford. This build-up of

Protestant indignation was embarassing for Rutherford, an Orangeman, supported politically by Protestants, who yet had to impart an aura of impartiality. On the other hand, defending free speech was more respectable than justifying meetings and parades that led to violence. In the council chamber the Irish nationalists were strongly opposed to making St Domingo Pit a meeting place. On *3rd April* Rutherford attended a meeting of the Finance Committee and asked them to support him in calling a special meeting of the council on *7th April,* in order to get a decision from the special committee on open spaces. He was hoping a decision could be made quickly that would allow Wise's meeting to go ahead and so pre-empt Wise's going to prison and martyrdom on the 8th. In fact the special committee report was only to be discussed at the May council meeting, so no action was taken. Meanwhile the pressure on local politicians continued. For example, on *2nd April* the Walton branch of the Protestant Union passed a resolution condemning the Chief Constable and calling on the councillors in Warbreck ward to 'maintain the right of free speech in the council chamber'.[66] Meanwhile the increasingly flustered Rutherford wrote to Wise on *6th April,* asking him not to address any outdoor meeting until after *6th May,* the date when the council would decide on the open-air meeting issue. In return, Rutherford would ask the stipendiary to see if the date for Wise to enter into recognisances could be put back until after then. Wise's frame of mind is indicated by his reply:

> It is very gracious of you to interpose in this case and I thank you for it; but you must permit me most respectfully to inform you that unless the altogether unprecedented decision of Mr Stewart (Stipendiary) is completely abrogated or suspended until the special committee give their report, and I am in the interim granted the privilege to hold open air meetings on the only permanent site in Protestant Everton, St Domingo Pit, I am bound by all conscience to go to Walton gaol and there suffer the cruel indignities imposed upon me by what I consider to be an unjust administration of the English law. Other Protestant speakers have held, and are holding, open air meetings in this city and in the name of justice I claim the same right . . . The only crime of which I am guilty is my popularity among Protestant workingmen and in order to ruin their influence, I am literally hounded to death by wicked and unrelenting police persecution. And now I am to go to prison because of Popish mob rule, misrepresentation of facts and garbled quotations of my public speeches.[67]

With a sure touch Wise turned his imprisonment on *8th April* into another Protestant demonstration, more dramatic than the meeting originally planned for that day. The police arranged with him that, in the absence of recognisances, he should report to Walton gaol by noon, where they would be ready with the warrant for his arrest. At noon Wise attended a meeting at the Y.M.C.A. in Mount Pleasant attended mainly by women. He said it was the most solemn and precious moment of his life. The crowded meeting showed he had more hearts sympathising with him than were against him. He had no idea when he took up his work that he would be subject to so much social ostracism and bitter persecution. He hoped that when he came out of prison they would have free speech. After the meeting, crowds of people tried to shake his hands. A crowd estimated at 5,000 was waiting as Wise got into a carriage to be driven to Walton. Enthusiastic supporters unharnessed the horses and pulled it down Mount Pleasant. Other supporters followed and the triumphant procession set out for prison, witnessed by crowds all along the way.[68] Significantly, in the cortege was Albert Stone, who had come up from London to take over the crusade whilst Wise was in prison.

In the weeks following, protest meetings and processions were held all over Liverpool and the Home Office was bombarded with petitions for Wise's release. Stewart's nerve was beginning to crack under the constant barrage of criticism. On *14th April* he wrote to the Home Office, enclosing cuttings from the Liverpool papers containing letters critical of his behaviour. He appealed to the Secretary of State to take action or prevent the repetition of such attacks, which, apart from being personally hurtful, he felt were bringing the administration of justice into disrepute.[69] But, apart from expressing regret that Stewart was subject to such attacks, there was nothing the Home Office could do. On *17th April* the council's special committee on open air spaces met and recommended that five sites be allocated for meetings, and it was agreed to seek parliamentary powers.

Dunning was clear in his own mind about Wise's motives. He wrote to the Home Office stating that Wise had chosen to go to prison to bolster his prestige and added:

> There is at present very bad feeling here between the Orangemen and the Roman Catholics due to Wise's demonstrations which will I anticipate, have vent in serious breaches of the peace before long.[70]

Meetings and resolutions continued unabated, and indicative of Wise's self-perception was one of his letters read out after he had heard of the special committee's decision to allocate St Domingo Pit as one of the open-air meeting sites.

> This is a wonderfully blessed morning for me and our work. Thank god! Victory is within sight. St. Domingo's Pit will be allocated. Remember, it is only by persistence that our rights are won; therefore let me dear friends, supporters and loyal fellow workers keep up the crusade, and still bring all the moral force possible to influence the Council in fixing the ultimate issue. Hard work will do everything. I am thankful that the Lord has thought me worthy to suffer for the Protestant cause.[71]

There is little doubt that he wished to be viewed as a martyr. The lady mayoress and her daughter visited him in Walton and Rutherford, the mayor, was heavily involved in the petitions to the Home Office.[72]

During the weeks leading up to Wise's imprisonment there had been no clashes between Catholics and his followers. On Sunday *19th April* a large crowd of supporters attended St Silas's Church in Pembroke Place. After the service they formed a procession and started to march back to Shaw Street *en route* for Everton. A number of attempts were made by Catholics to break up the procession but a large body of police prevented them doing so.[73] Some Protestants were convinced that the Catholics were trying to provoke retaliation in the hope that breaches of the peace would influence the council's decision regarding the open-air sites.[74] The constant meetings and processions were once again building up an atmosphere of trouble to come. On Saturday afternoon, *25th April* a large Protestant demonstration took place at St Domingo Pit and the incidents which followed illustrated the growing lawlessness. A procession marched to St George's Hall, where A. M. Stones addressed the meeting, referring to Ritualism, an issue almost forgotten in the furore over Wise's imprisonment. The meeting, on St George's Hall plateau, finished quietly but as the crowd was dispersing a fight broke out between two brothers, each wearing a Wiseite badge. Two policemen went to break it up, but the combatants turned on them, severely beating them. A tram inspector interfered and was also beaten; two more constables came to assist and were also beaten, but the four policemen managed to haul the brothers, struggling, down towards Dale Street bridewell. Several hundred men from the meeting gathered and some attempted to release the prisoners. Another policeman joined his comrades and one of the prisoners kicked him to the ground. It was alleged in court that the crowd were shouting, 'Let them go', 'No surrender-remember Derry's Walls.' The situation was becoming more and more threatening, and a reinforcement of sixty to seventy constables was brought from inside St George's Hall to surround the prisoners. The crowds were now so menacing that the police had to draw their staves and use them. Eventually the prisoners were got to the bridewell, but not before several policemen had received severe beatings. Four Protestants were arrested and the police identified one as being in the procession from St Domingo Pit. All four received prison sentences.[75] Meanwhile, Ritualist churches continued to attract attention. On Sunday *26th April* three men stood up in St Thomas's, Warwick Street, and shouted, 'We object to this, it is idolatrous.' One of the men arrested was a solicitor's clerk and another was a member of an Orange lodge. On Monday *27th April* Dunning presented a report on the special committee's recommendations concerning open-air sites. He opposed the use of St Domingo Pit on the grounds that it was not safe, and his dislike of Wise showed:

They may think he has exaggerated the chances of breaches of the peace but he would remind them that the principal demand for these sites has been made by, or on behalf of, the man whose abuse of free speech has provoked breaches of the peace and has bred the spirit of party rancour which now threatens the peace of the City.[76]

On 1st May Charles McArthur, M.P., presented a petition for Wise's release to the Home Secretary; it contained 42,895 signatures. On *13th May* he presented another petition with 19,674 signatures but the Home Secretary saw no grounds for releasing him.[77] On *13th May* the city council debated the issue of open-air sites. It developed into a battle between the Catholic councillors and their supporters, who opposed any allocation, against the Orange sympathisers, who did. Wise's behaviour over the previous two years was gone over, despite the attempt of the mayor to avoid any discussion of Wise. In the end the issue was put off for six months.[78]

Meanwhile the date for Wise's release approached. On *19th May* Dunning wrote to the governor of Walton gaol, asking if Wise could be released the evening before the day of his discharge proper, to try and avoid a demonstration by Protestants.[79] The political pressure was beginning to show. On *23rd May* the inaugural meeting of the *National Protestant Electoral Federation* was held. This Federation aimed at coordinating the various Protestant bodies, with the intention of securing Protestant objectives over Conservative priorities. On the platform were T. H. Sloan, M.P. (Belfast), and the Rev. J. McKinney. An example of the pressure on local politicians was a letter read out from C. H. Rutherford in which he refused to attend the meeting or a meeting of the George Wise defence committee - 'I am the Unionist candidate and a party man.' The chairman announced that in view of this the executive of the N.P.E.F. had asked the voters of the Anfield ward to remain neutral.[80] Rutherford (Nonconformist) was the Conservative nominee for a vacant seat on the council. He lost. Meanwhile the Kensit crusade continued, with several meetings in Birkenhead, where tempers had not cooled. On *Sunday 24th May* the Protestant Boys drum-and-flute band attended a meeting at the Queen's Hall. Afterwards, as they were marching away, a crowd attacked them, throwing bottles and stones and beating up some of the members.

Wise was released from Walton on *5th June* and wasted no time in getting back to business. On Sunday *21st June* he and an estimated 2,000 supporters crossed to Birkenhead to attend a meeting of the Protestant Crusade. Trouble was expected, and 100 Birkenhead police were on duty with 100 Liverpool in reserve. A clash took place between Catholics and Protestants and eight men were arrested, including the same John McKeever who had been charged with Kensit's murder the previous

December.[81] He was advised by the magistrate to emigrate. On *5th July,* in Birkenhead, St Mary's drum-and-fife band was attacked on the mistaken assumption it was connected with the Kensit campaign.[82] On *6th September* George Wise and his followers held a meeting near St Oswald's, Old Swan. A group of Catholics attacked them and nine were arrested, eight being remanded.[83]

Notes

1   Hugh Farrie was the chief leader writer of the *Liverpool Daily Post* in 1883 and he initiated an investigation into Liverpool's slums. The result was a series of articles entitled 'Squalid Liverpool'. See *Liverpool Daily Post,* 5th, 6th, 7th, 8th, 9th, 10th November 1883. For an account of prostitution in Liverpool at this time see *Liverpool Review,* 9th June, 21st July, 28th August, 11th, 18th September 1888 and 31st August, 7th, 14th September 1889.

2   *Liverpool Weekly Mercury,* 14th July 1877.

3   Ibid., 14th July 1877.

4   Ibid., 27th July 1878.

5   Ibid., 20th July 1878.

6   Ibid., 27th July 1878.

7   *Liverpool Mercury,* 3rd August 1878.

8   *Liverpool Weekly Mercury,* 31st July 1880.

9   Waller, op. cit., p. 144: 'In Liverpool nothing overtook fratricidal religion.'

10 Waller, op. cit., p. 141.

11 *Liverpool Courier,* 8th, 9th and 12th July 1889.

12 Not a great deal has been written about Wise, beyond bare biographical details. The biographical material used in this book is drawn from the following sources: R. F. Henderson, *George Wise of Liverpool* (1967); R. Griffiths, *Life Story of Pastor George Wise* (1909); *Liverpool Echo,* 29th November 1917 (obituary); *Liverpool Daily Post,* 30th November 1917 (obituary).

13 The Bramley-Moore Dock is in the North End and in the shanty 'From Liverpool to 'Frisco aroving went' the dock is mentioned.

14 For the politics of anti-Ritualism in Liverpool see Waller, op. cit., chapters 11, 12 and 13.

15 *Liverpool Mercury,* 19th July 1898.

16 *Liverpool Review,* 4th March 1898.

17 There were A. F. Warr (East Toxteth), J. H. Stock (Walton) and J. A. Willcox (Everton).

18 *Liverpool Daily Post,* 8th April 1901.

19 Ibid., 22nd April 1901.

20 *Liverpool Daily Post,* 27th May 1901. This contains an account of Wise's appearance in court on 25th May and describes the events of 15th and 16th May. See also *Liverpool Courier,* 27th May 1901.

21 *Liverpool Daily Post,* 27th May 1901.

22 Ibid.

23 Steward attended St Luke's Church in Southport, a Ritualist parish.

24 Rutherford was an Orangeman and a town councillor. Defending Wise was not only performing a duty towards a fellow Orangeman, it also won votes.

25 *Liverpool Daily Post,* 27th May 1901.

26 Ibid.

27 A precise account of the legal issues involved in Wise's behaviour in regard to his meetings is in the Law Report dealing with Wise's appeal. King's Bench Division, Wise v. Dunning, November 1901, pp. 167-80. F. E. Smith appeared on Wise's behalf. Smith was a keen cultivator of Orange votes.

28   As with Wise, not much has been written about Kensit other than bare biographical
     details and reports of his activities in organising anti-Ritualist meetings. Most useful
     is G. I. T. Machin, 'The last Victorian anti-Ritualism campaign, 1895-1906', in
     Victorian Studies, Spring 1982, pp. 277-302. The biographical details in this chapter
     have been taken from newspaper reports. See *Liverpool Courier,* 8th October 1902,
     also *Manchester Guardian,* 8th October 1902.
29   *Liverpool Courier,* 8th October 1902.
30   Machin, op. cit., pp. 283-9.
31   *Liverpool Review,* 6th September 1902.
32   *Liverpool Courier,* 30th July 1902.
33   P.R.O. HO 144/659/V36777/10. Kensit to Lane, 30th August 1902; also report on
     meeting by PC Hughes dated 30th August 1902.
34   *Liverpool Review,* 13th September 1902.
35   P.R.O. HO 144/659/V 36777/109. Report on meetings on 29th and 30th August 1902
     from Superintendent Thomas Clingan of Liverpool City Police and Inspector J. J.
     Keelan.
36   Ibid. Thomas Clingan.
37   *Liverpool Echo,* 8th September 1902; *Liverpool Courier,* 9th September 1902.
38   The local press coverage was enormous. The *Liverpool Courier* in particular gave
     prominence to the event. For example see 15th September 1902. For a hostile apprais-
     al of Kensit's imprisonment and his motives see *Liverpool Review,* 13th September
     1902; 'Liverpool is well able to protect itself against the dangers of mob law and the
     stipendiary has taken the first step in that direction by binding Mr Kensit over to keep
     the peace for twelve months as the leader of one mob . . .'
39   Ibid,, 20th September 1902.
40   *Liverpool Courier,* 8th September 1902.
41   Ibid., 11th September 1902.
42   Ibid., 12th and 16th September 1902.
43   lbid., 19th September 1902.
44   Ibid., 18th September 1902.
45   Though the meeting passed off without violence this was due to a large police presence.
     In fact there was an hostile Irish crowd who would have seriously harmed Kensit given
     the chance. P.R.O. HO 144/659/V 36777/90. Chief Constable of Birkenhead to Home
     Secretary, 27th September 1902.
46   *Liverpool Courier,* 22nd September 1902.
47   Ibid., 22nd September 1902.
48   Ibid., 23rd September 1902.
49   The most authoritative statement of events on the night of 25th September is the
     report of W. J. Davies, Chief Constable of Birkenhead. P.R.O. HO 144/659/V 36777/90.
     Davies to Home Secretary, 27th September 1902. See also *Liverpool Courier,* 26th
     September 1902; *Liverpool Echo,* 26th September 1902. *Liverpool Courier* 27th and
     29th September 1902.
50   P.R.O. HO 144/659(V 46777/109. Dunning to Under-Secretary of State at the Home
     Office, 2nd October, 1902.
51   P.R.O. HO 144/659/V 36777/142. Dunning to Under-Secretary of State, 7th October
     1902. Also *Liverpool Echo,* 3rd October 1902.
52   Dunning, op. cit. Also *Liverpool Echo,* 4th October 1902.
53   Dunning, op. cit.
54   L.R.O. Watch Committee Minutes, 6th October 1902. Report of Head Constable, p.
     215.
55   *Liverpool Echo,* 8th October 1902.
56   L.R.O. Watch Committee Minutes, 6th October 1902. Report of Head Constable, p. 215.
57   For details of Kensit's last days see *Liverpool Echo,* 2nd and 3rd October 1902;
     Liverpool Courier, 8th October 1902.

58   *Liverpool Echo,* 13th October 1902; *Protestant Searchlight,* 1st November 1902; *Liverpool Review,* 11th October 1902; *Manchester Guardian,* 8th October 1902.

59   P.R.O. HO 144/659/V 367777/181. Dunning to Under-Secretary of State, Home Office, 13th November 1902. 'There has been enough trouble in Liverpool through the so-called religious crusades and I venture to say this trial would be the means of reviving and aggravating the feeling of hostility between Catholics and Protestants.' Also P.R.O. HO 144/659/V 36777/182. Dunning to Under-Secretary of State, 15th November 1902. Dunning again went over his reasons for not wanting the trial to be held in Liverpool. 'Under these circumstances the trial of McKeever in Liverpool can produce but public excitement and ill feeling.' The Director of Public Prosecutions was irritated by Dunning's interference. See P.R.O. HO 144/659/V 36777/184, D.P.P. to H. B. Simpson, Under-Secretary of State, 18th November 1902. 'I cannot in my long experience in this office remember a case in which any Chief Constable or Chief Officer of Police has gone into court and opposed an application made, presumably, in the interests of justice on the part of the D.P.P. It is not, I hope, likely that such a course will be adopted by any police officer.'

60   For accounts of McKeever's arrest and trial see *Liverpool Echo,* 5th, 10th, 13th, 15th, 17th, 28th November; 8th, 9th, 10th, 11th, 12th December 1902.

61   Head Constable's Report, 'Protestant Demonstration announced for April 8th', presented to the Watch Committee on 23rd March 1903. Wise's intentions were widely publicised. For a critical view of his intentions see *Liverpool Review,* 1st March 1903.

62   Ibid., p. 5. His reference to Catherine of Siena and his justification for quoting her is given in 'Why I go to prison', *Protestant Searchlight,* April 1903, p. 96.

63   Head Constable, op. cit., p. 7.

64   P.R.O. HO 144/704/107039/13. Copy of information laid by Dunning. See also *Liverpool Daily Post,* 21st March 1903.

65   First Division status allowed a prisoner to have a cell to himself, to wear his own clothes, avoid prison work and buy extra food, newspapers, etc. Also, a First Division prisoner could have help while in prison.

66   *Liverpool Courier,* 4th April 1903.

67   *Liverpool Courier,* 7th April 1903. Copy of letter from Wise to Rutherford dated 4th April 1903. *The Protestant Searchlight* of April 1903 carried an article by Wise headed 'Why I go to prison'. In it he attacks Dunning's ability as Chief Constable and asks 'O God, send they people another Cromwell.'

68   *Liverpool Courier,* 9th April 1903.

69   P.R.O. HO 144/704/107039/2. Stewart to Secretary of State, 14th April 1903.

70   P.R.O. HO 144/704/107039/11. Dunning to Under-Secretary of State, Home Office, 20th April 1903.

71   The Special Committee met on 17th April and made its decision to allocate sites 'subject to parliamentary powers being obtained'. *Liverpool Courier,* 18th April 1903. Wise's letter was reproduced in *Liverpool Courier,* 21st April 1903, p. 3.

72   *The Liverpool Review* of 18th April 1903 carried a satirical account of the mayor's attempts to keep Wise out of prison ('Mrs. Malaprop to Wise, the Foolish'), p. 14.

73   *Liverpool Courier,* 20th April 1903. During this period Wiseites interrupted a service at St Margaret's, a Ritualist church in Warwick Street, shouting 'We must have another Oliver Cromwell here.' *Liverpool Courier,* 21st and 28th April 1903.

74   Letter, *Liverpool Echo,* 21st April 1903.

75   *Liverpool Courier,* 27th and 28th April 1903.

76   *Liverpool Courier,* 28th April 1903.

77   P.R.O. HO 107039/22.

78   *Liverpool Courier,* 14th May 1903. This edition carries a detailed account of the city council meeting on 13th May.

79   P.R.O. HO 144/704/107039/36. Dunning to governor, Walton Gaol, 19th May 1903.

80   *Liverpool Courier,* 23rd May 1903,

81   On his release from prison Wise announced he would stand for the council. *Liverpool Courier*, 8th June 1903. For police estimate of crowds at the prison for his release see L.R.O. Watch Committee Minutes, 8th June 1903, p. 13. For the trouble in Birkenhead see *Liverpool Courier*, 22nd June 1903.

82   *Liverpool Courier*, 6th July 1903.

83   L.R.O. Watch Committee Minutes, 7th September 1903. Report of Head Constable.

Chapter IX **Communal strife,** 1904-09

Following the events of 1903 Wise never again held a meeting in Islington Square but intercommunal relations did not improve. A split in the ranks of the Protestant preachers meant that no one was in complete charge, and while Wise remained the dominant figure in the North End, Albert Stones emerged as the South End leader and Louis Ewart, the organiser of the Liverpool Kensitites, took the initiative in Garston. Between 1904 and 1908 the working-class areas of the city were subject to regular sectarian clashes and the full extent of the alienation within Liverpool society was revealed publicly and tragically in 1909. The population movements which took place accentuated the existence of religious ghettoes and the events of that year represented a nadir in the city's history of sectarian violence.

I

Though Wise's activities at Islington Square and St Domingo Pit earned him the reputation of a rabble rouser, he displayed more positive talents. In 1903 'Protestant' candidates contested seats in the municipal elections, reflecting the disenchantment in their ranks with official Conservative resolve over the matter of Ritualism. They contested four seats and were successful in three, one of which was won by Wise in Kirkdale.[1] As a councillor Wise devoted a great deal of time and energy to the needs of his constituents but in December he became pastor of the Protestant Reformers' Church in Netherfield Road, totally supported by membership contributions.[2] As a full-time minister he had to give up his council seat. In his new role he displayed the same commitment that he had in his other activities, the most notable of the latter being his Bible class. Started in 1898, by 1909 it had grown to something between 1,600 and 1,700 members, almost entirely working men. Wise preached teetotalism, and his success can be judged by the fact that an estimated two thirds of the Bible class were abstainers. The Bible class was separate from the Protestant Reformers' Church, as was the George Wise Protestant Crusade. The church ran three women's Bible classes, a large Sunday school and the biggest cycling club in Liverpool. In addition, Wise regularly visited all Protestant children at the Netherfield Road Hospital; he was a member of the Liverpool Distress Committee and a member of the West Derby Board of Guardians.[3] He was also an Orangeman and became a chaplain to the Liverpool Province. Despite his good works, his anti-Catholic speeches over the years had dismayed many Protestants who were equally staunch anti-Ritualists.[4] More significantly, personal jealousies opened up a split in the ranks of working-class supporters of the George Wise Crusade and one important consequence was that no one was in control of the situation. Between 1901 and 1903 Wise had decided what meetings were to be called and parades held in connection with his Crusade. This gave the police someone to deal with when trying to control events. After 1903 the Protestant leadership was divided, Albert Stones quarrelled with Wise and took over the South End crusade while Louis Ewart became the leader of the Liverpool Kensitites and went his own way.

Albert Stones had been engaged in 1903 to look after the Crusade while Wise was in prison. In London, Stones had been the manager of Kensit's bookshop. His contract with Wise was for four months, at a wage of £1 10s a week, with 15s a week accommodation allowance. He was also allowed removal expenses from London to Liverpool.[5] At the end of his contract he was offered a permanent position in the South End, at £2 per week, and accepted. Stones was a strong character and, in the same way that Wise did not like playing second fiddle to the Kensits, so Stones disliked his subordinate role. After six months he asked for a rise. It was refused and the rift with Wise opened up.[6] Stones alleged that Wise was jealous of his popularity in the South End and referred to Wise as the 'Pope of the North'.[7] The final split came in April 1904, when the Crusade committee accused Stones of financial irregularities. Stones and his supporters set up a rival organisation and, in effect, Wise lost his influence in the South End.[8] It was another case of establishing territorial rights.

In the summer of 1904 the scene of sectarian clashes switched from the North End to Toxteth as Stones, Ewart and renegade Orange bands stomped the streets. Part of the problem was that the officials of the Orange Institution had no control over the 'scratch bands'. These did not belong to any particular lodge but were made up of musicians from a number of lodges who came together to play.[9] Frequently such bands initiated parades which became involved in clashes with Catholics. In 1904 the marching season opened in March and immediately there was trouble. On the 27th Stones led a procession following a George Wise Crusade meeting, estimated at 2,000. Accompanied by drum-and-fife bands it marched into Mill Street, where it was met by a large crowd of Catholics waving green flags. On this occasion an incident occurred which was to become a not uncommon feature of such confrontations. A Catholic leapt into the middle of a band, armed with a knife. His aim was to puncture the big drum. This was increasingly regarded as a test of courage for Catholic bucks.[10] A general free-for-all followed and the police had difficulty in restoring order. Immediately after the fracas a Protestant youth was beaten up by other Protestants who thought he was a Catholic.[11] On Saturday 16th April another serious clash occurred in Toxteth. A crowd of about 700 Protestants were following two bands, the *Sons of Derry* and the *Sons of William*. They marched into Mill Street, a mixed area, and a man in the procession left it to attack a man whose only offence was that he was wearing a green tie. The result was a riot. The next day a Catholic band was assaulted by Protestants.[12] The rest of the summer witnessed continual street fights in the South End, involving both Orange and Irish bands of music.[13] Many of the incidents involved terrifying experiences for innocent victims. For example, on 10th June a Protestant procession went into Essex Street, Toxteth, and paused outside No. 37. Three sisters were alone in the house. Their father was a Protestant but the mother was a Catholic and they had been brought up Catholics. For this reason alone the windows were smashed and two men ran into the house and kicked one of the girls in the head. The police dragged them out but another man climbed over the back wall and assaulted another sister, despite the police presence.[14] On 8th August a Catholic crowd following an Irish band attacked a Protestant house, and on Saturday and Sunday 13th and 14th August there were sectarian rows in several parts of Liverpool, in which houses were attacked and damaged.[15] The situation was anarchic, although the meetings of Stones and Ewart encouraged crowds to gather. From the police point of view, it was impossible to predict where trouble would break out next.

The officer with the difficult task of preserving peace in Toxteth was Superintendent Breeze, of C Division, and, like Dunning and Wise, Breeze and Stones were developing a healthy dislike of each other. On 30th January 1905 Stones was leading a large procession through the South End when Breeze and his men lined the road and asked people to disperse. An argument started and Stones was injured in the resultant melee. He subsequently claimed he was beaten up by the police; that he was injured was not in dispute. He was charged with inciting the riot and remanded on bail for the assizes.[16] Like Wise, Stones became convinced the police were anti-Protestant and that Breeze was out to get him. To complicate matters, the Kensitites, led by Louis Ewart started a campaign in Garston

and disturbances also occurred there throughout the summer.[17] The difficulties facing the police were illustrated by the events of 27th August
1905. The Irish National Forresters marched from the South End as part
of a recruiting campaign, to Garston. On arrival, many followers ignored
the meeting and tried to get into the Orange district of Garston, in particular Window Street. They were opposed by the residents and a pitched
battle ensued. The police arrived and both factions turned on them.[18]
During 1904 the Liverpool police were asked to prepare for trouble on 639
occasions, force had to be used on eighty of them and eighteen were
described as riots.[19] While the number of incidents fell between 1905 and
1908 there is no doubt that the excitement generated from 1901 onwards
had polarised the Catholic and Protestant communities and resulted in an
atmosphere of mutual dislike, in some cases hatred, which only needed a
particularly bad incident to trigger widespread disorder. It happened in
1909.

II

The rapidity with which Wise and his colleagues could find issues to
protest about was bewildering. Ritualism had been the centre of
Protestant demonstrations for ten years when, in 1908, attention was
switched to the provisions of the 1829 Catholic Emancipation Act. Among
other things the Act banned the carrying of the consecrated Host in
public. The relevence of this was that the Roman Catholic Church was
holding its Eucharistic Conference in London in September 1908 and in
Protestant circles rumours circulated that the Host *was* to be carried in
procession through the streets of London.[20] In fact this had been planned,
but on advice from the Home Office the idea was abandoned. Whether or
not this was widely known is not clear but the airing of the issue in the
press and in the House of Commons had alerted Protestants. If the
Catholics did publicly parade the Host it would be illegal, and as, in
practice, the 1829 Act was almost a dead letter in most towns it was
possible that any breach of the law might be ignored. It was this possibility which alarmed Protestants. On 5th September Wise and Louis Ewart
addressed a mass meeting in Liverpool to protest about the 'illegal procession' to be held in London. They also 'demanded' that no alteration
should be made to the Coronation and Accession oaths. Neither Wise nor
anyone else had any evidence that the procession would break the law, so
they were protesting about an illegality which *might* occur.[21] Under the
provisions of the 1829 Catholic Emancipation Act it was also illegal for a
Catholic priest or member of a Roman Catholic religious order to 'exercise
any of the rites or ceremonies of the Roman Catholic religion or wear the
habits of his Order save within the usual places of worship of the Roman

Catholic religion or in private houses . . .'[22] The Home Secretary had pointed out these provisions to the Archbishop of Westminster, and the law was strictly complied with at the opening ceremonies in London on 12th September. The following Sunday all the Catholic churches in Liverpool celebrated the opening of the congress. Militant Protestants regarded the Eucharistic Congress as something of a victory celebration and reacted accordingly. On 14th September John Kensit held a protest meeting in Preston even though the London procession had taken place.[23] In London Colonel Fitzpatrick, an Orangeman, placed a large notice outside his house stating that if the 'Papal Host' came out, 'ten thousand valiant Orangemen' would make sure it never returned to the 'Mass House'.[24] The meeting in Liverpool on 5th September by Wise and Ewart had been preceded by a procession with several fife-and drum bands. The process of winding up Protestant passions had begun again.

Early in 1909 the parish of Holy Cross in Vauxhall decided to celebrate the sixtieth anniversary of the founding of the Catholic mission in the parish, an area of extreme deprivation and overwhelmingly Irish Catholic.[25] On 8th April the chairman of the Health Committee received a request from Holy Cross, asking for permission to decorate the streets with flags and bunting and for permission to erect an altar at a road junction in the centre of the parish. In addition the parish was to hold a celebratory procession on 9th May. On 15th April the Committee approved the requests but had no authority to approve the erection of an altar: that came under the purview of the Finance Committee. Even more significant, Dunning, the Head Constable, knew nothing of these developments, although the Holy Cross festival committee informed Superintendent Smith on 23rd April of the arrangements. Thus, so far, there had been a simple administrative error. But in Liverpool, the erection of an altar in the street could never be a simple error, and on 30th April the Catholic Emancipation Act reared its head. Dunning received a letter from Alexander Colter, Liverpool Provincial Grand Secretary of the Orange Institution, writing on behalf of the Grand Lodge, saying that he 'understood' the Host was to be carried in the Holy Cross procession on 9th May and that it could lead to serious trouble with Orangemen and other Protestants.[26] Neither then nor subsequently could Colter state where he obtained his information regarding the Host.

This letter was Dunning's first intimation of trouble. He rang the organiser of the Holy Cross procession, Councillor Burke, who gave it as his private opinion that no Host or religious emblems would be carried. On this basis, Dunning reassured Colter that the law would not be broken. The ball was now rolling. On 4th May Dunning received a letter from the George Wise Crusade stating that the executive committee had 'strong reasons for believing that an attempt will be made to carry the Host (consecrated wafer) through the streets of Liverpool' and warning of trouble.[27] Later, under cross-examination, Richard Briggs, chairman of the Crusade Committee, subsequently admitted he had no evidence at all of any such intention. On 5th May Dunning received a letter from George Wise in similar vein. Again he reassured Wise but on 7th May he received more warnings of trouble from John Walker, Orangeman and president of the Protestant Labour Club, who likewise wanted reassurance. Dunning was by now uneasy and the same day he wrote to Councillor Burke, pointing out to him the relevant sections of the 1829 Act.[28] On the same day, too, the Orange Institution put an advertisement in the evening papers stating that the Head Constable had assured them that the Host would not be carried on 9th May.[29]

The procession took place and 4,500 people were gathered. The Italian community carried a life-size statute of the Virgin and Child on a litter, and laymen in the procession wore cassocks, including the altar boys. Significantly, two members of a religious order wore habits. A group of Protestants tried to interfere but the police easily contained them. It was only in the days following that Dunning found out that an altar had been erected in Marybone and his discovery coincided with a flood of complaints from Orangemen and other Protestants.[30] The gist was that the Catholics had broken their promise and carried illegal images and that men in the procession wore illegal dress: Dunning should have stopped the procession. These allegations were based simply on a misunderstanding of the law. The restrictions on dress in the 1829 Act applied to priests and members of religious orders. In the procession two priests had been wearing birettas and cassocks, and it was most unlikely that they were illegal. However, the two Benedictines wearing a habit had broken the law. The question of the statue of the Virgin and Child was more problematical; the Italians had been unwise but it was not clear it was illegal. Orangemen alleged also that the altar in Marybone was an obstruction, causing annoyance. In the heart of an almost totally Catholic area the complaint was clearly specious. On 14th May Dunning wrote to the Attorney General with details of the procession, including the information about the birettas, cassocks and habits.[31] In the eyes of Orangemen, Dunning had not fulfilled his responsibilities and was also guilty of a breach of faith.

Accusations of indifference to Protestant sensitivities were something Dunning had learned to live with but, unfortunately for him and Liverpool, the matter would not lie. The Finance Committee had given permission for the Catholic Young Men's Society to hold a rally on the St George's Hall plateau on 23rd May which coincided with an Orange procession to Holy Trinity Church, situated near by. Dunning feared a flare-up and asked the Orangemen to postpone their parade; they refused. He then asked Archbishop Whiteside to do likewise. He too refused and the joint events took place, without disorder.[32] Dunning was still receiving complaints about the 9th May procession and wrote to the Home Office, on the 24th May, in the course of his letter he pointing out that Liverpool was comparable to Belfast and he wanted more guidance on the interpretation of the provisions of the 1829 Act.[33]

By 14th June he had still not received a reply and he was becoming anxious, as St Joseph's Catholic church had announced a procession on Sunday 20th June. A report had just appeared in the press that the Host had been carried in a public procession in London and Dunning knew that Liverpool Orangemen would assume the same thing might happen on the 20th. On 17th June he received a reply from the Home Office to the effect that no action was to be taken regarding the 9th May procession but that he should warn the Roman Catholic authorities in the town that the 1829 Act was not a 'dead letter'.[34] At this point Dunning went to Ireland on holiday, leaving H. P. Lane in charge. The process of confrontation, typical of the Catholic-Orange quarrel, was now well under way. On 17th June the Provincial Grand Lodge of the Orange Institution proposed a counter-demonstration on 20th June. Significantly, Wise opposed the suggestion, on the ground it was madness. He was overruled. His opposition counters the view of him as an unmitigated rabble rouser.[35] On 18th June the *Evening Express* carried an advertisement, placed by officials of the Orange Institution, calling for a 'monster demonstration' in Juvenal Street, which was on the Catholic procession route. On 19th June H. P. P. Lane, the Deputy Chief Constable, sought assurances from Fr Rigby of St Joseph's that the procession would not break the law, and on receiving them immediately communicated the information to the Orange officials, asking them to call off the advertised demonstration. Obviously, at such a late stage, it was extremely difficult to do so and the only public statement was a verbal request from Colter at a Protestant Crusade meeting at Edge Hill.[36] To cover himself completely, on 19th June, Lane sent a written warning to Fr Rigby that if any images or emblems were carried in the procession he would stop it.[37]

III

During the week preceding 20th June people living in the streets and courts of St Joseph's parish were erecting small altars in their windows and lighting candles. It was a common practice in parts of Liverpool and such altars were frequently surrounded by women and children saying the rosary and singing hymns. By 12.30 p.m. on 20th June Protestant crowds were gathering in Juvenal Street East while Catholics were assembling in Juvenal Street West. In anticipation of trouble, Lane had 700 men on duty, including mounted police. He claimed afterwards that a fight broke out among the Protestant crowd of about 1,200 and quickly developed into a riot in which knives, swords and iron pipes were used as weapons. This is puzzling, in that there was no reason for Protestants to fight each other, and Protestants subsequently denied that a riot had taken place. It was alleged to have been an isolated drunken brawl.[38] Whatever the facts, Lane gave the order to clear Juvenal Street East, and it is fairly clear that the mounted police used considerable force. The incident was to be the centre of Protestant allegations against the police.[39] In neighbouring Prince Edwin Street, crowds of Protestants fought the police so fiercely that those on foot had to be assisted by the mounted police. While all this was going on, the Catholic procession in Juvenal Street had to be escorted on a shortened tour, back to the church. The fighting between groups of Protestants and police continued until midnight in the streets between Juvenal Street and Netherfield Road, and by that time Lane had 1,000 officers at his disposal.[40] There is no doubt that the clashes were vicious on both sides, and the Protestant areas in the North End were in a state of uproar. It was particularly shocking to Protestants that the police should have attacked them.

Had the events of 20th June been confined to fighting between police and Protestant crowds, together with some drunken brawls, the situation would have been not much worse than many previous upheavals. However, both the riot of 20th June and the animosity shown by Protestant leaders towards the St Joseph's procession, and Catholic bitterness at its curtailment, seemed to release a huge upsurge of anger. It was as if all the frustration arising from poverty, overcrowding and unemployment broke the surface and found outlet in sectarian violence at the readiest 'legitimate' excuse. The position of Catholics and Protestants alike who found themselves a minority in a street or neighbourhood became dangerous, and though the situation never approached the excesses of Belfast it was a near thing. The following examples serve to illustrate the terror that ordinary people experienced in the weeks following Sunday 20th June. These were reported, many such incidents were not. On the Monday and Tuesday following the procession, drunken fights occurred throughout the city, particularly in the North End. On Tuesday 22nd June, lunchtime, the children from St Polycarp's Church of England School in Gordon Street fought children from St Anthony's Catholic school in nearby Newsham Street. As word got round, both Catholic and Protestant mothers arrived on the scene, and an extraordinary series of fights took place between the women, stopped only when police reinforcements were brought from all over the city. At the same time the council school in Roscommon Street, All Souls' Catholic school in Collingwood Street and another school in Sackville Street were all invaded by gangs of women seeking reprisals for real or imagined grievances. Children and teachers were assaulted, and many of the invading women were armed, it being alleged that some Orange women carried swords.[41] The situation in the inner city was becoming more dangerous as rumours spread concerning the rioting. For example, in streets surrounding the Butler Street schools a rumour circulated that Catholics had burned down Heyworth Street school in Everton and were coming to attack Butler Street. Hysterical mothers rushed into the junior school and started to drag their children out, creating even more panic, made worse when a man arrived with a revolver, intending to defend the school.[42] In this growing hysteria the School Management Sub-committee met the same day and decided to close seventeen schools in the areas of the North End which were disturbed.[43] Anyone was liable to be attacked. In Catholic areas strangers were chased by gangs of women who suspected them of being Orangemen, rumours circulating that men had come from Belfast to burn down Catholic churches.[44] The police had been on duty continuously since Sunday morning and by 23rd June were exhausted. Commenting on the immediate aftermath of the St Joseph's procession, the *Liverpool Daily Post* of 23rd June said:

> This attack on schools and school children really constitutes the latest and most pitiful phase of the disgraceful proceedings of the last few days. Owing to the highly inflammable state of the crowds and the waywardness of their behaviour, the police find it extremely difficult to be 'on the spot' when a fresh row breaks out, but there is no doubt that but for the promptitude with which they have acted, in many instances, the results would have been far more serious.

In fact the situation *was* more serious than the *Post* realised in that Protestants and Catholics living as minorities began to be intimidated in quite a vicious manner.

Protestant dock workers were at risk because they had to pass through predominantly Catholic districts on the way to work; those living near the docks were exposed to intimidation. At 8.00 p.m. on the evening of 21st June Andrew Cathcart and two fellow carters were walking home through Hopwood Street, a predominantly Catholic area. Practically all carters were Protestants and the fact was well known. The three were attacked by a gang. Cathcart's colleagues escaped but he took a severe beating and subsequently died.[45] Another carter, George Shepherd, was known to be a Wiseite and on returning to the stables near Hopwood Street he was attacked. He fled, leaving his horse, but took some punches before he managed to hide in a loft, where he was rescued by the police.

He was never able to return to work in that district.[46] John Rawlinson, also a carter, lived with his wife and children in Vescock Street. On 21st June he was told the houses were going to be attacked and asked for police protection. None was forthcoming, probably because the police were over-stretched. During the night of 21st-22nd June the house was stoned and his wife injured. The family hid in a water closet next door until the police arrived.[47] Elizabeth Flynn, a Protestant, lived at 27 Westmorland Place. At 11.00 on the night of 21st June she was warned that she and her family should leave, as the house was going to be attacked because they were Protestants. A crowd of about thirty rushed up and stoned the building, smashing the door down. Mrs Flynn was alone with her child, her husband being at work. She sent the child for a policeman but when one arrived forty-five minutes later her bed had been dragged into the street and burned, together with the bedclothes. Next day the attackers returned after her husband left for work and the unfortunate woman wandered the streets looking for a policeman. The family abandoned their home.[48] Protestant workers at the Palatine Oil Cake Mills near the dock numbered only fifty out of a work force of five hundred. William Brown, a Protestant, was attacked by Catholic workers and escaped only by running up to the third floor and swarming down a hoist into the street. He had to give up his job.[49] Robert Taylor, another Protestant at the same mill, was beaten on the same night and had to leave his job for good.[50] William Daniels worked at the Palatine Mills. He was also the Worshipful Master of the Star of Kirkdale Orange Lodge and so was particularly at risk. He had been foolish enough to take a sword to work and sharpen it. After the riot on 20th June he was warned it was dangerous to go back to work but on Monday 22nd he returned and the situation was so threatening that the management sent for the police to escort him home. Despite an escort of six officers, he was attacked by a woman with tongs and received a head injury. Daniels never returned to his job and his brother was hounded out of the same mill.[51] The Rev. Sherwood Jones was the vicar of St Martin's in the Field, the Anglican parish between Scotland Road and Vauxhall Road, and he estimated that 80% of his parishioners were Roman Catholic. In the three weeks following the 20th June riot 110 Protestant families had to leave the parish through fear and intimidation.[52]

The attacks on Catholics living in or near predominantly Protestant areas were even more widespread. The Catholic parishes which bore the brunt of the Wiseite anger were Our Lady Immaculate in St Domingo Road, St Anthony's and All Souls'. Our Lady Immaculate presbytery was situated near the pit in St Domingo and hence was in the front line. Despite the strength of Orangeism in Everton, there was a sizeable Catholic community centred on Our Lady's, estimated at 5,500.[53] In the immediate area were the Catholic bishop's house, which was also a seminary, a convent in Everton valley and an orphanage in Beacon Lane. The parish priest in 1909 was Fr John Fitzgerald, who had been there since 1892 and so had experienced the effects of the Wiseite meetings in 1901-03.

Following the disturbances on 20th June Fitzgerald submitted a report to the town council, describing the position of Catholics in his parish and requesting action to stop Wise's meetings at the pit.[54] He claimed that since 1901 he and his fellow clergy, nuns and Catholic lay people had been subjected to non-stop harrassment which at times amounted to terrorism. In 1906 one of his curates was attacked and beaten in the street in broad daylight. In 1907 two nuns were pursued by a gang of youths, one of whom, he claimed, 'flung the contents of his nostrils over her'.[55] His church was invaded on two occasions, on one of which vestments were strewn over the floor and smeared with human excrement. Following the 20th June riots matters worsened. On 22nd June a crowd of Wiseite women were harrassing Catholic children leaving school, and when Fitzgerald intervened one attacked him with a poker. Throughout July, August and September incidents occurred regularly - Catholics were attacked, priests harrassed, Catholic shops and houses damaged. Fitzgerald alleged that in one incident Protestant youths urinated from a wall over Catholic infant schoolchildren and that a pregnant Catholic woman was kicked and beaten. By February 1910, he claimed, a total of 3,200 Catholics had left the parishes of Our Lady, St Anthony's and All Souls' for safer areas.[56]

Fitzgerald's document made a profound impression both in Liverpool and at the Home Office, and there was independent corroboration of some of the claims of intimidation in the Netherfield Road area.[57] Between 20th June 1909 and February 1910 twenty-two attacks took place on Catholic shops in that road.[58] There was also economic terrorism. Michael Sutton was a Catholic coal merchant with a yard in Netherfield Road. He was threatened by men who said they wanted 'Orange' coal, not 'Papist' coal, and he was forced to sell out at a loss.[59] In another street Catholics received leaflets signed 'The Sons of Death', ordering them out of their houses, and many took the advice.[60]

IV

This level of communal bitterness was causing extreme concern at all levels of society and the temperature was raised when George Wise forced another confrontation over processions. On 6th June 1909 his Bible class had held a parade in a Protestant district of Everton. Such parades had been going on for six years without trouble. On this occasion a woman had waved a green flag and was assaulted by two members of the class. They received prison sentences.[61] On 18th June Wise had informed the police of his intention to hold another Bible class procession on 27th June over the same route. Dunning suggested that in view of the 20th June riots and the excited state of the area it would be advisable not to hold the procession. Wise replied that it would go ahead. Not unreasonably, he argued, in a Protestant area it was not likely to provoke disorder. Dunning decided to act, on the basis that 27th June was only a week after the riots and a 'copy-cat' disturbance might take place.[62] On 25th June he laid an information before the stipendiary to the effect that the parade would lead to a breach of the peace. Wise was arrested and appeared before the stipendiary magistrate, where the case was adjourned until 1st July and he was released on bail. Next day the magistrates issued instructions to the police to use 'every means in their power' to preserve the peace. Dunning had the support of many Protestants. For example, on 20th July the Anglican bishop informed him that fifteen vicars in parishes in the North End had met and unanimously condemned party processions and also praised the police for their help. On 7th August the stipendiary ordered Wise to enter into his own recognisances in the sum of £100 and to keep the peace. Wise refused and was sentenced to four months in prison. Martyrdom was eagerly embraced and on 10th August he went to Walton gaol. As on previous occasions petitions and demonstrations were quickly organised for his release.[63] Inevitably the imprisonment increased the Wiseites' sense of persecution and brought calls for Dunning's sacking. It also triggered off more violence on the streets. There were ninety-eight convictions during August for crimes against property, sixty in the week following Wise's imprisonment.[64] On 18th August he was released to appeal before the King's Bench, an action which Dunning thought might cool Protestant tempers. In fact Wise lost the appeal and returned to prison on 23rd October, an occasion which was accompanied by more trouble, including an attempt to attack St Alphonsus' Catholic church, with clashes between police and Protestants.[65]

Wise's imprisonment was a matter of considerable concern and embarrassment to Dunning, Conservative politicians and anyone else who wanted to see peace on the streets. Wise could have secured his own release at any time by entering into recognisances to keep the peace for twelve months but he refused on the grounds that to do so would amount to admitting he had committed an offence. Shephard Little, the stipendiary magistrate, W. W. Rutherford, M.P. for West Derby, and Councillor Charles Rutherford had all told Wise that was not the case but he was adamant.[65A] To the further irritation of Protestants, Little was unsympathetic and would not allow Wise the status of a First Division prisoner and all the comforts that had been enjoyed by John Kensit, junior, seven years before. This was seen as another element of vindictiveness on the part of the authorities. Conservative politicians who had particularly allied themselves with the Protestant vote had to be seen to be doing something as the clamour over Wise's imprisonment grew. Charles McArthur, Unionist M.P. for Kirkdale, wrote to Herbert Gladstone, the Home Secretary, asking for a reconsideration of Wise's case, '. . . which has aroused a very strong feeling in this city and threatens consequences dangerous to peace and order'. He wanted Wise to have First Division status but the Home Office refused to interfere.[66] Harmood Banner, M.P. for Everton, went to the Home Office and explained that the situation in Liverpool was critical, pleading for Wise's release.[67] As a result the Home Secretary cabled Dunning on 18th August asking for a report on the state of public order. (Wise had entered Walton gaol on 10th August.) Dunning confirmed that the town was in an agitated state, which took the 'form usual in Liverpool', street processions, meetings and damage to property. Significantly, he made clear his recognition of Wise's positive virtues :

> Wise is supported by a number of respectable people, influenced by the good work he undoubtedly does as Pastor of what is known as the Protestant Reformers Church while in the character of George Wise of the George Wise Protestant Crusade, by his attacks on the Roman Catholic religion, he attracts the lower sort of Protestants whose motive is mere opposition to Roman Catholicism . . . he exercises a great deal of influence over electors and is a factor in local politics into which, as the Secretary of State is no doubt aware, religious differences enter to a large extent. In this particular crisis he has stated his intention of influencing the Conservative Party to take up his case at the November elections with a view to electing another Watch Committee.[68]

Dunning was referring to the fact that Wise and his supporters were after his scalp and wanted him sacked. W. W. Rutherford joined in the correspondence with the Home Secretary, stressing the unsettled state of the city and claiming that some people went 'in fear of their lives'. He said that tempers were kept up because many Protestants felt Wise had been treated unfairly; 'nothing is more dangerous to the peace of the community as a sense of injustice'.[69] As a senior Orangeman Rutherford was close to Protestant opinion and had to be seen to exert himself on Wise's behalf even though, like most Conservative politicians, he was appalled by the violence. The dilemma for Herbert Gladstone was that, while accepting the situation in Liverpool was dangerous and that Wise's imprisonment was an unsettling factor, he did not wish to interfere publicly in the stipendiary's administration of justice. No one believed Little, the stipendiary, would himself order Wise's release.[70]

Simultaneously with the campaign for Wise's release, Orangemen and Wiseites were pressing for an investigation into the behaviour of the Liverpool police, alleging brutality on 20th June and partiality towards Catholics. This latter charge seems ludicrous, given the experience of policemen in Vauxhall and other Irish areas, and it was based on the fact that the Orange leaders and Wiseites had a muddled understanding of the law and its applications. However, the city council, needing to repair the harm done to community relations, requested a government inquiry, following a petition signed by a large number of people, on 14th August. The council's request was favourably received and on 25th November the royal assent was given to the Police (Liverpool Inquiry) Act, to enquire:

(a) into the conduct of the police in the City of Liverpool in dealing with the disturbances in that city during the twelve months immediately preceding the passing of the Police (Liverpool Inquiry) Act, 1909.
(b) into the circumstances causing such disturbances.

This gave the Home Secretary the opportunity to release Wise without appearing to overrule the stipendiary's decision. Wise was advised to petition the Home Secretary for a discharge, promising not to speak at any open-air meetings until after the inquiry was completed and, further, to do everything in his power to assist in restoring peace in the city. He submitted the required petition and was released on 26th November.[71] The Home Office issued a press release, explaining that he had been freed to help him prepare his evidence for the forthcoming inquiry.[72] On the same day the Home Secretary wrote to the stipendiary, informing him of his decision and the reasons, reassuring him that it did not reflect on his actions in court.[73] The release of Wise was an unusual step for a Home Secretary and must be taken as an indication of the government's concern over the state of affairs in Liverpool. In judging the Home Secretary's decision it should be noted that demands for Wise's release were not confined to his friends and allies. For example, Dr Waddy, a physician in Liverpool, had been a friend of Wise's and had treated him before they quarrelled in 1905. On 20th November he wrote to E. G. Jellicoe, a barrister and Liberal politician in Liverpool, expressing the opinion that Wise was unsuited to prison life:

He is a soft flabby creature and one, who if he should get an attack of pneumonia, or any chest infection, would go out with scant notice . . . What if an accident occurs? There will be a riot such as never was known before in Liverpool and the blame, rightly or wrongly, will be put on the government . . . I believe even the Catholics are saying now they do not want Wise kept in any longer.[74]

Waddy was concerned that Wise's imprisonment was going to provide political ammunition to be used against the Liberals. Jellicoe sent the letter to the Home Office, which immediately asked the governor of Walton to give Wise a medical check-up.[75]

The Catholics were suspicious of the deal, particularly as the incorrigible Wise seemed to be resuming his old habits in defiance of the conditions agreed to in the petition which formed the basis of his release. The day he left prison he addressed two meetings, one at the St Domingo Pit, thus breaking his undertaking to the Home Secretary. At the second meeting, in his own church in Netherfield Road, he again attacked the Roman Catholic Church in general and the Jesuits in particular. This was reported to the Home Secretary, who told Dunning to take no action but to warn Wise that any more breaches of his agreement would not be tolerated.[76] However, George Lynskey, acting as solicitor for the Liverpool Catholic Emergency Association, wrote to the Home Secretary asking for a copy of Wise's petition. On receiving it he complained that Wise had broken the agreement; but to no avail.[77]

V

The inquiry was presided over by Arthur Ashton, appointed commissioner by the Secretary of State, and was in session from 31st January to 26th February, 1910. Five different interest groups were represented: Liverpool City Council, the Head Constable and police, the Loyal Orange Institution and the George Wise Protestant Crusade, the Roman Catholics, and, lastly, certain property owners and shopkeepers. During the twenty-five days the inquiry was in session 146 witnesses were examined, including nineteen Catholic priests. Significantly, only two Anglican clergymen gave evidence, reflecting the fact that Roman Catholics were the main complainants and that most Anglican clergy were not involved in the quarrel. Witnesses had been invited through advertisements in the press and so were a self-selected sample, with the result that evidence of many violent incidents never came before the commission. On 31st March the commissioner submitted a seventy-page report to the Home Secretary, a document based on 1,687 pages of evidence.[78]

The central conclusions are easily stated. The police were cleared of all charges of unnecessary force on 20th June 1909; with regard to the allegations that the police showed partiality to Roman Catholics, the police, and Dunning in particular, were exonerated. In fact Wise and other Protestants had dropped many of their charges before the end of the inquiry because the revelation of factual evidence rendered the charges worthless - for example, that Dunning had sanctioned the erection of the altar in Marybone.[79] In other cases simple ignorance of either the law or of Roman Catholic practices invalidated many charges. Illustrative was Wise's claim that Dunning should have charged the Roman Catholic

Bishop Whiteside for allowing the 9th May procession to take place. However, under cross-examination, he admitted he knew of no Act under which this could happen. The bishop had committed no crime.[80] Laymen in the 9th May procession had worn cassocks, being Tertiaries, a lay order. Orange leaders had assumed their garb was illegal under the 1829 Act, which it clearly was not.[81] Turning to the causes of the 1909 disturbances, the commissioner stated with reference to events from 1901 onwards:

> I therefore report that the manner in which the George Wise Crusade had been conducted from its commencement was one of the causes of the disturbances under consideration.[82]

In respect of the role of George Wise himself, on whom the Roman Catholics had placed sole responsibility for the disturbances, the commissioner said with regard to Wise's dual personality:

> I have endeavoured to solve this strange enigma to the best of my ability. I think Mr Wise is responsible to a far greater degree than he himself appreciates for the disturbances which happened last year. He is an excellent speaker and a born debater but I doubt whether he fully apprehends the effect which his language produces upon his followers and upon his opponents . . . I report that the manner in which Pastor George Wise has in the past conducted his propaganda against Roman Catholicism was one of the causes which led to the disturbances.[83]

Another conclusion was that Orange bands were a causal factor in the street disorders.[84]

The commission's findings seem reasonable; they did not place all the blame on Wise but recognised an element of responsibility in his actions. Given the terms of reference, the investigation concentrated on events immediately preceding the 1909 disturbances. Obviously any attempt to establish causality in social science is extremely difficult but it is clear that the chain of events leading to the riots went back to McNeile, the Irish famine and the political manipulation of the prejudices, fear, economic rivalry and xenophobia that existed long before Wise arrived in Liverpool. At one point in the report some oblique reference is made to these antecedents:

> The predisposing cause of these disturbances is to be found in the fact that the Roman Catholics and Protestants living in neighbouring districts, which imperceptibly shade into one another, are alike animated and at times dominated by intense sectarian feeling. In these districts, to sing 'The Boys of Wexford' on the one hand and 'The Boyne Water' or 'Derry's Walls', on the other is no light matter. St. Patrick's day or Orangeman's day always yields some trouble. And indeed, where the same external circumstances express to one man in very truth the presence of his God, and to his neighbour the idolatory of perishable matter, and where conviction is in each case saturated

> with feeling, slight causes may produce far reaching results. If the seeds of strife are sown in such soil, it yields abundantly the evil fruits of crime, oppression and misery.[85]

It is difficult to believe that Wise was unaware of the consequences of his inflammatory speeches on uneducated minds; it is equally difficult to believe that he approved of the undoubted violent repercussions of the sectarian quarrel. Perhaps the demands of his ego when facing large, adulatory crowds overcame his sense of responsibility; he had shown considerable skill as a self-publicist. Dunning revealed himself as an educated man and a dedicated professional. However, keeping the peace had exhausted him. He admitted that the task was extremely difficult and that, had he known how difficult, he would never have gone to Liverpool. With regard to the period since the 20th June riot in 1909, and the Protestant campaign against him, 'life had been hell'.[86]

The investigation revealed that Protestants and Catholics *could* live together. Many Catholic priests said they had Protestant friends. Fr John Oldham of St Alban's parish said that, on the occasions of Catholic processions, Protestants helped with the decorations.[87] Similarly Fr Pinnington, parish priest of St Alphonsus' church, claimed that Protestant and Catholics got on well together.[88] A similar view was expressed by Fr Clarkson of St Oswald's, Old Swann, and Fr Jackson of St Anne's, Edge Hill.[89] More significantly, Fr John Fitzgerald of Our Lady Immaculate, St Domingo, said he was on friendly terms with many Orangemen and, up to Wise's campaign, had never been insulted. The Catholic clergy distinguished between Protestants and Wiseites. Fr Fitzgerald told the inquiry he used the term 'Wiseites' 'to distinguish them absolutely from the Protestants of the city'.[90] The Rev. R. Graham Bell, vicar of St Paul's, Kirkdale, was personally friendly with Catholic priests in his neighbourhood and was of the opinion that it was quite possible for Anglican and Roman Catholic priests to work together to restore harmony.[91] These opinions supported the view that the basic antagonism since 1901 had been between Wise and his followers, on the one hand, and Roman Catholics, on the other. Anglicans in general were bystanders in this particular squabble, although the history of the previous seventy years indicates that the Irish Anglicans had been a central element in the sectarian conflict.

VI

It needs to be remembered that the inquiry was asked for by the town council, not the Roman Catholics. A *Times* special correspondent subsequently alleged that the motivation for the request came from three prominent councillors who wanted the police to be found guilty. He did not name anyone, but the Orangemen element on the council were well known. The correspondent alleged that, following the unwanted conclusions of the commissioner, the town council quietly shelved the report and its implications.[92] An important recommendation had been that there should be a conciliation conference, but it appeared to be forgotten the year following publication of the report. Certainly the report was not followed by any sign of positive action. On 26th May a large deputation of Catholics, led by Bishop Whiteside, met the Lord Mayor and asked that inflammatory meetings at the Pit be banned. He said Catholic processions had been abandoned for the year and promised that no images or decorations which might cause trouble would be allowed in any future Catholic processions. However, he reiterated the view that Liverpool's sectarian violence was caused by Wise and his campaign.[93] The Lord Mayor had not the power to comply but the police were taking action to establish more clearly their power with regard to open-air meetings in public places.

The early signs as to whether a new spirit prevailed after the report were not encouraging. Soon after the meeting between Bishop Whiteside and the mayor in 1910, several hundred young members of the Catholic Defence League broke up a meeting of the George Wise Crusade in Edge Hill.[94] On Sunday and Monday 19th and 20th June 1910, a year after the Juvenal Street riot, mobs of people attacked a house in China Street, Everton, because it was thought the woman of the house was a Catholic and had a portrait of the Pope on her wall. The ringleaders received prison sentences. In fact the woman was not a Catholic.[95] On 12th July the crowds following the Orange parade seemed bigger than ever and the street celebrations wilder. It appeared to be almost a gesture of defiance. Many more streets were decorated and effigies burnt in Catholic and Orange areas.[96] A serious riot occurred in St Helens, ten miles away, when Orangemen marched through the Irish quarter of Greenbank.[97] 1911 brought little improvement; in June a Catholic funeral was held in Kew Street - the deceased was a youth said to have been injured in the sectarian fighting of twelve months before. The funeral procession met a hostile crowd and a fight ensued.[98] At the same time an elderly Protestant carter was attacked and beaten unconscious. He was an Orangeman. His horse found its own way home, raising the alarm.[99] On 11th June the Carneys, a Catholic family, were in bed when they were woken by knocks on the door and a voice asking who lived there. The daughter of the house went down and, the mother alleged, a voice asked, 'What religion?' The girl replied, 'Catholic,' and there was a scuffle. The daughter was found on the floor with no apparent injuries, but she died later. The inquest verdict was pneumonia but Catholics believed she had been killed. The Carneys' house had been marked 'Roman Catholic', and Mrs Carney alleged one of the attackers said, 'These are Coggers here' (a Liverpool expression for Catholics).[100] On 18th June a confrontation occurred in Netherfield Road between Catholics and Protestants, and the police lost control, allowing a Protestant mob to sack a Catholic house.[101] Throughout the summer there were continued incidences of sectarian violence, a lot of it arising from drunkenness. A potentially dangerous development was a new militancy among young Catholics. On 31st July the Catholic Defence League again attacked a George Wise Crusade meeting.[102]

The unfortunate Dunning was under more strain when, in August 1911, Liverpool was engulfed in a bitter transport strike which brought its own difficulties in police-public relations.[103] One would have thought the intensity of the strike, affecting all the working class, would have diverted attention from the sectarian quarrel. However, it was not so. There were *some* hopeful signs. In the rioting associated with the labour dispute the troops shot and killed two Liverpool men. One of them, Michael Prendergast, a Catholic docker, was buried at Ford Catholic cemetery: 250 members of the Netherfield Road Protestant Reformers' Church walked in his funeral procession and the crusade sent two wreaths 'from a few sympathisers in Netherfield Road'; yet on the same night an extraordinarily fierce fight took place between Catholics and Protestants in streets bordering Great Homer Street.[104]

Clearly the situation was intolerable, and in September 1911 steps were taken to set up a conciliation conference on the lines Commissioner Ashton had suggested in his report. This came about during discussions regarding industrial relations, arising out of the transport strike.[105] The object would be to try to bring an end to the sectarian feuding, and Lord Derby was asked to be chairman. It is probable that pressure was being exerted on the Liverpool M.Ps' and others by the government. Thirteen prominent citizens were invited to attend, including George Wise, Dr Whiteside, Catholic Bishop of Liverpool, and the Anglican bishop, Chevasse.[106] This body met fairly quickly and came up with a number of recommendations concerned with legislation regarding processions, the allocation of space for meetings, the rigid enforcement of the law concerning unlawful assemblies and a proposal to adapt certain features of the St Helens Corporation Act of 1911, which gave power to the Corporation for 'the prohibition of the use of emblems or weapons or the playing of music likely to create a disturbance'. Wise argued that socialists and secularists should come within the terms of any new legislation. Many of the recommendations were eventually incorporated in the Liverpool Corporation Bill, which became law in October 1911.[107]

Little seemed to change after the conciliation conference. Wise still made anti-Catholic speeches at open-air meetings and Conservative politicians still played the Protestant card. Politicians and zealots remained preoccupied with issues that seemed marginal elsewhere. Thus Liverpool tempers were rising over the King's Declaration Bill which became law in August 1910. In July the death of Charles McArthur brought about a by-election at Kirkdale, and Kyffin-Taylor, the Conservative candidate, had to exhibit his Protestant credentials.

> He did not want to be considered a one-sided man. Talk about the Protestant drum being sounded, well, so it would be but that was not the only thing. He stood where the late member stood for the Principles of the Reformation but at the same time it was essentially important for the safeguarding of the commerce of the country and to enable the toiling millions to work, that they should have an army as strong as it was today, indeed, much stronger.[108]

However, although, under Salvidge's leadership, the Conservatives still courted the Protestant vote, the events of the last decade meant that circumspection was necessary. At the same election meeting at which the above speech was made Salvidge replied to attacks from Cameron, the Socialist candidate, by denying the Conservative Party had a sectarian platform and were 'raising sectarian bitterness'.[109] That Salvidge was treading thin ice was demonstrated when, simultaneously with his denial of sectarianism, Wise stated that he was 'prepared on any occasion to support any Protestant candidate, irrespective of political party'.[110] The Parliament Act of 1911 meant that the Lords could delay a Home Rule Bill for only two years and the Liberal government had to try to meet the demands of the Irish members of Parliament. Home Rule had implications for Liverpool, where the Orange Institution took a firm stand and there were threats of a volunteer force going to Ulster should civil war break out. An incident occurred at the time which illustrates both the class divisions within the Conservative Protestant ranks and the indispensibility of Wise to Liverpool Tories. In October 1912 Carson, the Ulster Protestant leader, had landed at Liverpool to a rapturous welcome. During the evening he said to Salvidge that in the excitement of the day he had promised some 'chap' called Wise to speak at his Bible class. He did not want to go - 'I'll be the laughing stock of my pals in London.' Salvidge's reply was brief and to the point: 'You must keep the appointment.[111]

Up to August 1914 sporadic street clashes continued. Between the outbreak of war and November 1917, 800 men from Wise's Bible class joined the forces. Of this number, 149 had been killed or were missing and over 130 were wounded. Wise displayed his usual energy and drive during the war years. He received more than 5,500 letters from his men at the front and answered them all personally. Every one of the servicemen received a parcel of comfort each year, and it is easy to appreciate why he was held in such high regard by his flock. In February 1917 he fell ill. He knew he was dying and arranged his own funeral, choosing the hymns to be sung. On 29th November he died at his home in Kirkdale. He was buried on 4th December at Anfield cemetery.[112] The chief mourners were John Kensit, junior, and the trustees of the Protestant Reformers' Memorial Church. Salvidge did not attend but was represented by S. E. Murch, secretary of the Liverpool Constitutional Association and the rising light in Liverpool Conservatism. The Orange Institution was represented, but not the Bishop of Liverpool, and there were relatively few Anglican clergy.

VII

It might have been expected that the shared experience of Catholic and Protestant working men in the horror of the trenches would have finally broken down sectarian antagonisms and that the removal of such a strong character as Wise would have completed the healing process. It did not happen. Between 1918 and 1959 street clashes continued to occur, varying in the intensity. The number of people involved in violence during this latter period was probably small, a few hundred; the real tragedy was that the bitterness and hostility was more widespread than fist fights indicated. Mixed marriages in particular caused much unhappiness. While Catholic clergy had never indulged in public attacks on Protestantism, their opposition was total and they would go to extraordinary lengths to prevent mixed marriages or to 'safeguard the souls' of the children of such unions. Over a hundred years of Orangeism in Liverpool had, by 1919, produced a strong working-class culture, with its own music, songs, traditions and social organisation of benefit clubs, burial societies and quasi-religious ceremonies. It continued to be faced by a huge Catholic population, increasingly well led, still identified with Ireland, poverty, charity, a burden on the rates, competition for jobs, etc. Nothing had changed. Wise's mantle was taken up by the Rev. H. Longbottom, and the Protestant Reformers' Memorial Church prospered for a while in the 1930s. However, Longbottom was no copy of George Wise. Yet the strength of the Orange tradition was such that the stereotype of the Irish Catholic continued to excite the same kind of passions. At the same time, there is little doubt that the Orange Order brought colour to the drab streets of central Liverpool and many Catholics remember the 12th July processions, the decorated streets and the violence almost with nostalgia. Even today the decorations in China Street and Essex Street are talked of.

Writing in the 1930s, Pat O'Mara describes the day he and some of the Catholic boys took their courage in their hands and ventured up into Netherfield Road to watch the processions on King Billy's day:

> A crowd of our enemies [the Orangemen] with band and banners carrying
> inscriptions that made our blood boil surged round us. Orange everywhere
> and not a bit of green! I had never known there were so many enthusiastic
> Protestants. I had always been brought up to believe that Protestantism was
> a dying cult and its adherent cowards and easily frightened; but this mob up
> here, led by that magnificent white horse bearing a little boy dressed as a
> perfect duplicate of Prince William, did not look frightened at all.[113]

O'Mara goes on to tell how the day ended in a fight in which he and his
pals were lucky to escape a severe beating. The incident recaptures
entirely the atmosphere of certain areas of pre-1960 Liverpool (where, for
example, a ham shank was frequently hung from a lamp post with a sign,
'Cured at Lourdes'). O'Mara's idea that Protestantism was a dying cult
was a fairly common view among Liverpool Catholics, many of whom
would be brought up in entirely Catholic communities, frequently without
any contact with Protestants. The same kind of nostalgia for the raw
aggressions of Liverpool life in pre-slum clearance days is echoed in the
biography of James Sexton, the dockers' member of Parliament. In 1906
Sexton stood as the Labour Party candidate in the West Toxteth division,
an Orange stronghold. Jim Larkin, the Liverpool Irish Labour leader,
turned up to help his campaign. Sexton tells us:

> Larkin displayed an energy that was almost superhuman. The division was
> one of the storm centres of religious strife and the stronghold of the Orange
> Order, through whom Mr. Houston held the seat. My being a Roman Catholic
> naturally made the situation still more lively. But nothing could frighten
> Jim. He plunged recklessly into the fray where the fighting was most furious,
> organised gigantic processions against Chinese labour on the road, faced
> hostile mobs saturated with religious bigotry, who were howling for our
> blood . . .[114]

The fury of working-class Protestants was something many Labour candidates and politicians had to face in Liverpool elections, and not only in
Toxteth. Bessie Braddock and her husband Jack sometimes held meetings
in an open-air meeting space at the St Domingo Pit, right in the middle of
the stronghold of the Orange Order. Many of the Protestant 'Mary Ellens'
were fearsome fighters and became involved in brawls as often as the
menfolk. For the Braddocks to get to and from St Domingo required a
strong police escort. A biographer of Bessie Braddock describes such an
occasion:

> Speakers proceeded through Everton like lead in a pencil, Police packed on
> either side of them. Bill Sharp was Ma Bamber's bodyguard and later he
> donned knuckle dusters in defence of Bessie, staying close when she walked,
> working his way through the audience at the first whisper of a riot. Ma
> Bamber, Enid, Jack and Bessie, flanked by police, proceeded through this
> stronghold of Orangeism at their own peril, an army of occupation in hostile
> territory.[115]

The second world war was followed by significant changes in Liverpool society; as in the rest of the country there was full employment until the early 1970s and working-class people could enjoy television, a car, holidays abroad and other diversions. By 1958 there was only one city councillor returned under a 'Protestant' ticket but in that year Archbishop Heenan was stoned by some Orange women and children when visiting a sick Catholic woman in Robsart Street,[116] Slum clearance in the inner city broke up the religious ghettoes, although the Pope's visit in 1982 resulted in street decorations which clearly indicated that the town centre is still predominantly Catholic.[117] The visit, unaccompanied by disorder, was the final proof that physical combat between Catholics and Protestants is a thing of the past almost. In 1985 the author witnessed a stone-throwing attack on an Orange lodge which injured a woman in the procession.

Notes

1   Waller, *op. cit.*, p. 202.
2   Many of the references in this chapter are from the Minutes of Evidence to the inquiry set up under the Police (Liverpool Enquiry) Act, 1909, referred to hereafter as the 'Inquiry'. Also references are taken from the report of the Inquiry Commissioner, hereafter referred to as the 'Report' (see p. 237).
3   Inquiry, qq. 11937-54, G. Wise.
4   Without naming Wise, Archdeacon Madden told a conference of his personal experiences of the effects of religious controversy on Liverpool's slums. *Liverpool Weekly Post*, 21st October 1911.
5   *Liverpool Courier*, 27th April 1904.
6   *Liverpool Courier*, 23rd April 1904. This contains a long account of Wise's view of the differences with Stones and details of Stones's contract with the crusade.
7   *Liverpool Weekly Post*, 18th March 1905. Stones used this phrase on 16th March 1904, according to Sergeant Collins, giving evidence in a court case in March 1905. For Stones's statement concerning Wise's jealousy see *Liverpool Courier*, 27th March 1905. In his court case Stones made the claim under cross-examination.
8   *Liverpool Courier*, 27th April 1904. This edition contains copies of the correspondence between the George Wise Crusade Committee and Stones.
9   Throughout the disturbances in the years up to 1909 Orange bands were blamed for creating an atmosphere of excitement. Inquiry, qq. 1402-3. R. Segar, solicitor for Roman Catholics. During the inquiry the L.O.I. passed a rule making it necessary for all band members to be members of the L.O.I. inquiry, qq. 22288-91, S. G. Thomas.
10   *Liverpool Courier*, 12th April 1904, Account of court case. 'Buck' is a Liverpool term for a hard man. See also L.R.O. Watch Committee Minutes. 28th March 1904, p. 718.
11   *Liverpool Courier*, 1st April 1904.
12   *Liverpool Courier*, 18th and 19th April 1904.
13   For example see *Liverpool Courier*, 23rd April, 23rd May, 10th and 30th June, 6th, 14th and 22nd July, 3rd, 8th, 9th, 10th, 15th, 20th and 24th August 1904; *Manchester Guardian*, 10th August 1904.
14   *Liverpool Courier*, 22nd July 1904, court case regarding events of 10th June.
15   *Liverpool Courier*, 8th and 9th August 1904.
16   *Liverpool Weekly Post*, 11th and 18th March 1905.
17   Ewart was secretary of the Liverpool Kensit Crusade and a member of the Protestant Truth Society. Following a disturbance in Garston he appeared in court charged with

'unlawfully and wilfully obstructing the passage of a certain footpath'. He was found guilty but refused to pay or to give any guarantees he would not hold any further meetings. He was on the martyr's trail. See *Liverpool Courier*, 5th April, 25th and 31st July, 13th, 15th, 28th August 1905.

18 *Liverpool Courier*, 28th August 1905.
19 Waller, op. cit., p. 209.
20 Report, p. 1.
21 *Liverpool Echo,* 7th September 1908.
22 Report, p. 8.
23 *Liverpool Echo,* 15th September 1908.
24 Ibid.
25 Report, p. 2; also P.R.O. H045/11138/186474. Dunning to Home Office, 17th May 1909. For a police opinion of the parish see Inquiry, q. 19717. Sergeant E. Green.
26 Report, p. 3.
27 Ibid., pp. 4-5.
28 Ibid., p. 6. Wise to Dunning; Dunning to Wise, p. 7; Walker to Dunning, p. 8; Dunning to Burke, p. 7.
29 Ibid., p. 9, copy of newspaper advertisement.
30 Ibid., pp. 10-14.
31 Ibid. p. 14. Dunning to Home Office, 14th May 1909.
32 P.R.O. HO 45/11138/186474. Dunning to Bishop Whiteside, 17th May 1909. Dunning to Attorney General, 24th May 1909. See also Report, p. 19. Bishop Whiteside to Dunning, 18th May 1905.
33 Dunning, op. cit.
34 Report, p. 25. Home Office to Dunning, 17th June 1909.
35 Ibid., p. 27, Inquiry. Wise, qq. 13302-6.
36 Inquiry. Wise q. 13313.
37 P.R.O. HO 45/11138/186474. Lane to Fr Rigby, 19th June 1909.
38 Lane's account of the riot in Juvenal Street is contained in the Inquiry, qq. 17497-645. See also *Liverpool Courier*, 29th June for an account of court proceedings regarding those charged with respect to the riot in Juvenal Street.
39 Inquiry, qq. 13927-35. Wise.
40 Inquiry, q. 17539. Lane.
41 *Liverpool Daily Post*, 23rd June 1909.
42 Ibid.
43 Ibid.
44 Ibid.
45 Report, p. 73.
46 Inquiry, qq. 22034-46. See also evidence of J. J. Hesketh, carter, qq. 22086119.
47 Report, p. 78. G. C. Rees alleged Protestant doors were marked, indicating that they were to receive visits from Catholic gangs.
48 Inquiry, qq. 22120-160. E. Flynn.
49 Inquiry, S. G. Rees, p. 81.
50 Ibid.
51 Ibid., qq. 10335-80.
52 Ibid., qq. 9815-930.
53 Our Lady's presbytery is in St Domingo Road, in an area which is still regarded as Orange.
54 Fr John Fitzgerald was the parish priest of Our Lady's. He gave evidence to the inquiry, qq. 20180-405. He also submitted a report to the town council concerning the harassment of Catholics in his parish. P.R.O. HO 144/704/ 107039; 36. Fitzgerald to Town Council, November 1909. This report forms the basis of the material used in the text concerning events in his Parish. H. B. Simpson, Under-Secretary of State at the Home Office, described it 'as a powerful indictment of Wise's followers'.

55   Fitzgerald, p. 7.

56   Ibid. p. 2.

57   Inquiry; see evidence of Catherine Owens, Florence Brodigan, Kate O'Laverty, Sarah Morgan, Susan Gallagher, Elizabeth Hammond, Margaret Cassidy, Eliza Ann Parkins.

58   Ibid., q. 22267. Inspector Hammond.

59   Ibid., qq. 21177-80. M. Sutton.

60   Ibid., qq. 21083-94. Mrs Connolly.

61   Ibid., qq. 13669-77. Wise.

62   Report, pp. 30-1.

63   It was claimed by Harmood Banner that 100,000 were asking for Wise's release. P.R.O. HO 144/704/107039/56.

64   Report, p. 38.

65   Inquiry, qq. 20105-10. Superintendent Tomlinson. Qq. 22279-80. Inspector Hammond.

65A P.R.O. HO 144/704/107039/68. Rutherford to Secretary of State for Home Affairs.

66   P.R.O. HO 144/704/107039/49. Charles McArthur to Herbert Gladstone, Home Secretary. McArthur asked Gladstone to receive a deputation. 'The deputation was anxious to bring to your notice special circumstances in the case which appear to call for a reconsideration of the treatment of Mr Wise, which has aroused a very strong feeling in this city and threatens consequences dangerous to peace and Order.' He was probably referring to the fact that Wise was a Second Division prisoner.

67   P.R.O. HO 144/704/107039; 56.

68   P.R.O. HO 144/704/107039; 58. Dunning to Under-Secretary of State, Home Office, 18th August 1909.

69   P.R.O. HO 144/704/107039; 69. Rutherford to Gladstone, 23rd October 1909.

70   P.R.O. HO 144/704/107039; 76. The opinion in the Home Office was that the stipendiary would not agree to release Wise, even if the chief magistrate was in favour of release without Wise entering into sureties.

71   HO 144/704/107039; 124. Petition, Wise to Home Secretary.

72   P.R.O. HO 144/704/107039; 124. Dunning to Home Office. Dunning suggested that Wise should be released two days earlier than planned, to coincide with the announcement of the setting up of the inquiry.

73   P.R.O. HO 144/704/107039; 124. Home Secretary to Stipendiary.

74   P.R.O. HO 144/704/107039; 131. Waddy to Jellicoe, 20th November 1909.

75   P.R.O. HO 144/704/107039; 131. Home Office to Jellicoe, 20th November 1909.

76   P.R.O. HO 144/704/107039; 136. E. Troup to Dunning, 7th December 1909; Dunning to Troup, 9th December 1909.

77   P.R.O. HO 144/704/107039; 137. Lynskey to Home Secretary, 11th December 1909.

78   The report and the minutes of evidence (two copies) are available at Liverpool City Local History Library.

79   Report, p. 49.

80   Inquiry, qq. 13209-55, Wise. He stated he was sorry the charge had been made.

81   Ibid., qq. 20559-64. Fr J. Browne explained that the Tertiaries had taken no vows of religion. See also qq. 20325-49, Fr J. Fitzgerald.

82   Report, p. 68.

83   Ibid., p. 69.

84   Ibid., p. 66.

85   Ibid., p. 63.

86   Inquiry, q. 16571-80, Dunning.

87   Ibid., qq. 21823-33; qq. 21860-4, Fr Oldham.

88   Ibid., qq. 21909-12, Fr Pinnington.

89   Ibid., qq. 20669-73, Fr Jackson; qq. 20689-94, Fr Clarkson.

90   Ibid., qq. 21910-12, Fr Pinnington; qq. 20206-9, Fr Fitzgerald.

91   Ibid., qq. 9997-10,000 and 10,005, Rev. R. G. Bell.

92   *Liverpool Weekly Post*, 1st October 1910. This quotes the *Times* correspondent.

93   Ibid., 28th May 1910.

94   Ibid., 4th June 1910.

95   Ibid., 30th July 1910.

96   Ibid., 16th July 1910.

97   Ibid., 30th July 1910. In a sectarian row on 11th September a youth was stabbed in Kew Street. See *Liverpool Weekly Post,* 24th September 1910.

98   *Liverpool Weekly Post,* 20th and 24th June 1911. The Catholic Defence League took part in the funeral.

99   Ibid.

100 Ibid., 8th and 29th July 1911.

101 Ibid., 1st July 1911.

102 15th and 22nd July 1911. In another sectarian row, two Catholic brothers attacked a Protestant, one holding him while the other brother stabbed him repeatedly. See *Liverpool Weekly Post,* 8th July 1911. *Liverpool Daily Post,* 19th June 1911, account of disturbances in Netherfield Road. *Liverpool Weekly Post,* 5th August 1911, disturbances at Edgehill.

103 For an account of the politics of the strike see Waller, op. cit., chapter 15, pp. 249-62.

104 *Liverpool Daily Post and Mercury,* 14th August 1911. A police inspector described the fight as the fiercest clash seen for years. Troops were used to bring it to an end. For a report of Prendergast's funeral see *Liverpool Weekly Post,* 26th August 1911.

105 *Liverpool Weekly Post,* 16th September 1911. The Home Office conciliation team, consisting of T. P. O'Connor, Kyffin Taylor and D. J. Shackleton, was concerned primarily with the effects of the labour dispute but also enquired into sectarian troubles.

106 *Liverpool Weekly Post,* 30th September 1911.

107 Ibid., 18th November 1911. This contains an account of their recommendation to the Watch Committee.

108 *Liverpool Courier,* 19th July 1910.

109 Ibid.

110 Ibid.

111 Quoted by Salvidge's son in S. Salvidge, *Salvidge of Liverpool: Behind the Political Scenes* (1934), p. 121.

112 *Liverpool Echo,* 29th November 1917; *Liverpool Daily Post,* 30th November and 5th December 1917.

113 P. O'Mara, *The autobiography of a Liverpool-Irish Slummy* (1934), p. 87.

114 E. Larkin, *James Larkin: Irish Labour Leader,* 1876-1947 (1965), p. 12.

115 H. Toole, *Mrs Bessie Braddock* (1957), p. 56.

116 Waller, op. cit., p. 349.

117 St Andrew's Gardens, a huge circular block of flats at the top of London Road, was completely covered in the Papal colours. The author toured the inner city on the day of the Pope's visit and many council flats were decorated with the Papal colours. Orangemen called off a threatened demonstration following negotiations with Bishop David Shepherd.

Postscript

It would be an attractive conclusion if the events described in this book could be explained by a single all embracing theory. This is not possible, yet we are left with the need for an explanation of some kind. Certain tentative conclusions present themselves. More than in any other town in England, the experience of Liverpool supports Clarke's thesis regarding the strength of Tory Anglican ideology. Long after 1829 its spokesmen appeared on Liverpool platforms, addressing enthusiastic audiences, and McNeile was archetypal.

Foster, Kirk and Joyce have each, from their different perspectives, confirmed the existence and strength of the Tory Anglican hegemony in the Lancashire mill towns during most of the nineteenth century.[1] It might be tempting, therefore, to assume that Liverpool was simply typical, only more so, of a more general pattern of social structure in northern industrial towns. Clearly, that was not so. Liverpool was not an industrial town. The culture of the factory, the paternalism of factory employers and the sense of community engendered by paternalism were not a feature of working-class Liverpool. Manufacturing industry never played a significant part in the local economy. Joyce has convincingly made the case that it was the immediate circumstances of living, the family and the neighbourhood, within the orbit of the factory, that brought a remarkable degree of stability to those Lancashire communities based on manufacturing. More important, he argues, to the satisfaction of this author, that the sense of community predominated over the sense of class. Deference, however, was not a feature of the Liverpool working class; the almost total absence of the culture of the factory town left a gap which was filled by a popular Protestantism, reflecting the anti-Irish/Catholic resentment arising from Liverpool's peculiar position as the centre of Irish immigration.

The Orange Order, with its lodge meetings, anniversaries,

ceremonies, benefit clubs, parades and political activities, provided the *raison d'être* for a large section of Liverpool's unskilled Protestant working class, who, under the guise of patriotism, could indulge their hostility towards the Irish invaders. In Joyce's words:

> In Lancashire even more than elsewhere, the Irish comprised a pool of often cheaper and unskilled labour. As the 'external enemy' they can also be understood as the 'poor whites' of the north, healing the wounds of dependence felt most by the less skilled.

This point was made by Marx:

> The ordinary English worker hates the Irish worker as a competitor who lowers his standard of life . . . thus antagonism is kept alive by the pulpit, the comic papers, in short, by all the means at the disposal of the ruling class.[2]

If this was true of the mill towns, how much more so of Liverpool. While Joyce was correct in stating that in the mill towns the Orange Order could be controlled, in Liverpool, as Waller and this work have shown, such was not the case. The Orange Order in Liverpool gave an opportunity for men of humble origins to attain positions of authority in an organisation which had wide grass-roots support. The lodge masters had a level of influence in the local community which mirrored that exercised by employers in the mill towns; hence the strength, fanaticism and persistence of Liverpool Orangeism. Kirk and Foster also illustrate the role of the Orange Order in the mill towns as an organ of Tory politicians and the extent to which Orangemen were amenable to Tory control. Even in the Lancashire and Cheshire mill towns violence could erupt, reflecting underlying ethnic animosities, but these large-scale disturbances were 'one off' phenomena: Stockport (1852), Oldham (1861), Aston under Lyne (1868) and, outside, Chesterfield (1862) and Tredegar (1882). This is not to say that ethnic hostilities did not simmer just beneath the surface, until the end of the century, but it was only in Liverpool that the fabric of working life was permanently scarred by open sectarian violence.

Central to an understanding of the strength of this tradition of sectarian bitterness is an appreciation of the reality of the conflict, in the concrete and individual experiences. To come home at night and find a brother, father or sister bleeding and battered after a fight over 'religion' was a traumatic experience which entered into the family stock of stories and prejudices, to be embroidered over time. The strength of the verbal tradition of story-telling in the working class has received little attention. The writer knows of a family *at the present time* whose relative, a Catholic Irishman, was sentenced to transportation following the Garibaldi riots in 1862. The family have a garbled idea of what happened in 1862, but the events are a part of their folk lore. The author is still told, with relish, of fights between Catholics and Protestants on 12th July, up to the second world war. An uncle still tells of his fear as a boy in the 1920s when he heard the Orange drums and fifes: as a Catholic he had been brought up to believe that those people were out to hurt him. This verbal tradition was central to the process of embedding stereotypes in the minds of the two communities and it was not simply the large-scale riot which set the tone of the inter-communal dialogue; it was the thousand and one quarrels and fights, many unreported, which established animosity in the streets, public houses and workplaces.

With regard to the pattern of violence over the period of this study, long periods of simmering communal hostility were punctuated by serious street-level disturbances. The pattern of violence goes some way to support Bohstedt's view on the role of stress in producing disturbances. In the burgeoning urban centres in the 1840s the newly arrived, restless populations were settling down and establishing a new urban culture. For example, in Liverpool in 1851, 72% of the population aged twenty years or over were born outside the borough. As English, Irish, Scots and Welsh sought to establish their position in local society any attempt by minority groups to overstep their allotted role would be resisted. Thus, for example, in 1850 the restoration of the Catholic Hierarchy raised the status of Catholics, most of whom were Irish, and the following year Liverpool witnessed the largest-ever Orange demonstration. In 1908 the Eucharistic Conference was seen by Protestants as a flaunting of success by the Catholic Church and riots followed. This type of behaviour has overtones of the poor whites in the southern states of the USA and their perception of the role of blacks in their society.

However, we are still left with considerations about the role of individuals. The underlying social structure of the working class was constant over the period, as was the level of personal sectarian conflict. If on this scene a strong character is imposed, does it explain the large-scale disturbances? Between 1841 and 1852 McNeile was at the height of his No Popery oratory, and that period witnessed a growing level of violence, culminating in the 1851 riots. Between 1901 and 1910 George Wise held the attention of the Protestant working class, with consequent disorder. Though both McNeile and Wise were No Popery orators they were of different moulds from Murphy, Camin and Gavazzi. Wise could clearly be described as a rabble-rouser but he had his roots in the Protestant community of the North End. There his influence was in many ways beneficial to the community. Whether this was outweighed by the deterioration in inter-communal relationships is an open question. An important factor, difficult to measure, is simple tribalism, with all territorial and symbolic connotations. The Irish were resented as outsiders and had to be confined to their districts. Attempts to overstep the demarcations were to be resisted. In all cases, crowds and riots attract young men for whom fighting is fun and for whom ideological motivation is often difficult to sustain.

The Orange Institution still flourishes in Liverpool among the least advantaged of society. Lip service is still paid to anti-Catholicism and 'Paddy is a bastard' is still sung in the streets on 12th July, though 'The sash my father wore' has replaced 'Boyne Water' as the most popular Orange song. But the role of the present-day Orange Institution is more complex than before the second world war. It provides a support system and sense of identity and community to people who have been battered by the upheaval involved in slum clearance and unemployment caused by the collapse of much of the local economy. It is doubtful whether there is a great deal of real anti-Catholicism among its members, so that now 12th July has more of the character of a folk festival. It is true, however, that the troubles in Northern Ireland have injected new life into Orangeism, at least for a small minority. Catholicism has changed. The reforms introduced by John Paul II have resulted in a form of Catholicism that is unrecognisable to those raised in the old Liverpool style. Attendance at Mass has dropped, mixed marriages are common and the cause of few problems, while divorce rates are relatively high. It could be argued that Orangeism has survived in rather better shape than Catholicism.

Notes

1   J. Foster, *Class Struggle and the Industrial Revolution* (1974); P. Joyce, *Work, Society and Politics* (1980), especially chapters 5 and 7; N. Kirk, *The Growth of Working Class Reformism* (1985), especially chapters 6 and 7.
2   For Marx's full statement on the Irish see K. Marx and F. Engels, *On Britain* (Moscow, 1953), pp. 123-7.

Appendix 1

**MEMBERS ATTENDING THE GRAND LODGE ON 4th JUNE 1832
AT PORTMAN SQUARE, LONDON**

LOYAL ORANGE INSTITUTION OF GREAT BRITAIN.
(ROYAL ARMS)

At a Meeting of the Very Right Worshipful the GRAND LODGE ; assembled at
No. 9, Portman-square, on Monday, the 4th day of June 1832 :

PRESENT:

Field-Marshal H. R. H. Prince Ernest Duke of Cumberland, K. G. &c. &c. &c.
Grand Master of the Empire.
The Very Right Worshipful and Right Honourable Lord Kenyon, F. S. A. &c. &c.
Deputy Grand Master of England and Wales.
General the Very Right Worshipful and Most Noble The Duke of Gordon, G. C.B. &c.
Deputy Grand Master of Scotland.
The Rev. James Harris, Deputy Grand Chaplain, A.M.

MEMBERS OF THE GRAND COMMITTEE :

The Marquis of Thomond, K.P.	Lieutenant-Colonel Fairman
The Viscount Cole, M. P.	Captain Morris
Sir Edmund Hayes, Bart. M. P.	Ensign Losack, 69th reg.
Henry Maxwell, esq. M. P.	John Eedes, esq.
Colonel Perceval, M.P.	John Augustus Knipe, esq.
Honourable Colonel Wingfield Stratford	William Augustus South, esq.

DIGNITARIES OF THE GRAND LODGE OF IRELAND :

The Earl of Roden, D. G. M.	Robert Nettles, esq. G. S. Cork.
Lord Langford, D. G. M.	N. D. Crommelin, esq. G. M. County Down,
Edward S. Cooper, esq. M. P - M C.	Drury Jones Dickinson, esq. G. T.
Anthony Lefroy, esq. M.P M. C.	Trinity College
Bev. Charles Boyton, G. C.	James Lendrum, esq. M.C.
Robert H. Dolling, esq. M . C.	

The Right Worshipful Lieut. - Col. Fairman, Deputy Grand Master for London,
and Master of the Metropolitan Warrant.
William French, Deputy Grand Master of Birmingham.
John Kenworthy, Deputy Grand Master of Oldham.
The Worshipful John Rainer, Master of Warrant 59.

Joseph Clowes, Master of Warrant 60.
John Condell, Master of Warrant 223.
John Earl, Master of Warrant 234.

RECENTLY ADMITTED MEMBERS.

The Right Rev. Sir Robert Peat, D. D. Vicar of Brentford, and Prelate of the
Sovereign Order of St. John of Jerusalem.
Rev. Robert Spranger, LL. B. Rector of Low Toynton, near Horncastle.
Edward Nucella, esq. of Vauxhall-place, South Lambeth.
Edwin Savil, esq. Copper Mills, Esher, Surrey.
Lieutenant-general Sir Thomas Bowser, K. C. B.
Charles W. Marr, esq. Southampton-street, Hampstead-road
Captain William Synon, 18th Regiment, High Sheriff elect for the City of Dublin.

PROXIES.

For Ayr, Brother Adams - For Rochdale, Brother Bostock.

VISITORS.

Brothers Oldis, 59 - Adams and Lacy, 223 - and Shepherd, 234:
Brother John Condell, Acting Grand Mace Bearer.
Brothers John Condell and David Sayers, Acting Grand Tylers.
Prayers being read by the Rev. James Harris, Deputy Grand Chaplain.
The lodge was opened by the Duke of Cumberland, the Grand Master of the Empire.

APOLOGIES.

The most noble the Marquis of Chandos, through previous unavoidable
engagements, was unable to attend the meeting.

Apologies were also received from other distinguished characters and various
provincial members at present unable to attend, including one from the Rev.
Thomas Comber rector of Oswaldkirk, one of the deputy grand chaplains, whose
letter breathes those ardent and energetic sentiments which have ever character-
ized his exertions on behalf of the Orange Society; as also an animated letter from
the Rev. G. S. Bull, rector of Bierley, near Bradford, York, subsequently to the
meeting of the grand lodge.

Source: S.C. Report on Orange Lodges in Great Britain (1835), Appendix 2.

Appendix 2

MEMBERS OF THE TOWN COUNCIL OF THE BOROUGH OF LIVERPOOL 1842-43

Name	*Ward*	*Occupation*
Conservative		
Aspinall, James	Pitt Street	Gentleman
Birkett, William	Rodney Street	Warehouse keeper
Blundell, R. B. B. H.	St Paul's	Cotton broker
Brancker, Thomas (Sir)	Castle Street	Sugar refiner
Bramley-Moore, J.	Lime Street	Merchant
Brassey, Thomas	St Anne's	Gentleman
Bushell, Christopher	Abercromby	Wine merchant
Chilton, Thomas (Ald.)	Great George	Merchant
Cooper, Joseph	Great George	Ironmonger
Copeland, Henry	Vauxhall	Brewer
Crook, R. S. (Ald.)	South Toxteth	Barrister
Edwards, Joshua	St Paul's	Stonemason
Gladstone, Robertson	Abercromby	Merchant
Griffith, Richard (Ald.)	St Paul's	-
Harbod, Richard	North Toxteth	Gentleman
Hodgson, David	Everton and Kirkdale	Gentleman
Holmes, Isaac	Scotland	Schoolmaster
Holmes, Samuel	St Peter's	Builder
Houghton, Richard (Ald.)	Scotland	Gentleman
Houghton, Richard (Jnr.)	Scotland	Timber merchant
Jones, Robert	St Anne's	Brewer
Kilshaw, John	Lime Street	Gentleman
Lace, Ambrose	South Toxteth	Attorney
Lawrence, G. H.	West Derby	Merchant
Lawrence, Henry	Rodney Street	Barrister
Lawrence, James	Great George	Brewer
Leigh, John Shaw	West Derby	-
Lloyd, John Buck	Lime Street	Attorney
Molyneaux, Edmund	Vauxhall	Shipbroker
North, John	Exchange	-
Parker, James	St Anne's	Brewer
Proctor, James	Abercromby	-
Plumpton, James	West Derby	-
Rae, Ebeneezer	St Peter's	Merchant ship's chandler
Rigby, Robert	Lime Street	-
Sand, Thomas	Exchange	Merchant

Name	Ward	Occupation
Shand, Francis	Everton and Kirkdale	Merchant and shipowner
Shaw, Thomas	Everton and Kirkdale	Canvas merchant
Sheppard, John	North Toxteth	Gentleman
Smith, Alexander (Jnr.)	North Toxteth	Merchant
Thompson, J. Caton	St Paul's	Attorney
Trotman, S. Lee	South Toxteth	Merchant
Toulmin, Thomas	Pitt Street	Attorney
Turner, John H. (Ald.)	Pitt Street	Broker
Wood, John Nelson	Rodney Street	Merchant

Reformers

Aiken, James	Castle Street	Merchant and shipbroker
Barclay, T. B.	Everton and Kirkdale	Merchant
Blackburn, Thomas	Vauxhall	Surgeon
Bulley, Thomas (Ald.)	North Toxteth	Gentleman
Earle, William, Jnr. (Ald.)	Exchange	Merchant
Evans Eyre (Ald.)	Rodney Street	Merchant
Fawcett, William	Pitt Street	Engineer
Freme, W. Purser (Ald.)	St Peter's	Merchant
Holmes, Henry	Exchange	Merchant
Holmes, John	Castle Street	Merchant
Holt, Thomas (Ald.)	Abercromby	Merchant
Hornby, Hugh	Castle Street	Merchant
Moon, James (Ald.)	West Derby	Merchant
Platt, John	South Toxteth	-
Preston, William	Vauxhall	Engineer
Priestley, John	St Peter's	-
Thornhill, William	Scotland	Gentleman

Appendix 3
LIST OF ORANGE LODGES AT NOVEMBER 1830

No.	CITY OR TOWN. ·	PLACE OF MEETING.	Time of Meeting
	London, The Grand Lodge	Lord Kenyon's, Portman-square	May & Nov.
1	Manchester	York Inn, Shude Hill	3d Monday.
2	Oldham	Dog and Duck, Eagle-street	2d Monday.
3	Manchester	Buck and Hawthorn, St. Anne-st.	Last Monday.
4	Stockport	Castle, Market-place	1st Monday.
5	Oldham	Stag's Head, West-street	2d Monday.
6	Bury	White Bear, Wild-street	2d Monday.
7	Bolton	Three Arrows, Old-hall	2d Thursday.
8	Newton Heath, near Manchester	Church Tavern	3d Monday.
9	Mottram, Cheshire	The Gun Inn	Last Saturday.
10	Halifax, Yorkshire	Waterhouse Arms, Nelson-street	Last Monday.
11	Wigan	The Old Dog, Market-place	Last Saturday.
12	Rochdale	Moulder's Arms	4th Tuesday.
13	Bridge-end; near Glossop, Derbys.	Howard's Arms	1st Saturday.
14	Ashton-under-Line	Pitt and Nelson Inn, Old-street	2d Wednesday.
15	Shaw Chapel, near Oldham	Duke of York	Last Monday.
16	London	D. G. M. C. E. Chetwode.	
17	Knot Lanes, Oldham	Horse Shoe	Last Saturday.
18	Houghton, near Denton, Lancash	Clarke's Arms	2d Saturday.
19	Gorton, near Manchester	Bull's Head	2d Monday.
20	Dobcross, Yorkshire	Woolpack	Last Monday.
21	Wigan, Lancashire	Dog and Partridge, Wallgate	2d Saturday.
22	Hadfield near Glossop, Derbysh,	Hope and Anchor	2d Saturday.
23	Exeter, Devonshire	Three Cranes, Butcher's-row	1st Tuesday.
24	Devonport	Commercial Inn, Fore-street	3d Monday.
25	Middleton, Lancashire	Dusty Miller Inn	3d Saturday.
26	Blakeley, near Manchester	White Lion Inn	2d Monday.
27	Edinburgh	142, Canongate	1st Tuesday.
28	Winchester	Mr. Horton's.	
29	Girvan, (Ayr)	M'Winey's Inn.	
30	13th Light Dragoons.		
31	Royal Sappers & Miners, 7th Com	June 1825.	
32	Ipswich	Waggon and Horses	2d Thursday.
33	24th Regiment of Foot	June 1825.	
34	Cambridge	The Ram Inn	1st Wednesdy.
35	Ditto	Crown and Woolpack, Sidney-st.	2d Wednesdy.

36	Plymouth	Mason's Inn, High Broad St.	
37	Monmouth	The Bell Inn	Every 2d Mond.
38	Kidderminster	Plough Inn, Church-fields	1st Monday.
39	Nant-y-Glo, Wales.		
40	Manchester	Fox Tavern, Deansgate	2d Monday.
41	Blackburne, Lancashire	Mason's Arms, North-gate	1st Monday.
42	Sheffield	King William, Solly-street	Last Tuesday.
43	Edinburgh	9 Greenside-place	2d Monday.
44	Glasgow	Deputy Grand Master's Warrant.	
45	Morpeth, Northumberland	Howard Arms Inn	3d Monday.
46	Huddersfield	White Hart Inn	Last Thursd.
47	Portsmouth	White Horse, White Horse-street	2d Tuesday.
48	Liverpool	J. Taylor's, Gilbert-street	1st Monday.
49	Barnsley, Yorkshire	The Nelson Inn	1st Saturday.
50	Norwich	Waggon and Horses, Tombland	1st Wednesday.
51	Bristol	The Coffee Pot	1st Wednesday.
52	North Shields	Tyne Inn, Camden-street	Last Tuesday.
54	Wibsey	The Black Dog.	-
55	Lowton, nr Warrington, Lancas.	Ram's Head.	-
56	Upholland, near Wigan	White Lion	1st Monday.
57	Prestwich, Lancashire	Ostrich, Church-gate	3d Monday.
58	59th, or Rifle Brigade.		
59	London	The Swan	2d Monday.
60	Birmingham	Lamp Tavern, Edmund-street	3d Wednesday.
61	Greetland, near Halifax	Golden Fleece	Last Saturday.
62	Sowerby, Yorkshire	Royal Oak	2d Saturday.
63	Sunderland, County of Durham	Black Lion Inn, High-street	2d Monday.
64	35th Regiment.		
65	Royal Artillery Drivers.		
66	43d Regiment	Renewed to Samuel Morris.	
67	Royal Artillery.		
68	Rochdale	The Blue Balls	2d Saturday.
69	Newcastle-upon-Tyne	Cock Inn, Head of the Side	2d Tuesday.
70	Leeds	The Rodney Inn, Cull-lane	Last Monday.
71	Brecon		1st Tuesday.
72	London		4th Thursday.
73	St. Helens, near Wigan.		
74	Newcastle-upon-Tyne	Dolphin Tavern, Close	Last Monday.
75	Norwich	The King's Head, St. Stephen's	1st Monday.
76	Skelmersdale, near Wigan.		
77	Royal Horse Artillery.		
78	Bradford, Yorkshire	Old Bishop Blaze	2d Tuesday.
79	Honley, near Huddersfield	George Inn	3d Saturday.
80	Charlesworth, near Glossop	George and Dragon Inn	3d Saturday.
81	Chapel-en-le-Frith	Bull's Head	2d Saturday.
82	Gloucester	The Fountain Inn.	
83	Glasgow	John Falconer's, Iron-gate	1st Monday.
84	42d Foot (Highlanders)		
85	Southowram, near Halifax		2d Monday.
86	Ripponden, Yorkshire	Prince of Orange Inn	3d Saturday.
87	59th Foot.		
88	Worcester	The New Greyhound Inn, New-st	1st Tuesday.
89	Gloucester	Three Cock's-lane	1st Wednesday.
90	Preston	Dog Inn	3d Saturday.
91	Holmfirth, near Huddersfield	Rose and Crown	2d Saturday.
92	Bolton, Long Moor-gate	The Starkie's Arms	
93	Brieghtmet, near Bolton, Lancash.	Hare and Hounds	2d Saturday.
94	Rifle Brigade, 2d battalion.		
95	Bury, Lancashire	Buck and Joiner's Arms, Rock-st.	

96	Shelf, near Leeds.		
97	Dumfries, North Britain.		
98	London	40 Bermondsey-street, Southwark	4th Monday.
99	Southwark, Surrey	Three Tuns, St Margaret's-hill	
100	Norwich.		
101	London.		
102	Paisley	M'Leas' Moss-street	1st Friday.
103	Shrewsbury	The Castle and Falcon	1st Saturday.
104	42d Regiment.		
105	Durham City	Red Lion	1st Tuesday.
106	Glasgow	Mr. Wilkie's, Gallowgate	1st Monday.
107	Leicester	The Generous Briton, Wharf-st.	1st Monday.
108	Little Lever, near Bolton	The Unicorn	1st Monday.
109	Wigan	King's Head, Market-place	3d Saturday.
110	Darlington, county of Durham	Hat and Feather	Last Saturday.
111	Hollingwood, near Oldham	Waggon and Horses	1st Monday.
112	Ratclifie, near Bury	Royal Oak, Radcliff-street	3d Saturday.
113	Three Lane Ends, Aspull	Red Lion	2d Saturday.
114	Rifle Brigade.		
115	Manchester	Weaver's Arms, Cock Pitt Hill	1st Monday.
116	Horwich,near Bolton, Lancashire	Brown Cow.	
117	Hindley, Lancashire	Lord Nelson	3d Saturday.
118	Musselburgh, near Edinburgh.		
119	Bradford	The Horse and Groom.	
120	31st Foot.		
121	Northampton	Plumbers' Arms, Sheep-street	1st Monday.
122	London	Mr.Birt,Gloucester-house,Bishops-gate-street	
123	Girvan, (Ayrshire) North Britain	James Kennedy's	2d Tuesday.
124	New Springs Haigh, near Wigan	Packet Horse	Last Saturday.
125	7th Dragoon Guards.		
126	Stranraer, Scotland.		
127	Whitehorn, Wigtonshire.		
128	Southampton	The Rose and Crown, French-st.	
129	Cross-hill, near Girvan, Ayrshire	James M'Neidger's	1st Friday.
130	Dundee	Ancient Freemason's Lodge, Murrowgate.	2d Monday.
131	16th Light Dragoons.		
132	Wigton, N. B.		
133	Sheffield	Royal Oak, Pond-street	2d Tuesday.
134	Little Horton	Lester's Arms.	
135	Sheffield	The Dolphin, Edward-street	1st Tuesday.
136	Kilmarnock	Black Bull, Portland-street	1st Monday.
137	Carlisle	The White Ox, English-street	2d Saturday.
138	Whitefield, near Bury	Bull's Head	4th Monday.
139	Cheetham Hill, near Manchester.		
140	Milnrow, near Rochdale	Woolpack Inn	1st Saturday.
141	Congleton	Black Horse	Last Monday.
142	Rochdale	The Collier's Arms	1st Saturday.
143	Warrington	Old Coffee House, Horse-market	Last Saturday.
144	Merthyr, Wales	The Bee Hive	4th Wednesday.
145	Hammersmith, near London		
146	Tredegar, Wales	The Black Prince.	3d Saturday.
147	Little Bolton, Lancashire	Bull and Wharf Inn	4th Saturday.
148	Harwood, near Bolton	Nab Gate	Last Saturday.
149	Kendal, Westmoreland	White Lion Inn, Strickland-gate	2d Saturday.
150	Stricker-lane, near Bradford, Yorkshire.	Hand and Shuttle, Dudley-hill	
151	Carlisle.		
152	Silkston, near Barnsley	Angel Inn	Last Saturday.

153	Scarborough	Old Globe, Globe-street	1st Monday.
154	Liverpool	Duke of York, Richmond-row	1st Monday.
155	Goberhall near Barnsley	The White Lion Inn	3d Monday.
156	Creeton, Scotland.		
157	Bretton, near Barnsley	The Beaumont Arms	Last Saturday.
158	Wigan.		
159	Furness, near Whalley-bridge, Derbyshire.	Soldier Dick	3d Saturday.
160	Manchester	Wheat-sheaf, Hulme	1st Wednesday.
161	South Shields	Burn's Head, Long-row	2d Wednesday.
162	Chowbent, Lancashire	Red Lion, Market place	Last Monday.
163	Blackburn, Lancashire	King's Arms, North-gate	2d Monday.
164	Nailor's Green, near Bury	King's Arms, Bowling-green	1st Saturday.
165	51st Light Infantry.		
166	Chorley, near Blackburn	Swan Inn, Water-street	1st Saturday.
167	Glasgow	Mr. Falconer's, Iron-gate	2d Monday.
168	Manchester.		
169	Pemberton, near Chowbent.		
170	Caldermoor, near Rochdale	Dog and Partridge	Saturday on or before full moon
171	Heywood, near Middleton	King's Arms	1st Saturday.
172	Chorley.		
173	Dumfries, N. B	Mr. Black's, English-street.	
174	Burnley.		
175	Bacup, near Rochdale	The Bull's Head	3d Saturday.
176	Glasgow	Christie's Tavern, Argyle-street	Last Monday.
177	Chester	Pointed Dog, Watergate-row	1st Wednesday.
178	Paisley	Donaldson's Tavern, Main-street	1st Monday.
179	Liverpool	The Sign of the Letters, Gilbert-st.	3d Monday.
180	Stainland, near Huddersfield	Coach and Six	1st Saturday.
181	6th Foot.		
183	Wilson's Town, Lanarkshire	Clarkson's Inn	2d Monday.
185	Sheffield	Deputy Grand Master's Warrant.	
186	Whitehaven	Globe Inn, King-street	1st Saturday.
187	Small Bridge, near Rochdale	Waggon and Horses	3d Saturday.
188	Leicester	Sailor's Return, Bridge-street	2d Monday.
189	Wilsons Town, Lanarkshire	M'Cullock's Inn	1st Monday.
190	6th Dragoon Guards.		
191	Oldham	Rope and Anchor	1st Monday.
192	Todmorden, near Bury	The Golden Lion	2d Saturday.
193	Duilly, Ayrshire, N. B.		
194	Worsley, Lancashire	Swan Inn	Last Saturday .
195	Hindley, Lancashire	Swan Inn	3d Saturday.
196	Burnley, Lancashire.		
197	Newton, Ayrshire, N. B.		
198	Northowram, Yorkshire	The Marquis of Granby.	
199	Leigh, near Chowbent, Lancash.	Millstone Tavern	1st Saturday.
200	Glasgow	Webster's Tavern, 62, Trongate	1st Monday.
201	Pollock Shaws, near Glasgow	James Walker's, Main-street	Last Monday.
202	Burnley, near Bury, Lancashire	Royal Oak	3d Saturday.
203	Great Horton, Yorkshire	King's Arms, Knight-street	Last ditto.
204	5th Dragoon Guards.		
205	Royal Artillery, 4th Battalion.		
206	Nailsworth	The King's Head	1st Wednesday.
207	Stanningly, near Leeds	Golden Fleece Inn	Last Saturday.
208	Stranraer, Ayrshire	Andrew M'Masters	1st Friday.
209	London	The Three Neats' Tongues, Pearl-street, Spitalfields.	1st Monday.
210	Little Hulton, Lancashire	Golden Lion	2d Saturday.

211	Fenton, Staffordshire	Royal Oak	1st Saturday.
212	Kirkcudbright, North Britain.		
213	Norwich	Two Quarts Tavern	2d Monday.
214	Coln, near Haslingdon	The Commercial Inn	3d Tuesday.
215	Glenluce.		
216	Newton Stewart, Wigton, N. B.	James Vernon's	1st Monday.
217	Stoney Kirk, Wigton, N. B		
218	Lark Hall, near Hamilton, N. B.	William Frames, Main-street	1st Friday.
219	Port Glasgow	Mr. James Erskine's	1st Monday.
220	Dalkeith, North Britain.		
221	Worksop, Notts	Greyhound Inn	1st Monday.
222	Darcy Lever, near Bolton	Farmer's Arms	1st Saturday.
223	London.		
224	Manchester	Wellington Inn, Old Garrett-road	3d Monday.
225	Burnley	The Cross Keys.	
226	Wallsend, Northumberland	Swan Inn	1st Monday.
228	Maybole, (Ayr) N B	James Edgar's	2d Friday.
229	St. Hellier's, Island of Jersey	The Navy and Friends Inn, Waterloo-street.	1st Wednesday.
230	Glasgow	Mr. Nisbet's, Laigh Kirk Close	1st Monday.
231	Mexico, South America	Granted to Brother J. Connybear.	
232	7th Battalion Royal Artillery	St. Hillier's, Jersey	1st Friday.
233	Woolwich, Kent.		
234	London	The Phoenix, Stacey-st., 7 Dials	4th Tuesday.
235	Whitehaven	Globe, King street	Last Tuesday.
236	Bilstone, Staffordshire	The Seven Stars.	
237	Halifax, Yorks	Wheat Sheaf Inn, New Market-st.	2d Monday.
238	67th Foot		
239	Horseforth, county of York	The Old King's Arms	Last Saturday.
240	Stayley Bridge, Lancashire	Dog and Partridge	3d Saturday.
241	29th Regiment of Foot.		
242	Hemsworth, near Barnsley	The King's Head Inn.	
243	Royal Sappers and Miners.		
244	Hollingwood, near Oldham	Coach and Horses	
245	Gatehouse of Fleet, N. B.		
246	Kersley, near Bolton	Rawson's Arms.	
248	Royal Artillery, 5th Battalion.		
249	Pont-y-pool	The Duke of Wellington.	
250	Leeds	The Star Inn.	
251	Idle, near Bradford	The White Hart Inn	1st Saturday.
252	Wortley-lane, near Leeds	The Star Inn	1st Saturday.
253	Chatham	The Old George.	
254	Royal Artillery, 6th Battalion.		
255	Manchester.		
256	Manchester		
257	Woodmill, Yorkshire.		
258	94th Foot.		
259	Neilson, near Paisley	Mrs. Anderson's	1st Tuesday.
260	17th Foot.		
261	Maisemoor, near Gloucester	The Ship	2d Wednesday.
262	Stanningley	The Sun Inn	2d Saturday.
263	Pudsey	The White Cross Inn	3d Saturday.
264	Milnrow, Lancash. near Rochdale		
265	Brickfield, ditto, ditto		

Warrants Dormant. - 53. 145. 182. 184. 227. 247.

Source: S.C. Report on Orange Lodges in Great Britain (1835), Appendix 19.

Appendix 4

COUNCIL OF THE LIVERPOOL CONSTITUTIONAL ASSOCIATION, 1852

Name	Occupation	Name	Occupation
Bold, James	Merchant	Longton, J	-
Bold, Thomas	Merchant	Moss, G.	-
Berereton J.	-	Neill Hugh	Surgeon
Byeford, Ambrose	Apraiser & Auctioneer	Peacock, J.	Attorney
		Peel Lawrence	Attorney
Byeford, Edward	Pawnbroker & Navy Agent	Prowse, Joshua	Shipowner
		Rankin Robert	Merchant
Chapman, Henry Cleaver	Merchant (Metals)	Satchell Thos. Henry	Hat Manufacturer
		Shand, A.	Merchant
Clint, Francis Anderson	Merchant	Shand, Francis	Merchant
		Shaw, J	-
Clint, Thomas Tolson	Merchant	Sherlock Randley Hopkins	Proprietor Liverpool Mail
Deane, Edward Guy	Attorney	Stavely, F.	Chemist & Druggist
Ellison, R.	-		
Fleming Thomas	-	Steele, Henry	Timber merchant
Foster W. F	-	Taunton, George Edward	Assurance Agent & Share Broker
Frodsham, Robert	Attorney		
Gardner, J.	-	Torr John	Broker
Gibb Duncan	Timber merchant	Trotman S. L.	Merchant
Graves, Samuel Robert	Merchant	Turner T.	-
Gregory, G. H.	Attorney	Tyrer J , W,	-
Hamp Francis	Attorney	Wagstaffe	Attorney
Henderson, Arthur	Merchant	Warrell J.	-
Holme Samuel	Builder	Warrington, C. J.	-
Hodgson, Adam	-	Williamson J.	-
Horsfall, G. A.	Merchant	Williams, R.	-
Horsfall, W. J.	Merchant	Wolfe, J. S.	Merchant
Leather, Peter	Attorney		
Lister, Charles	Surgeon		

Appendix 5

OFFICIALS OF THE LIVERPOOL PROVINCE OF THE LOYAL ORANGE INSTITUTION, 1885

Name	Status	Address	Occupation
Ball, Henry	D. D. M.	109 Granton Rd, Everton	Relieving Officer
Ballard, John Wm.	Pro G.M. and D.M.	86 Queen's Rd	Tin/iron trunk maker and shop
Barton, Alexander	W.M,	3 Town Row, W. Derby	Ironmonger
Bennet, James	W.M,	8 North Dingle, Kirkdale	Boilermaker
Birch, Frederick	D.S.	56 St Georges Hill, Everton	Bookkeeper
Bonner, Samuel	W.M.	16A Falkland St	Brassfinisher
Booth, James Freeman	D.M.	21 Oakfield Rd, Everton	Gentleman
Brown, George	W.M.	67 Abbot St, Heyworth St	Bricklayer
Buck, Robert	D.D.M.	30 Clint Rd	Joiner
Buchanan, E.	W.M.	3 Seacombe Bldgs	
Carl, J.	D.S.	46 Netherfield Rd, 8th	Bricklayer
Carter, Thomas	W.M.	9 Sales Terrace, Roscommon St	-
Clarke, J.	W.M.	29 Newstead Rd, Toxteth	Bootmaker
Cook, John	W.M.	37 Arthur St, Walton (Rice Lane)	Joiner
Carmode, Charles	D.O.M.	13 Roach St, Toxteth	Porter
Crowe, S,	W. M.	37 Fonthill Rd, Kirkdale	-
Davies, Frederick	W.M.	14 Faraday St, Everton	Bookkeeper
Davies, Joseph	P.M.	25 Dorritt St, Toxteth	Boilermaker
Dillon, G. W.	D.T. and R.O.	82 Stansfield St, Everton	Bookkeeper
Dixon, Charles	W.M.	28 Luther St, Scotland Rd	Painter
Dobbie, John	W.M.	30 Kent Sq, Kent St	Tin plate worker
Downey, James	W.M.	6 Rivington St, Everton	Engine fitter
Eccles, Thomas H.	D.T. and R.O.	4 Arthur St, Toxteth	Joiner
Edwards, William	W.M.	14 Beatrice St	Carter
Fee, William	W.M.	14 Premier St	Porter
Follest, William	D.M.	77 Skelhorne St	Warehouseman
Forshaw, John	W.M.	217 Grafton St, Toxteth	Shipwright
Gabrielson, William	W.M.	73 Great Mersey St	Boatman
Gilling, Robert	W.M.	35 Mount Vernon St	Bootmaker
Harkness, John sen.	W.M.	25 Denbigh St, Bootle	No occupation given
Harrison, John	W.M.	43 Squire St, Edge Hill	No occupation given
Hedderick, James	W.M.	58 Rose Vale, Everton	-
Higginson, Samuel	W.M.	131 Park St, Toxteth	-
Holden, Thomas	W.M.	3 Backmill Lane, Hawthorne Rd	-
Holmes, R. G.	W M.	39 Old Hall St	Caretaker
Johnston, R.	W.M.	16 Vienna St	No occupation given
Lang, John	Pro G.T. and P.T.	9 Wilton St	Relieving Officer
Lindop, R. A.	W.M.	292 Crown St	Tinsmith
Lightfoot, George Samuel	W.M.	35 Hyslop St, Toxteth	Plasterer
Littler, Samuel		71A Boaler St	Warehouseman
Lloyd, John	P.T. and R.O.	76 Upper Essex St, Toxteth	Shipwright
Lloyd, John H,	W.M.	94 Gwendoline St	Shipwright
Lovett, Richard	W.M.	40 Molville St, Toxteth	Joiner
Magee,	D.T. and R.O.	140 Brownlow Hill	Butcher
Maudsley, Joseph Jackson	W.M.	10 Chester St, Garston	-

Name	*Status*	*Address*	*Occupation*
McClean, John	D.D.M.	19 Drayton Rd, Walton Village	-
McCoy, George	W.M.	2 Harewood St, Everton	-
McCoy, Stewart	W.M.	8 Mona St	-
McKeown, J.	W.M.	9a Portland Pl, Roscommon St? (116 Portland Pl.)	Mariner
Miller, George	W.M.	46 Northbrook St	-
O'Neill, John	W.M.	398 Mill St	Angle Iron Smith
Owen, William	D.S.	54 Kirkdale Rd	-
Palmer, Samuel	W.M.	80 Delamere St	-
Parry, John	D.D.M.	26 Potter St	-
Plane, William T.	D.T. and R.O.	330 Kensington, Elm Park	Bookkeeper
Preston, James	W.M.	33 Holmes Rd, Litherland	-
Price, J.	W.M.	137 Buckingham St. Netherfield Rd	-
Ranicar Charles	W.M.	61 Seacombe St	Cooper
Rawlinson, H.	W.M.	29 Winchester Rd	Baker
Rawlinson John	W.M.	35 Rutter St	Whitesmith
Riiter, William	W.M.	14 Clint Rd Edge Lane	Coal merchant
Robinson, R. H.	W.M.	10h 63 Court, Upper Mary St -	
Samuelson, William C.	W.M.	142 Hamilton Rd	-
Scott, Thomas	D.D.M.	131 Burlington St	No occupation given
Sebastian, John A	D.S.	29 Conyers St, Kirkdale	Shipwright
Sewell, William Luther	D.S.	1 Dorritt St, Toxteth	Joiner
Shadwell, Allen	W.M.	64 Bismark St, Everton	Warehouseman
Shaw, W.	D.T. and R.O.	168 Field St, Everton	-
Smith, William	W.M.	43 Geraint St, Toxteth	Foreman
Smyth, Isaac W.	W.M.	195 Mill St, Toxteth	Earthenware dealer/ Clog and pattern maker
Smythe, Jacob	W.M.	151 Park Rd	-
Snodden, George	W.M.	10 Carmel St, Everton	-
Somerville, Francis	D.M.	196 Scotland Rd	Clothier
Steaaman, George	D.S.	67 WoodruffeSt, Toxteth	Bricklayer and Plasterer
Thomas, Harry	Pro G.S. and D.D.M.	25 Fitzclarence St	Plumber
Thornton, Willtam	D.S.	50 Eastlake St, Everton	Lithographic printer
Towers, William	D.M.	40 Sandhayes St, Walton Rd	Timber Salesman
Trevitt, Henry	D.M.	Hall Lane	Manager
Vallant, J.	W.M.	45 Back Salisbury St	Brewer
Verner, E.	W.M.	36 Olive St	Woodturner
Waugh, James	W.M.	County Rd, Walton	Funeral Furnisher
Walker, Robert	W.M.	61 Summerseat	-
Wilday, William	D.M.	39 Windsor St	-
Williams, T.	D.R.O.	29A St Annes St	Watchmaker
Wood, John	D.O.M.	33 Windsor St, Toxteth	-
Woxthington, James	W.M.	47 Kinmel St, Toxteth	Foreman
Wynne, Adam	W.M.	17 Dunkeld St, W. Derby Rd	-

Index